MW01062778

Female Circumcision
and the
Politics of Knowledge

African Women in Imperialist Discourses

Edited by

OBIOMA NNAEMEKA

Westport, Connecticut
London

Library of Congress Cataloging-in-Publication Data

Female circumcision and the politics of knowledge : African women in
imperialist discourses / edited by Obioma Nnaemeka.
    p. cm.
  Includes bibliographical references and index.
  ISBN 0–89789–864–8 (alk. paper) — ISBN 0–89789–865–6 (pbk. : alk. paper)
  1. Female circumcision—Africa. 2. Body, Human—Social aspects—Africa.
3. Africa—Colonial influence. I. Nnaemeka, Obioma, 1948–
GN484.F43 2005
392.1—dc22   2005006044

British Library Cataloguing in Publication Data is available.

Library of Congress Catalog Card Number: 2005006044

ISBN: 0–89789–864–8
    0–89789–865–6 (pbk.)

First published in 2005

Praeger Publishers, 88 Post Road West, Westport, CT 06881
An imprint of Greenwood Publishing Group, Inc.
www.praeger.com

Printed in the United States of America

The paper used in this book complies with the
Permanent Paper Standard issued by the National
Information Standards Organization (Z39.48–1984).

10 9 8 7 6 5 4 3 2 1

To
Women of African Descent
with Affection and
in Sisterhood

Contents

Acknowledgments

My most profound gratitude goes to all contributors to the volume for their patience and collegiality during many years of collaboration. I thank John Harney for believing in this project and finding a publishing home for it. To my extraordinary editors, Jane McGraw and Alexander Andru-syszyn, I say: "You are the best. Your professionalism and generosity made the work easy." Jane and Alexander did everything to ensure a flawless product. If after all their effort flaws are still lurking somewhere, I deserve a punch in the face. I thank my Chair, Gabrielle Bersier, for valuing my work, being very supportive, and providing inspiring leadership. I am very fortunate to have a competent and hardworking research assistant, Joanna Fields, whose boundless energy, commitment, and laughter are infectious. I thank you, Joanna, for the joy you bring to my work.

PART I

Introduction

The Challenges of Border-Crossing: African Women and Transnational Feminisms

Obioma Nnaemeka

> *Le barbare, c'est d'abord l'homme qui croit à la barbarie* / The barbarian is first and foremost he who believes in barbarism.
>
> CLAUDE LÉVI-STRAUSS[1]

> Each man calls barbarism whatever is not his own practice.
>
> MICHEL DE MONTAIGNE[2]

> [W]hen Africans get in trouble, whom do they call? Everybody. They call on people they shouldn't even talk to. . . . So they can accept what I—someone who loves my former home—am saying. They don't have a leg to stand on, so they better not start hopping around me!
>
> ALICE WALKER[3]

The contributors to this volume draw from a wide range of fields, including gender/women's studies, cultural studies, law, film studies, literary studies, history, feminist studies, African studies, and anthropology, to engage from "the other side" the hot-button issue of female circumcision. All the contributors condemn the practice and have, through their scholarly writing and publishing, fieldwork, and collaboration with nongovernmental organizations, registered their opposition to the practice and worked vigorously to end it. Although collectively we are concerned about the worldwide abuse of the female body, whether culturally sanctioned, aesthetically inspired, or politically motivated,[4] we do not intend here to defend the offended part in female circumcision as my African female friend once urged me: "Sister Obi, now that they have placed our *toto*[5] on the curriculum, we have to defend it." It is not necessary to defend it; not after Alice Walker dedicated an entire book to it!

> This Book is Dedicated
> With Tenderness and Respect
> To the Blameless
> Vulva[6]

It is also not our intention to dwell on the nature, history, and practice of female circumcision. Rather, we seek to engage the discourse on female circumcision and in the process (re)trace, expose, and map a long lineage of imperialist and colonial discourses.

Echoing many of the contributions to the volume, Sondra Hale's chapter uses the discourse on female circumcision to explore the relationship among knowledge, politics, and history—the politics of knowledge and the history of gender, race, and class in shaping imperialism. Hale, a Sudanist, who became aware of female circumcision three decades ago while teaching in Sudan, attributes her thirty-year silence on the issue partly to her vacillation between ethnocentrism and cultural relativism and partly to her difficulty working in an anti-Muslim and anti-Arab, racist environment in the United States, where female circumcision and the veil construct Muslim female identity. Raising questions about location, voice, and agency, Hale exposes the racism and ethnocentrism that color feminist and human rights struggles: "Western feminists (white and of color) have been given license to let their ethnocentrism free associate! A broader but related issue is, of course, that one part of the world is defining human rights for the rest of the world."[7] Further, she notes that the Western, feminist-led insurgency against female circumcision in Africa has more to do with what is happening to Western feminists and to their countries and less to do with the African women themselves and, of course, often concerns the eagerness to erect the "we" versus "them" hierarchy that objectifies and inferiorizes African women:

> We might also ask how and why so many Westerners, especially (but not only) white feminists, are becoming active in either scholarship or politics around this issue without knowing anything about the practices or without having had a single conversation with a circumcised woman! In this sense and in others, we seemed to have engaged in a great deal of "arrogant perception," which really relates not so much to what we think of something, but what we do with that information and, especially, how we use our analyses to set ourselves apart from *them*.[8]

This volume creates a prominent space for Africans to participate in the debates as producers of knowledge. The African voices at the center of the volume speak to the complexity of the imperialist project by exposing it as a question of location ("where one is coming from," literally and metaphorically) that transcends race and history. Identifying the problem as a mindset that emanates from a specific location (Western), the African contributors expose the ways in which women of color (from the United States and Asia), through their writings, films about, and condescension towards Africans, mimic the imperial arrogance of white explorers, imperialists, and colonizers, which is at the heart of imperial and colonial discourses. Insisting that the hierarchy on which rests the imperialist project is not bipolar but multilayered and more complex, the contributions show how imperialist discourses complicate issues of gender, race, and history. Not surprisingly, the two feminists under scrutiny in many of the essays in the volume—Alice Walker and Pratibha Parmar—are both women of color. Their unsolicited interventions on behalf of African women and their discourse on female circumcision and African women reflect a mindset that emanates from specific locations. Recognizing the centrality of the issue of location, one of the contributors, Chimalum Nwankwo, asserts that "imperialism and Western Feminism share the same ancestry, the same pedigree."[9]

The chapters in the volume trace the "travels" of imperial and colonial discourses from antecedents in anthropology, travel writings, and missionary discourse to modern residues and configurations in films, literature, and popular culture. The authors are concerned about the possibilities of transnational feminism agendas. Significantly, the volume has implications for transnational feminism and development in the sense that it interrogates foreign/Western modus operandi and interventions in the so-called Third World and shows how the resistance they generate can impede development work and undermine the true collaboration and partnership necessary to promote transnational feminist agendas. L. Amede Obiora, in her contribution to the volume, zeroes in on the flawed modus operandi of Western feminist insurgency to explore why it has failed to register any significant success in promoting change. At the heart of the failure is the continued marginalization of indigenous women in crucial issues in their lives and the incapacity and unwillingness of Western feminists to create a site for true collaboration and equal partnership:

> The relevance of this for the question of female circumcision is that there is no substitute for the involvement of the women who provide the pillar for the practice. A crucial dimension of collaborative schemes and viable strategies entails developing a rapprochement with the affected population, tapping into the indigenous perspectives about the rhythms of change, and conceding the local women the right to take the lead in identifying their needs and formulating their solutions. If female circumcision is an everyday reality or province that they control, it is inconceivable that it could be eradicated without their input. Radical approaches that covertly and overtly shun them bode ill for enduring change and reduce reformist efforts to little more than intellectual masturbation.[10]

Discussions of women and imperialism have been extensively documented by women historians, but their focus has to a large extent been limited to Western women and their complicity in the imperialist project. Earlier scholarship on women and imperialism by feminists and female historians presented the limited notion of the category "women" that was endemic in the early feminist scholarship and theorizing of second wave feminism.[11] This restricted notion of the category "women" has also influenced the nature and scope of more recent scholarship on women and imperialism. Works by white (feminist) women historians, such as Helen Callaway and Claudia Knapman,[12] fail to engage fully in a race, gender, and class analysis of the colonial system. They focus more on the relations between white men and white women and how those relations colored the colonial agenda but do not in any significant way extend the gender analysis or distinction to the silenced colonized who are no more than tools for elaborating on the main focus of the works—that is, white men/white women relations.

This focus on Western women in scholarship on women and imperialism results, even in more recent scholarship, in works that read like a gendered variant of the navel-gazing, mainstream Western scholarship on imperialism, in which the West is talking with the West about the West. These accounts of women and imperialism by feminists and scholars of women's history focus primarily on white women as participants and tools or "victims"[13] of the imperialist project. Focusing on women (mostly white) as complicit in and resistant to imperialism, *Western Women and Imperialism*[14] delineates and critiques earlier scholarship on women and imperialism. Although the editors claim that the essays in the collection "encourage the reader to consider the multiplicity of voices,"[15] the reader hears multiple voices that are no more than Western women's different takes on the imperialist agenda that do not absolve them from the fundamental issues of racism, classicism, superiority, and power implicit in the imperialist project. Although they may have critiqued the project with varying degrees of intensity, the Western women were bound by their endorsement of imperialist adventurism.

Contrary to Knapman's attempt to present white men as sole proprietors of the evil empire, it is obvious that white women, as beneficiaries of colonial protective laws against native male "savages," reveled in images of themselves as angels, superior and pure. Knapman's ascription of "benevolence" and so forth[16] to white women does not in any way exonerate them from culpability in actively participating in a violent, racist operation. These scholars of women's history strive to disprove the impression in earlier scholarship on empire that the imperial space was a male space by re-gendering the space through the reinsertion of women as participants. However, in inserting women (Western women specifically) into the colonial/imperialist space as participants, the scholars seem to be more interested in presenting the women as better and more benevolent colonizers than their male counterparts.[17] If these Western women were also "victims" of the imperialist project, as some of the women historians claim, they are certainly "speaking victims" whom these historians have given a space in which to speak their "victimhood" while denying the same space to the silenced colonized victims similar to those speaking in the present volume.

In spite of the restraints put on them by the masculinist colonial apparatus, white women in colonial Nigeria, for example, still found ways to participate actively in the colonial agenda. When they circumvented these restrictions in order to "meet African society in innovative and positive ways,"[18] they did not deal with Africans as equals but as inferior and helpless creatures that needed help but could not help themselves. White women's "friendship" with Africans, especially women, was too maternalistic and condescending to be taken seriously. In presenting white women's acts of "benevolence" during the colonial era, an attempt must be made to separate episodic anecdotes and guilt-ridden "personal accounts" from active participation by white women in an oppressive system, and highlight not what individual women did or said they did but what white women in the system represented.

Earlier works on women and imperialism fail to include in any meaningful way the voices of the real victims of imperialism—colonized women. On the contrary, this volume inserts the voices of women (colonized women) who were/are the real victims of imperialism. Contrary to earlier works on women and imperialism that locate imperialism in the past and sometimes dismiss it as an aberration, the present volume presents imperial arrogance as cutting through different historical periods and implicating different races. The volume brings into the debate the suppressed voices of indigenous women, not by locating imperialism in far away periods in Africa, Asia, the Pacific or South America, but by focusing on a contemporary debate, circumcision, to show that imperialism is a will to dominate that haunts us even today.

Sustained by a bipolar logic, the polemic at the core of the circumcision debates is fuelled by Enlightenment universalism on the one hand and cultural relativism on the other. Asserting that the female body as sign is a site for the construction of individual as well as community identity, Françoise Lionnet explores the extent and ramifications of positions taken by cultural relativists on the one hand, and universalists on the other, as they lock horns in the 1980s over the female circumcision question. In her analysis of trials of African circumcisers in French courts, Lionnet problematizes the use of global solutions for local questions, a method that may ultimately vitiate correct responses to issues of women's rights, individual versus group rights, human needs versus human rights, and bodily integrity. Bronwyn Winter goes further to show how the universalist/cultural relativist divide accounted for the different perspectives on criminalization of circumcisers that prevailed in France in 1991:

> In France in 1991, the Paris trial of an *excisieuse* (circumciser) further polarized the long-standing debate between a feminist pro-criminalization position on the one hand and cultural relativism on the other. While the point of depar-

ture for many people on both sides of the polemic was a reaction against the abuse of a non dominant class by a dominant class, the pro-criminalization feminists concentrated on the excision as the abuse of female children, whereas the cultural relativists saw criminalization campaigns as continuing abuse by a hegemonic Western power of people it had once colonized. [19]

To understand the nature, limits, and arguments in the debates, it is important to identify the participants and delineate the battle lines. Who speaks? From where?[20] The West is arguing with itself for/against women used as tools to affirm and perpetuate a long history of political, imperialist, and racist positions anchored in moralizing (but morally bankrupt) assertions of superiority. The two feminist camps of universalists and cultural relativists (or difference feminists) are less concerned about the women at the center of the controversy as full-fledged human beings deserving of dignity and autonomy and more interested in using the context and texture of their lives to assert power and dominance and justify colonial nostalgia: "It is about the use of women as ammunition in a polemic of central concern to their lives, but where the issue at stake is not the women's own interests but, rather, the consolidation of the power of others to define those interests."[21]

Chima Korieh's contribution to this volume investigates how female circumcision becomes the impetus for the objectification of African women in the media, where African women are presented as mutilated, abject bodies. Vicki Kirby goes further to underscore the complicity of ethnocentricism and phallogocentricism in the production of the abject female body that is at the center of the debates about the primitive practice called circumcision: "If the African Body lacks integrity, and is not whole(some), then intervention is necessary, even if it means we must save them from themselves."[22] Kirby identifies two camps in the debates and insurgency—those who argue that female circumcision is an "unspeakable" act so heinous that it demands intervention, and on the other hand, the cultural relativists who assume the transparency and translatability of cultures. In both instances, the propensity to speak for others implicates Western feminists in the same violent economies.[23] Focusing on the works (overwhelmingly by women) that argue against the practice, Kirby notes that the discourse that argues against the practice is clinical in its unfolding under a medical gaze:

> The object of concern is uncovered before us, the truth of its deficiency pinned down between inquiring pages, opened out to photographic scrutiny or simply documented into readable, textual comprehension. The peculiar and prurient fascination of the viewer/reader is swiftly sanitized behind the impassivity of a medical gaze. In fact, medical discourse provides the common thread which weaves through this entire cluster of texts, providing its classifications and, implicitly, the "real" meanings which authorize the argument.[24]

In his contribution to the volume, Jude G. Akudinobi shows how the mythologies of African femininity propped the British imperial project and

Victorian expansion, and how these mythologies of "de-normalized" femininity are linked to the European notion of self as it is embedded in the zone of normality and superiority. Akudinobi probes the unfolding of these imperial fictions and their implications in the construction of identities in the colonial context in three films—*Mountains of the Moon*, based on William Harrison's novel, *Burton and Speke*; *Mister Johnson*, based on a novel of the same name by Joyce Cary, and *Warrior Marks*, a film about female circumcision by Alice Walker and Pratibha Parmar. The rehashing of the same fictions from earlier films and novels by white men to the more recent *Warrior Marks* by women of color supports Akudinobi's argument that the construction of African femininity is not bound by history or truth but flows from the imperial Western gaze.[25] Echoing Akudinobi's argument about Western notions of self, Eloïse A. Brière asserts that "focusing on genital mutilation enables the West to view itself in a positive light, just as Keith Richburg's obsession with all that is wrong with Africa enables him to view U.S. culture favorably and to be thankful that slavery brought his ancestors to the New World."[26]

Placing female circumcision in history and identifying its global reach, Korieh's contribution shows how cultural illiteracy can fuel the racist assumptions upon which imperial discourse on circumcision is grounded, and proposes genuine cross-cultural understanding as a mitigating factor. Cultural literacy/illiteracy is at the heart of the comparative analyses in which Brière, Omofolabo Ajayi-Soyinka, and Chimalum Nwankwo engage. Brière undertakes a comparative analysis of two films on female circumcision by two black women, one non-Western and the other Western—*Femmes aux yeux ouverts/Women with Open Eyes* by Anne Laure Folly from Togo and *Warrior Marks* by Alice Walker from the United States—to show to what extent imperial ideology and cultural illiteracy can inflect what the imperial gaze sees/captures and reproduces. While the narrator's voice (Western) dominates the film *Warrior Marks* and silences the African women whose lives are commented upon, Anne Laure Folly's film creates a space for African women to speak for themselves. Nwankwo, in turn, compares the work on female circumcision by an African, Olayinka Koso-Thomas and that of Western feminists such as Alice Walker, whose intentions he questions: "It is obvious that their programs are quite remote in intent from that of the more serious and well-meaning researchers such as Olayinka Koso-Thomas."[27] He further exposes the lack of cultural understanding that produces the misreadings of African literature by non-African critics of African literature such as Florence Stratton and Elleke Boehmer: "Elleke Boehmer's Oxford vantage point should not be allowed to read as authoritatively as that of Igbo women who know better than the kind of claims replete in Boehmer's universalistic presumptions and conclusions. We know that in assertions or contentions of this nature, as Chinua Achebe inimitably put it several years ago, 'theories and bogeys are no substitutes for insight.'"[28]

Pushed to the edges of feminism and transnationalism, these objectified Africans are knocked down if they dare speak or demand a conversation. How else can one interpret, for example, Alice Walker's arrogant dismissal of Africans in her interview with Paula Giddings?

> When Africans get in trouble, whom do they call? Everybody. They call on people they shouldn't even talk to—trying to raise money, appealing to people to fight their battles, buying guns from Russia and the United States. They [Africans] invite all of these experts from Europe and the United States to go there to say their bit about AIDS to sell them condoms. So they can accept what I—someone who loves my former home—am saying. They don't have a leg to stand on, so they better not start hopping around me![29]

I do not know the Africans to whom Walker refers. The Africans I am most familiar with, Igbo women, stand on two firm legs. They do not hop around; they pounce. The historical records are there. Walker's suggestion here touches on my earlier comment about the provenance of imperial arrogance and discourses. As far as imperialism and its discourses go, the realtor's mantra is applicable: location, location, location. Walker's chiding of Africans for attacking her—a black woman—instead of whites echoes Parmar's interminable complaints in an interview,[30] although despite her assertion that Kenya is her birthplace she erroneously confers Nigerian citizenship on the best known Kenyan writer, Ngugi wa Thiong'o![31]

The imperial arrogance that permeates the encounters in Africa and Ithaca discussed in Ajayi-Soyinka's contribution in this volume underscores the issue of location. The encounters are not between African women and whites; they are between African women on the one hand and non-African women of color on the other hand. In raising the issues of location and imperial arrogance in her encounter with Gayatri Spivak at a conference coincidently entitled "Feminisms and Cultural Imperialism," Ajayi-Soyinka explores the hierarchies within Third World women and women of color configurations of the feminist project, and the marginalization of African women in knowledge production. Focusing on the relationship amongst women of color—between Asian women and African women, between continental African women and Diaspora African (African American) women—Ajayi-Soyinka shows how in each instance, African women are demoted to an inferior status, spoken for and against. Ajayi-Soyinka's comparative study of the works of Ama Ata Aidoo (Ghana) and Alice Walker (United States of America) explores the tensions that undergird these relationships but more importantly, shows how the imperialist discourses of works by Western women of color that demote Africans below human level are allied to the imperial arrogance prevalent in works by white imperialists and colonizers. Ajayi-Soyinka's comparison of Walker and Aidoo in their construction of knowledge about the African identity is instructive:

> Between Aidoo's and Walker's creative efforts, there is a phenomenal world of difference in the construction of the identity of the African and the person

of African descent. The production of knowledge in *Dilemma* and *Possessing* communicates radically contrasting pictures of self-awareness, concept of self and ways of knowing. . . . On the one hand, Aidoo strives for unity of two different peoples by investigating and understanding their common differences and by striving to overcome their superficial similarities. Critically informed by the present, Aidoo digs perceptibly deep into history, reexamining facts and fiction in order to build a more solid future. . . . Alice Walker perches on a pedestal placing her [African] characters below her in a hierarchical paradigm she has constructed. It is a sad commentary that *Possessing* perpetuates and most uncritically reproduces the most abject stereotypical images of African women as ignorant, fatalistic, and malicious partners in their own victimization. *Warrior Marks* reeks of sheer contempt for its subjects.[32]

Decoding the inner workings of cultural imperialism is indeed complex. I find useful John Tomlinson's suggestion for a point of entry: "One way of putting this is to speak of the *discourse of cultural imperialism*. To speak of the discourse rather than the thesis is to recognize the multiplicity of voices in this area and the inherently 'unruly' nature of these articulations."[33] The story by Rumi, the thirteenth-century Sufi teacher, about the blind men and the elephant has often been framed as an issue of perspective. It is certainly a question of perspective but beyond that, it is an issue of misrecognition and misnaming of what lies beyond one's zone of intelligibility. Michel Foucault's insightful analysis of the boundless nature of discourse and its taming in social interactions and knowledge production can also illuminate the notion of barbarism and its co-optation in imperialist discourses: "In every society, the production of discourse is at once controlled, selected, organized and redistributed by a certain number of procedures whose role is to ward off its powers and dangers, to gain mastery over its chance events, to evade its ponderous, formidable materiality."[34] This taming and pruning—what Foucault calls "procedures of rarefaction"[35]—pushes back a whole teratology of knowledge beyond its margins. According to Tomlinson,

> A "teratology" is the tale of the marvelous or the monstrous. Foucault reminds us that anything can be said: mundane, rational, marvelous or monstrous. What academic practices do, in one sense, is to "police the boundaries" of this saying, keeping the marvelous and the monstrous at bay. . . . This is perhaps especially important when we speak in the language of Western rationalism of the cultural practices of other cultures. We should remember that the "monstrous" is only a way of describing what lies beyond our intellectual boundaries, in the same way as the medieval cartographers imagined monsters to inhabit the lands beyond the known world.[36]

Arrogant notions of superiority propel "barbaric" from its original meaning of "foreign" (*barbarikos, barbaros*) to an over-determined configuration of baroque proportions—monstrosity, abnormality. Transnational feminists and cultural workers are seriously studying the role of the media in constructing and perpetuating colonial tropes of "civilized" West versus "barbaric" non-West where the former are "rescuers" perched on high moral ground ready to swoop and rescue the latter who are incapable of helping themselves.[37] At the heart of cultural imperialism is limited knowledge's tendency to demonize what lies beyond its zone of comprehension. Constructing itself as a site of moral superiority, the West is incapable of interrogating its claims. Its location permits it to voice unexamined moral outrage against what lies beyond its borders without taking into account its complicity in creating the conditions against which its moral outrage speaks:

> It is unfortunate but unavoidable that the "moral superiority" of U.S. geopolitical discourse has become part of the new global feminism emerging in the United States (and worldwide, though in the interest of diverse agendas). The dominant discourse in regard to international issues constructs U.S. feminists as saviours and rescuers of "oppressive women" elsewhere within a global economy run by powerful states. This new discourse of a global sisterhood . . . creates hegemonic notions of freedom and liberation, refuses to acknowledge the power of dominant groups in the United States, feminist and non-feminist, and wishes to "rescue" "Other" women rather than address the imperial policies and practices of the United States that create conditions of exploitation elsewhere.[38]

Pertinent to this line of thinking is Nawal El Saadawi's insistence in this volume and elsewhere[39] on the importance of context in understanding female circumcision and devising strategies for its eradication. The factors that subtend oppressive situations—race, gender, class, politics, and so on—are not immutable and isolated categories in their functioning, influences, and determination; they derive their impact and complexity from their capacity to travel and join forces with other categories to create contexts of oppression. El Saadawi is unyielding in her insistence that we take into account the nexus of oppression:

> A few years ago while speaking in an international women's conference, I made a connection between George H. W. Bush (then president of the United States) and female circumcision. Many people laughed because they did not see the link. . . . The results of research done in Egypt in 1987 show that the incidence of female circumcision increased with the revival of the religious political powers by so-called religious fundamentalism. It is a known fact that the Ronald Reagan and George H. W. Bush administrations encouraged religious fundamentalist groups internationally and inside the United States to fight against communism, the Soviet Union, and democratic movements all over the world.[40]

As they join transnational feminist forces, Third World women face a double-pronged challenge—the fight against patriarchal nationalism on the one hand and the resistance against colonialist and imperialist feminism on the other hand. We are well aware of the challenges of transnational feminists "dialogues" where the speakers (usually from the North) are hearing their own voices, not those of their supposed "interlocutors" (usually from the South). Nowhere are these "no-dialogue dialogues" more prevalent than in the so-called international conferences proliferating with sustained intensity during the two UN decades for women (from Mexico City in 1975 to Beijing in 1995). Marked as sites of transnational feminist struggles, these international conferences are often hijacked by Northern participants who insist on framing the agenda—usually replete with colonial and imperialist discourses of powerful states.[41] The U.S. official delegation (led by Maureen Reagan) to the 1985 UN women's conference in Nairobi, Kenya, threatened to pull out if the issue of apartheid was included in the agenda, insisting that the conference should be limited to discussions of "women's issues"! Two issues dominated the Beijing UN women's conference—female circumcision[42] and American perspectives on Sino-American relations. Participants were bombarded with interminable tirades about lack of freedom for women and other gender-based abuses in China as if the United States is immune from denial of freedom and a whole range of abuses inflicted on minorities. In these encounters, it is all about the North.

The North/South divide can also reconfigure along the fault-line of education and the lack thereof, academy and activism. Tahera Aftab articulated this problem with great clarity in her account of the first meeting of the International Network of Women's Studies Journals (INWSJ), held in September 2001 at Mt. Saint Vincent University, Halifax, Canada, whose objective "was to set up a network for interdisciplinary feminist and women's studies journals with a focus on the development and inclusion of a transnational feminist understanding of women's development issues."[43] Aftab's probing questions reflect the source of the scepticism and resistance from feminists and non-feminists in the South:

> How does feminist knowledge impinge upon grassroots activism, how does academic scholarship infringe upon it, and how could feminist knowledge and academic scholarship be used for the benefits of those for whom it was supposed to have been created? What role could women's studies journals play in bridging this gap?. . . What voices would be heard? Who would be the listeners? Will the voices coming from directions less familiar be heard and understood? What can we do to make these voices not only heard but also respected? How can the INWSJ network remove or at least minimize the inequalities of opportunities for the less heard voices?[44]

Championing the infusion of more action-oriented research in feminist agenda, Aftab and like-minded feminists wonder "whether this might be the time to recast feminist models of scholarship, to step out of the classrooms and libraries, and mix and mingle with the multitudes of women in the rest of the world."[45]

Internationally, second wave feminism generated two major responses: (1) the global sisterhood approach that overplayed homogeneity and paid little or no attention to issues of difference based on race, class, culture, ethnicity, sexuality, beliefs, and so on; and (2) the development approach in its different mutations—Women in Development (WID), Women and Development (WAD), Gender and Development (GAD)[46]—that institutionalized the helper/helped dichotomy. Both responses failed to fully account for and address the issues of hierarchy, power, and inequality. Then along came the transnational feminists schooled in postcolonial studies, cultural studies, globalization, and "new" anthropology, ready to go beyond, challenge, and address—in theory and practice—the shortcomings of the two major feminist responses mentioned above. Transnational feminism engages border-crossing at boundaries of race, class, gender, ethnicity, and nation but more importantly, it asks crucial questions about who is crossing which border and from where to where. Walker and Parmar can easily afford to travel to Senegal and Gambia on their voyeuristic trip to document the oppression of African women, but will the women in the villages they visited be allowed to wander freely in urban and rural United States and Britain to document women's oppression in all its disguises? Of course not; they will most likely be denied visas. Even if they were granted visas, they cannot afford the travel funds, camera crew, equipment, and so on, needed for such an undertaking.

Unequal power relations and privilege determine the nature and frequency of and reasons for border-crossings. The unequal power relations that determine the nature, boundaries, and integrity of knowledge produced prompt scholars on both sides to ask crucial questions about the ethical issues involved in the knowledge production.[47] Often, circulating and possibly colliding at the border are power, imperial arrogance, and imposition on the one hand, and dissent and resistance on the other: "Just as women of color in the United States have challenged feminists to recognize that their categories of analysis assumed the universality of white middle-class experience and defined equality and opportunity in ways that marginalize the political interests of working-class women and women of color, so also have women from the neo-colonized South challenged the dominant voice of women from the North."[48]

But the border also presents the possibilities for the crossing of true partners and collaborators united by mutual needs, interests, and respect. Transnational feminism is cognizant of the fact the unequal power relations produce the contestations at the heart of the female circumcision controversy. Transnational feminist practices create the space for a critique of the inequality and point to the possibilities of new international alliances in spite of asymmetries of power and location:

> Thus, if we speak of transnational circuits of information, capital, and labor, we critique a system founded on inequality and exploitation. . . . Transnational feminism, for example, is not to be celebrated as free of these oppressive conditions. In fact, there IS NO SUCH THING as feminism free of asymmetrical power relations. Rather, transnational feminist practices, as we

call them, involve forms of alliance, subversion, and complicity within which asymmetries and inequalities can be critiqued.[49]

Believing that much can be accomplished in this regard, the contributors to this volume join Sondra Hale in her call to Western feminists of all colors: "[I am] calling for *us*—and I am mainly (but not exclusively) addressing white feminists—to self-interrogate, calling on us always to be suspicious of our ideas and beliefs, and to work on ways of being effective *invited* allies. Whenever we become engaged in the affairs of the *Other*, we should be circumspect. Whenever we take on, uninvited, *their* plight as *ours*, in the face of so much political work to do in our own oftentimes pitiful society, it is useful to examine the timing, the actors, and the rhetoric."[50]

The concluding chapter in the volume, by Ange-Marie Hancock, answers the call with specific proposals and strategies. Hancock looks beyond the limitations of feminist theory to embrace its potential by arguing for the possibility of a theory of egalitarian coalitions that can emerge from the framework of feminist theory. Placing the voices of African feminists and scholars (Molara Ogundipe-Leslie, Salem Mekuria, Philomena Okeke, and Obioma Nnaemeka) at the center of her theorizing and addressing issues in African feminisms, Hancock hopes to bridge the gulf between Western and indigenous women: "To repair this broken bond, I propose a theory of egalitarian multicultural coalition building which aspires to repair the linkages broken between Western feminists and African women. This approach builds on work in the areas of feminist theory, politics, and international development in hopes of creating an empowering approach to coalition development."[51]

Noting that Western feminist practice in the campaign against female circumcision disempowers and antagonizes African women and ends up alienating an important constituency necessary for fashioning homegrown and easily adaptable strategies that could produce positive results, Hancock reminds us that African women on the continent have, in various ways and through organizations, done more than Western salvationist interventionists to bring an end to the practice in many African countries.[52] Echoing El Saadawi's warning against the dangers of ignoring contexts—cultural, political, socioeconomic, and so on—of African women's lives,[53] Hancock proposes the campaign against female circumcision in Burkina Faso as a possible site for the flowering of multicultural egalitarian coalitions. To accomplish her goal of fashioning a new theory of coalition building, Hancock proposes a three-step undertaking that would pursue intersubjective understanding, envision women as contextualized subjects with agency, and minimize differential power among coalition member groups. A successful implementation of these strategies could produce the type of successful outcome that greeted the INWSJ conference and is powerfully articulated by Tahera Aftab: "We emerged from long deliberations with decisions that were arrived at jointly. We worked together, we worked separately, and again we worked in small groups. We were like waves reaching the shore, then returning to our source. The lesson for me was: we merge to work for a common cause; we do not merge to shed our selves."[54]

NOTES

1. Lévi-Strauss 1961, 22.
2. Montaigne 1965, 152.
3. Giddings 1992, 60.
4. See discussion in Nnaemeka 1994.
5. "Vagina" in pidgin English.
6. Walker 1992, no folio.
7. Hale in this volume.
8. Hale in this volume.
9. Nwankwo in this volume. See also Jacobs 1992.
10. Obiora in this volume.
11. For example, in 1995 Americans celebrated the seventy-fifth anniversary of "women" getting the right to vote when in fact only a particular category of women—white women—was accorded that right in 1920.
12. See Haggis 1990 for discussion.
13. See Haggis 1990, 112.
14. Chaudhuri and Strobel 1992.
15. Chaudhuri and Strobel 1992, 6.
16. See Haggis 1990, 107.
17. See also Blake 1992.
18. Haggis 1990, 108.
19. Winter 1995, 316.
20. See Okin 1999. See also Nnaemeka 2004 for comment on Okin. Alcoff 1995 provides a useful articulation of the issue of "speaking for others."
21. Winter 1995, 315.
22. Kirby in this volume.
23. See Alcoff 1995.
24. Kirby in this volume. See also Pratt 1985 and 1992.
25. See also Pratt 1985 and 1992.
26. Brière in this volume.
27. Nwankwo in this volume.
28. Nwankwo in this volume.
29. Giddings 1992, 60.
30. See Kaplan 2000. It is interesting to note that Parmar had, in an essay published two decades ago (Amos and Parmar 1984), accused white women of the imperial arrogance against which she now defends herself.
31. "I was born in Kenya, East Africa and schooled in England, yet I was brought up to think of India as home. . . . Kenya gained independence in 1963, and my family moved to England a few years later" (Walker and Parmar 1993, 89). "Film being directed by the Nigerian writer Ngugi" (Walker and Parmar 1993, 214).
32. Ajayi in this volume.
33. Tomlinson 1991, 9; emphasis in the original.
34. Foucault 1981, 52.
35. Foucault 1981, 49.
36. Tomlinson 1991, 10.
37. Bacchetta et al. 2001, 3.
38. Grewal 1998, 511–512.

39. See El Saadawi 1980.
40. El Saadawi in this volume.
41. See Nnaemeka 2005.
42. See Hale in this volume.
43. Aftab 2002, 154.
44. Aftab 2002, 155.
45. Aftab 2002, 155.
46. See Snyder 2004.
47. See Patai 1994, and Nnaemeka 2004.
48. Brenner 2003.
49. Grewal and Kaplan 2000.
50. Hale in this volume.
51. Hancock in this volume.
52. See Lionnet and Nnaemeka in this volume.
53. See El Saadawi in this volume.
54. Aftab 2002, 154–155.

WORKS CITED

Aftab, Tahera. 2002. "Lobbying for Transnational Feminism: Feminist Conversations Make Connections." *NWSA Journal* 14 (2): 153–156.

Alcoff, Linda Martín. 1995. "The Problem of Speaking for Others." In *Who Can Speak: Authority and Cultural Identity*, ed. Judith Roof and Robyn Wiegman, 97–119. Urbana, IL: University of Illinois Press.

Amos, Valerie, and Pratibha Parmar. 1984. "Challenging Imperial Feminism." *Feminist Review* 17:3–19.

Bacchetta, Paola, Tina Campt, Inderpal Grewal, Caren Kaplan, Minoo Moallem, and Jennifer Terry. 2001. "Transnational Feminist Practices against War: A Statement." http://www.geocities.com/carenkaplan03/transnationalstatement.html (accessed July 2002).

Blake, Susan L. 1992. "A Woman's Trek: What Difference Does Gender Make?" In *Western Women and Imperialism: Complicity and Resistance*, ed. Nupur Chaudhuri and Margaret Strobel, 19–34. Bloomington, IN: Indiana University Press.

Brenner, Johanna. 2003. "Transnational Feminism and the Struggle for Global Justice." *New Politics* 9 (2).

Callaway, Helen. 1987. *Gender, Culture and Empire: European Women in Colonial Nigeria.* London: Macmillan.

Callaway, Helen, and Dorothy O. Helly. 1992. "Crusader for Empire: Flora Shaw/ Lady Lugard." In *Western Women and Imperialism: Complicity and Resistance*, ed. Nupur Chaudhuri and Margaret Strobel, 79–97. Bloomington, IN: Indiana University Press.

Chaudhuri, Nupur, and Margaret Strobel, eds. 1992. *Western Women and Imperialism: Complicity and Resistance.* Bloomington, IN: Indiana University Press.

El Saadawi, Nawal. 1980. *The Hidden Face of Eve: Women in the Arab World.* Trans. and ed. Sherif Hetata. London: Zed Book.

Foucault, Michel. 1981. "The Order of Discourse." In *Untying the Text*, ed. Robert Young, 48–78. London: Routledge and Kegan Paul.

Giddings, Paula. 1992. "Alice Walker's Appeal." *Essence* (July): 60–62.

Grewal, Inderpal. 1998. "On the New Global Feminism and the Family of Nations: Dilemma's of Transnational Feminist Practice." In *Talking Visions Multi-Cultural Feminism in a Transnational Age*, ed. Ella Shohat, 501–530. Cambridge, MA: MIT Press.

Grewal, Inderpal, and Caren Kaplan. 2000. "Postcolonial Studies and Transnational Feminist Practices." *Jouvert* 5 (1): 4–7.

Haggis, Jane. 1990. "Gendering Colonialism or Colonizing Gender?" *Women's Studies International Forum* 13:105–115.

Jacobs, Sylvia M. 1992. "Give a Thought to Africa: Black Women Missionaries in Southern Africa." In *Western Women and Imperialism: Complicity and Resistance,* ed. Nupur Chaudhuri and Margaret Strobel, 207–228. Bloomington, IN: Indiana University Press.

Kaplan, E. Ann. 2000. "An Interview with Pratibha Parmar." *Quarterly Review of Film and Video* 17 (2): 85–105.

Knapman, Claudia. 1986. *White Women in Fiji, 1835–1930: The Ruin of Empire?* Sydney: Allen & Unwin.

Lévi-Strauss, Claude. 1961. *Race et histoire.* Paris: Gonthier.

Montaigne, Michel de. 1965. *Complete Essays of Montaigne,* ed. and trans. Donald Frame. Stanford: Stanford University Press.

Nnaemeka, Obioma. 1994. "Bringing African Women into the Classroom: Rethinking Pedagogy and Epistemology." In *Borderwork: Feminist Engagements with Comparative Literature,* ed. Margaret Higonnet, 301–318. Ithaca, NY: Cornell University Press.

———. 2004. "Nego-feminism: Theorizing, Practicing, and Pruning Africa's Way." *Signs: Journal of Women in Culture and Society* 29 (2): 357–386.

———. 2005. "International Conferences as Sites for Transnational Feminist Struggles: The Case of the First International Conference on Women in Africa and the African Diaspora (WAAD)." In *Dialogue and Difference: Feminisms Challenge Globalization,* ed. Marguerite Waller and Sylvia Marcos, 53–77. New York: Palgrave/Macmillan.

Okin, Susan Moller. 1999. "Is Multiculturalism Bad for Women?" In *Is Multiculturalism Bad for Women?* ed. Joshua Cohen, Matthew Howard, and Martha C. Nussbaum, 9–24. Princeton, NJ: Princeton University Press.

Parmar, Pratibha, producer/director. 1993. *Warrior Marks* [videorecording]. A Hauer Rawlence Production. New York: Women Make Movies (distributor).

Patai, Daphne. 1994. "U.S. Academics and Third-World Women: Is Ethical Research Possible?" In *Feminist Nightmares, Women at Odds: Feminism and the Problem of Sisterhood,* ed. Susan Ostrov Weisser and Jennifer Fleischner, 21–43. New York: New York University Press.

Pratt, Mary Louise. 1985. "Scratches on the Face of the Country; or, What Mr. Barrow Saw in the Land of the Bushmen." *Critical Inquiry* 12 (1): 119–143.

———. 1992. *Imperial Eyes.* London: Routledge.

Snyder, Margaret. 2004. "Women Determine Development: The Unfinished Revolution." *Signs: Journal of Women in Culture and Society* 29 (2): 619–632.

Tomlinson, John. 1991. *Cultural Imperialism.* Baltimore, MD: The Johns Hopkins University Press.

Walker, Alice. 1992. *Possessing the Spirit of Joy.* New York: Harcourt Brace Jovanovich.

Walker, Alice, and Pratibha Parmar. 1993. *Warrior Marks: Female Genital Mutilation and the Sexual Blinding of Women.* New York: Harcourt Brace.

Winter, Bronwyn. 1995. "Women, the Law, and Cultural Relativism in France: The Case of Excision." In *Rethinking the Political: Gender, Resistance, and the State,* ed. Barbara Laslett, Johanna Brenner, and Yesim Arat, 315–350. Chicago: University of Chicago Press.

PART II

Cultures, Sexualities, and Knowledge

Imperialism and Sex in Africa

Nawal El Saadawi

When I was seven years old, I used to look up to the sky and ask my mother, "Who created all these stars?" "God created them," my mother replied. "And who created God?" I used to ask, as children did ask in the past, do in the present, and will do in the future. This childish question, "Who created God?" can open the way to a new knowledge or a new philosophy different from the dominating patriarchal class philosophy. However, the question is never encouraged to survive. It is lost in the amnesia that happens to children through the fear of God. Inhibiting all the questions related to God is the basis of education all over the world, not only in Egypt or Africa.

As a child, more than fifty years ago, I noticed that female circumcision, discrimination between boys and girls, the impurity of menstruation, virginity blood, marriage, divorce, abortion, and other similar sexual matters were all related to God's orders. I noticed also that King Farouk, the ruler of the country was related to God. In fact, the two personalities of God and the king appeared to me to be one personality. People used to laugh at me, but when I grew up and studied history in school, I discovered that the king of ancient Egypt, "the Pharaoh," was king and God at the same time.

A few years ago while speaking in an international women's conference, I made a connection between George H. W. Bush (then president of the United States) and female circumcision. Many people laughed because they did not see the link. But for me the link was as clear as the links I had made in my childhood between God and sex or God and the king. Since my childhood, I have come to know three words that are linked in one chain: God, sex, and the king. The results of research[1] done in Egypt in 1987 show that the incidence of female circumcision increased with the revival of the religious political powers by so-called religious fundamentalism. It is a known fact that the Ronald Reagan and George H. W. Bush administrations encouraged religious fundamentalist groups internationally and inside the United States to fight against communism, the Soviet Union, and democratic movements all over the world.

Modern or postmodern capitalism is a neocolonial system based on old class and patriarchal family values. Economic and sexual exploitation of women and the poor are linked, and both lie at the core of the system, which could never have been possible or maintained without a range of cruel devices used to keep a woman's sexuality in check and limit her sexual relations to only one man, the husband. In a patriarchal class system, history shows that the father was keen on knowing whom his legitimate children were so as to hand down his property to them. It was necessary to build up a system of legal, moral, cultural, and religious values capable of protecting the father's economic and political interests. Confounding children of the husband and those of the lovers would mean the collapse of the patriarchal class system built around knowing the name of the father.

As a medical doctor, I have been writing for more than thirty years against female circumcision and other cruel rites which deprive millions of women all over the world of one of their basic human rights: the right to bodily integrity. It has often been proclaimed that female circumcision relates exclusively to black African or Moslem societies. But in fact, it is performed on women regardless of their religious beliefs. When I was in primary school in Egypt, all my schoolmates were circumcised: Christians and Jews as well as Moslems. In African and Asian countries, it is performed on women who believe in one God as well as those who belong to polytheistic or atheistic communities. In the past, women in Europe and America were not exempted from this practice. Today, it is estimated that in the United States, approximately 40,000 women, most of whom are immigrants from different parts of the world, are circumcised every year. Many women who are not necessarily subjected to surgical removal of the clitoris are victims of the removal of other body parts as well as psychological and educational ectomy.

Sigmund Freud promoted psychological circumcision of women when he formulated his theory that maturity and mental health in a woman required that orgasm related to the clitoris cease and be transferred to the vagina. The abolition of the functions of the clitoris is equal to its absence. It might even be considered more malicious because it produces the illusion of being complete, whereas the body has lost an essential organ.

I am against all types of circumcision including male circumcision, which is not as detrimental as female circumcision, but is still harmful and may cause serious complications. To cut away any part of the human body for nonmedical reasons should be considered a crime. I oppose all attempts to deal with female circumcision or any other sexual problem in isolation, severing it from its links with historical, economic, and political factors, at the national and international levels. Not long ago, a Togolese woman, Fauziga

Kasinga, who claimed she had fled her country because she did not want to be circumcised, came to the United States seeking asylum but was instead incarcerated for two years. Miss Kasinga was exposed to double crime: the old tribal rites and the postmodern U.S. immigration denial of her rights. She is a female facing circumcision, but she is an alien and therefore not credible. In her prison cell, she dreams of her home country, Togo. Sometimes, the family rites are less cruel than the denial of alien rights.

Many people say that we live in the postcolonial era. But in Egypt and Africa we are still in the colonial or neocolonial era. Imperialism changes its methods and colors but it maintains its basic patriarchal, class, and capitalist philosophy. God, sex, and the king are still linked but in less obvious ways, and names have been changed. The king may be called the president and God may be called the superpowers, and sex may be replaced by gender. However the link is there. Imperialism as a patriarchal class system cannot survive without sexual and economic exploitation of women and the poor.

Africa is looked upon as the poorest of the poor, although in reality, it is one of the richest continents. Historically, Africa is one of the continents most ruined by imperialism. The riches of Africa have been robbed by imperialism, colonialism, and neocolonialism, leaving the continent with a per capita income of less than one U.S. dollar per day and at the mercy of neocolonial institutions such as the World Bank. The ruin of Africa was not only due to military and economic exploitation but also to social, cultural and sexual exploitation.

If there is something the imperialists or colonizers fear more than anything else, it is the power of knowledge or the extension of the domain of reason in the conduct of public and private affairs among colonized men and women. In Egypt, the British and French colonizers started their activities by building missionary schools where they taught girls and boys the fear of God. The primary school that I attended in Menouf, Egypt, was an English school. Miss Hamer, the British head of the school, used to read parts of the Bible every morning before we went to our classes. Religion was taught more than any other subject. There were Moslem, Christian, and Jewish girls in the school, and the three monotheistic religions were taught. As a Moslem, I had to believe in the three holy books. Obedience was the most praised virtue. Obedience to God was linked to obedience to all other authorities, from the school's British head down to my mother and father. My mother was not respected as much as my father by the British school head. Miss Hamer was a woman, but she looked down upon her own sex and raised the flag of Great Britain. She told us that we, Egyptians and Africans, were barbaric, uncivilized, morally and mentally debased, and that the British came to Egypt to civilize us. I was nine years old and the year was 1940. In April 1996, Jacques Chirac, the French president, came to Egypt on a visit. The intellectuals of the upper ruling class opined that the French came to Egypt to civilize us, and that Napoleon Bonaparte's expedition to Egypt was fundamentally an emancipatory and not a colonial project. Their views remind me of Miss Hamer's views more than half a century ago.

History shows us that the French, like the British, or Americans, Germans or any other imperialist power, did not come to emancipate us. De Lesseps built the Suez Canal under the Khedive Ismail to open Egypt up to colonial rule. In 1882, Britain occupied Egypt. Bonaparte admitted that the main objective of his expedition to Egypt was to outflank Britain by cutting off the route to India, and his lieutenant, Kléber, who was credited with much of the cultural or emancipatory achievements of the expedition, was killed by Soliman El-Halaby, an Egyptian in the resistance movement, after Bonaparte had secretly fled from Egypt. Through technical superiority in the art of warfare, the imperialists were able to wage savage, barbaric wars against us, the Africans, and were able to commit atrocities in order to force open the doors of our countries, not only for unequal trade or unprecedented material plunder, but for sexual, cultural, and human exploitation.

Imperialist scholars could write about us Africans as barbaric, uncivilized, morally, mentally, and sexually debased people while ignoring their barbaric, uncivilized aggression against our men and women. They could use old patriarchal habits, such as female circumcision, to label us and justify their colonization as an emancipatory effort. African popular revolts are labeled terrorism. Freedom fighters are terrorists, but imperialist wars and massacres are legal action for which God and the global superpowers are to be praised. When I was a child, I used to listen to the radio and hear the king praise God because He, God, was always with the king. In the Gulf War in 1991, I heard George H. W. Bush praise God because He was with George Bush.

I wonder why God is always with those who have military and economic power. God is now against the Africans. He is no longer against the Asians. The Chinese who were labeled by imperialists as the "Yellow Peril" are nowadays a respected world power due to China's position as a nuclear and economic power. China's economic growth reaches an annual average of 9 percent (from 1978 to 1994) with the expectation that in 2025, China's economy will be by far the largest in the world (1.5 times the size of the U.S. economy and 75 to 80 percent that of America, Japan, and Western European economies combined).

The economic development in any country is not merely the result of appropriate economic growth. It is also the result of political, social, educational, cultural, and economic transformations, without which it is impossible to force imperialist powers out of the country. The imperialists possess both nuclear power and economic power, and we cannot get rid of them by writing articles or books, or praying to God. Real peace can happen only when there is justice, and there is no real justice in an environment of inequality.

This we know from the history of liberation movements in all countries. Powerless women cannot change patriarchal family values. Men dominate women by their economic and muscular power, in addition to the power of God. God is always with men against women. I learned that in childhood. The three books of God confirm this fact. When I was a child in primary school, I had to struggle against these three holy books of divine justice.

Imperialist double standards ignore issues like peace, democracy, and human rights when it comes to their allies in Africa and our Arab region. Just look at the so-called peace between Israel and the Palestinians. Israel is using the situation of unequal relations to pursue a unilateral peace process, to ensure that the territories remain as cantons governed by a "functional" Palestinian authority, rather than a sovereign Palestinian state.

The five nuclear states (the United States, Russia, France, Britain, and China) in addition to Israel are accumulating and developing their nuclear military power. Israel refuses to sign the Nuclear Non-Proliferation Treaty and does not provide vital information to the International Atomic Energy Agency. While fifty-three African nations signed the African Nuclear Free Zone Treaty in Cairo in April 1996, Israel's Demona nuclear reactor was leaking radiation and threatening all those living in the region. Nuclear disarmament is forced upon Egypt and Africa, although no African country can afford nuclear-powered industries. The nuclear threat to Africa is essentially external, from the imperialist powers. In Egypt, the threat is very close to us in the Negev Desert—the Israeli nuclear reactor at Demona, with its weapon-grade plutonium that is dangerously toxic and ten times more so than enriched uranium. The Declaration on the Denuclearization of Africa does not stop nuclear powers from carrying out their nuclear tests and dumping their nuclear waste in Africa.

In view of the foregoing, can one really believe the nuclear powers when they talk about human rights, women's rights, or female circumcision?! Female circumcision in Africa has become a profitable issue for imperialists. It can be a sensational subject of discussion on CNN. Sex in Africa can be discussed as a cultural or multicultural issue. The imperialists are experts in separating sex from economics, politics, and power relations. In the name of diversity and cultural differences, they fail to recognize the danger in organizing conferences on African culture, in which they watch African dances, listen to African music and songs, gaze at black female flesh, and enjoy sexual liberation in African brothels. Sex, culture, multiculturalism, African festivals, and conferences become an exhibition, a spectacle for the pleasure of imperialists to see, to consume. The prominence of Africans in certain areas of the media, particularly in sex, dance, music, and sports, equals their exclusion from the upper echelons of political, military, and economic power.

I still remember the words of Mumia Abu Jamal, the black American activist journalist on death row, uttered in his prison cell as he waited to

die: "The color of power can often be white, and the color of disempower-
ment can often be black. But the most consistent variable that determines
power is the color green, the color of money." He goes on to say, "The
spirit of freedom, of human liberation cannot be held in one vessel. It is
like holding air in a glass: the rest of the area around that glass is not a vacuum; it doesn't stop there. It is the same for the spirit of revolution. I am
just one vessel and there are many other vessels. Let's keep pouring it and
pouring it on until it becomes the air we breathe."

NOTE

1. See Arab Women's Solidarity Association (AWSA), Field Research on Women's
Participation in Cultural Activities in Rural and Urban Egypt, Cairo: AWSA, 1987.

African Women, Colonial Discourses, and Imperialist Interventions: Female Circumcision as Impetus

Obioma Nnaemeka

THE 1980S AND THE "RAJ REVIVAL"

In the 1980s, moviegoers and television viewers were regaled by a bumper harvest of feature films and television series on India and former colonies in Africa—*Out of Africa, White Mischief, The Far Pavilion, Jewel in the Crown, Clive of India, A Passage to India,* and so forth. The colonial nostalgia grounded in the belief that colonialism was good for the colonized because it rescued them from backwardness and barbarism was aptly called the "*raj* revival"[1] by Salman Rushdie. The "*raj* revival" went beyond the lay public's fascination with empire to include its formal inscription in scholarship, including Western feminist scholarship that sometimes linked women's emancipation to the imperialist agenda: "There can be little doubt that on balance the position of women in imperialist, i.e. advanced capitalist societies, is for all implications more advanced than in less developed capitalist and non capitalist societies. In this sense the changes brought by imperialism to Third World societies may, in some instances, have been historically progressive."[2] The *raj* revival in Britain spoke to a past that was tolerated in the present: "The politics involved do not relate solely to the past; they involved justification for a late twentieth-century conservative ideology of white racial superiority as well. Defense of the empire certainly became more acceptable during Margaret Thatcher's Conservative administration of the 1980s."[3]

Thatcher's closest ally was Ronald Reagan. The conservative Reagan-Bush administrations of the 1980s also made "the defense of empire acceptable." The environment was conducive for a *raj* revival in the context of female circumcision debates and insurgencies. The imperialist notion of the inferiority of the colonized intensified racial intolerance that colored anti-immigration policies directed mainly against people from the ex-colonies in Africa.[4] Françoise Lionnet's study of developments on the other side of the Atlantic shows the extent to which the criminalization of female circumcision in France based on laws passed in the 1980s put African immigrants at great risk of arrests, trials, fines, and imprisonment.[5]

The polemic at the heart of the debates about female circumcision revolved around the questions of rights, culture, and civilization—individual versus communal rights, cultural relativism versus universalism, and barbarism versus civilization. Variants of these bipolarities have also figured in development discourses for decades.

DEVELOPMENT AND ITS DISCONTENTS: HUMAN RIGHTS WITHOUT HUMAN DIGNITY

Iji nma, jide ji.
You have the knife and the yam.

IGBO PROVERB

Ngwelenine makpu amakpu na amaro nke afo nalu.
Because all lizards lie on their stomach, it's difficult to know which one has a bellyache.

IGBO PROVERB

Despite the billions of dollars purportedly spent in the past four decades to develop Africa and her peoples, many parts of Africa are worse off than before. The failure is due not so much in the fact that Africans are not "developable" but, rather, in the mythology of development itself, mythology in the Barthesian sense of the word—a lie, a cover-up. Indeed, the irony of the development enterprise is that an intervention intended to herald and maintain progress has, to a large extent, become an impediment to progress. To move forward, an archaeology of the mythology of development is pertinent, imperative, and urgent. Vincent Tucker ably engages the archaeology in his essay "The Myth of Development: A Critique of Eurocentric Discourse" that unmasks the "cover-up" called development:

Development is the process whereby other peoples are dominated and their destinies are shaped according to an essentially Western way of conceiving and perceiving the world. The development discourse is part of an imperial process whereby other peoples are appropriated and turned into objects. It is an essential part of the process whereby the "developed" countries manage, control, and even create the Third World economically, politically, sociologically, and culturally. It is a process whereby the lives of some peoples, their plans, their hopes, their imaginations, are shaped by others who frequently share neither their lifestyles, nor their hopes, nor their values. The real nature of this process is disguised by a discourse that portrays development as a necessary and desirable process, as human destiny itself.[6]

The language of development is the language of necessity and desirability (the so-called Third World needs and must have "development") and, by implication, the language of the indispensability and relevance of those who believe it is their prerogative to make development happen. It is the language of those who "have the knife and the yam" (as my people say). But the illusion of indispensability carries in its articulation the seed of resistance—the resistance of those for whom development is manufactured as a panacea. It is in this respect that the issue of female circumcision has become one of the contested terrains in development discourse and engagement. The disagreement is not about the urgent need to put an end to a harmful practice—most people (both Africans and non-Africans) agree that the practice must end. The resistance from Africans is not necessarily against the termination of the practice; rather, it is against the strategies and methods (particularly their imperialistic underpinnings) used to bring about this desirable goal. The resistance is against "an imperial process whereby other people are appropriated and turned into objects"[7]—exhibited, gazed at, and silenced.

The danger of globalization lies in its preponderant unidirection and hegemony which dam the multiplicity of voices (particularly voices of marginalization, dissent, and resistance) and create a wide gulf at all levels—class, gender, racial, economic, digital, and so on. Globalization and the internationalization of African women's issues have produced a recontextualization and rearticulation of such issues. For example, about two decades or so ago, female circumcision was addressed primarily as a health issue, and the question of widowhood practices in Africa was addressed largely as an economic issue (specifically because of their economic impact on widows). The past decade has increasingly witnessed the tendency to herd all categories of human suffering into one battlefield: human rights. Human rights have become the mantra for all the causes célèbres generated in recent times; they become a cure-all for all African women's problems. Not surprisingly, international human rights documents—conventions, protocols, and so forth—proliferate in reports, essays, and books on African women produced recently inside and outside Africa.

To mobilize Africa against female circumcision, many have called on African governments and organizations (the AU, for example) to live up to the spirit and letter of their state constitutions as well as international human rights documents—the Convention on the Elimination of All Forms of Discrimination against Women (CEDAW), for example—to which they are signatories. One critic is quick to remind Nigerians that

> Chapter IV of the Constitution of Nigeria delineates the "fundamental rights" of Nigerian citizens. It states that "[e]very individual is entitled to respect for the dignity of his person, and accordingly, no person shall be subjected to torture or inhuman or degrading treatment." In light of the explicit language in these provisions, Nigerians need look no further than their own

constitution for injunction against female circumcision as violation of women's and children's constitutional rights.[8]

Well said. But "respect for the dignity of his person," and "degrading treatment" demand scrutiny. Indeed, the word "dignity" is at the core of all the basic human rights documents that have emerged from the United Nations since its formation over fifty years ago. The first sentence of the Universal Declaration of Human Rights[9] contains the word: "Whereas recognition of the inherent dignity and of the equal unalienable rights of all members of the human family is the foundation of freedom, justice and peace in the world."[10] The first sentence of the oft-cited 1981 CEDAW includes the word: "Nothing that the Charter of the United Nations reaffirms faith in fundamental human rights, in the dignity and worth of the human person and in the equal rights of men and women."[11]

Female circumcision has been condemned as a "torture" or "degrading treatment" that lacks any "respect for the dignity" of women and girls. And it should be. Unfortunately, some of the most egregious manifestations of "degrading treatment" and lack of "respect for dignity" lie in the modus operandi of many Westerners (feminists and others) who have intervened in this matter. The resistance of African women is not against the campaign to end the practice, but against their dehumanization and the lack of respect and dignity shown to them in the process. For the Western interventionists and insurgents to lay claim to any credibility and legitimacy, they must first put respect and dignity back where they belong. In my view, the ultimate violence done to African women is the exhibition of their body parts—in this instance, the vagina—in various stages of "unbecoming." This acute voyeuristic inclination would have fizzled out if the victim had been Western.[12] What is good for the goose is also good for the gander! It is not necessary to violate African women in order to address the violence that was done to them. In effect, African women are doubly victimized: first from within (their culture) and second from without (their "saviors").

The images (as photographs) of African and Muslim women in books, magazines and films about circumcision are disturbing at best, and downright insulting at worst. A couple of examples will suffice—the first is explicit; the second is more subtle. Not too long ago, I received an e-mail offering me a book on circumcision that had just been published. I acquiesced, and a couple of weeks later the book, titled *The Day Kadi Lost Part of Her Life*,[13] was in my mailbox. After reading the book and looking at the pictures, I retitled it: "The Day Westerners Lost All of Their Mind"! A promotional insert in the book reads as follows:

> We "meet" Kadi on the morning she is to be circumcised when she is still blissfully ignorant of what is about to happen to her. We see her at home, going about her daily chores, eating her breakfast and then accompany her on the journey to the village where the operation is to take place. Photos

depict the sacrifice of a chicken as precursor to her own circumcision and then witness as Kadi is taken by the "buankisa" (circumciser), made to undress, held down and then cut. While the photographs are very confronting, they are portrayed with sensitivity and delicacy, yet evoke sadness and anger, which we hope will serve to rally readers against this practice.[14]

This book—which, incidentally, was short-listed for the Australian Award for Excellence in Educational Publishing—gives a bad name to "sensitivity and delicacy." The book is replete with photos of Kadi (this poor girl from a nameless African country) in different states of undress—the most disconcerting being the pictures where she is held down (legs spread out) by the emaciated legs of an old woman, and screaming her head off as her clitoris and a razor are held in full view for the reader. The photos come with captions such as:

> With the first incision, Kadi's screams cut the heavy air of the sky, threatening a storm. The *buankisa's* hands are covered with blood, again. . . . The pain is unbearable and Kadi fears the incision will never end. . . . The strength of the old woman is insufficient against the instinctive reactions of Kadi's pain, and the cuts of the razor, used on each girl until the point of bluntness, are repeated despite her movement.[15]

In fact, in the picture that carries this last caption, the child that is being cut does not look like Kadi (although the name is ascribed to her)—she's much younger and has more baby fat than Kadi—and the hands circumcising her are different from the ones circumcising Kadi. This observation may seem minor or insignificant, but it certainly reveals the making of "Kadi," on behalf of whom money will be raised (like other Kadis who have been used to swell bank accounts). The reader is reminded in the promotional insert that "*part* of the proceeds of profits" (my emphasis) will go to FORWARD—the Foundation for Women's Health, Research and Development. Similar to other "development" promotional materials before it, this insert is silent on where the *bulk* of the proceeds will go.

This choreographed text (like most such texts) is presented to us as a chance meeting of two journalists from Spain who stumbled into Africa with cameras and films to "meet Kadi on the morning she is to be circumcised." This may not be as fortuitous as one is made to believe. The text was written by Isabel Ramos Rioja, editor of *La Vanguardia* newspaper, and the photographs are by Kim Manresa, who has won many photojournalism awards, some of which were probably given to him for taking photographs of little girls' clitorises in Africa. Kadi's predicament is cause for concern, but so should be the predicament of the emaciated hungry-looking old woman who is holding her down. Fortunately, Manresa's camera documents a wider and more complex landscape: Kadi and the context (human and material) of her existence. Unfortunately, the book, in its articulation, ignores the complexity of the context and focuses instead on Kadi's clitoris and the razor that eliminates it. So goes the mythology of circumcision as it is thrust on to the international stage. So are the contextualization and banalization of African women's lives as they take the center stage in the narratives of feminist insurgence against female circumcision.

It is no secret that Westerners and Western media organizations have offered money and used all sorts of coercion to have girls circumcised so that Westerners could shoot pictures for their magazines, newspapers, books, and documentaries. Pratibha Parmar's account of the encounter with Bilaela in Gambia is instructive:

> Our first meeting with Bilaela went badly. I felt cheated and upset that she had not been straightforward. We'd made a monetary agreement by phone from London, which I'd confirmed in writing by fax. . . . Bilaela now says she has spent all the money we had allocated. . . . I am afraid Bilaela thinks we are like the crew members from a major U.S. television network who were here three weeks ago. According to Bilaela, they had plenty of money, stayed in five-star hotels, and had many rest days at the pool and on the beach. Bilaela was the American crew's local liaison, and apparently had problems getting the money they owed her and thinks we are probably not going to pay her either. Bilaela said . . . that if we were willing to pay for some girls to be excised, she could arrange for us to film it. She said she'd done that for the New York crew.[16]

And these voyeurs want me to believe that they are fighting for the human rights and dignity of African females! The role that money, the politics of poverty, and the politics of the belly play in these campaigns and interventions demands extensive research. In the so-called Third World, poverty makes people more vulnerable and exploitable.[17] Such vulnerabilities cast a shadow on the authenticity of claims about "Third World collaborators."

In March 1999, Germany was hit by a barrage of billboard announcements developed by the advertising agency Young & Rubicam for the German-based organization (I)NTACT, whose main focus is the campaign against female circumcision. (I)NTACT used what Young and Rubicam produced to: "(1) inform the public about FGM; (2) make known the organization (I)NTACT; and (3) stimulate giving."[18] There are four announcements, each of which has a picture of an object: an old, rusty, crooked, blood-stained knife; a long threaded needle; a rusty, bloodstained pair of scissors; and a rusty, bloodstained razor. Tobe Levin, a dedicated feminist advocate for the end of female circumcision, translates the German inscriptions on the announcements as follows:

> Above the scissor, for example, subway passengers can read: "Whoever thinks about cutting hair has never seen the eyes of a child who, without anesthesia, is having her clitoris cut out." Above the needle, bus riders can read: "Whoever thinks about darning socks has never held the trembling hands of a baby whose vagina was sewn up." Above the knife, pedestrians can read: "Whoever thinks about peeling potatoes has never experienced the torment of a bride

whose vagina is cut open on her wedding night." Above the razor blade, motorists can read: "Whosoever thinks about shaving has never heard the screams of a four-year old whose labia are being cut off." Under all four objects is written: "Each year worldwide two million girls and women are mutilated, physically and spiritually, as a result of circumcision. (I)NTACT helps." With thousands of posters attracting attention throughout the nation, the action has inspired hundreds of newspaper articles, a swollen treasury, and not a little criticism from African women.[19]

(I)NTACT's effort is supposedly intended as a counterpoint to the prevailing exposure of African and Muslim women's genitalia. However, even this "kinder, gentler" and more subtle version is devastating in its commodification of African women—African females are pushed as one would push detergent, toothpaste, or shaving cream in a television commercial. Obviously, the language, the disturbing parallels, and troubling juxtapositions are intended to attract attention and shock readers/viewers into opening their wallets to (I)NTACT. It worked: (I)NTACT laughed all the way to the bank.

RENAMING TO MISNAME: STRATEGIES AGAINST SPEECH AND RESISTANCE

If you want to see the way that the world has treated the Igbo man, look at the names his children bear.

CHINUA ACHEBE

It is not what you call me; it is what I answer to.

IGBO PROVERB

Until the lion has a voice, the tales of the hunt will be only those of the hunter.

ERITREAN PROVERB

Censorship, as an imposition of silence on others, works in different ways. In the debate about female circumcision, the tactic of renaming to misname and silence has been deployed to marginalize voices which are making legitimate arguments against the pitfalls and wrongheadedness of campaigns by Westerners against female circumcision. African women who have objected to the modus operandi of the Western insurgents have been labeled, indicted, and dismissed as defenders of female circumcision. The Western-inspired name game that obfuscates the real issues in this matter is a diversion that the campaign to bring an end to female circumcision does not need. Many years ago, a conference on women responding to racism was held in Connecticut. One of the participants, Audre Lorde, exposed the renaming-to-misname tactic used by the local print media:

Women responding to racism is a topic so dangerous that when the local media attempt to discredit this conference they choose to focus upon the provision of lesbian housing as diversionary device as if the *Hartford Courant* dare not mention the topic chosen for discussion here, racism, lest it became apparent that women are in fact attempting to examine and to alter all the repressive conditions of our lives.[20]

Renaming to misname (changing the subject) has been used by anti-abortion advocates in the United States to put pro-choice activists on the defensive—a tactic that is tantamount to censorship and resistance to self-affirmation and self-determination. The abortion debate in the United States polarizes with the shifts in the language to articulate it, primarily owing to the entrenched ideological positions and profound ethical questions that have been injected into it. The naming and renaming of the combatants in this bitterly contested terrain—from pro-abortion/antiabortion to pro-choice/pro-life—is instructive. Claiming to be sole custodians of life, pro-lifers brand voices of opposition as anti-life ("baby-killers"), thus putting the pro-choice advocates in the difficult position of spending time and energy to defend themselves against a name they did not call themselves and at the same time, assert that pro-choice and pro-life are not mutually exclusive.

Female circumcision has also been thrust into the name game—from gruesome sexual castration and female genital mutilation to the "kinder and gentler" female genital surgeries, and now female genital cutting. But in this instance, one must not underestimate the impact of the renaming for people (Africans) whose cultures attach an importance to naming so profound that ceremonies are performed to mark it. From people like Alice Walker who has labeled African cultures "mutilating cultures"[21] to the German Bundestag, which declared in a 1998 multi-party motion that "the term 'circumcision' shall no longer be used by the government," Westerners are quick to appropriate the power to name, while remaining totally oblivious of and/or insensitive to the implications and consequences of the naming. In this name game, although the discussion is about African women, a subtext of barbaric African and Muslim cultures and the West's relevance (even indispensability) in purging the barbarism marks another era where colonialism and missionary zeal determined what "civilization" was, and figured out how and when to force it on people who did not ask for it. Only imperialist arrogance can imagine what Africans want, determine what they need, and devise ways to deliver the goods.

The relevance or indispensability of the West in African affairs thrives on the availability of problems and crises. If the problems are not there, they are kept alive in our collective consciousness through imaginings, speculations, manufacture, and reinvention. Western fascination with African women's body parts and sexuality has a long history. In 1810, Sara Baartman—a twenty-year-old Khoisan woman—was taken from her home in South Africa to London to be exhibited as a freak of nature, because of her "larger-than-normal" (by European standard) buttocks. In 1814, when the British had had an eyeful, they shipped poor Sara to France, where the French used her for "scientific research" until her death in 1815. The "scientific research" continued after her death, with her body parts—sexual organs and brain—displayed in the Musée de l'Homme in Paris for one hundred and seventy years. In the nineteenth century, the problem was the African woman's buttocks. The current debate is about another body part—the vagina. Indeed, Alice Walker dedicated her novel *Possessing the Secret of Joy* to the offended body part: "This Book Is Dedicated with Tenderness and Respect to the Blameless Vulva." Who knows what the next body part for discussion will be! Ultimately, the circumcision debate is about the construction of the African woman as the "Other."

But naming, renaming, and misnaming have their impetus, goals and consequences. During the apartheid regime, for example, naming and renaming of people based on shades of skin color was linked to the right to vote or disenfranchisement. Not much is accomplished by substituting what the people who engage in the practice under discussion call it—female circumcision—with "female genital mutilation" except to (1) exhibit the arrogant claim to the power to name;[22] (2) justify the indictment and opprobrium heaped on Africa and the Muslim world; and (3) create the urgency necessary for effective fundraising. Indeed, the third reason relates also to the number of circumcised African women that is floated around—over a hundred million. What we have not been told is whether the hundred million were circumcised in one year, ten years, or since Africa and Africans came into existence. As far as I know, when the statistics of people murdered in the United States or women raped in Germany are given, the time period is specified—usually a six-month or one-year period. More importantly, we are often reminded that in Africa, female circumcision is such a taboo that people are hesitant to talk about it. If people are silent on the issue, who provided the figures bandied about for circumcised African? In my view, it makes no difference if two, three, or a trillion African females circumcised. If one is circumcised, it is one too many. The point I am raising here is that of trust between the helper and the "helped." Trust among collaborators, and between giver and recipient, is the most important ingredient in fashioning meaningful change with regard to female circumcision and similar issues. During their 1993 two-week whirlwind tour crisscrossing the Senegambia region for their documentary *Warrior Marks*, Alice Walker and Pratibha Parmar came to grips on a few occasions with the issue of trust/mistrust and its consequences. Pratibha Parmar notes with disappointment and frustration her unsuccessful interview with Madame Fall:

> After all the waiting, the interview turned out to be a great disappointment. In our previous conversation, Madame Fall had spoken of the joys of sex, how important it was to her, how circumcision took this pleasure from women. She had laughed, had been informative, entertaining, persuasive. None of this occurred in our filmed interview, and none of our promptings

produced what we were looking for. Instead, she talked about her "leader" and the political party she belonged to. Fortunately, the interviews with the two sisters were inspiring. One of the sisters said, "you cannot ever come to terms with pain."[23]

Obviously, Madame Fall did not trust Pratibha Parmar and her group enough to give them "what [they] were looking for." More important, Parmar and company are not interested in what Madame Fall wanted to talk about—politics. This encounter reveals some of the salient issues at the core of the debate about and campaign against female circumcision—the unequal power relations between the West and the so called Third World; the reduction of the myriad issues facing African women to female circumcision; the disregard of the complexity and integrity of African women; the obsessions, prejudices, and deafness of the West.[24] Parmar and her group came to Africa in search of Africa. Their documentary was already made before they set foot on African soil. Any African whose interests, concerns, and priorities ran contrary to the group's already-made documentary (in their heads) was irrelevant and what he/she had to say was worthless. African women see and live their lives in ways that are much more complex than the obsessive one-dimensional and one-issue-oriented depictions that appear in books and films about female circumcision.

People name themselves and things in their environment for specific reasons and particular purposes. Africans do. TOSTAN, a Senegal-based nongovernmental organization (NGO) that has registered significant success in its campaign against female circumcision, calls ending the practice "abandonment," not the popularly used "eradication." The former term has a specific meaning for the people on behalf of whom TOSTAN has launched its campaign. To insist that TOSTAN use the "accepted" latter term instead of the term that works for the communities it serves will certainly undermine the work of the NGO. "Abandonment" makes sense if one examines closely the context in which female circumcision occurs. In the Ivory Coast,[25] female circumcisions are performed in a hut during initiation ceremonies. But what goes on in the hut is much more than female circumcision. Young girls are taught hygiene, sex education, and other lessons of life they need. Outsiders who demand that the "circumcision hut" be destroyed meet with resistance from the community. The community is not resisting because they can no longer circumcise their girls due to the demolition of the hut; they are resisting because the destruction of the hut will mean the erasure of all the educational activities that occur in it. What the local NGOs did, with government support, was to argue for the retention of the hut minus one activity (female circumcision) that takes place in it. This seems to me to mark the difference between "abandonment" and "eradication." One can "abandon" one aspect (female circumcision) of the context without "eradicating" the entire context (the hut). Also, by renaming female circumcision "female genital mutilation" in which knives, razors, and other instruments are used, Western inurgents have inadvertently narrowed the field of struggle. Little do they know that female circumcision is not always about knives and razors. There are communities that use hot water to numb the clitoris. I am—in collaboration with an Africa-based NGO—in the midst of a campaign against this practice. The communities will remain nameless for fear of the spectacle of Westerners rushing off with cameras to these communities looking for women with buckets of hot water to photograph and/or harass.[26]

IN SEARCH OF SOLUTIONS: A QUESTION OF METHOD

Those who fight against circumcision have always blamed it on "tradition" and culture" and consequently, have proceeded to exorcize Africa's and Islam's past. Tradition is not about a reified past; it is about a dynamic present—a present into which the past is projected, and to which other traditions (with their pasts and presents) are linked. It is to the present, and to how we as members of local and global communities are implicated in creating and maintaining traditions, that we must respond. Pratibha Parmar worries about the "return" to reified tradition in nationalist movements, its nefarious consequences for women, and

> the worrying and dangerous tendency in cultural nationalist movements, which in their bid to return to traditional values deny women their free agency. It is women who bear the brunt of these patriarchal traditions. For instance, women in Iran have been forced to put back the veil in the Islamic drive for a return to traditional values. While a sense of cultural nationalism is often crucial to the fight for self-determination, this should not be at the expense of half the nation's population?[27]

But two decades ago, in her preface to *The Hidden Face of Eve*, Nawal El Saadawi wrote a more probing analysis of the rise of Islamic fundamentalism and its manifestations (for example, the upsurge in the use of the veil) in the Arab world in general, and Iran in particular.[28] In her analysis, El Saadawi linked the rise of fundamentalism to foreign—particularly American—intervention in the region. This intervention, the ousting of the Shah, the return of Ayatolla Khomeini, and the rise of Islamic fundamentalism are linked. In this instance, as in others, "traditional values" and "these patriarchal traditions" (according to Parmar) are invoked by internal forces purportedly to protect the inside from the outside. Foreign intervention, therefore, becomes an alibi for enforcing and justifying repression within. In the final analysis, women become pawns in the struggle between repressive, authoritarian internal forces and external imperialistic forces. What is at issue here is our collective responsibility for the so-called traditional practices. Unfortunately, those who have invented globalization are quick to grab the benefits, but renege on the responsibilities.

The problem with this circumcision business is that many Westerners who plunge into it do so thoughtlessly. It is not sufficient to read about female circumcision, then quit your job, set up shop, and raise tons of money "to save young girls from being mutilated." Of course, there are many who are thoughtful and genuinely committed. But as my people say, "because all lizards lie on their stomach, it's difficult to know which one has a bellyache." At any rate, a noble, thoughtless cause is a dangerous oxymoron. To combat female circumcision, we must first diagnose the problem; and to do that effectively, we must ask questions (lots of questions); we must have a sense of history; we must have the humility to learn (not to teach); we must have the capacity to listen (not to preach). In "dialogues" between Africa and the West, one party is listening and not speaking; the other party is garrulous and deaf. Not only do such "dialogues" not promote social change, they undermine attempts to bring genuine social transformation. One of the most memorable graffiti I read at the University of Minnesota as a graduate student was the following exchange between two students—first student: "Jesus is the answer." Second student: "What was the question?" Many Western insurgents against female circumcision have all the answers, but ask no questions. But we must ask questions: Why was circumcision done and, more importantly, why is it still done? Who brought it to an end? Why is it done in certain African countries and not in others? Why is it done in one community and not in another within the same country? Where else, other than in Africa and the Islamic would, has it been done? Why and when?

The global sweep of female circumcision is not disputed (although many would claim to be ignorant of it). Female circumcision is not just an African or an Islamic problem; it is a global problem. It was not imported into the West by "Third World" immigrants, as some would suggest. It happened in the West before the immigrants arrived.[29] Nawal El Saadawi raised this issue during the heated debate about circumcision that erupted at the 1980 mid-Decade for Women conference in Copenhagen:

> In Copenhagen, we had a lot of disagreement, we women from Africa and the Third World, with her [Fran Hosken, publisher of *WIN News*]. In our workshops, we argued that clitoridectomy has nothing to do with Africa or with any religion, Islam or Christianity. It is known in history that it was performed in Europe and America, Asia, and Africa. It has to do with patriarchy and monogamy. When patriarch was established, monogamy was forced on women so that fatherhood could be known. Women's sexuality was attenuated so as to fit within the monogamous system. But she doesn't want to hear any of this.[30]

In my view, the important question should not be about "tradition," geography (Africa or the Middle East), or religion (Islam). The crucial question should be: Why is the female body subjected to all sorts of abuse and indignity in different cultures and different places (including the West)? Western feminist insurgents need to link their fight against female circumcision to an equally vigorous fight against the abuse of the female body in their immediate environment. Charity, they say, begins at home. Their first task should be to straighten out their own men by inviting other women ("Third World," Muslim, and so on) to join them in their endeavor (a task "Third World" women will perform creditably!). Such collaboration will earn Western women a place in "Third World" struggles. It is unwise for Western women to think that they are very capable of solving their own problems, whereas "Third World" women need their help because they are totally incapable of taking care of their own problems. Such thinking breeds resistance. The problem of women living under patriarch is a global one that requires global action.

The issue I raise here is that of agency. African women do not lack agency, whether others wish to attribute it to them or not. My earlier questions— Why is it no longer done in certain places? Who brought it to an end?—are pertinent here. Female circumcision is no longer practiced in some African communities not because Fran Hosken published *WIN News* (which most women in Africa do not read) or because Alice Walker produced the film *Warrior Marks* (which most African women have not seen and probably will never see). Walker's "dream" for *Warrior Marks* makes the point: "While planning the film, I dreamed of taking it from village to village, but by now I've visited many African villages, and there are absolutely no audio-visual facilities. Barely, sometimes, drinking water. None that we foreigners could drink."[31] It does not occur to Walker that there may be a relationship between female circumcision and this "absolute" lack she documents in her book *Warrior Marks*. Who is Fran Hosken writing for? Who is Alice Walker filming for? Certainly not for the African women who are there on the ground working tirelessly against female circumcision. There is a huge difference between writing and filming *about* African women, on the one hand, and writing and filming with/for African women, on the other. That difference may determine the success or failure of the campaign against female circumcision.

Indeed, foreigners and foreign organizations have contributed money and material resources to women and organizations in Africa campaigning against female circumcision, and these individuals and organizations should be applauded. However, it is grossly erroneous to conclude that things are changing in Africa because of Beijing (or any such UN gatherings). The fight against female circumcision in Africa predates 1975 (the beginning of the first UN Decade for Women). Involvement by outsiders since then has accelerated progress in some respects and impeded progress in other areas. But much of the credit for what has been achieved must go to African women (men too!) and Africa-based NGOs that actually do the work. African women do not lack agency. What they lack may be the material and structural conditions necessary for the accomplishment of their goals.

CULTURE, THE HUMANITIES, AND DEVELOPMENT

The rest of this essay will be devoted to the work of two Africa-based NGOs that have been successful in their campaigns against female circumcision: Women's Issues Communication and Services Agency (WICSA) in Nigeria and TOSTAN in Senegal. To understand and appreciate these NGOs' success, it is necessary to examine how they do their work. But before getting into the specifics of their strategies, I would like to address briefly the limitation of the notion and articulation of development. In an earlier essay I argue that the inordinate focus on politics and the economy in development studies and work needs to be relaxed to create room for what I call cultural forces—culture as a positive force in development,[32] culture (cultural practices, cultural values, cultural impositions, and so forth) is often evoked as a negative element that impedes development. I argue that culture and its manifestation in different media play a positive role as well, and should be put in the service of development. Africa-based NGOs are cognizant of this fact, and have designed and executed their work accordingly.

Also, there are the issues of context, complexity, and interrelationships. Each "cultural practice" is a link in a chain whose demise may depend not on a surgical removal of the link but, rather, on adjusting the other links to which it is attached. It has been shown that many people in the "Third World" would have fewer children with an improvement in the context of their lives—education, material conditions, and so forth. It is not sufficient to preach to the woman who sends her child to hawk goods in a Lagos market about child labor and child abuse when the child's very existence depends on the hawking/labor; when the economy has so broken down that the mother had to withdraw her child from school because she could not afford the fees; when forces beyond her control—internal fiscal irresponsibility coupled with the unfair and strident monetary policies of international institutions such as the International Monetary Fund—have paralyzed her economically.[33] The child is not abused by his or her mother (who is devising ways to ensure the child's survival); the child is abused by the internal and external forces mentioned above. For the child to be saved from hawking, the context of his or her existence must change—a change that can be brought about by the meaningful collaboration and genuine commitment of the internal and external forces that abuse the child. We must not lose sight of contexts and interrelationships.

The Africa-based NGOs that I have observed, and with which I have been fortunate to work, are mindful of context, complexity, and interrelationship as they engage in their campaigns against female circumcision. Unlike some of the organizations that are mushrooming in Europe and America, with only one item on their agenda—female circumcision—Africa-based NGOs campaign against female circumcision as part of an overall campaign for and against other myriad issues. (Africans have things to campaign for, too!) Furthermore, they place culture and cultural expressions (visual and performing arts, for example) as a positive force at the center of their work. The importance of the humanities (particularly the visual and performing arts) in development can be neither underestimated nor ignored, particularly in view of the fact that the majority of the people for whom the campaigns are launched are illiterate. The Nigerian NGO, WICSA, has put in place a "traveling museum" of paintings and sculptures for its campaign against female circumcision. WICSA gathered both male and female artists for its project. This point is important, and will be addressed below. The works of art are contextualized, and the accompanying literature (brochures and so on) is in European languages and more importantly, in local languages as well. WICSA brings the "museum" to the people in their immediate environment (both urban and rural)—a strategy that encourages the participation of a wider audience, which would not have been possible if the "museum" were housed in one location to be viewed by communities for whom transportation is either inadequate or nonexistent. WICSA has also succeeded in bringing its work to the attention of international audiences. In 1998, it was invited to participate in the second Women in Africa and the African Diaspora conference on "Health and Human Rights" held in Indianapolis. One of the conference participants, Tobe Levin, was so impressed by the workshop organized by WICSA that she collaborated with the NGO to organize a six-month exhibition tour of Germany.

TOSTAN (literal meaning: "breaking out of the egg"), a Senegal-based NGO directed by Molly Melching, has truly engineered a breakthrough by bringing cultural understanding to bear on development, and achieving outstanding results. TOSTAN, supported by funding from UNESCO and UNICIEF, played a pivotal role in the banning of female circumcision in Senegal in 1998. Through its eighteen-month modular basic educational program (developed by a group of Senegalese villagers and African and American non-formal education experts) that links basic education to life skills, TOSTAN has been able to teach rural women reading and writing skills in their local languages, encourage them to start and maintain income-generating projects, train them in health-related issues, give them self-confidence, and mobilize them to initiate and participate in social change— for example, the successful campaign to ban female circumcision. The groundswell of opposition to female circumcision in Senegal has its roots in the relationship between TOSTAN and the women of Malicounda Bambara who participated in the TOSTAN basic education program. Armed with knowledge about health, leadership, and human rights, the literate, confident graduates of the TOSTAN program decided to tackle the issue of female circumcision. The women did their homework, and argued their case in the presence of the village council, which subsequently banned female circumcision in their community in 1997. Word spread to other communities, which also decided to endorse "the oath of Malicounda." In the community of Ker Simbara, the campaign was spearheaded by two men who had participated in the TOSTAN program. The February 1998 "Dia-bougou Declaration," which got thousands of villagers to commit to the cessation of female circumcision, was drawn up by the village authority and the women.

A common thread runs through these two success stories—sensitivity to context and complexity, cultural understanding and its integration in project design, participatory processes, use of local languages, collaboration between women and men, participation of local religious and "traditional" authori-ties, and genuine, meaningful collaboration between local communities and foreign entities. TOSTAN provided a context of empowerment for the women of Malicounda Bambara, allowed them to determine what their pri-orities were, and encouraged them to pursue and accomplish their goals. The women invited the participation of men because they are culturally attuned to such thinking, coming from an environment in which women's issues are village/community issues requiring the participation of villagers regardless of sex. The women are politically astute in ensuring the partici-pation of all branches of local authority, regardless of which gender holds the authority. They also believe, as many African women do, that if the men are part of the problem, they should also be part of the solution. The problem with Western feminist insurgents against female circumcision is that they go to Africa to interview women, while alienating and putting down the men. The one man whom Alice Walker and Pratibha Parmar dis-cuss interminably in *Warrior Marks* is their Gambian driver, Malign. The one time Walker made an attempt to talk to the men who hold authority in the village was when she visited the chief's compound:

> The men around here are blandly gracious, like slave-masters, I suppose. We paid our respects to three graying patriarchs representing the *marabout* or *alacar* (not sure of the word they were using for chief; something Arabic) of the village, who was away on business. The men sat on chairs, the women on the ground. As a guest, I got a chair but could barely stay in it. The women had to recite in detail, and several times, everything we'd done since arriving in the village. They seemed bored, weary of their own subservience. I hadn't realized no one can leave the village, even guest, without this ritual of being "released" by the chiefs, who are, of course, always men. This answers the question of why women don't run away. And, too, where would they go?[34]

To decode and analyze Walker's statement would require another essay. Suffice it to say that the arrogance and disrespect that turn a courtesy call into a treatise on bondage account for the failure of many interventions in Africa that are spearheaded by Westerners. One does not have to look too far to see why WICSA, TOSTAN, and similar NGOs succeed where self-serving projects like Alice Walker's have failed to make any positive and lasting impact on the lives of African women.

NOTES

An earlier version of this chapter appears in Celeste Schenck and Susan Perry, *Eye to Eye: Women Practicing Development across Cultures* (London: Zed Press, 2001).

1. Rushdie 1984.
2. Molyneux 1981.
3. Chaudhuri and Strobel 1992, 1.
4. The Reagan administration granted a blanket amnesty to *illegal* immigrants who had been in the United States for five years. By limiting the amnesty to *illegal* immigrants, the policy disqualified millions of Africans immigrants because the majority of African immigrations enter the United States *legally* as students.
5. Lionnet 1995.
6. Tucker 1999, 1–2.
7. Tucker 1999, 1.
8. *Harvard Law Review* 1993, 1954.
9. United Nations 1948.
10. United Nations 1948.
11. Center for the Study of Human Rights 1996, 1.
12. In February 2000, within one week, two tragic accidents occurred in two parts of the globe. A Kenyan Airline, with almost 170 crew and passengers (mostly Nigerians) on board, plunged into the Atlantic Ocean off the Ivory Coast. There were only ten survivors. A few days later, an Alaskan Airline plane crashed into the Pacific off the California coast, killing all 88 people on board. During the recovery period, the Western media updated viewers with the number of victims recovered off the California coast (viewers heard about the numbers, but did not see the victims). But the same Western media exhibited on television grisly images of bloated and decomposing bodies/body parts recovered off the coast of Ivory Coast. Such disrespect is shown to the African dead or alive.
13. Rioja and Manresa 1998.
14. Rioja and Manresa 1998, no folio.
15. Rioja and Manresa 1998, no folio.
16. Walker and Parmar 1993, 161–162.
17. Betsy Hartmann 1995. Hartmann has documented cases in India where population control experts and organizations can get women to "accept" sterilization in exchange for a couple of saris and a bag of rice.
18. Levin 2005, 294.
19. Levin 2005, 294–295.
20. Lorde 1984, 128.
21. Walker and Parmar 1993, 73.
22. When the Europeans came to Igboland, they met people who called themselves *ndi Igbo* (Igbo people). Claiming that they could not pronounce "gb" and did not have the time nor inclination to learn how it is said, the Europeans renamed *ndi Igbo* "Ibo people," and eternalized the renaming and misnaming in their books. The same Europeans told the Igbo people that they could not pronounce *anya* (eye), but Igbo people have recently discovered that Europeans can pronounce "Netanyahu" correctly and with ease!
23. Walker and Parmar 1993, 207.
24. I am aware that the two major figures in the making of the documentary—Alice Walker and Pratibha Parmar—are women of color. By referring to them as Westerners, I wish to state that what is at issue here is not skin color but the mindset (mentality) that emanates from a particular location. It is instructive that Parmar conferred Nigerian citizenship on the well-known Kenyan writer Ngugi wa Thiong'o—

"film being directed by the Nigerian writer Ngugi" (Walker and Parmar 1993, 214)—despite her claims of affinity to Kenya: "I was born in Kenya, East Africa and schooled in England, yet I was brought up to think of India as home. . . . Kenya gained independence in 1963, and my family moved to England a few years later" (Walker and Parmar 1993, 89).

25. The Ivory Coast case was narrated by the Ivoirian minister for health during the second international conference on "Women in Africa and the African Diaspora: Health and Human Rights" held in Indianapolis (October 1998).

26. During a recent visit to Germany, I listened to a presentation by the wife of top German politician who is leading a campaign in Germany against female circumcision. She proudly exhibited the knives and razors she confiscated from circumcisers during one visit to Benin, I believe. How naïve to think that the circumcisers have been put out of business because a couple of their knives are now in Germany!

27. Walker and Parmar 1993, 213.

28. El Saadawi 1980.

29. Some would argue that female circumcision as "female genital mutilation" was not performed in the West. But this is the case in many African communities where the practice goes on. Many of these communities have never heard of or practiced the radical versions that can conceivably be called mutilation. The problem with the Western-driven campaign is that it chooses the worst-case scenario and makes it a generic term for the practice. The issue of "urgency" I raised above applies here as well.

30. Patterson and Gillam 1983, 190–191.

31. Walker and Parmar 1993, 81–82.

32. Nnaemeka 1997.

33. See Okafor 2001.

34. Walker and Parmar 1993, 43.

WORKS CITED

Center for the Study of Human Rights. 1996. *Women and Human Rights: The Basic Documents.* New York: Columbia University.

Chaudhuri, Nupur, and Margaret Strobel, eds. 1992. *Western Women and Imperialism: Complicity and Resistance.* Bloomington, IN: Indiana University Press.

El Saadawi, Nawal. 1980. *The Hidden Face of Eve: Women in the Arab World.* Trans. and ed. Sherif Hetata. London: Zed Book.

Hartmann, Betsy. 1995. *Reproductive Rights and Wrongs: The Global Politics of Population Control.* Boston, MA: South End Press.

Harvard Law Review. 1993. "What's Culture Got to Do with It? Excising the Harmful Tradition of Female Circumcision." *Harvard Law Review* 106 (8): 1944–1961.

Levin, Tobe. 2005. "Female Genital Mutilation: Campaigns in Germany." In *Engendering Human Rights: Cultural and Socioeconomic Realities in Africa and the Africa Diaspora,* ed. Obioma Nnaemeka and Joy Ezeilo, 285–301. New York: Plagrave/Macmillan.

Lionnet, Françoise. 1995. "The Limits of Universalism: Identity, Sexuality, and Criminality." In *Postcolonial Representations: Women, Literature, Identity,* 154–166. Ithaca, NY: Cornell University Press.

Lorde, Audre. 1984. *Sister Outsider.* Trumansburg, NY: The Crossing Press.

Molyneux, Maxine. 1981. "Socialist Societies Old and New: Progress towards Women's Emancipation." *Feminist Review* 8:1–34.

Nnaemeka, Obioma. 1997. "Development, Cultural Forces, and Women's Achievements in Africa." *Law & Policy* 18 (3 and 4): 251–279.

Okafor, Chinyere. 2001. "Beyond Child Abuse." In *Eye to Eye: Women Practicing Devel-*

opment across Cultures, ed. Celeste Schenck and Susan Perry, 259–276. London: Zed Press.

Parmar, Pratibha, producer/director. 1993. *Warrior Marks* [videorecording]. A Hauer Rawlence Production. New York: Women Make Movies (distributor).

Patterson, Tiffany, and Angela Gillam. 1983. "Out of Egypt: A Talk with Nawal El Saadawi." *Freedomways* 23 (3): 186–194.

Rioja, Isabel Ramos, and Kim Manresa. 1998. *The Day Kadi Lost Part of Her Life*. Melbourne: Spinifex Press.

Rushdie, Salman. 1984. "The Raj Revival." *The Observer* (April 1): 9.

Tucker, Victor. 1999. "The Myth of Development: A Critique of Eurocentric Discourse." In *Critical Development Theory: Contributions to a New Paradigm*, ed. R. Munck and D. O'Hearn, 1–26. London: Zed Books.

United Nations. 1948. "Universal Declaration of Human Rights." Available at: http://www.un.org/Overview/rights.html.

Walker, Alice. 1992. *Possessing the Secret of Joy*. New York: Harcourt Brace Jovanovich.

Walker, Alice, and Pratibha Parmar. 1993. *Warrior Marks: Female Genital Mutilation and the Sexual Blinding of Women*. New York: Harcourt Brace.

Transcending the Boundaries of Power and Imperialism: Writing Gender, Constructing Knowledge

Omofolabo Ajayi-Soyinka

At a conference on "Feminisms and Cultural Imperialism" held in 1989,[1] I drew an analogy between African and African-American women's reserved reception of white-based feminist criticisms and theories while bringing out the subtle but significant cultural and political differences in their methodological approaches to feminism. Although located in the same cultural space as the American woman of European descent, the African American's specific experiences with slavery and racial discrimination are crucial to any feminist theory relevant to her. Similarly, gender cannot be the only organizing principle for African feminism: colonial imperialism brings in its wake multiple levels of sociocultural destabilization that affect both men and women located in that colonized space. Correspondingly, even as colonial oppression and exploitation are common experiences for African and African American women, the politics of location creates important differences in how they are oppressed by their respective patriarchal cultures. The way the dynamics of colonial imperialism frames gender hierarchy differs from how racial discrimination structures its overall power domination. These differences must be confronted and dealt with to effect any meaningful changes. Regarding current theories in feminist analysis, I specifically questioned the relevance of deconstruction to the analysis of African women's conditions. Despite its subversion of the very basis of power hierarchy, deconstruction is essentially Eurocentric and male-focused. I believe deconstruction and a number of white-based feminist theories negate the specific experiences of African women constructed twice over as subordinate under what I call *double patriarchy*. African women have to endure the patriarchy of European colonization and cultures in addition to the patriarchal structures of their own cultures.

My contributions were peremptorily ridiculed and dismissed by Gayatri Spivak, a well-known scholar who is considered one of the voices of authority for "Third World" women in the United States. She took particular issue with my critique of deconstruction and ignored all else I said regarding the multiple oppression of African women under colonial imperialism. Characterizing my opinions on Eurocentric theories for African conditions as a genetic fear on the part of Africans for theory and an inability to conceptualize ideas, she virtually inferred that Africa has never contributed and will never contribute significantly to human progress and knowledge. What a revelation! Yet, only two years earlier, Wole Soyinka, an African playwright, had won the Nobel Prize for literature. To claim authenticity and demonstrate her authority on the subject, she had cited a couple of African scholars and their works. However, in order to justify her conclusions, she had also situated them inappropriately in a controversy that questioned their contribution to knowledge. Not only was I rendered irrelevant but in a most insidious manner, I became the means by which Africa and its scholarship were trashed and declared worthless.[2]

This *déjà vu* systematic erasure of Africans and their production of knowledge is reminiscent of European imperialists' denigration of African lifestyles to justify their exploitation of Africans and the resources of Africa. Thus, despite the deliberate manipulation of facts in Spivak's analysis, there is a long-standing tradition of distortions and lies about Africans since colonial times. Evident in my exchange (assuming that what occurred was indeed an exchange) with Spivak was an overtone of cultural imperialism and the affirmation of an intragender hierarchy. When what purportedly started out as a feminist analysis assumes the overtones of imperialism, it becomes glaringly obvious that gender analysis is an inadequate basis for constructing the different forms of oppression facing *all* women. In addition to gender hierarchy,[3] women invariably take on the socioeconomic, political, and in this instance, the "assessed" intelligence status of their collective cultural/ethnic group. With the history of documented colonial policy of color-based discrimination among colonized peoples,[4] the continental and cultural differences between Professor Spivak (Asian) and me (African) take on added significance, further revealing the implications of power hierarchy and imperialist ideology.

It is indeed a travesty of intentions that a conference organized to interrogate imperialist discourses and geared towards understanding and transcending the "common differences" among women should turn out to be the site that reifies the contrary. It is even more ironic that the contention is over deconstruction, a theory that posits a breakdown of power structures. With its focus on the "politics of differences," the conference held a special significance for me as an African feminist recently located in America. Although only about six months in the country at that time, I was already aware of a prevalent inability even in feminist studies to accommodate or acknowledge different forms of construction and production of knowledge outside the Western canon and experience. I had been virtually stunned into silence at the arrogance and presumptuousness of mainstream American feminism for positing its experience and derivative critical theories as universal and normative. When analyzed in the context of these "other" theoretical formats, African women invariably emerge as caricatures of themselves, leading me to wonder who are these African women that keep popping up across the pages of American feminist analysis. This conference was to be a space to reclaim my voice and also re-inscribe African women within relevant and contextual precepts. I thus welcomed the opportunity to participate at the conference and also be part of the organizing team. I had envisioned the conference as a forum where women, "Third World" women in particular, could freely learn and exchange critical ideas, enhance perceptions of each other without anyone being constructed as the exotic "other" under imperialistic analytical gaze. Such anticipations had not been made in a vacuum, and to a considerable degree they were justified until the encounter that took place at the last event of the two-day conference.

Obviously, being African, I am only too aware of the fossilized status of African cultures and the persistent primitive status that anything African occupies in Western heuristic analysis to justify the enslavement of Africans. More recently in the early stages of Western feminist research, the status of African women became an impetus to re-create an evolutionist theory of gender oppression; thus suggesting that while women in the West had evolved into the civilized state of gender emancipation, African women were still lagging behind in their primitive state of oppression. Nonetheless, well into the 1980s, and in an era of coordinated global feminisms, I had expected more education on the different forms of women's oppression, resistance and survival. The critical works by women of color in America especially provided enough background for awareness, and I wanted to believe that such regressive revision of imperialism was a thing of the past. Definitely, a conference aimed at investigating cultural differences was the last place I expected the reinvention of new structures of cultural imperialism. The problem, however, was that in my anticipation I had overlooked the fact that charges of imperialism have been made almost exclusively within a colored/colonized and noncolored/colonizer cultural dichotomy. Often indicted are white women whose association with the class and cultures of the race of colonizers gives them a privileged status over other oppressed women and men. They are accused of reinstituting and perpetuating the structures and privileges of imperialism, even within women's coalitions. Not much attention has been paid to investigating the possibility of power hierarchy even among women traditionally marginalized by colonization. Obviously, there are manifestations of power hierarchy *among* women of color.

Given this background, it becomes clear that it was not *what* I said as such, that is, questioning the universalism of generic feminist theories, or even trying to contextually locate African women's experience, that provoked the confrontation, but *who* said it. Although similar points have been made before,[5] in the American rapidly expanding postcolonial space, African women's voices are still a rarity. The norm has been for them to be "spoken for" and "spoken of" by non-African women located in the Western Hemisphere. Thus the questions posed urgently by this incident revolve around the production of knowledge and construction of identity. Revisiting the encounter is to foreground and contextualize, in a sense, the broad focus of this chapter.

Specifically, the chapter investigates the implications of structures of imperialism in the production of knowledge between and among people who have collectively and variously suffered oppression, marginalization, and erasure under colonial powers. As colonized peoples whose perceptions of selves and knowledge of each other have been formed under the gaze of imperial forces, what and how are the new ways of knowing being produced to transcend the distortions and falsehood? With the established structures of imperialism, the control of the language of discourse and means of disseminating information, how can we transcend Western models of thought that impose themselves so relentlessly on our consciousness and reach a more objectively critical understanding of one another? The debate continues, whether to reject these models or be critically selective in our adaptation. Postcolonial studies in particular foreground the politics of location as a crucial factor investigating the means by which new structures of knowledge and identity are produced. It also problematizes the issue of authenticity and objectivity in analytical theories, especially between those located in the West and those located in the so-called Third World countries; each group is confronted with different problems which demand their own solutions. Yet if postcolonial studies are truly a revision of the colonial discourse, they must engage in a thorough interrogation of all levels of structures of power, between the colonizer and the colonized, as well as among the colonized. However, what is the focus of these revisions and how are they structured? More specifically, who constructs what knowledge for whom and from whose or what standpoint?

Nowhere do these questions converge more viscerally than among Africans and people of African descent on both sides of the Atlantic. Viciously torn asunder in slavery and located in radically different geopolitical space, we are further separated by different sociocultural experiences and influences. New cultural forms emerge and new alliances are established either through coercive forces or as survival strategies. Nonetheless, the ancient roots of a common origin linger in the subliminal recesses of our consciousness, simultaneously intersecting with and transcending the manifestations of colonial or racial imperialism. In biographies, fictional works, and personal anecdotes and relationships, continental and Diaspora Africans individually and collectively attempt to grapple with the tenacious control of imperialist forces and investigate those strings of relationship no matter how seriously frayed at the edges. How successful are these attempts to reestablish a communication system? Using a number of available resources, but especially concentrating on the works of Ama Ata Aidoo and Alice Walker, this chapter investigates the strains of imperialism in the construction of knowledge about us across the gulf of temporal and spatial distance and differences.

WAYS OF KNOWING: OLD BARRIERS, NEW BRIDGES

Imperialism as a metalanguage for domination and oppression manifests itself variously on the platforms of culture, nationalism, ethnicity, gender, sexuality, class, and/or physical (racial) features. In a strategic move to assert its power and control, the dominant group uses these structures to develop stereotypes of the dominated through which the dominated create individual and intragroup identities. But in an amazing sleight of hand, the deliberate distortions, along with the dehumanizing effects of colonial conditions, become reconstructed as the natural attributes of the colonized and touted as evidence of their incapacity. Such are the conditions under which perceptions about peoples of Africa and the Diaspora are formed. Thus African peoples on both sides of the Atlantic are denounced as indolent, stupid, and shiftless. By keeping colonized subjects apart and preventing them from knowing and understanding each other beyond the chasm of power and powerlessness, imperialism further sustains and perpetuates its power. The control of the means and forms of communication and knowledge, and of social production and reproduction, constitute the classic tactics of "divide and rule," which have served tyrants only too well over the ages.

In the exclusively British-structured educational system in colonial Nigeria, for example, America was a well-kept secret. In history classes, North America was nothing more than a disembarking port for slave ships that was referenced only within the larger context of the humanitarian efforts of the British abolitionist movement. If the teaching of America was a brief footnote in the infamous history of European slave trade, talking about the victims—subjects of the trade (the transplanted Africans in the Americas)—was absolutely taboo. To break this code of silence was to run the risk of being charged with treasonable felony, and every employee of the colonial government was fully aware of the penalty. In his autobiography, Nnamdi Azikiwe (Zik) recounts how as schoolboys, he and others came to learn about Diaspora Africans in colonial Nigeria in the 1920s.[6] Their only source was an old, faded, and badly mutilated issue of *The Negro World* that was secretly and fearfully passed around on school premises. Significantly, that edition was a clarion call for all oppressed peoples, including non-Africans, to unite and fight for their liberation. Young Zik was impressed and motivated enough to risk his budding civil service career to try to stow away to America. He endured several obstacles, including threats to his life, in his search of African Americans as the apostles of freedom who had successfully fought to end their oppression. He ultimately succeeded in getting to America legally, and fulfilled his schoolboy dream of knowing and learning about African Americans and their historic struggles against racial oppression. Azikiwe himself later became a prominent leader in the struggle to end European colonization in Africa. The example of Zik clearly demonstrates why the association of people with related conditions of oppression is definitely injurious to the health of colonial power interests.

Unfortunately, even in postindependence Nigeria, knowledge about Diaspora Africans was still obtained outside formal educational structures. The enduring strength of imperialist structure manifests itself in the fact that colonial policy continued unexamined and unchallenged by the new leaders. One of the ways of sustaining American invisibility in colonial Africa was to insist that its system of education is inferior to the British. The few Nigerians who, like Azikiwe, studied in the United States rather than in Britain or any European country were usually treated as inferior scholars and were sometimes subjected to some form of restraint upon returning home. The educationally sanctioned ignorance about Africans in the Diaspora continued, although it could be argued that at that time many independent African states were also just beginning to insert their own history and general African-centered disciplines in the school curriculum. Similar to Azikiwe's generation, mine had to learn about the Diaspora outside the classroom. Fortunately, my generation's education took place in the less repressive, more self-affirming and politically vibrant atmosphere of anticolonial struggles, and the Civil Rights and Black Power movements.

This unstructured, haphazard means of the production of knowledge about Africans and peoples of African descent in the Diaspora is a serious impediment to opening up smooth-flowing communication channels and meaningful relationships across the Atlantic. For centuries, Africans and African Americans have seen each other essentially through the prejudicial and distorted lens of imperialist forces: colonialism in Africa, slavery and racism in America. Overwhelmed with deliberate misinterpretation of our existence, we remain oblivious of the controlling power structures that initiated such misrepresentations and end up relating to one another with thinly veiled hostility, and in a worse case scenario, self-denigration and hatred. We continue to assimilate and uncritically reproduce these negative impressions that keep changing according to global economic and geopolitical realities. To many Africans, the African American is lazy, unwilling to be educated, aggressive, and violent. The assessment is fully reciprocated by most African Americans, who denounce Africans as being uncritical of, and too easily satisfied with minuscule crumbs from the white man's table. The current political instability of many African governments, the monetary quagmire of many African economies, and the devastating social and physical health reports from several African nations become sources of shame and provide reasons for many African Americans to proudly proclaim their non-Africanness.[7]

Apart from the stereotypical nature of such criticisms, they are made outside the historical contexts that provide the canvas for brushing on these broad strokes of condemnations. Beyond the field of political rhetoric, we need to seriously examine and re-evaluate how we arrived at this critical moment in our history and investigate the processes of our current culture of knowledge. Failure to review and historicize our conditions of existence and cross-Atlantic relationship leaves us with no alternative than to continue inscribing ourselves within this cycle of falsehood and ignorance. The slave trade that created the African Diaspora is a sore point of contention in the efforts to open up channels of communication. Most information on this infamous trade, a most horrendous chapter in human history, is still written or controlled by white historians, most of whom cover up the calculated brutalization of a continent and the systematic decimation of six million people over three centuries. Even the "Freedom Narratives,"[8] though written from the perspectives of the struggles to end slavery, were aimed at white readers who had the power and means to end it. Therefore, the focus was essentially to demonstrate the humanity and intellectual capacity of the narrators rather than criticize white slavers and risk antagonizing potential sympathizers. The white control is perhaps more pronounced in women's narratives usually recorded by white women who more or less appropriated black women's voices. Stetson's study of black women's freedom narratives reveals that white women were eager to use black women's experiences as a mask to express their "overt protest against their subordination, and of their hostility toward men as well as toward the Victorian home."[9] Overall, there is a concerted effort to gloss over the deed, the guilt, and the pain. Among the victims, especially African Americans, the pain cannot simply be wished away; it keeps cropping up at strategic moments, asking pertinent questions without receiving satisfactory answers.

Who sold whom into slavery? To Diaspora Africans, far removed from the scene of the crime, but always the palpable, enduring evidence, the answer seems straightforward. Unquestionably, the Africans who are familiar with and remain at the scene are culpable and should accept the blame. Frederick Douglass implied as much while responding to calls on African Americans to return to Africa to help "civilize" the people in 1859,[10] and Alice Walker made several references to it in *The Color Purple*. In a desperate moment of pain and confusion, Nettie, the authorial voice in the novel cries out, "Why did they sell us? How could they have done it? And why do we still love them?"[11] On two occasions, I have since met my own real-life

"Nettie." Similar questions were first posed through my nine-year-old daughter in 1988, by a twenty-one-year-old man, and the second time was in 1993 by an African American female professor at a college in Washington, DC.[12] A number of African Americans feel resentful that Africans are not on a permanent guilt trip, and most Africans do not want to acknowledge responsibility for that chapter in their history. Rather, Africans too are trying to comprehend why the same cultural group, and sometimes extended families are suddenly split up, separated by barbed wires, and prevented from communicating with each other across the Babel of French, English and/ or whatever language is spoken by the colonial power that grabbed a piece of land *including* the owners.[13]

The effects of these arbitrary regroupings and callously imposed new forms of identity still reverberate today—in Somalia, Sudan, Rwanda, and God knows where else, it is simmering, ready to explode any moment. The fact is, there are victims of the human traffic on both sides of the Atlantic. Unfortunately, this reality has not been given the attention it deserves. Among the few African intellectuals and writers who have tried to revisit the anguish of those whose loved ones had been abducted during slavery, Ama Ata Aidoo and Ousmane Sembène are truly noteworthy for their sensitive yet critical examination of history. In a short story, "Tribal Scars,"[14] Sembène re-creates how a man becomes an accomplice in the slave trade in order to locate his abducted daughter. While clearly condemning slavery, Sembène makes it clear in the story that not all Africans who participated in the European slave trade did so out of greed or sheer malice. He also demonstrates that the slave trade continued not from lack of positive and communal inspired struggles against foreign slave raiders and their local collaborators. In some parts of Africa, oral traditions still survive about local struggles against the slave trade and about the destabilizing effects of slave raids in communities and the psyche of survivors. There are also stories about professional slave raiders who become victims of their greed, are caught and sold into slavery. Ama Ata Aidoo explores one such story of retribution as a subtheme in *Anowa*, a play that examines the unending social upheavals of the slave trade in general. Giving the local lore of the Ashanti people of Ghana a critical twist, Aidoo focuses on the conspiracy of silence that surrounds slavery to demonstrate that, rather than take away the pain, the forced silence only perpetuates the tragedy of slavery. Anowa, the feisty, independent, and free-spirited heroine who gives her name to the play, rejects the culture of silence built around the slave trade in her community. She remembers the horror stories of slave raids her grandmother told her and is tormented by vivid nightmarish dreams of screaming humans being torn away from their loved ones. Thus, when later exposed to the lure of power, easy life, and quick monetary rewards that the slave trade promised, she condemns and spurns it unequivocally. Her husband, who on the other hand succumbs to the communal desensitization, eagerly joins in the dehumanizing traffic, thus identifying with the seductive trappings of white power that is rapidly overtaking his land. Although he does not end up being sold into slavery, he loses the meaning of life and contaminates those around him (including his wife) who love him, and consequently commits suicide.

While African Americans have been more forthcoming on the discussion of slavery, it is more of an identity quest than a rigorous interrogation of slavery. Discriminated against and still unwelcome as full citizens in the land they had literally slaved to build with their soul and blood, African Americans' urge to know their origins and discover their true identity understandably assumes some urgency. However, even though efforts have been made towards reconnection—from Phillis Wheatley's occasional poetic references to "The land of errors, and Egyptian gloom,"[15] and Olaudah Equiano's (Gustavus Vassa) vivid recollections of his capture,[16] to W. E. B. Du Bois's actual resettlement in Ghana in the 1960s—they have been fraught with problems. As in the African experience, the lack of informed and systematic education about the old and new forces that separate us and shape our current cultural experiences and political awareness prove to be a crucial shortcoming. Adelaide Cromwell Hill is able to pinpoint a serious flaw in the cross-Atlantic relationship when she characterizes Africa as a "fragile source of identity" for African Americans. Africa, she explains, is present in the self-image of African Americans only because it forms the basis of their nonwhite status in America.[17] The expression "nonwhite" is a significant element in this construction of self-image: it presupposes a crisis of identity. Being "nonwhite" presents an identity constructed by a *lack*, a lack determined not by that individual, but by an "other," a whiteness that is considered the norm. As a "being" constructed in negativity, it reduces the wholeness of that identity and erodes the confidence of the individual. Thus the African component of that identity as the basis of the "lack" and its "non-whiteness" is already compromised, making its fragile nature even more susceptible to further fractures and absences. Consequently, it is short shrift for a number of African Americans to reject and denounce what has been constructed as barbaric, the cause of their nonwhite identity, and the source of the racism and discrimination they experience in America.

The process of reconstructing the African American identity since emancipation serves only too well to underline the fragility of the image. Besides the settlement of a number of freed people in Liberia during the eighteenth century, one of the more common means of knowing Africa has been through Christian missionary evangelism. Missionary activities in Africa had their own imperialist foundations. The missionaries' statements and subsequent collusion with the colonial administration to take over African lands and destroy African cultures seriously compromised their (the missionaries') claims of religious altruism and commitment to equality of all before God. The popular saying in many African cultures that "the white man came with the bible in one hand and the sword in the other, and while the Africans' eyes were shut in prayers, he took all the land" illustrates that there is really no difference between the missionaries and the colonial establishment. African American missionaries to Africa find themselves in an ambiguous relationship. Linked by way of a "fragile source of identity" to their potential converts, yet members of the white converting team, they vacillate between holy righteousness and racial apologia. A letter in Carter Woodson's book on African American letters during the first half of the nineteenth century illuminates this point. Writing to his mission, the American Colonization Society (ACS), an African American evangelist states: "We too have a great work to perform. To the Anglo and Africa-American is committed the redemption and salvation of numerous people, for ages sunk in the lowest depth of superstition and barbarism."[18] It is noteworthy that the ACS, which also supported the resettlement of freed slaves in Africa, has been criticized for its racism. A number of its white founders and supporters made it clear that their intention was really to get rid of black people, whom they considered unfit to be American citizens, rather than make a genuine effort to correct the ills of slavery. The letter symbolically denounces the African or "nonwhite" part of the writer's identity while its evangelical fervor masks the anguish that accompanies such a rejection. It is by no coincidence that Alice Walker, who in a recent interview claims she regards Africa as her "former home," should begin her creative explorations into the continent via a missionary family team in the award winning *The Color Purple*.

The Black Power movement is the most recent, independent, and politically significant effort in the series of "back to Africa" initiatives by the African Diaspora. But the disappointment and problems encountered by many of these cultural pilgrims underscore the multitude of differences that separate the "returnees" and the "home folks." Fired with romantic notions of returning to the ancestral homeland, several African Americans went to African countries expecting automatic and unquestioning welcome. Many could not cope with the vast cultural differences or comprehend why as "Africans," they should be required to produce passports and obtain entrance visas. Even the "home folk" Africans have been divided up in unfamiliar territorial boundaries and given new forms of nationalism that have no relationship with their former linguistic associations or cultural identities. Rather, the newly created African countries were carved up for the benefit of the European powers scrambling for a piece of the "magnificent African cake."[19] Even those African Americans who were not so naive were not prepared for the vast cultural differences, political priorities, and economic conditions they encountered in Africa. The various public services that had been taken for granted in the United States were either nonexistent or presented to them as privileges for which they had to be exceptionally grateful. Africans responded to the naivety of these Americans with amazement and intolerance and could hardly wait to get them out of their lands. The crossed wires of purposes, intentions, preparations, and receptions produced some volatile and unpleasant situations.

I am reminded of a particular group of African American exchange students who came to Nigeria during a politically trying time. It was 1971, and Nigeria was just emerging from a fratricidal civil war that had depleted national resources for the war efforts and diverted funds from national institutions such as higher education to postwar reconstruction. Expecting a certain minimal level of comfort at the university, the exchange students were not prepared for the situation, nor were they sympathetic. Nigerian students, in turn, were only too eager to denounce them as "over pampered Westerners." Feeling unwelcome, a large number of the African American students retaliated by declining to represent the university any further at the interuniversity sports competition that was just two weeks away. The soured relationship suddenly produced from the closet various worn-out records with "his master's voice" labels of "racial" stereotypes. The vicious exchange of falsehoods across the board sometimes deteriorated to fisticuffs. It was a sad contrast to the high expectations and enthusiasm that preceded the exchange program on both sides. Fortunately not all of these cross-cultural encounters ended in regrets and painful memories. There were a number of people on both sides who were aware that cultural differences do exist and took the trouble to get to know each other by comparing notes and exchanging histories. Prejudices and preconceived notions were reassessed, and new ways of knowing were established. Even among the usually self-centered, impatient students, lasting friendships were formed over the improved communication networks.

That a new knowledge of self and awareness of the other is possible even after the ritual of bitter recriminations appears to be the focal point of Ama Ata Aidoo's *Dilemma of a Ghost*. Eulalie (Eu), an African American woman, comes "home" by way of marriage to Ato, a Ghanaian who had been in the United States as a student. "Home" to Eu is where she "will not be poor again"; it is full of "the palm trees, the azure sea, the sun and golden beaches."[20] In Ghana, however, harsh realities begin to surface, conflicting with the "tourist brochure" image. It becomes a struggle to keep their marriage from collapsing while they grapple with the problem of their ignorance of each other's history. Unable to comprehend Eu's status as a person of African descent outside Africa, in fact outside their immediate Fanti culture, Ato's family members are contemptuous of the conditions of slavery that gives her an American citizenship. Is it a collective amnesia that frames such reaction or collective guilt? Slavery, the taboo subject in *Anowa* resurfaces again in more contemporary times and with more urgency. The ambiguity that makes Eu an African physically but not culturally almost destroys her already fragile sense of identity. Had Ato's African American wife been white and behaved the way she did, perhaps she would have been more readily forgiven and given a better reception even if grudgingly; the cultural differences would have been more obvious and therefore more tolerated. More-over, it is with pride and without any sense of contradiction whatsoever that Ato is conferred with the title "our white master," a nickname of honor he earns by the virtue of his possession of the white man's form of knowledge and culture. While the victim of slavery is ostracized, the perpetrator, the white man, remains sacrosanct, and desirable in his powerfulness. African men qualifying as the new "white masters" assure the perpetuation of the very power that made colonialism possible in the first place. Such seduction of power prevents us from recognizing our own being and potentials, binding us to new forms of powerlessness under neocolonialism or postcolonialism.

While men like Ato go in search of imperialist-prescribed new ways of knowing and associated powers, women are enjoined to preserve African traditions and ancient ways of knowing. Consequently, under such a pres-sure, women as a group usually become more unforgiving of cultural trans-gressors than men. The normally accommodating female community of grandmother, mother, and other women relatives and neighbors find it dif-ficult to offer Eu the traditional hospitality and welcome her into their midst. But more than anybody else, Monka, Ato's sister, who is closer in age to Eulalie, is especially vicious. She refuses to acknowledge her name, deri-sively referring to her as "Hureri," "my Lady" "my brother's morning sun." When Monka acknowledges her presence at all, it is to sneak on her and give a distorted account of Eu's activities to her mother, Esi Kom. Consis-tently chipping away at Eu's fragile identity, she creates a gaping hole with the song she says reminds her of her sister-in-law:

> She is strange,
> She is unusual,
> She would have done murder
> Had she been a man
> But to prevent
> Such an outrage
> They made her a woman
> Look at a female.[21]

With a tenuous American citizenship and a hostile Ghanaian nationality, Eu is now in danger of losing her only certain form of identity, her female-ness. That Monka draws from existing cultural musical repertoire is indica-tive of the marginalized position of women in that culture. Essentially the song implies that women are disapproved of if they assert their uniqueness. To deviate from the norm is as horrific as committing murder. The song thus helps to understand the background of Monka's unrelenting attack and the more pronounced hostility of the women in general to Eu's cultural differences.

Because of her gender and the newly emerging economic structures in her society, Monka's education has been passed over so that her brother can have the best education money can buy. She has neither forgotten nor forgiven the burden of the sacrifices she is compelled to make as a female. For once, she directs her frustration at the appropriate quarters, her family, when she complains:

> A great part of the land was sold and even that was sufficient for nothing. . . . Finally the oldest and most valuable of the family heirlooms, *kente* and golden ornament, which none of us younger generation had ever seen before, were all pawned. They never brought them into daylight . . . not even to celebrate the puberty or marriage of a single girl in this house.[22]

For her brother to have married a woman who is black like her but has the added advantage of benefiting from Western social and educational opportunities is rubbing salt to the injury. It is a double slight that reverses the construction of power and gender as is being currently reformulated in the new cultural space circumscribed by imperialist strategies. The acquisition of Western culture and knowledge firmly assures Ato's position in the new emerging cultural space in Ghana, while his status as a man in the traditional culture was never threatened. In order to afford Ato's new form of knowing, Monka's interests and ability to fully adjust to the newly emerging society are sacrificed. By pawning its heirlooms, Monka's family has deprived her of economic security and traditional values. Thus, while Ato's new concept of self is shaped by a surplus, his sister's is constructed by a scarcity that changes her personality and perception even towards a fellow woman under similar gender oppression. Gender marginalization, cultural ignorance, and imperialist construction of false perceptions culminate in a bitter exchange between husband and wife:

EU: I must always do things to please you and your folks. . . . What about the sort of things I like? Aren't they gotten any meaning on this rotten land?

ATO: (*With false forcefulness*) When in Rome, do as the Romans do.

EU: (*Contemptuously*) I thought you could do better than clichés. . . . Can't you preach to your people to try and have just a little bit of understanding for the things they don't know anything about yet?

ATO: Shut up! How much does the American Negro know?

EU: Do you compare these bastards, these stupid, narrow-minded savages with us? Do you dare?[23]

Here is a case of the pot calling the kettle black. What a dilemma! Haunted by the ghost of an unexamined and distorted past, the two people find their genuine love tottering on the brink of destruction. Repressed antagonism, mutual disrespect, denigration, suspicion, and centuries of guilt-tripping for millions of people come pouring out from these surrogates from across two continents. Nonetheless, it is a revealing, powerful moment of truth and self-discovery. Each gets to know a little bit more about the other, and more importantly, what one thinks of the other. A true healing process has begun.

Marriage, the union of two different individuals where romantic idealization or other social considerations often tend to suppress differences, becomes Aidoo's tool for problematizing the politics of location in the construction of knowledge and identity. The nearly jeopardized love between Eu and Ato is symbolic of the relationship between the two larger entities they respectively represent, the African American and the African. Significantly, the healing hand that wields the tool of reconciliation is Esi Kom, Ato's mother, not Ato with his Westernized knowledge. In fact he has become so confused that he is no longer able to communicate with either his foreign wife or his own people. Esi Kom identifies the root of the problem as education or more appropriately the lack thereof. More importantly, she ponders the value of Ato's knowledge acquired through Western education if he is unable to apply it to common daily problems: "But do you never know anything? I thought those who go to school know everything. . . . So your wife says we have no understanding and we are uncivilized. . . . We thank her, we thank you too. . . . But it would have been well if you knew why she said this."[24] Later, advocating a systematic process that allows no room for distortion or confusion, Esi Kom emphasizes a re-education, the construction of new ways of knowing. Appropriately, she admonishes her son: "No stranger ever breaks the law. . . . (*another long pause*) Hmm . . . my son. You have not dealt with us well. And you have not dealt with your wife well in this."[25]

The institution of marriage also becomes a metaphor for Aidoo to examine the specificity of women's identity under both indigenous and colonial cultures. The plight of Eulalie as a woman is particularly instructive of the different standards that women in general often experience in cross-cultural contexts. As a woman and a colonized, she is faced with a double jeopardy. Inscribed within a colonial context that is patriarchal in its concept and structure of power hierarchy, the woman also has to adjust to the patriarchal structure of the host culture.

WOMEN AS BATTLE-BODIES IN IMPERIALISM AND COUNTER STRUGGLES

Monka's reconstituted cultural identity and gender status in *Dilemma* serves as a significant subtext underlining the intersection of imperialism with gender, race, economic conditions, and changing cultural values and priorities. New and urgent conditions force colonized peoples to reevaluate their lifestyles as they are touched by the new ruling system. Consequently what is called African "traditional" culture has undergone significant if not radical changes in the contemporary era. In his study of the Ibos, Basden laments that "what now passes for native law and customs is but a travesty of what it was in the old days; it is but a shell; the kernel has been destroyed."[26] While such a condition may not be completely true all the time, Basden's statement is, nonetheless, a powerful indication of the nature and form of the European/African contact. The encounter did not, and still does not take place under a normal acculturation process in which there is a mutual exchange and acknowledgement of ideas. On the one hand, there has been a consistent denial by Europeans of any African influence on their ways of life, creativity, or technology. On the other hand, the European/African contact has been a cultural encounter of the most unequal and brutalizing kind for the African, in which, in too many cases, a single-minded imperialist agenda succeeds in imposing the pace and nature of the contact. The African experience is best summed up as a headlong collision with an absolute-power-driven hierarchical machine.

Both the colonized and colonizer emerge from two patriarchal systems, one seeking to dominate and the other fighting against domination. Thus during anticolonial struggles, women are invariably reconstructed as the battle bodies upon which the power contests are fought out. On either side of the contest, society's definition of appropriate roles for women intensifies and stereotypes are more rigorously applied. Subsequently, the traditional roles of women as cultural custodians assume new meanings of purity and authenticity. In such instances, gender differences in both cultures become magnified and distorted as each side strives to test, gain, and retain dominance through the bodies of their women.

A prime example of anticolonial struggles literarily turning women's bodies into battlegrounds for patriarchal power is "female circumcision."[27] Wielding the big stick of religious and cultural superiority, colonialists see female circumcision as more evidence of the barbarism and ungodliness of the "natives." It is denounced as unchristian, sinful, and of course, savage. To some nationalist leaders, by contrast, female circumcision assumes the magnitude of symbolic freedom and cultural pride wherever it is practiced. In *Facing Mount Kenya*, Jomo Kenyatta, who later became the first premier of independent Kenya, demonstrates how both colonial imperialism and missionary evangelism acting in concert destroyed the basis of existence of many African peoples. Denouncing the way the missionaries had manipulated female circumcision to undermine further Kikuyu indigenous values, Kenyatta advocates retaining the practice, insisting that no Kikuyu man should marry an uncircumcised woman.[28]

At the same time, to not be circumcised was the only way girls could, in a number of instances, be allowed into the Western educational system. The Christian/colonial missionary crusade against female circumcision in Kenya and in other African cultures where it is practiced constitutes an arrogant denigration of the people and their existence. The campaign against the practice did not express concerns over women's health or their sexual rights and enjoyment. The focus was more on the various communal activities, particularly the dancing that usually accompanies the practice, and how they conflict with the European sense of community. The colonialists saw the Africans as having no values of their own, they were "clean slates" upon which to write Western culture in its entirety for the Africans' "own good." Their actions and pronouncements were therefore designed to belittle and ridicule any thing emanating from the colonized cultures that appeared substantive or symbolic enough to threaten their self-imposed mission. The unrelenting patriarchal overtone of colonialism is reflected in the fact that the missionaries banned female (not male) circumcision because it is "sinful." Since male circumcision is sanctioned in the Bible, to declare it "savage" would be to damage the integrity and the implied superiority of the colonialist culture. Consequently, women become the convenient and safe site for the manifestation of imperial power. There is overwhelming evidence that both the colonial administrators and missionaries collaborate in selectively stripping female institutions of their political and economical power[29] in order to effectively impose European cultures and systematically eradicate indigenous structures of knowledge and cultural identity.

Propelled to the forefront of the international feminist movement in contemporary times, female genital excision is no longer a religious morality issue but a sexual construct. Rallying round gender solidarity, the movement to end the practice extends beyond national and cultural boundaries. But did the imperialist attitude associated with the earlier missionary intervention disappear in the spirit of sisterhood? A highly complex subject, clitoridectomy has become *the symbol* in the construction of the African woman's identity, as well as a brutal manifestation of male dominance over women. Yet, not all African cultures observe the practice, or practice it for the same reasons. Awa Thiam, a pioneer in the struggle to eradicate the practice, cautions in her book *Black Sisters, Speak Out* that in discussing genital mutilation, distinctions must be made among groups that practice it by focusing on the different reasons for the practice by a particular group. She carefully analyzes the differences between two different cultural groups in Mali that engage in the practice—the Dogon and the Bambara. Nonetheless, just as I (an African woman) have become the trope for reinventing some preconceived notions of the Africans' inferiority on a universal scale, so has female circumcision, in fact its most brutal form—infibulation—become the sole form of identifying and/or identifying with African women.

In *Possessing the Secret of Joy* (hereafter *Possessing*) and the follow-up documentary, *Warrior Marks*, Alice Walker actually reduces the different personalities and multiple identities of African women to one thing—the vulva. Focusing on genital mutilation, the novel is specifically "dedicated with tenderness and respect to the Blameless Vulva." Walker makes it clear that *Possessing* is her crusade against genital mutilation and it is undertaken on behalf of women, or more appropriately, daughters betrayed by their mothers who perform it on them.[30] The archetypal genitally mutilated daughter in the novel happens to be an African from the fictional country of Olinka, thus the novel can also be considered as another stage in the series of Alice Walker's return journey to Africa. Although presented as having been mutilated physically, sexually, and psychologically, Tashi, who was not circumcised as a child, has not been betrayed by her mother. Her mutilation is self-inflicted as a demonstration of her loyalty to the struggles against colonial powers in her country and an affirmation of her identity as a woman in Olinkan culture. But according to the author, rather than be a true affirmation of self, Tashi's new identity becomes a source of torture bringing her close to a state of dementia. Like all daughters who have undergone this genital surgery, Tashi is presented as a woman who knows no single moment of health or happiness for the rest of her life.

Despite its avowed commitment to a humane cause, the artistic recreation of the horrors of genital mutilation in the novel only results in an astounding compilation of the most derogatory, age-old racist stereotypes about Africans. Tashi, the archetypal "mutilated" African daughter, is on a closer analysis, the colonial imperialist-created archetypal African, a perpetual child, helpless and uncomprehending of the more complex world around her. *Possessing* is a tragic story, but rather than a heroic "classic" tragic figure, Walker's creation is a disabled protagonist who comes across most of the time as petulant, confused, and helpless. Tashi evokes not sympathetic admiration for her struggles against forces beyond her control, but pure pathos for her dependency on others and the misery she inflicts on their lives. She is made to suffer from self-inflicted wounds but unable to see beyond blind loyalty to a practice that imprisons her and many others. Tashi's problems are rooted in the same ritual that the missionaries in their "wisdom" had denounced as barbaric and successfully prevented her from going through as a child. Nevertheless, she is naturally without the slightest clue to solving her problems; it would seem that the missionaries have a better insight to Africa's problems and how to solve them. Still committed to the salvation of the "natives" in spite of themselves, the missionaries bring in their colonial partners for longer lasting solutions. Thus, Walker brings in a team of experts—psychoanalysts (Old Man), mystic psychoanalyst (Raye) and psycho-anthropologist (Pierre), who descend on the mind and body of Tashi to help her. And once again, Africa's problems are solved by a crew of Westerners with Western knowledge.

By virtue of her exposure to Western influence in America where she is eventually located, Tashi is able to know the full impact of her folly. Her puny efforts to reconstruct herself according to Olinkan structures of knowledge are revealed as mired in ignorance, corrupt leadership, and lack of motivation among the people. Her tortured lifestyle is symbolized in a recurring nightmarish dream of being imprisoned and tortured in a "tall, dark tower." Slight relief is provided only through the combined efforts of those Western experts who relentlessly and conscientiously chip away at her enigmatic dream. Finally cracking the code, Pierre presents the riddle of her horrors in simplified picture-frame images to Tashi. The tower is the termite hill so common in Olinka, Tashi is the queen termite, and the torture she is subjected to is the castration of her genitalia. Although Tashi is indeed later imprisoned for the death of M'Lissa, the expert circumciser, the dream extends beyond her. In the same way that Tashi stands for every African, and Olinka, any African country, her nightmare is a code for the fate of Africans who refuse to listen to the wisdom of the Western experts. Significantly, the cause as well as the solution to the archetypal African's problem is right there in her country and culture. All Pierre has to do is arrive in the country, see the dwelling places and the termite hills and the final piece in the puzzle falls into place. So simple, yet neither Tashi nor any of her fellow citizens is intelligent enough to see it. Like the wingless, blind termites of her dream, Tashi and her people are the "generations of visionless offspring."

In a novel committed to speaking up and taking decisive action, the affected characters are curiously rendered passive and blissfully unaware of their oppression. Readers are bombarded with the pontificating opinions, racist judgment, and assessments of "experts" detached from the situation, but are met with the silence of the *victims* of an obviously redundant and painful ritual. When their voices attempt to rise above the contemptuous din of the experts, they are rendered worthless, impotent, and ineffective. Clearly, the Olinkans cannot articulate their pain or be trusted to speak for themselves, much less take any form of meaningful action. They are portrayed either as ignorant, undiscerning masses who are incapable of any independent judgment, or as despots like the Olinkan leader, or as bitter and frustrated individuals like M'Lissa, the circumciser. Amazingly, this ritual surgery of the female genitalia was not always an Olinkan tradition; it was instituted simply on the capricious whim of a ruler. There even exist in living memory, women who remember the better times in their society when they actually possessed the joy of "full" sexual satisfaction (orgasm included). In addition, some of them continue to pay homage to the goddess of this libidinal pleasure, albeit in secret. Yet they remain silent in the face of this abject tyranny and allow their daughters to be subjected to its horror. Not one of them possesses the strength, courage, or the sense of outrage to organize a movement to abrogate an imposed and obviously destructive decree. M'Lissa herself, scarred for life and fully aware of the cause, unconscionably subjects other women to the same debilitating procedure. Tashi's tortured voice comes through in a final sweeping condemnation and self-denigration, "women are cowards."[31] Thus, the message of the novel is one of hopelessness; the women of Olinka do not possess the will to save themselves from sure destruction.

Even though Tashi purportedly speaks in her own voice throughout the novel, it is a mutilated voice tortured by misguided and unrequited loyalty.

Moreover, it has been heavily impacted by her endless trips to too many psychoanalysts. Ultimately, the direction of her new-found knowledge of activism is not much different from the disappointing results of her participation in the freedom struggles. A lost soul herself, she has nothing positive to bequeath to other women. Like the crime she cannot commit (the murder of M'Lissa), but for which she is sentenced to death, she dies without passing on the knowledge of "possessing the secret of joy" to anybody because she has not found it. The only suggestion of "joy" comes from the American contingent of experts, Adam, Olivia, Benny, and Pierre, who throw themselves into charitable work in the prison, administering to hopeless cases of AIDS victims. The last scene of the novel, the site of Tashi's execution, is a highly symbolic paraphrase of the whole story. While the banner inscribed with the phrase "resistance is the secret of joy" is unfurled by the same American regulars that now include Raye, and an Olinkan woman (Mbati), the crowd of other Olinkan women who have assembled as a clear gesture of defiance, remain mute. Their presence is just that—a gesture—not the desired action, or even a suggestion of moving forward. To the end, the novel represents Africans as "voiceless" and "visionless."

It is highly ironic that in a work entitled *Possessing the Secret of Joy*, not sarcastically but ambitiously dedicated to unlocking that secret supposedly on behalf of Olinkan women, none of the characters experiences any joy in her life. The only character in the entire novel that experiences any form of joy and personal fulfillment is Lissette, a French woman and Adam's lover. Without being tied down as a "wife," Lissette enjoys the love, respect, and companionship of a man she desires and is blessed with an adorable and intelligent son that she wants. No Olinkan woman or any other character in the novel is so blessed. The presence and power of their oppression is so overwhelming that it has crushed their spirits and wiped even the faintest smile off their faces.

Perhaps the most devastating and revealing in the unmitigated demeaning image of the African woman and her offspring painted throughout the novel is summed up in Pierre's solemn and authoritative verdict upon translating Tashi's dream code: "You who are fat, greasy, the color as you have said of tobacco spit, inert; only a tube through which generations of visionless offspring pass, their blindness perhaps made up for by their incessant if mindless activity, which never stops, day or night. You who endure all this, only at the end to die, and be devoured by those to whom you've given birth."[32] If ever there was a statement that condemned a people to perpetual ignorance, irredeemable hopelessness, and powerlessness, this is it. The nouns and their qualifying adjectives have not been randomly selected; each is loaded with meaning calculated to belittle and is dismissive of whoever or whatever Tashi stands for. Pierre's decoding system is another set of codes for racial stereotypes: tobacco (dark and smelly); spit (a gesture of disgust); inert (brain-dead, stupid); tube (inanimate, incapable of action), and the "incessant mindless activity" implies that the Olinkan are all brawns and no brains. Finally, the last phrase in the quote refers to their cannibalistic self-destruction. As if this is not enough, Walker moves from Tashi's dream world to the more palpable tragic reality of the dying AIDS patients packed behind prison walls. Olivia's firsthand and practical experience with these AIDS patients gives her the undisputed authority to offer a personal "testimony" which serves to reinforce and confirm Pierre's racist psychoanalysis of the Olinkans:

> No one has any idea why he or she is sick. That's the most difficult thing. Witnessing their incomprehension. Their dumb patience, as they wait for death. It is their animal-like ignorance and acceptance that most angers Tashi, perhaps because she is reminded of herself. She calls it, scornfully, the assigned role for the African: to suffer, to die and not knowing why.[33]

Even the designated Olinkan intellectuals whom we encounter briefly as dying AIDS patients do not escape this congenital, nationally genetic mental retardation. The presentation of the Olinkan questions the spirit of help and sisterhood Walker claims inform her thematic concern in the novel. It exposes instead a deeply rooted imperialist ideology.

A crucial question remains: How truly representative is Tashi as an African woman? African women are typically known for their industry and in addition to being homemakers, they are in many instances professionals or at least wage earners in some capacity. On the contrary, because Tashi is presented as unfit to pursue any significant occupation she comes across as a lady of leisure who is solely preoccupied with her sexuality. Her lack of engagement in any occupation feeds into Pierre's tendency to dismiss the preoccupations of Olinkan women as "mindless activity." Too ill to even take care of herself, Tashi cannot be called a homemaker. She is totally dependent on the stoic devotion of Adam and the emotionally detached and clinical care from Olivia, her sister-in-law. More importantly, the decision to kill M'Lissa—who has become a national icon in the same way that female circumcision has attained national symbolism in the political expression of some actual African countries—is self-serving. It is in no way representative of the reputed African high sense of community. To every M'Lissa killed, ten more are alive and practicing. Her motivation to kill the national symbol therefore is not for the sake of all women, so they can possess the secret of joy, it is a personal revenge, for making her life so miserable. Why does she not, who now knows better, mobilize other women into vigorous protest movements? The answer is that she is too wrapped up in her pain to be fully aware of her surrounding and be of any use to anybody. Tashi is a self-centered young woman, not necessarily the coward she wants to make us believe. The parable of Lara, the panther with which Tashi introduces herself in the opening pages of the novel, is narcissism par excellence. Her joy, if she did discover it at all, is in self-absorption and aggrandizement.

Where did Alice Walker get all these images she heaps on the African woman? One crucial source that literarily leaps out at every page very authoritatively is Marcel Griaule, the early twentieth-century French anthropologist. Direct references are made to him and his works among the Dogons who inhabit what has been described as the ultimate in the land of termite hills. Pierre acknowledges his indebtedness to the French anthropologist when he concludes that "the Creation itself began with mutilation and rape."[34] The Dogon myth of creation is intricately interwoven with termite hills, the natural phenomenon that dominates their landscape and transcends the sexuality so luridly hashed out before young Tashi by the old men of Olinka.[35] Moreover, the sexual section of the myth, as pointed out by Awa Thiam, serves as a rite of purification for *both* boys and girls, and she finds no evidence to support a phallocentric theory, even though she denounces it as genital mutilation.[36] The myth in its entirety is the Dogons' complex ways of knowing and the foundation of their sociopolitical organization, creativity, and in particular, their philosophical concepts. Therefore, they did not need any Marcel Griaule to interpret it for them. Nonetheless, the Frenchman is reincarnated in Walker's Pierre, the "new age" psycho-anthropologist who rediscovers the wheel all over again. One wonders for whose benefit is the interpretation. Is it for the "natives" who created the code in the first place or the foreigners who come already handicapped with an agenda specific to their own experience and by the "natives's" language of discourse? But rather than acknowledge his ignorance, the Westerner parades the "native" as unknowledgeable and incapable of producing knowledge.

In conformity with this imperialist's tradition of appropriation, manipulation, and control of knowledge, Alice Walker's *Possessing* completely ignores the fact that there are African activists who have spoken against, and taken decisive steps to stop the practice of clitoridectomy and infibulation in their different societies. The radical and pioneering efforts of women like Awa Thiam and Nawal El Saadawi stand out among others.[37] No one who is seriously committed to eradicating genital excision, except those blinded by a superiority complex, can claim ignorance of the works of these two women in particular; both are internationally known for their published works and extensive research on the subject. Incidentally, the "classic Olinka walk" frequently referred to in the novel is too close to the description of the "excised walk" given during a woman's testimony in Awa Thiam's *Black Sisters Speak Out*.[38] Yet unlike the authoritative voices of Marcel Griaule, and Pierre, his fictionalized re-incarnation, no African character, fictional or real, is given any such authority in the novel. To acknowledge African women's critical concern and committed activism in stopping the practice will be to reduce the significance of Western expertise and highlight Africans as knowing, enabling, and capable.

Although *Warrior Marks* (both the film and the book) feature and interview other Africans in various walks of life who are fighting through religious, political, local or international forums to end this dated and needless practice,[39] Alice Walker still emerges as the sole knowing voice of authority. Criticizing this star-syndrome in her review of the film, Leasa Farrar-Frazer concludes that it "obscures the fact that the lives of the women at stake are ultimately more important than Walker's own vision."[40] Walker hugs the limelight, remaining center stage throughout and masking the visibility of the practice she claims she wants to make noticed, including the dangers it poses to young girls, the true victims of the practice. Although a lot of sentimentality dribbles on the pages on behalf of children, the focus is more on Walker than on the real welfare of the children. Witnessing one "outing" ceremony where a little four year old had been excised, Walker describes how "blood splattered, some of it on little Mary's feet. Her feet, the smallest of all, wrecked me. I thought of the circumciser grabbing her or what was sought. I finally started to weep, looking at those small feet."[41] Rather than what has actually happened to little Mary, we learn more of Walker's own emotional state.

Alice Walker displays an unbelievable level of intolerance and arrogance towards her informants, particularly in Senegal and Gambia, the two countries where she gathered the materials for the documentary. Her "interviews" with informants in either of the two countries are typically conducted in the following manner:

> I asked what kind of circumcision she did on the children. That too was a secret. I could not resist telling her it was not a secret to us. I described the various forms of circumcision: Sunna, intermediate, and pharaonic. I pantomimed infibulation, the sewing shut of the vulva after all external sexual organs are removed. She seemed genuinely surprised to know I had this information. . . . The circumciser wore a face of saccharine sweetness. She was wearing some of her "gold." Very cheap and white-looking, one pendant in shape of Queen Nefertiti, who was said to have been circumcised. It was chilling to think that for many African women this ritual of circumcision is the only real link they have with their ancient Africa-Egyptian heritage.[42]

Clearly, these women are no more than "strawfigures" propped up only to be knocked down in order to show off Walker's strength. She has nothing but utter disrespect and scathing contempt for the bulk of people that serve as "research materials" for her project, because after knocking them down, she proceeds to stamp on them by ridiculing their appearance. No matter how repulsive the practice, it must be kept in perspective that it is the deed that needs to be eradicated, not the victims. There is no genuine interest on the part of Walker to communicate effectively with the people; rather, she projects a lot of antagonism and negativism. A truly committed activist should have some respect and understanding for the people in question and the cause in which she is engaged. Without the slightest modicum of understanding and regard for the practitioners, how can she hope to fulfill her objectives? In the end, like Tashi, Alice Walker passes on no legacy of positive achievement except a strong sense of self-importance.

Contrary to what Walker thinks of the Senegalese and Gambian women, they are not stupid, and her arrogant demeanor is not lost on them. Thus, most counter her "American-know-all" arrogance and obvious "Westerness" with a "what-do-you-know?" "it's none of your business" attitude, and refuse to tell her much. It is almost like the confrontation scene between Eulalie and Ato.[43] Rather than strive for better understanding and come down a notch from her high horse of self-righteousness, Walker proceeds to give judgment on impressions formed under this mutually antagonistic situation. Even indigenous field researchers from the same culture, often speaking the same language as their informants and who know better than approach them with an arrogant attitude, meet with such protectionist, "it is your culture, you-should-have-known" attitude from their informants. It is the classic anticolonial syndrome. The people believe that colonialists have eroded their ways of knowing and demolished their means of identity for too long and they should start fighting back with the limited resources left at their disposal. They have seen how they and their cultures have been caricatured and misrepresented in European and Hollywood feature films, fictional and documentary texts, post cards and so on, by foreigners they had generously shared their customs with or who simply recorded their impressions. Rightly, or wrongly, the current "protectionist" attitude, particularly towards foreign researchers, is a method of fighting back against the invasion of their lives and what they accurately perceive as a resurgence of imperialism.

Parmar, Walker's co-author of *Warrior Marks*, complains that the steady onslaught of rich television crews, amateur anthropologists, and other Western experts on African genitalia-curio has jeopardized their own tighter budget. This might well be. However, what is the impact of all the uninvited attention on the Gambians and the Senegalese themselves? These are two small countries forced to play hosts to a crowd of uninvited foreigners with the technological and economic power to invade their cultures and the privacy of their lives. Obviously, too wrapped up in their own interests, neither Parmar nor Walker has given any thought to how their sudden and constant harassment of these people will affect them economically, morally, psychologically, and perceptually? One immediate result is that a supposedly humanitarian project has become a circus show with audience jostling for vantage points. Western interests in the practice have become so voyeuristic that Bilaela, "who is the head of an organization that educates women away from harmful traditional practices,"[44] and who often serves as the contact person for many of the Western crews, sees no contradiction in regularly arranging special circumcision "ceremonies" solely for the cameras and for her own pocket. As Parmar exclaims incredulously, "Female genital mutilation has become a media commodity!"[45] The lure of capitalism has corrupted Bilaela's initial, more altruistic objectives and distorted her vision of promoting women's welfare. Bilaela's case raises an important question about the truth-quality of the information being "sold" in a situation where "demand" outstrips the "supply." Naturally, prized information will go to the highest bidder, and conversely, the highest bidders will demand the most for their money. Within the circus context of the "market," sensationalism overrides authenticity. The sensationalization of female circumcision thus becomes *the event* paraded before the Western world as more "proven" evidence of the unequaled extremity of African women's oppression and helplessness. A serious health issue has become another platform of power to resuscitate imperial grandeur and titillate some Western morbid fancy.

The issue is not that a Westerner has joined in calling needed attention to the health hazards of infibulation and the hidden power play in this dangerous game of sexual hierarchy. As Awa Thiam states, "Bringing the mutilation of any human being whatsoever to public attention is a positive move." What is objectionable is the compulsive need to denigrate in their entirety the cultural values of the people that practice it, and not taking "the trouble to get to know the women who have been excised and infibulated."[46] Alice Walker refuses to get to know the human elements of her cause. The language, style, presentation, and the uncritical and uneducated use of sources and materials in both *Possessing* and *Warrior Marks* detract from and debase whatever objectives that were set out to achieve. Even though Parmar has a more reflexive approach to the presentation of her materials, the resounding message, nonetheless, is that once again Africans have proved incapable of constructing their own knowledge. Forever childlike, they remain dependent on the expertise of the West to extricate them from the mess they have mindlessly caused on themselves. Rather than the voice of care and sisterhood, it is the voice of contempt and disgust that reverberates. The organizing concepts of the two works are already problematic and controversial from the African woman's perspective. The vulva as the metonymy for African women fiercely conflicts the way African women want to be considered. I believe Awa Thiam speaks for most when she says African women reject being reduced to the vagina by polygamous, patriarchal societies. In the same way, we African women reject being reduced to vaginas by our imperialist, Western feminist "sisters." Walker admits in an article, "One Child of One's Own" that the vagina is a crucial construct of her "nonwhite" identity. She calls attention to how black women are often constructed differently by white women and feminists and cites the instance of an art exhibition entitled "The Dinner Party: a Feminist Statement," by Judy Chicago. Of the set of plates laid at the table in the exhibition, only The Sojourner Truth plate, representing black women, depicts a face whereas all others representing white women are "creatively imagined vaginas." Walker comments, "It occurred to me that perhaps white women feminists, no less than white women generally, cannot imagine Black women have vaginas."[47] Walker's project foists on African women this perception, formed within the American racist context and which Cromwell Hill aptly describes as the "nonwhite" identity. Although her objection to the art exhibit is meaningful and relevant in the general American cultural context, extending the same perceptions to Africa and African women that are under entirely different conditions is arbitrary and objectionable.

Furthermore, conceived as a crusade on behalf of "daughters *betrayed* by their mothers" both *Possessing* and *Warrior Marks* engage in a judgmental finality that precludes any rigorous interrogation of female circumcision. Since women are automatically condemned as culpable and as maliciously inflicting the pain of circumcision on their daughters, it follows that there is no point investigating either the deep cultural network associated with the practice or the various obstacles the mothers have to overcome in order to stop it. Feasting, dancing, and other social activities interwoven with excision rituals and outing ceremonies are consequently interpreted by Walker as undeniable proof of the callousness and unnaturalness of these African mothers. The desire to prove maternal betrayal overrides any other possible interpretation in normal mother/daughter relationship; it beclouds the mother's love for her daughter that makes her persist in wishing for her daughter to grow up like her peers. Both projects have arrived at the conclusion that African mothers are incapable of loving their daughters. Even little acts of motherly affection are twisted through the prism of betrayal in order to condemn the women; for example, the candies given by mothers to the newly circumcised girls as a gesture of feeling and an attempt to mitigate the pain of the surgery is seen by Walker as creating problems of obesity in the future for the girls. It is indeed laughable that Walker holds such a view of candy and children, given the role candy plays in American child-rearing system and the general problem of overweight in the United States. The pervasive, judgmental tone in these works is reminiscent of the earlier-mentioned letter to the ACS in the nineteenth century by an African American missionary. It echoes young Nettie's bitter but uninformed, self-righteous condemnation of contemporary conditions of African countries: "Today the people of Africa—having murdered or sold into slavery their strongest folks—are riddled by disease and sunk in spiritual and physical confusion. They believe in the devil and worship the dead. Nor can they read or write."[48] Who is speaking here? The African American girl miseducated about Africa and in search of a wholesome identity, or the speculating, greedy slave trader and/or colonialist on the prowl for forced African labor, fertile lands, rich mineral deposits, and a soothing balm for his conscience? The same ventriloquist voice is clearly audible in *Possessing* when Pierre revives the ghost of Marcel Griaule. It is the same continuous imperialist power play and the denial of African people's capacity for intelligence and meaningful action. For Alice Walker, time stands still for Africans, and the racist stereotyping continues. As it was in the nineteenth century and earlier, it remained so in the 1920s and the 1990s and will remain for evermore.

CONCLUSION

When the axe came into the forest, the trees said the handle is one of us.[49]

Across the field of knowledge, ways of knowing abound, which variously implicate and validate our existence and being within the specificity of our respective experiences. However, imperialism, for its own self-aggrandizement, has consistently demoted colonized peoples, particularly Africans and people of African descent, below human level. The need to investigate if and how forms of imperialism intersect with and impact the reconstruction of our identity and notion of self cannot be overstated. Our efforts to reconstruct ourselves should be wary of the pervasive structures of imperialism, in whatever forms and wherever such materialize. As with theoretical precepts, so should it be with creative ventures; fictional works should be equally wary of regurgitating the myths created by imperialism. While exercising the right to present and fictionalize her subject to the best of her creative talent, an artist must not overlook her responsibility to truth and fact. The responsibility is even greater in re-creating real life events; fictionalization must not be confused with or substituted for distortion. Fictionalization does not mean blatant disregard for truth, neither does it call for an evasion.

Between Aidoo's and Walker's creative efforts, there is a phenomenal world of difference in the construction of the identity of the African and the person of African descent. The production of knowledge in *Dilemma* and *Possessing* communicates radically contrasting pictures of self-awareness, concept of self, and ways of knowing. In the presentation of a people and their complex history of "racial" relationship, there are such diametrically opposed attitudes to similar problems. On the one hand, Aidoo strives for unity of two different peoples by investigating and understanding their common differences and by striving to overcome their superficial similarities. Critically informed by the present, Aidoo digs perceptibly deep into history, reexamining facts and fiction in order to build a more solid future. Even though Aidoo has been criticized for the naive way she portrays the African American life and problems,[50] there is no overtone of contempt, and there is a clearly discernible attempt to critically examine any problem within its appropriate context. More importantly, she places her characters on the podium with her and works with them from there. Consequently, she achieves a clear, unambiguous, two-way communication system between two people long separated by the structures of imperialism.

Alice Walker, on the other hand, appears perched on a pedestal and arranges her characters in hierarchical order below her. As a result, her creative vision becomes distorted. It is a sad commentary that *Possessing* perpetuates and most uncritically reproduces the most abject stereotypical images of African women as ignorant, fatalistic, and malicious partners in their own victimization. *Warrior Marks* reeks of sheer contempt for its subjects. It seems that Walker is caught up in the frenetic attempt to stamp out a practice that victimizes women, and is too hastily dismissive of whatever efforts the victims themselves have achieved. She fails to see those who, like the Somali woman, construct themselves as survivors rather than victims.[51] Haunted by the ghost of an unexamined and distorted past, her sisterhood activism is fraught with serious problems and inappropriate foreign solutions. Unlike Aidoo's Esi Kom, the Ghanaian mother who ultimately discovers the "secret of joy" by investigating the strengths and weaknesses of her people, Walker creates an inarticulate Tashi and brings in a team of Western experts who impose their own solutions, thus perpetuating the endless cycle of imperialism. Walker's journey back to Africa is like another missionary venture featuring the colonial imperialist on a civilizing project where the indigenes are accorded no respect, and the only interests worthwhile are those of the "experts." Alice Walker has often been criticized before for her Western views of African women. Gay Wilentz sees "Walker's Western perceptions of African society become increasingly problematic" leading her (Walker) among other things, to a "misreading of African society and women's role in it."[52]

When people of color reach across differences to communicate, they must be mindful of falling into the seductive pit of narcissism, arrogance, and power tripping. The remark of AAWORD still holds true: "Solidarity can only exist alongside self-affirmation and mutual respect."[53] Anything short of this, will lead to a breakdown of communication in the alliance. What Alice Walker has achieved in *Possessing* and *Warrior Marks* is not much different from what black women accuse white feminists of—imperialism couched in feminist cause and solidarity. It is too uncomfortably similar to the above mentioned incident at the "Feminisms" conference when a critical comment is catapulted far outside its immediate frame of reference and becomes a trope for trashing the scholarship of a whole continent. Situations such as these prompt the Yoruba people to caution that "when a handshake of friendship extends beyond the elbow, the intended solidarity becomes suspect." At such instances, there is need to reassess the basis of the friendship. When Walker's purported creative activism on behalf of African women becomes the basis for belittling the same women and sensationalizing their problems, obviously, her handshake of solidarity has extended beyond the elbow. The time has come to investigate the fundamental ideological background of such attitudes and critically review the alliance itself.

The issue of the trees and the ax quoted above aptly underscores the problematic of who produces knowledge for whom and through what means. (Although this same quote appears as an epigraph in *Possessing*, the intended meaning is not clear within the context of the novel.) Surely when the trees rejoice at the visit of the ax, they do not forget that the metal has given the wooden handle a new form of identity and perception. Does its attachment to metal mean the handle is a better wood than the trees? Should the ax-handle now consider itself superior to the trees lacking the metal? Or do the trees construct the ax-handle as a lack, lacking in the tall majesty of full "treeness" intact with roots, leaves, and branches? Being still able to recognize the bond of kinship is important; it could be an indication that a mutually rewarding association is possible. It is equally important to acknowledge the differences, so that the charges of betrayal, arrogance, or self-seeking promotion could be avoided. What is being advocated especially within the context of postcolonial studies is not a revisioning that glosses over fundamental problems and covers up uncomfortable truths. At the same time, the truth of what is presented should be informed and balanced. As writers and critics, women of Africa and of African descent have produced significant theoretical perspectives whose validity and strength rest on the truth of their varied experiences. This is what should be sustained.

NOTES

This chapter is a greatly modified version of a paper, titled "Getting to Know You, Sister of My Skin," that I presented at the conference on "Black Women in the Academe: Defending Our Name."

1. "Feminisms and Cultural Imperialism: Politics of Difference," Cornell University, Ithaca, New York, April 22–23, 1989.

2. I wish to seize this opportunity to thank my friends who, even at the risk of their own careers, stood by me and helped me to survive this traumatic experience. I will like to call attention to the fact that scholars of Asian origin were among this group of supportive friends. Professor Spivak and I met later at another conference, and at her initiative, we had some useful discussions and reached some understanding.

3. There were actually attempts to pass the incident off as a male/female gender issue. In the ensuing furor, Biodun Jeyifo, a male African scholar, wrote a widely circulated but unpublished paper, "'Race' and the Pitfalls of Ventriloquial Deconstruction" (1989) in defense of African scholarship. In her article, "Reading *Satanic Verses*," Gayatri Spivak interpreted Jeyifo's paper as a paternalistic intervention and tried to recast the whole event as a patriarchy-based controversy. My circulated response, "A Question of Power," was in reaction to this development. Bell hooks, who was also present at the conference and was in fact the keynote speaker during this exchange, refers to the incident in *Yearning: Race, Gender and Cultural Politics* (1990, 93–94).

4. For example, many Asian Indians were "brought" to a number of African countries by the British as the preferred source of labor and accorded much better status than the indigenes. South Africa, Uganda, and Kenya are good examples. The economic advantage that such color hierarchy created in Uganda fueled resentment among the indigenous population who hailed Idi Amin, upon his coming to power in 1970, for his policies that forced many of the Indians to migrate to Britain. Although resident in Uganda, most Indians had retained the British citizenship accorded them since during colonial administration, even though the last three generations had never set foot in India or Britain.

5. See Christian 1985; hooks 1989; Walker 1983.

6. Azikiwe 1970, 34.

7. While discussing racism and its effects in America during one of my classes, an African American, nontraditional female student who had been active in the Black Power movement said that she preferred the racial discrimination of America to the disease-ridden and appallingly abysmal lifestyle of Africans. When I tried to

put the condition of African countries in perspective citing the inner-city problems in America for analogy, a much younger, white, male student who had been on the defensive thus far asked me what made me come to America if Africa was so good.

8. Although they are more commonly referred to as "Slave Narratives," I prefer the term "Freedom Narratives" because the narratives are about freedom.

9. Stetson 1982, 71.

10. Douglass 1969, 164.

11. Walker 1982a, 145.

12. The recurring question is: "Why did you people sell us into slavery?" My daughter was visibly upset and confused because she did not understand the basis of the question. We were just a few months in the United States. I took the opportunity to educate the two of them the best way I could about our common heritage. More recently, in 1993, during a conversation with an African American professor in Washington DC, I mentioned my daughter's experience, and she immediately shot back: "Well, is it not true? Did you not sell us for beads and alcohol?" It was devastating, but I thought we could still dialogue. I had to give up any further attempt after she literally threw it at me that it is a scientific proof that AIDS came from Africa. A good friend of mine who had in fact introduced me to this person, and was present during the conversation was utterly speechless. My friend, also an African American woman and a professor, studied and taught for several years in Nigeria and had traveled to other African countries.

13. Along the Ghana/Togo borders, one half of the same family resides in Togo controlled by the Germans and subsequently by the French, whilst the other half lives in Ghana controlled by the British. Ancient Yorubaland is divided between British colonized Nigeria, and French controlled Republic of Benin and parts of Togo. Meanwhile, Gambia was carved out of Senegal by the English to thwart the French control of the area. The issue at stake for the colonials was the land and its mineral or agricultural resources, the people just happened along as labor supply.

14. Sembène 1987.

15. Wheatley 1969, 46.

16. Equiano 1967.

17. Hill 1968, 131.

18. Berghahn 1977, 44.

19. Statement credited to King Leopold of Belgium at the Berlin Conference in 1879 during the "Scramble for Africa."

20. Aidoo 1965, 3.

21. Aidoo 1965, 29.

22. Aidoo 1965, 31.

23. Aidoo 1965, 45.

24. Aidoo 1965, 48.

25. Aidoo 1965, 49.

26. Basden 1966, xiii.

27. "Female circumcision" will be used to refer to how the practice was known before the contemporary and international feminist movement renamed it. Unless otherwise stated, it will refer to the three types of female circumcision: excision, clitoridectomy, and infibulation.

28. See Walker and Parmar 1993, 268, where Walker expresses disappointment at this statement by Kenyatta (1938).

29. For analysis of how African women are systematically stripped of their political powers while their men are co-opted by the colonial government and its trappings of power, see Okonjo 1976; Mba 1982; Amadiume 1989; Ayandele 1966, 260–270; Nassau 1904, 48–261. The last two offer interesting comparative analysis.

30. Walker and Parmar 1993, 21.

31. Walker 1982a, 25.
32. Walker 1982a, 233.
33. Walker 1982a, 249–250.
34. Walker 1982a, 234.
35. Walker 1982a, 236–238.
36. Thiam 1986, 69.
37. Alice Walker apparently tried without much success to have an interview with Awa Thiam in Gambia while working on the documentary, *Warrior Masks*. It appears that Awa Thiam has decided to take her battle against genital excision to the political arena and was busy on the campaign trail and so could not meet with Alice Walker.
38. Thiam 1986, 61
39. These include Efua Dorkenoo, Head of FORWARD International and the rebellious Aminata Diop, whose escape to France from Senegal on the eve of her infibulation ritual made international headlines. See Walker and Parmar 1993, 27–32, 241–251, 255–262.
40. Farrar-Frazer 1994, 41–42.
41. Walker and Parmar 1993, 47.
42. Walker and Parmar 1993, 48.
43. Aidoo 1965, 45.
44. Walker and Parmar 1993, 51.
45. Walker and Parmar 1993, 162.
46. Thiam 1986, 79.
47. Walker 1982b, 43.
48. Walker 1982a, 145.
49. Bumper sticker. Also appears in Walker 1992, no folio.
50. Hill-Lubin (1982) discusses this issue at length. I am indebted to Obioma Nnaemeka for calling my attention to Hill-Lubin's article.
51. In Walker and Parmar (1993, 251), Efua Dorkenoo refers to the Somali woman who although infibulated, describes herself and others like her at a UN convention as "survivors" and rejects the term "victims."
52. Wilentz 1992, 73.
53. AAWORD 1983, 217.

WORKS CITED

Aidoo, Ama Ata. 1965. *The Dilemma of a Ghost.* Accra: Longman.

Amadiume, Ifi. 1989. *Male Daughters, Female Husbands.* London: Zed Press.

Association of African Women for Research and Development (AAWORD). 1983. "A Statement on Genital Mutilation." In *Third World Second Sex*, ed. Miranda Davies, 217–220. London: Zed Press.

Ayandele, Emmanuel A. 1966. *Missionary Impact on Modern Nigeria, 1842–1914.* London: Longman.

Azikiwe, Nnamdi. 1970. *My Odyssey: An Autobiography.* New York: Praeger Publishers.

Basden, George. 1966. *Niger Ibos.* New York: Barnes & Noble.

Berghahn, Marion. 1977. *Images of Africa in Black American Literature.* Totowa, NJ: Rowman and Littlefield.

Christian, Barbara. 1985. "Toward a Black Feminist Criticism." In *The New Feminist Criticism*, ed. Elaine Showalter, 168–185. New York: Pantheon Books.

Douglass, Frederick. 1969. "African Civilization Society." In *Apropos of Africa: Sentiments of Negro American Leaders on Africa from the 1800s to the 1950s.* Compl. and ed. Adelaide Cromwell Hill and Martin Kilson, 161–166. London: Cass.

El Saadawi, Nawal. 1980. *The Hidden Face of Eve: Women in the Arab World*. Trans. and ed. Sherif Hatata. London: Zed Press.

Equiano, Olaudah. 1967. *Equiano's Travels: The Life of Olaudah Equiano or Gustavus Vassa the African Written by Himself*. New York: Praeger.

Farrar-Frazer, Leasa. 1994. "An Opportunity Missed: A Review of *Warrior Masks*." *Black Film Review* 8 (1): 41–42.

Hill, Adelaide Cromwell. 1968. "What Is Africa to Us?" In *The Black Power Revolt: A Collection of Essays*, ed. Floyd B. Barbour, 127–135. Boston: P. Sargent.

Hill-Lubin, Mildred A. 1982. "The Relationship of African-Americans and Africans: A Recurring Theme in the Works of Ata Aidoo." *Présence Africaine* 124:190–201.

hooks, bell. 1989. *Talking Back: Thinking Feminist, Thinking Black*. Boston: South End Press.

———. 1990. *Yearning: Race, Gender and Cultural Politics*. Boston: South End Press.

Jeyifo, Biodun. 1989. "'Race' and the Pitfalls of Ventriloquial Deconstruction." Unpublished paper.

Kenyatta, Jomo. 1938. *Facing Mount Kenya: The Tribal Life of the Gikuyu*. London: Secker & Warburg.

Mba, Nina. 1982. *Nigerian Women Mobilized*. Berkeley: University of California Press.

Nassau, Robert Hamill. 1904. *Fetichism in West Africa: Forty Years' Observation of Native Customs and Superstitions*. London: Duckworth and Company.

Negro World, The. 1917. New York: African Communities League.

Okonjo, Kamene. 1976. "The Dual Sex Political System in Operation: Igbo Women and Community Politics in Midwestern Nigeria." In *Women in Africa*, ed. Nancy J. Hafkin and Edna Bay, 45–58. Stanford: Stanford University Press.

Parmar, Pratibha, producer/director. 1993. *Warrior Marks* [videorecording]. A Hauer Rawlence Production. New York: Women Make Movies (distributor).

Sembène, Ousmane. 1987. *Tribal Scars and Other Stories*. Trans. Len Ortzen. Portsmouth, NH: Heinemann.

Spivak, Gayatri. 1989. "Reading *Satanic Verses*." *Public Culture* 2 (1): 79–99.

Stetson, Erlene. 1982. "Studying Slavery: Some Literary and Pedagogical Considerations on the Black Female Slave." In *All the Women Are White, All the Blacks Are Men, But Some of Us Are Brave*, ed. Gloria Hull, Patricia Bell Scott and Barbara Smith, 61–84. New York: The Feminist Press.

Thiam, Awa. 1986. *Black Sisters, Speak Out: Feminism and Oppression in Black Africa*. Trans. Dorothy Blair. London: Pluto Press.

Walker, Alice. 1982a. *The Color Purple*. New York: Harcourt Brace Jovanovich.

———. 1982b. "One Child of One's Own." In *All the Women Are White, All the Blacks Are Men But Some of Us Are Brave: Black Women's Studies*, ed. Gloria T. Hull, Patricia Bell Scott, and Barbara Smith, 37–44. New York: The Feminist Press.

———. 1983. *In Search of Our Mothers' Gardens*. San Diego: Harcourt Brace Jovanovich.

———. 1992. *Possessing the Secret of Joy*. New York: Harcourt Brace Jovanovich.

Walker, Alice, and Pratibha Parmar. 1993. *Warrior Marks: Female Genital Mutilation and the Sexual Blinding of Women*. New York: Harcourt Brace.

Wheatley, Phillis. 1969. "To the University of Cambridge in New England." In *Life and Works of Phillis Wheatley, Containing Her Complete Poetical Works, Numerous Letters, and a Complete Biography of This Famous Poet of a Century and a Half Ago*, ed. G. Herbert Renfro, 46–47. Miami, FL: Mnemosyne Publishing Company.

Wilentz, Gay Alden. 1992. *Binding Cultures*. Bloomington, IN: Indiana University Press.

Woodson, Carter, ed. 1926. *The Mind of the Negro as Reflected in the Letters Written during the Crisis, 1800–1860*. Washington, DC: The Association for the Study of Negro Life and History.

PART III

Bodies That Don't Matter

Out of Africa: "Our Bodies Ourselves?"

Vicki Kirby

"Unspeakable." The term is meant to say it all, to conjure something so terrible that it defies comprehension and simply stops the mouth. It is as if a moral limit has been breached so thoroughly that the difference between human and animal is dangerously unclear and the failure of words to remedy the situation cannot be risked. And yet one of the ironies about "the unspeakable,"[1] as we see in the case of what are termed genital mutilations, is that this "horror" does not effect a pause in our perceptions but an incitement to discuss it. However, "discuss" is perhaps the wrong word in this instance. For the interventionist urgency that attaches to these writings tends to censor considered reflection and debate, the give and take of different positions, possibilities, and the weighing up of sides. It is as if a judgment must be authorized so powerfully that the conceptual and ethical commitments that explain it are immured against interrogation. Beyond discussion, our adjudications assume the status of incontrovertible truths. Could the "unspeakable" more accurately refer to our own position in Western metropoles and the violence that maintains its privilege and authority as the arbiter of justice?

I began to suspect a degree of complacent self-righteousness in my own assumptions about these practices when I started reading Continental philosophy and poststructuralist criticism. Prior to this, I had been aware that there was something troubling about the way that "otherness" was routinely feminized and represented in terms of deficiency. Even such common assumptions as the mind/body, culture/nature divisions were inflected through this political asymmetry, with woman positioned as primitive "other" to a more evolved and rational male subject. Woman appears as body to his mind, "*the* sex" as Simone de Beauvoir described her,[2] a creature whose compromised sense of agency could be explained by her closeness to Nature and its vicissitudes. However, the arguments I brought to bear on these political prescriptions about "woman" now returned to mock me in my representations of the abject body of the African woman. Was she simply an object to be diagnosed and rescued, a victim so worn down by the barbarity of her miserable existence that she lacked the capacity to understand it and/or the agency to refuse it?

I was uncomfortable with the notion that the custodial arbitration of an acceptable cultural diversity could, or should, be determined in Western metropoles. Such patronizing salvage operations are informed by an evolutionary narrative of "development"—those theories and economic strategies that work on the principle of an inevitable, marketable "progress." Coupling these insights with a growing appreciation that subject formation is a *corporealized* process, where meanings and significances are the lived stuff of our sexualities and identities, I was increasingly unsure about how the truth of the body and its pleasures could be decided. Calls to a "global sisterhood" simply deny the purchase of the question, as if some final decision has been made about "what woman wants." Indeed, phallogocentrism's complicity with ethnocentrism is evident here in the protective lamentation about this primitive spectacle.[3] If the African body lacks integrity, and is not whole(some), then intervention is necessary, even if it means we must save them from themselves.

Although debates around clitoridectomy are not always uniformly organized, two recognizable positions can be discerned from the literature. Most common is the position that clitoridectomy is a self-evident violence that is so heinous that it compels intervention. However some women, very often ethnographers as well as some health-care workers, adopt a relativist position by opposing or qualifying active intervention, arguing instead that these practices can only be comprehended from within a particular culture's specific configuration of meanings.[4] Interestingly, this latter belief does not construe another culture's frame of signification as opaque to an outside. Instead, it assumes that cultural translation is possible when sensitively undertaken. The possibility that translation is itself a transformation that erases the evidence, or "residue," that the colonization of meaning incurs, is not entertained.[5] In the discussion that follows I will confine my attention to the sorts of arguments exemplified in the first position, that is, to those views that express their opposition to these practices and which actively argue for Western intervention against their continuation.[6] I will concentrate on the way these calls to action are typically expressed and suggest why their presumptive justice actually silences many of the complex contingencies that inform these behaviors.

First, the relevant literature is overwhelmingly written by women and is self-consciously situated within the political coordinates of a feminist/liberationist discourse that argues against unfair practices.[7] The object of concern is uncovered before us, the truth of its deficiency pinned down between inquiring pages, opened out to photographic scrutiny or simply documented into readable, textual comprehension. The peculiar and prurient fascination of the viewer/reader is swiftly sanitized behind the impassivity of a medical gaze. In fact medical discourse provides the common thread that weaves through this entire cluster of texts, providing its classifications and, implicitly, the "real" meanings which authorize the argument.[8]

A mind/body dualism is an essential ingredient for these arguments. The necessary "objectivity" with which the medical penetration of this body is exercised can only be achieved as its flesh is anaesthetized into passivity. The vitality of this body's subjectivity, the beliefs and values that are incorporated into its existential significance are pared away as extraneous. A biological reductionism, Reason's disinterested arbiter of "what a body is," translates cultural specificity through a universalizing template of sexuality. Although clitoridectomy and infibulation are practiced in thirty countries in Africa alone, the diversity of its cultural, political, and historical experience is summarily negated: medical discourse provides the definitive guarantee for this Western assertion of "what you are."

In countries where genital excision is practiced, there are women within the indigenous population who are vehemently opposed to its continuation. It is not my intention to dispute the meanings these women give to explain their own life experiences. However, what can be decided for one group of women has been made the ethnographic alibi that re-inscribes it as valid for all African women. What is "other" for the West must thereby forfeit its own internal contradictions and diversities in this homogenizing identification of alterity.

Consequently books about genital excision written by African women carry a sense of national authenticity within the role of their author function. For example, Raqiya Abdalla, a Somali woman, and Asma El Dareer, who is Sudanese, each writes about genital excision and infibulation in their respective countries. And yet their medicalized arguments, research methods, and bibliographical material make the results almost interchangeable. However, the voices from the medical profession are not always uniform. Dr. Shehida Elbaz, an Egyptian woman, opponent of excision and member of the Arab Women's Solidarity Association, is much more circumspect about intervention despite her own commitments. In an interview with Angela Davis, Elbaz recalls her attendance at a conference in London where these issues were raised, and recounts her opposition to the argument that female mutilation is a pivotal issue for women's liberation in such countries as Egypt, the Sudan and Somalia: "I originally came from the countryside, . . . but all my life I have lived in Cairo. I can't assume that I have the right to talk about women in the countryside. . . . So how can you decide for us, so far away?"[9]

It is worth taking just one of these books and following the logic of its narrative construction. By staying within its familiar terms of reference we can read the text against the grain of its argument and consider why the "truth" of this different body seems to escape ineluctably and disappoint our explanations of its grotesque effacement. I will concentrate on the Sudan because it has been made the representational condensation or topos of the problem. El Dareer's *Woman, Why Do You Weep?: Circumcision and Its Consequences* (1983) will take us into this "other" place and provide an exemplary illustration of what will remain resistant in these seemingly transparent texts.

The history of intervention in the Sudan achieved a significant success in 1946 when the British legislated against pharaonic circumcision. Although the Sudanese government has campaigned against its less drastic forms ever since, the response to both the earlier and more recent forms of prohibition and deterrence has been consistent in its refusal to comply with such directives. Of the 3,210 Sudanese women who participated in El Dareer's study almost 99 percent had been genitally excised.[10] The numbers have been *increasing* since colonization.

The type of excision tends to follow an urban/rural division, with the more educated classes preferring *sunna* to the more severe "intermediate" or "pharaonic" operation.[11] However, El Dareer's contention that the educated classes are leading the way out of their primitive heritage seems a wishful assertion when considered against information elsewhere in her book.[12] Ethnic groups such as the Fur and Nuba, for example, groups for whom such practices were not traditional custom, have adopted them more recently.[13] El Dareer explains that this shift has come about "since they had come in contact with the urban areas, and due to the introduction of midwives."[14]

The wealthier professional classes have also introduced a new "fashion" (El Dareer's description) by opting for genital reinfibulation after childbirth, and medically trained midwives have introduced this practice into country areas. Untrained midwives, much preferred by country people, are generally unfamiliar with it.[15] El Dareer responds to these anomalies with chastening descriptions of the women as "ignorant" and "conforming," "accepting of a position merely as instruments for men's pleasure."[16] These accusations of complicity are underlined by the fact that the practice is an exclusively female affair, involving mothers, sisters, aunts, and other women friends in the community.

Although patriarchal pressures are sufficiently pervasive to exert a controlling influence even in the absence of men, there remains a frustrating ambiguity in the literature not addressed satisfactorily by El Dareer's gloss of female stupidity/passivity. For example, responding to a question about the preferred type of excision, almost 59 percent of the 3,210 women respondents preferred the more extreme forms (intermediate and pharaonic) to the milder operation (*sunna*). The male response was the reverse of this. Less than 20 percent of a sample of 1,545 men preferred the pharaonic or intermediate, compared with 64 percent who preferred the least severe type. If patriarchal oppression seems somewhat qualified in these figures, El Dareer attempts a quick bit of repair work with an authorial intrusion. "It should be noted that the term *sunna*, when used by men, is somewhat misleading because they tend to think there are only two types—the pharaonic and *sunna*."[17]

However, this need to reinterpret the masculine response because it could otherwise begin to rupture her argument merely works to relocate the contradiction. For if we are to accept El Dareer's explanation, then the men whose desires police and explain the continuation of such practices seem strangely ignorant of their details and of the degree of their severity. Surely this male ignorance offers a space in which women could maneuver a little and at least take the less severe option, if that is their preference. An issue related to this, and just as puzzling, is the apparently passive role of fathers in the excision of their daughters:

> We found that the majority (75 percent) said that they did not interfere because they consider this to be an entirely feminine affair. . . . According to the women respondents, their husbands' opinion was sought in 43 percent of the cases, and of those, 50% agreed to have their daughters circumcised. The daughters of the other half, however, were circumcised *in spite* of their father's opposition.[18]

Given El Dareer's own description of the situation, it seems reasonable to wonder why the women don't take advantage of this latitude. A Western reader might be perplexed by this lack of action and conclude, as does El Dareer, that there is something lacking in these women, something indicative of a general deficiency in the culture as a whole. But there are more of these anomalies. In western Sudan, the wedding night can prove something of a "test" for both husband and wife, often turning the nuptial bedroom into a chamber of horrors. A tight infibulation may send women back to midwives and hospitals for surgical solutions when penetration proves impossible. Men risk public condemnation and as a result may resort to artificial methods to escape the shame of failure:

> Fearing the gossip and derision of the community some husbands prefer to take a longer time rather than use artificial aids or seek advice. One man said that he would prefer to die rather than ask for help. . . . This attitude is quite incredible since we found one woman who had remained tight for more than six years. . . . From the results of the survey, I found three pharaonically circumcised women who said that to achieve full penetration had taken eighteen months. Five men said it had taken six to eighteen months. . . . Out of the total sample of 3,210 women and 1,545 men, seven women and five men had not experienced full penetration. The duration of their marriages varied between three months and two years.[19]

From a Western standpoint the benefits that might accrue to men after what appear to be such unnecessary ordeals are further diminished when the reader learns that women can easily obtain divorce.[20] This seems to qualify the claim that these women are entirely powerless regarding the control of their bodies. Moreover the assumption that female sexuality has been commodified or "locked up" through the securing stitches of infibulation is inconsistent with El Dareer's expressed reason for disapproving of the behavior of many of these same women:

> This false appearance of virginity produced by recircumcision (reinfibulation) is why girls who have premarital intercourse have it done. Thus, rather than preventing immorality, circumcision can encourage misbehavior, because girls know they can always be stitched up again. This point is also emphasized by the midwives. . . . "They are like dogs, because they will not stick to one partner."[21]

Religious reasons were also offered to explain the adherence to these practices. Many said it was necessary because they were Muslims[22] while others claimed it was abhorrent and against their religion, again because they were Muslims.[23] Although there were only fifty-eight Christians in the sample, all practiced the most severe (pharaonic) form of excision. The complications that ensue are considerable and can result in death. Despite this, El Dareer tells us that "people will never reveal the name of the operator; they would sacrifice the life of their daughter first, because it is thought to be shameful to be an informer and it is not accepted in society."[24]

In the full knowledge of the risks to women's health that accompany these operations, 82.6 percent (2,652) of the women interviewed supported the continuation of the practice,[25] overwhelmingly preferring untrained to trained midwives and consistently refusing medical assistance.[26] This is evident in the survey figures, where of the 790 immediate complications that followed the practice, only 11.9 percent of these cases were reported to medical personnel.[27] A political economy of health frames some of this behaviour—health services are not always financially or geographically accessible to the rural poor. However, the modern construction of the Sudan, a nation-state which must incorporate the heterogeneity of different cultures and different languages into one social body, one identity, has relied in part upon medical practice to effect this homogenization. Even where medical assistance is available, it seems that very often women resist its caring ministrations.

As the birth of the bourgeois nation-state or "social body" was accompanied by the birth of the bourgeois subject or citizen, the health of both has been inextricably intertwined. Sexuality, as Michel Foucault explains, becomes a crucial site for the forging of this new individuality, with medical surveillance as supervising midwife. Indeed, the history of interventionist campaigns in the Sudan reveals the way in which a power/knowledge nexus locates women's bodies as the vehicles through which homogenization and docility of the whole population is attempted; an illustration of Foucault's biopower.[28]

El Dareer applauds this history of interference. British colonialists, with the cooperation of educated Sudanese men,[29] were persistent in their attempt to punish operators (women) and to relocate "tribes" such as the Jellaba, Fur, and Fallata. These groups were considered "at risk." As they were beginning to adopt these practices, their protection from the further contamination of neighboring tribes had to be ensured. It appears that genital excision was a behavior that located a dangerous pathology within the newly constituted social body of the Sudan. Thus, the control of women's bodies proved fundamental to the maintenance of the entire State's political health.

By 1946 a government campaign, encouraged by the Sudan Medical Services, succeeded in securing the legislation of certain prohibitions against the practice. The educational system was mustered into support for these new laws, and Islamic leaders were persuaded at last to condemn the custom. And yet it continues to flourish. With the failure of legal countermeasures, the battery of disciplinary regimes that map the country in a grid of welfare surveillance now attempts to police and eradicate this continuing recalcitrance.[30] Nevertheless, even these subtler forms of persuasive coercion are clearly resisted. El Dareer herself confronted a wall of noncooperation. Many women scurried away to avoid her questions, while others generously gave detailed answers that she later discovered were quite false.[31]

Although the use of different methods and approaches could secure a much better fit in the reading of these cultures, there will always remain a "certain something" that continues to escape the reader's template. We can fasten our comprehension against this "something" that threatens the boundaries of our knowledge by excising the difference as if it is of no real significance. But what questions might persist within an argument's *in*coherence that might reveal something problematic about our own self-certainties?

If we allow the possibility that sexuality locates the end product of the humanist subject's specific historical trajectory, then we are confronted with a dilemma. Questions about African women using the peculiar taxonomy that has come to organize Western genital pleasures, may be the inadvertent projection of ethnocentric assumptions.[32] Foucault has argued that the "truth" of the individual in Western societies has gradually been constructed around a libidinal economy of self;[33] a person's individuality—that singular mark of a specific identity—is anchored by the monitoring and expression of sexuality. Although numerous disciplinary practices (medical, pedagogical, familial, and architectural, etc.) have produced what we take to be this essence of our personhood, we have reclaimed this cultural effect as an essential biological fact. Consequently, what has come to secure the "truth" of Western bodies becomes problematic when it is used as a universal, explanatory grid: the pleasures and desires of a body situated in other histories and other cultures may not be so readily comprehended.

An example of this can be seen in Abdalla's small community study in Somalia. Twenty-five of the sixty circumcised married women maintained that they enjoyed intercourse with their husbands—an unexpected response from women who cannot, at least according to Western medical discourse, enjoy sex at all. Another five women "could not explain how or what they felt during intercourse."[34]

Any attempt to explain these responses as false consciousness or simple ignorance turns the difference between women and between cultures into a nonsense that the West alone can explain. If, however, meaning is produced through culture, corporealized, lived and experienced, then desires and pleasures may be context specific when it comes to subject formation. Just as many feminists argue that knowledge is itself sexually inflected, positioning women differently from men within the frame of Western values, so this critique of phallogocentrism can be extended to the positioning of so called Third World bodies within First World knowledges. A Third World voice will not be heard within the terms of a First World discourse in any straightforward way. There is no place for it there that will not neutralize/translate its foreignness into comprehensible familiarity.

In light of this, the example of the Sudan illustrates the way in which Third World people must constantly renegotiate their identities through the grids of Western knowledges[35] that attempt to fix them as subjects. Medical discourse is just one method of mapping bodies. Anthropology has also engaged in this construction of the Sudanese subject. For example, the anthropologist S. F. Nadel was financed by Rockefeller money to assist the British government to penetrate the Nuba "social body." Its 300,000 members had no apparent political hierarchy into which indirect rule could easily insinuate itself:

> A new policy phase had indeed opened in British imperialism, and in the Sudan, Nadel was one of its local agents. He provided the information necessary for the Administration to "make use of" local customs. . . . Overriding indigenous societies had become too dangerous and uneconomical—controlling people with sociology was easier than controlling them with troops, and "making use of" their customs not only facilitated Administration and kept them controlled, but under the policy of Indirect Rule, it had the additional and very critical effect of keeping them Nuba.[36]

This story is not unusual. Evans-Pritchard was employed to study the Nuer after their rebellion against the British[37] and Malinowski, writing about indirect rule, praised the productive and positive effects that it would have on the native:

> If from the outset it were possible to make quite clear in preaching the gospel of civilization, that no full identity can be reached: that what are being given to Africans are new conditions of existence, better adapted to their needs but always in harmony with European requirements, the smaller would be the chances of strong reaction and the formation of new, potentially dangerous nationalisms.[38]

It would be a mistake to regard anthropology as a mere reflection of imperialism, assisting the British administration in the context of "routine colonialism" or indirect rule. Discourse, in this case anthropology, made African
cultures into comprehensible and knowable entities for the West. A massive cultural mapping took place. "We might employ a staff of trained anthropologists to make a complete comprehensive and elaborate anthropological
survey of the Sudan. Such anthropologists would be appointed for an indef-
inite period and their work be comparable to that done by the Geological
Survey."[39]

As "tribes" were created for the British, they came to engender a conceptual and material reality for Africans as well. As Iliffe notes in relation
to Tanganyika:

> The British wrongly believed that Tanganyikans belonged to tribes. Tangany-
> ikans created tribes to function within the colonial framework. . . . Cameron
> and his disciples erected indirect rule by "taking the tribal unit." They had
> the power and they created a new political geography. This would have been
> transient however had it not coincided with similar trends among Africans.
> They too had to live amongst bewildering social complexity which they
> ordered in kinship terms and buttressed with invented history. Moreover,
> Africans wanted effective units of action just as officials wanted effective units
> of government. . . . Europeans believed Africans belonged to tribes; Africans
> built tribes to belong to.[40]

A history of violent appropriation and Western indebtedness is simultaneously negated and justified through these representations that mirror
Western desires. Given this, how might we "unlearn our privilege as our
loss?"[41] as Gayatri Spivak has encouraged us to do? I can at least gesture in
this direction by returning to the literature on clitoridectomy that illustrates how a history of indebtedness and contamination between speaker
and object is consistently written out of interventionist texts. I will concentrate on the source most relied upon by other writers on this topic:[42] *The Hosken Report: Genital and Sexual Mutilation of Females* (1979), edited by Fran P.
Hosken and part of a Women's International Network News, meant to be
read with an accompanying booklet subtitled, *The Facts and Proposals for
Action* (1980).

Hosken's arguments express the unquestioning faith that medical discourse can determine the truth of woman's sexuality. Western feminists,
such as Shere Hite, are also cited to supplement the evidence that women
who practice clitoridectomy have been alienated from their real needs and
desires. *The Hosken Report* locates those sites through which modernizing
changes are most likely to be effected, encouraging readers to work through
the private foundations, government agencies, and international development programs that have already infiltrated the African continent. This list
of avenues considered desirable includes: the U.S. State Department, U.S.
Ministry of Foreign Affairs, WHO, UNESCO, UNICEF, USAID, international

family planning organizations, International Planned Parenthood Federation, and the Ford and Rockefeller foundations. Such philanthropy assumes that the myriad problems that confront Third World countries can be explained by the conventional views of "underdevelopment": "Economic development will only work if countries in Asia, Africa and Latin America adopt the social institutions and values of the West."[43]

The cultural intransigence of traditional societies becomes the impediment to modernization, which European achievement attests is possible.[44] However, this view conveniently ignores the causal relationship between the overdeveloped world and the underdeveloped world—a relationship that reveals how the prodigious economic advances in Europe from the sixteenth century to the present were obtained by a simultaneous dismantling and plunder of economies elsewhere in the world. Traditional economies were destroyed and rearticulated according to the needs of colonial metropoles. Factors of production were moved from the subsistence to the export sector, thereby dismantling and diminishing their indigenous sustainability. This expropriation of an economic surplus from the African continent became the unilateral transfer of wealth consolidating European industrial development. Even today, national independence has been unable to break this nexus as the very economic infrastructure in these countries is now a dependent one.[45]

The myths of conquest in which "history" or "colonialism" become the reified culprits that explain the international economic and political order are akin to the self-preserving First World fictions that serve to maintain global power asymmetries. The question one must address is how such injustices are rehearsed, reproduced, and finally legitimized through a process that circumvents scrutiny of its own internal workings. In its contemporary guise, the misnomer of "aid" achieves just such a sleight of hand, allowing the First World recipient to masquerade as philanthropic donor.[46]

If we recontextualize Hosken's proposals for action, it becomes apparent that we are inadvertently being asked to support, or at least endorse, the ongoing exploitation of these countries. Every source of information or recommended intervention is confounded by the terms with which it is named. For example, the neo-Malthusian "population time bomb," promoted in the 1960s by theorists such as Paul Ehrlich,[47] contained an economic imperative that dictated the funding strategies of that era: "The Population Council in New York, supported by the Population Reference Bureau Inc. in Washington, launched an extensive publicity campaign . . . with massive financial help from the Ford and Rockefeller Foundations, which contributed millions of dollars."[48] Medical aid from the West is very often tied to the recipient accepting the presence of these population control organizations.[49] And such organizations are themselves caught in a larger network of multinational pharmaceutical interests.[50] These are the same interventionist networks that Hosken would rally us to support so unequivocally.

My argument against these interventionist programs has focused upon the asymmetrical power relations that endorse such intrusive action. This capillary network of control attempts to immobilize the body of the Sudanese woman by rendering her docile and receptive to Western "philanthropy," just as the entire social body is made vulnerable to the penetration of foreign financial interests. Although the conventional framework of a Marxist analysis of power is adequate to this section of the discussion, it is unable to engage or even entertain questions about corporeal difference and the experience of lived sexuality. In a traditional materialist approach, medical practice can still retain its privileged epistemological status, authorized by its scientific credentials as part of that "progress" which is of unarguable benefit to humankind. The truth of the biological body underwrites these assumptions, where Culture becomes the superstructural variable that merely interprets this universal tabula rasa: nature/culture, body/mind—the neat dualism of Western metaphysics that permits no reflexive interrogation. For Marxists, the problem can then be transferred onto the social misuse of this knowledge, to the "forces and actors within medicine . . . the same forces that determine the overall social formation."[51] What remains unquestioned within this account is "precisely the quality that endows medicine with such great potential ideological and cultural power. It hides its apparent distance and distinctiveness from other social practices."[52]

The discovery that medicine is never independent of social forces does not so much "catch it out" as unscientific, but rather implies that all knowledge, including scientific knowledge, is essentially a social enterprise. A materialist analysis which fails to interrogate just what it is that circumscribes medical knowledge as medical, unwittingly adopts the positivist metaphysic of capitalism's conceptual framework: the objective/subjective, fact/value dichotomies are left intact.

It is the sexual "truth" of this medical body that legitimates Western interventionist views of female genital mutilation. What is of interest here is how a medicalizing discourse has become the science founding all the sciences of Man in the West. The history of this secularization of body management whereby health replaces salvation has had an effect on Man's being: "The importance of Bichat, Jackson, and Freud in European culture does not prove that they were philosophers as well as doctors, but that, in this culture, medical thought is fully engaged in the philosophical status of man."[53]

The social sciences, including anthropology, begin from a biological base that is *already* a cultural product. Therefore the most potent of cultural investments is located in the Western belief that scientific and medical knowledges are in fact acultural. The certainty that "everybody else got it wrong," both across histories and across cultures, is fundamental to this view. However, a materialist analysis of power does not separate discourse or knowledge from reality: discourse is not just *about* objects, *it actively constitutes them as "knowable."*

If the "individual" can be understood more accurately as a specifically historical social emergent, an "effect and object of power, as effect and object of knowledge,"[54] then the sexed subject is a relatively recent "invention" which may not be transhistorical or transcultural.[55]

In speaking *for* "the other," Western feminists are inevitably implicated in these same violent economies. Although the notion of a pure and uncontaminated speech is impossible and is itself invested with utopian/theological desires, we can at least consider whether our rush to judge, rescue, or salvage "the other" is not a self-congratulatory exercise in disguise, and one whose results may well be quite opposite to its stated motivations.

NOTES

1. Probably the best-known source on this subject reiterates this sense of "the unspeakable" in its title. "African Genital Mutilation: The Unspeakable Atrocities," in Daly 1978.

2. See de Beauvoir 1953.

3. See Said 1978 and 1985.

4. See, for example, Llewelyn-Davies 1981—the anthropologist's work with the Masai concerns these practices. See also Calder et al. 1993 and Engle 1992.

5. For an explanation of how the resistance to translation might remain invisible, see Derrida's (1988) criticisms of John Searle, a speech-act theorist whose work is in many ways consistent with this naive hermeneutic approach.

6. I have criticized the assumptions which inform the second position elsewhere. See, for example, Kirby 1989 and 1993.

7. See, for example, Daly 1978; Hosken 1979 and 1980; El Dareer 1983; Abdalla 1983; Minces 1982.

8. The bibliographies from the texts already mentioned draw heavily from medical journals and medical conferences. Abdalla (1983) is typical of this reliance on medical discourse. She cites: *The Lancet, Sudan Medical Journal, Tropical Doctor, East African Medical Journal, Surgery and Clinical Pathology in the Tropics, Journal of Obstetrics and Gynaecology of the British Commonwealth, American Journal of Obstetrics and Gynaecology, WHO Reports, The Magazine of The WHO, WHO Conference of Obstetrics and Gynaecology,* and Dr. R. Cook's *Review of the Medical Literature.* The authors of three other works about genital mutilation, in the Sudan (El Dareer 1983), Somalia (Abdalla 1983) and Egypt (El Saadawi 1980) are all doctors. El Saadawi is also a psychiatrist.

9. S. Elbaz quoted in Davis 1985, 328.

10. El Dareer 1983, 1.

11. Female circumcision, cutting of the prepuce or hood of the clitoris, is known in Muslim countries as "*sunna*" which means "tradition" in Arabic. This, the mildest type, affects only a small proportion of the millions of women concerned. It is the only type of operation that can correctly be called circumcision, whereas there has been a tendency to group all kinds of practices under the misleading term "female circumcision." Excision or clitoridectomy is the cutting of the clitoris and all or part of the labia minora. Infibulation is the cutting of the clitoris, labia minora, and at least the anterior two thirds and often the whole of the media part of the labia majora. The two sides of the vulva are then pinned together by silk or catgut sutures. This is often referred to as pharaonic circumcision. Intermediate Excision has varying degrees between *sunna* and pharaonic. These medical classifications are followed by all the interventionist texts.

12. El Dareer 1983, 67.

13. El Dareer 1983, 23.

14. El Dareer 1983, 9.

15. There is an apparent contradiction here in the suggestion that a Western trained midwife could actively promote the introduction of such practices. However, it has to be allowed that these women are also Sudanese and at the very bottom of the medical ladder. El Dareer tries to resolve this anomaly with the explanation that because trained midwives are not preferred by country people, they are unable to make sufficient money from the deliveries they are allowed to perform. Consequently they are forced to break the law and encourage women to adopt new practices that will require their continued services (El Dareer 1983, 17–18). Of course, this still doesn't explain why these women are persuaded. The gloss that it is a "kind of fashion" just begs more questions.

16. El Dareer 1983, 65. "Men's pleasure" is synonymous here with a mechanical functionalism. A raft of scholarship in gender and queer studies would challenge normative prescriptions about marginal and marginalized identities and sexualities. But more importantly for this argument, it also suggests that male heterosexuality is itself a heterodox and not a conforming set of predictable practices with one simple goal.

17. El Dareer 1983, 66.

18. El Dareer 1983, 88 (emphasis added). For further evidence that many men don't support the practice while women do, see Lowenstein 1978.

19. El Dareer 1983, 46. El Dareer also notes that the average time taken to achieve penetration varies from one to eighteen months.

20. Abdalla 1983, 89. In fact the literature on Somalia that describes a similar situation refers to a very high divorce rate, with women frequently initiating changes in their sexual partners.

21. El Dareer 1983, 57

22. El Dareer 1983, 71.

23. El Dareer 1983, 21. For a discussion of the construction of a monolithic and menacing Islam, see Ahmed 1992.

24. Ahmed 1992, 28.

25. Ahmed 1992, 66.

26. Ahmed 1992, 17

27. Ahmed 1992, 28.

28. See Foucault 1980, 140–143.

29. Foucault 1980, 93–94.

30. The organizations involved include the Ministry of Health, Ministry of Education and Guidance, the Higher National Council for Religious Affairs, the National Council for Social Welfare and Development, the Ministry of Culture and Information, Women's Secretariat and Sudanese Women's Union, The Family Planning Association, the Welfare and Youth Training Centre and the Medical Council (El Dareer 1983, 97).

31. El Dareer 1983, 20. I don't wish to imply that resistance is ever total or predictable. Some people were responsive, and indeed their answers are often consistent with El Dareer's own assumptions. My intention here is to concentrate on the inscrutable or difficult parts of these texts rather than on the apparently "readable" and relatively transparent material.

32. The "truth" of our sexual selves as tabulated by such taxonomists as Kinsey, Masters and Johnson and even Shere Hite are taken as a universal reference by all interventionist texts. See, for example, Abdalla 1983, 25.

33. Foucault 1980.

34. Foucault 1980, 92.

35. This body of work is vast. Briefly, to mention just four disciplines where this conclusion has been made: history—Fox-Genovese 1982; philosophy—Lloyd 1984; psychoanalysis—Irigaray 1985; science—Harding 1986, 15–29.

36. Faris 1973, 157. "Keeping them Nuba" should be understood to require the initial task of constructing their identity as Nuba. An example of the type of grid through which this new "identity" was to be extruded is given in the appendix mentioned in MacMichael's letter to the Financial Secretary of the Sudan Government (dated October 1, 1929). He requested a professional anthropologist be employed to assist the colonial government's administration. See Ahmed in Asad 1973, 268–269.

37. Feuchtwang 1973, 93.

38. Feuchtwang 1973, quoting Malinowski, 92.

39. Ahmed 1992, quoting MacMichael, 267.

40. Iliffe 1979, 318–324. For other references which discuss anthropology's construction of the tribe, see Mafeje 1972; Ranger 1982.

41. See Creed, Freiberg, and McLaughlan 1985, 27.

42. For example, Daly 1978; El Dareer 1983; Abdalla 1983; McLean 1980. Even newspaper articles rely upon this source; for example, Brisset 1979.

43. Hoselitz 1960, 55.

44. Despite their differences, works such as the following have provided these views with academic legitimacy. Lewis 1955; Rostow 1991; Hoselitz 1960; Hagen 1962; Brandt 1980; Galbraith 1979.

45. See, for example, Amin 1973; Frank 1978; Gutkind and Wallerstein 1976; Oxaal, Barnett, and Booth 1975; Hoogvelt 1984.

46. See, for example, Hayter 1983; Hayter and Watson 1985; Pearse 1980.

47. Ehrlich 1971.

48. Rose and Rose 1976.

49. Doyal and Pennell 1976.

50. See, for example, Hayter 1983; Silverman, Lee, and Lydecker 1982; Barnet and Muller 1975.

51. Navarro 1979, vii.

52. Wright and Treacher 1982, 11.

53. Sheridan 1980, 44.

54. Foucault 1977, 192.

55. "Before the end of the eighteenth century, man did not exist. . . . He is a quite recent creature . . . an invention of recent date." See Foucault 1973, 308 and 387.

WORKS CITED

Abdalla, Raqiya. 1983. *Sisters in Affliction: Circumcision and Infibulation of Women in Africa.* London: Zed Press.

Ahmed, Akbar S. 1992. *Postmodernism and Islam: Predicament and Promise.* London: Routledge.

Amin, Samir. 1973. "Underdevelopment and Dependence in Black Africa—Their Historical Origins and Contemporary Forms." *Social and Economic Studies* 22 (1): 177–196.

Asad, Talal, ed. 1973. *Anthropology and the Colonial Encounter.* London: Ithaca Press.

Barnet, Richard J., and Ronald E. Muller. 1975. *Global Reach: The Power of the Multinational Corporations.* London: Jonathan Cape.

Beauvoir, Simone de. 1953. *The Second Sex.* Trans. H. M. Parshley. Harmondsworth: Penguin.

Brandt, Willy. 1980. *North-South: a Program for Survival. The Report of the Independent Commission on International Development Issues under the Chairmanship of Willy Brandt.* London: Pan.

Brisset, C. 1979. "Thirty Million Mutilated Women." *Le Monde,* February 28, 5.

Calder, Barbara L., et al. 1993. "Female Circumcision/Genital Mutilation: Culturally Sensitive Care." *Health Care for Women International* 14 (3): 227–238.

Creed, B., F. Freiberg, and A. McLaughlan.1985. "Interview" (with G. C. Spivak). *Art Network* 16:23–27.

Daly, Mary. 1978. *Gyn/Ecology: The Metaethics of Radical Feminism.* Boston: Beacon Press.

Davis, Angela. 1985. "Women and Sex: Egypt" In *Women: A World Report,* comp. New Internationalist publication staff, 325–348. New York: Oxford University Press.

Derrida, Jacques. 1988. *Limited Inc.* Trans. S. Weber. Evanston: Northwestern University Press.

Doyal, Lesley, and Imogen Pennell. 1976. "Pox Brittanica: Health, Medicine and Underdevelopment." *Race and Class* 18 (2): 55–72.

Ehrlich, Paul R. 1971. *The Population Bomb.* 2nd ed. New York: Balantine.

El Dareer, Asma. 1983. *Woman, Why Do You Weep? Circumcision and Its Consequences.* London: Zed Press.

El Saadawi, Nawal. 1980. *The Hidden Face of Eve: Women in the Arab World.* London: Zed Press.

Engle, Karen. 1992. "Female Subjects of Public International Law: Human Rights and the Exotic Other Female," *New England Law Review* 26:1509–1526.

Faris, James C. 1973. "Pax Brittanica and the Sudan: S. F. Nadel." In *Anthropology and the Colonial Encounter,* ed. Talal Asad, 153–170. London: Ithaca Press.

Feuchtwang, Stephan. 1973. "The Discipline and its Sponsors." In *Anthropology and the Colonial Encounter,* ed. Talal Asad, 71–100. London: Ithaca Press.

Foucault, Michel. 1973. *The Order of Things: An Archaeology of The Human Sciences.* New York: Vintage Books.

———. 1977. *Discipline and Punish: The Birth of the Prison.* Harmondsworth: Penguin Books.

———. 1980. *The History of Sexuality 1: An Introduction.* New York: Vintage Books.

Fox-Genovese, Elizabeth. 1982. "Placing Women's History in History." *New Left Review* 133:5–29.

Frank, Ande Gunder. 1978. *Dependent Accumulation and Underdevelopment.* London: Macmillan.

Galbraith, James K. 1979. *The Nature of Mass Poverty.* Harmondsworth: Penguin Books.

Gutkind, Peter Wolfgang Claus, and Emmanuel Wallerstein, eds. 1976. *The Political Economy of Contemporary Africa.* Beverly Hills, CA: Sage Publications.

Hagen, Everett Einar. 1962. *On the Theory of Social Change.* Homewood, IL: Dorsey.

Harding, Sandra. 1986. "From the Woman Question in Science to the Science Question in Feminism." In *The Science Question in Feminism,* 15–29. Ithaca, NY: Cornell University Press.

Hayter, Teresa. 1983. *The Creation of World Poverty: An Alternative View to the Brandt Report.* London: Pluto Press.

Hayter, Teresa, and Catharine Watson. 1985. *Aid: Rhetoric and Reality.* London: Pluto Press.

Hoogvelt, Ankie M. 1984. *The Sociology of Developing Societies.* 2nd ed. London: Macmillan.

Hoselitz, Bert Frank. 1960. *Sociological Aspects of Economic Growth.* Glencoe, IL: The Free Press.

Hosken, Fran. 1979. *The Hosken Report: Genital and Sexual Mutilation of Female.* Lexington, MA: Women's International Network News.

————. 1980. *Female Sexual Mutilations: The Facts and Proposals for Action*. Lexington, MA: Women's International Network News.

Iliffe, John. 1979. *A Modern History of Tanganyika*. Cambridge: Cambridge University Press.

Irigaray, Luce. 1985. *Speculum of the Other Woman*. Trans. G. Gill. Ithaca, NY: Cornell University Press.

Kirby, Vicki. 1989. "Corporeographies." *Inscriptions: Journal for the Critique of Colonial Discourse* 5:103–119.

————.1993. "Feminisms and Postmodernisms: Anthropology and the Management of Difference." *Anthropological Quarterly* 66 (3): 127–133.

Lewis, Arthur. 1955. *The Theory of Economic Growth*. London: Allen and Unwin.

Llewelyn-Davies, Melissa. 1981. "Women, Warriors, and Patriarchs." In *Sexual Meanings: The Cultural Construction of Gender and Sexuality*, ed. Sherry B. Ortner and Harriet Whitehead, 330–358. Cambridge: Cambridge University Press.

Lloyd, Genevieve. 1984. *The Man of Reason: "Male" and "Female" in Western Philosophy*. London: Methuen.

Lowenstein, L. 1978. "Attitudes and Attitude Differences to Female Genital Mutilation in the Sudan: Is There a Change on the Horizon?" *Social Science and Medicine* 12 (5): 417–421.

Mafeje, Archie. 1972. "The Ideology of Tribalism." *The Journal of Modern African Studies* 9 (2): 253–261.

McLean, Scilla, ed. 1980. *Female Circumcision, Excision and Infibulation: The Facts and Proposals for Change*. London: Minority Rights Group.

Minces, Julie. 1982. *The House of Obedience—Women in Arab Society*. London: Zed Press.

Navarro, Vincente. 1979. *Medicine under Capitalism*. London: Croom Helm.

Oxaal, Ivar, Tony Barnett, and David Booth. 1975. *Beyond the Sociology of Development*. London: Routledge & Kegan Paul.

Pearse, Andrew. 1980. *Seeds of Plenty, Seeds of Want*. Oxford: Oxford University Press.

Ranger, T. O. 1982. "Race and Tribe in Southern Africa: European Ideas and African Acceptance." In *Racism and Colonialism: Essays on Ideology and Social Structure*, ed. Robert Ross, 121–142. The Hague: M. Nijhoff Publishers.

Rose, Hilary, and Steven Rose. 1976. *The Political Economy of Science: Ideology of/in the Natural Sciences*. London: Macmillan.

Rostow, Walt W. 1991. *Three Stages of Economic Growth*. Cambridge: Cambridge University Press.

Said, Edward. 1978. *Orientalism*. New York: Vintage Books.

————. 1985. "Orientalism Reconsidered." *Cultural Critique* 1:89–107.

Sheridan, Alan. 1980. *Michel Foucault: The Will to Truth*. New York: Tavistock Publications.

Silverman, Milton, Philip R. Lee, and Mia Lydecker. 1982. *Prescriptions for Death: The Drugging of the Third World*. Berkley, CA: University of California Press.

Wright, Peter, and Andrew Treacher. 1982. *The Problem of Medical Knowledge: Examining the Social Construction of Medicine*. Edinburgh: Edinburgh University Press.

Women's Rights, Bodies, and Identities:
The Limits of Universalism and the
Legal Debate around Excision in France

Françoise Lionnet

Dramatic changes have occurred in the 1990s with regard to the practice of female genital mutilation, or FGM, as it is known in the West. Numerous communities in Senegal and in a few other parts of Africa have agreed to abandon this practice. In a recent essay, "Abandoning Female Genital Cutting in Africa," Molly Melching documents the exceptional results obtained by TOSTAN, a nongovernmental organization. Through education and "the use of innovative pedagogical techniques inspired by African traditions and local knowledge,"[1] TOSTAN—a Wolof word meaning "to break out of the egg"—has been instrumental in transforming the lives of women in more than 282 villages since 1997. This NGO owes its success to their "participatory" form of educational outreach. The group organizes health education classes, encourages women to share their knowledge with each other, and promotes a process of exchange and dialogue very much rooted in African local traditions. These exchanges led to the realization that it was not sufficient for women to decide to abandon the practice for their own daughters; they needed to ritualize that decision by involving the whole community in a public declaration or pledge that reflected the communal will to make such changes. These public declarations were the culmination of a process of social mobilization that allows members of the same extended family or ethnic group or even entire village to agree to put an end to the practice of FGM.

During the 1980s, however, a debate raged among feminists about the respective merits of cultural relativism and the universalist approach to the question of bodily integrity. This chapter is an attempt to understand the mediating role that the female body has always played in the construction of identities—not just individual female identity, but the identity of the communities of which women are part. Communities have much at stake in the symbolic construction of the body of their female members, and FGM is part of that process of symbolization. It became the center of renewed controversies and public debates in the United States, debates that featured the work of Alice Walker and its militant Western stance against this African practice. I will attempt to outline here some of the limits that the universalist approach revealed during that decade of feminist conflicts.

My purpose is to suggest that local questions cannot have global solutions, and that all totalizing responses to the question of rights and needs are bound to be problematic. While the Universal Declaration of Human Rights has had some success in promoting women's rights and the elimination of discriminations in the public sphere, it does not address the problems of patriarchal hierarchies and issues of family life. This declaration will remain a dead letter for many women so long as the artificial and unrealistic distinction between private/public continues to be made. Basic issues of survival often lead to conflicts between human *needs* and human *rights*, and it behooves us as literary and cultural critics to keep in mind the complexities that underlie any kind of "rights talk."

I think that my role as a critic is not to offer clear and simple solutions, but rather to muddy up the waters, to blur the categories between public and private, and to show that a straightforward formulation such as Article 5 of the Universal Declaration of Human Rights, which states: "No one shall be subjected to torture, or to cruel, inhuman, or degrading treatment or punishment,"[2] is not as easily invoked as it may seem, since within the strictly familial private sphere, issues such as "torture" do not come up. Indeed, what we (Westerners) might consider cruel and inhuman treatment of women is not *named* as such by many cultures, since practices like female genital excision are simply part of a technology of the body that remains unquestioned, given that they form part of a network of social values that are the scaffolding upon which the equilibrium of the culture rests.

The practice of female genital excision and the cultural debates surrounding issues of needs and rights in relation to immigrants from Mali who now live in France provide an important framework for the present discussion. In the 1980s, excision had become the subject of public opinion in France and other western European countries because immigrants were having it performed on their daughters. Medical and school professionals, social workers and lawyers, anthropologists and psychiatrists were called upon to attest to the existence of the practice, to interpret its meaning, to testify to its effects on the physical and mental health of children, and to speculate about the merits of criminal repression by the courts. The fact that the practice exists in Europe began to surface at a time when the rights of all children were also being widely debated, fostering new legislation to protect them from various forms of physical and sexual abuse.

On February 2, 1981, a new law was introduced in the French penal code with the express purpose of repressing violence against minors. Article 312-3 of the code states the various types of legal sanctions that can be used to punish those found guilty of assault and battery or "coups et blessures volontaires à enfants de moins de 15 ans." During the following decade, several interesting judicial cases that raised complex cultural questions would be tried on the basis of this law. They all involved African families whose daughters were subjected to this custom. Viewed as intolerable by Western critics since colonial times, excision consists primarily of clitoridectomy, but can also be accompanied by the excision of all or part of the labia, and by infibulation (or the stitching together) of the two sides of the vulva. It can be fatal, and is increasingly considered—in the West—as a violation of basic human rights.[3] (In 1992, another new law was added to the penal code: it is Article 229-10 which states that in the case of mutilation—especially premeditated mutilation—of minors under the age of fifteen, perpetrators can be sent to jail for up to fifteen years.)

Transferred by immigrants from their own countries to their new homeland, this rite of passage is meant to mark entrance into adulthood, and is normally accompanied by extensive psychological preparation in the form of religious teachings and ritualized observances. When performed in France, however, much of the ritual apparatus is absent, and the operation is sometimes performed at an extremely young age, resulting in death, such as that of Mantessa Baradji, a five-week-old baby girl who died of a slow but fatal hemorrhage on April 3, 1983, the day after she had been excised. This case and two other nonfatal ones involving Batou Doukara and Assa Traoré were tried in criminal court and suspended jail terms of one to three years were given to the parents. Several other cases are pending, and the justice system is becoming ever more severe in its attempt to suppress the practice. But at the same time, a serious legal controversy has emerged around these decisions.

The debate opposes two apparently conflicting versions of human rights, one based on the Enlightenment notion of the sovereign individual subject, and the other on a notion of collective identity grounded in cultural solidarity. Critics of the Enlightenment version of human rights have opposed to it the more culturally specific concept of human dignity, stating that "concepts of human dignity do indeed vary. They are embedded in cultural views of the nature of human beings, which in turn reflect the social organizations of particular societies," and adding that "in Africa, idealized versions of human dignity reflect idealized interpretations of pre-colonial structure."[4] When emphasis is on the group, protection of the individual *qua* sovereign individual subject can be at odds with her development as a fully functioning member of her own society. By criminalizing the practice and sending to jail the parents of the excised girls, the French courts have judged individuals guilty of an act of violence which they had, in fact, no intention of committing, since their behavior was in accordance with deeply held socio-

cultural and religious beliefs about the nature of femininity and the function of sexuality in their respective collectivities. Anthropologists and social
critics have argued that such sanctions will have little if any positive impact,
since families may continue to have the excision performed either clandes-
tinely in France (and with greater risk to the girls' life and health) or back
in Africa during school vacations.

Geneviève Giudicelli-Delage has pointed out that France is the only European country confronted with this issue that actually prosecutes "*les auteurs
et complices d'excision*/those who operate or aid and abet in the operation of
excision."[5] This, she says, presents serious judicial risks since "*le prétoire
pénal est le lieu où l'on juge exclusivement des comportements individuels et non un
lieu où l'on débat de pratiques collectives*/the criminal court is the place where
individual behavior only is to be judged, it is not an arena for debate about
collective practices."[6] Despite these warnings, the most recent jury trial at the
Paris *Cour d'assises* on March 6, 7, and 8, 1991, concluded with the harshest
punishment ever: a five-year jail term for Aramata Kéita, a resident of France
and a member of the caste of women ironworkers who traditionally perform
excision in Mali, and five years' suspended sentence with two years' proba-
tion for the parents, Sory and Sémité Coulibaly, who had had their six
daughters excised by Kéita in 1982 and 1983.

As *Le Monde* reported in its coverage of the trial, the presence of the
three accused in the dock seemed but "a pretext, were it not for the fact
that they were risking imprisonment."[7] Although three individuals were sent
to jail, it seems as though the courts tried the practice rather than the persons involved: "The three accused listened to proceedings without understanding them. Their two interpreters did not translate the debate being
conducted in court—which occasionally took the air of a symposium."[8] The
woman public prosecutor dismissed experts' arguments regarding the pressures of ethnic customs and the ways in which such a practice forms part of
a whole social system. She stressed the fact that Kéita received a financial
reward for her services (ostensibly the symbolic and documented offering
of a *pagne* and some soap, but presumably other unacknowledged monies
totaling approximately one hundred francs) and because of this, the prosecutor demanded—and got—an exemplary decision from the jury, stating:
"From today on, it must be made quite clear to every African family that
excision has become a money making activity which risks incurring a very
heavy sentence."[9] Under the guise of protecting young girls from a "barbaric mutilation," the French legal system has victimized three individuals
who were not themselves treated as persons in their own right during the
trial, since it was clear that intentions, motivations, and responsibilities—
which are the foundations of individual guilt before the law—could not be
interpreted as criminal.[10] As the respected ethnopsychiatrist Michel Erlich[11]
has explained, the reasons for the continued performance of this practice
are compelling psychosexual ones for those involved, since it is embedded

in a cultural context that encodes it as a beautifying and enriching phenomenon without which girls do not become women, and will therefore never be able to marry, have some degree of economic security, and lead "full" female lives.

However objectionable the practice (and many women and men in Africa and the Middle East have denounced it), experts agree that putting complex "strategies for eradication"[12] in place in countries like Senegal, Sierra Leone, or Egypt require education as the essential tool, whereas legal action cannot even be justified on judicial and juridical grounds, since there exists no law in France that specifically forbids excision. The only one is the abovementioned Article 312-3 that must be *interpreted* as relevant to these particular cases in order for it to apply. The social, economic, and psychological consequences of jail for the families of the condemned parties are ignored by the courts, which thus manifest a blatant disregard for collective, familial, and community values, and under the pretext of protecting the abstract rights of an individual child, penalize the child by arbitrarily sentencing her parents for the purposes of making an example of them.

It is to reflect upon the contradictions and difficulties that arise from these complex human rights issues that a working group or "Atelier Droits des Peuples et Droits de l'Homme" was created at the Centre Droit et Cultures of the University of Paris-Nanterre. The first series of essays pertaining to excision was recently published in the journal of the center, *Droit et Cultures*, and I would like to briefly survey the preliminary results of this workshop because of the importance that they will have in defining the discourse about identity and sexuality within immigrant communities in France, and because this discourse reopens the question of universal rights in an unprecedented way.

The increasing diversity and plurality of French society has given rise to cultural conflicts that continue to erupt around topics such as citizenship, habitation, schooling, dress, and the rhetoric of difference and equality, or integration and xenophobia, that characterized political discourse in the 1980s. These forced a reexamination of the principles of universal democracy and natural rights that had theoretically been taken for granted since the Revolution of 1789. As Raymond Verdier explains, it has become necessary to rethink the familiar Western dialectic based on the oppositional paradigm of the individual versus society, and to conceptualize in its place "*des droits dits de la solidarité/* rights based in the concept of solidarity":

Cessant de prendre pour point de départ le sujet individuel mais envisageant l'homme comme membre d'une communauté humaine diversifiée, l'approche proposée entend échapper tant à un pur relativisme culturel qui mettrait en pièce l'unité du genre humain qu'à un pseudo-universalisme totalitaire et impérialiste qui méconnaîtrait tout droit à la différence et conduirait à la négation de toute identité culturelle et religieuse, selon "la configuration moderne individualiste des valeurs." Difficile conciliation à promouvoir

qui nécessite d'un côté la connaissance profonde des traditions culturelles, de leur évolu-
tion et de leur transformation, de l'autre un regard critique sur la notion d'identité qui
nous évite de tomber dans les pièges de l'ethnocentrisme.[13]

[The approach we propose would not take the individual subject as its point
of departure, but would look at the human being as a member of a diversi-
fied community. This would avoid the recourse to either the pure cultural
relativism that undermines the unity of the human race or the totalitarian
pseudo-universalism that would refuse the right to difference and lead to the
negation of all cultural and religious identity, in keeping with "the modern
individualist configuration of values." This is a difficult conciliation, and it
requires a deep understanding of cultural traditions, of their evolution and
transformation, on the one hand, and, on the other, a critical look at the
notion of identity so as to avoid falling into the traps of ethnocentrism.]

The practice of female excision is a kind of ideal test case, since it apparently illustrates absolute and total cultural conflict between the rights of the
individual to bodily integrity on the one hand, and her need to be satisfactorily integrated into a community on the other. But, as Michel Erlich
reminds us, this right to bodily integrity is by no means an absolute value in
Western society, since male circumcision, tonsillectomy, and appendectomy—
which can be viewed as ritual forms of surgery comparable to ethnic "mutilations," and which have been the object of controversy among medical
professionals—are culturally acceptable, and thus do not fall under Article
312-3 of the penal code. Furthermore, what Erlich calls a form of "*miso-
gynie médicalisée*/medicalized misogyny" was the reason why excision was
frequently performed, (as were ovariectomy and hysterectomy) from the
seventeenth to the early twentieth century: to treat nymphomania, hyper-
trophy of the female genitalia, masturbation, and lesbianism. A famous
seventeenth-century French surgeon named Dionis is credited with being the
first one to recommend excision "*comme remède à la lascivité feminine*/as a
remedy against female lasciviousness."[14] To defend the practice on strictly
cultural relativist grounds is thus as misguided as to condemn it on universalist and humanitarian ones, since complex psychosocial phenomena both
in Europe and elsewhere have motivated its existence, and only education
and information combined with an open and tolerant approach to different definitions of identity and community would eventually help eradicate
excision.

Can one oppose the practice on a feminist epistemological ground? Ideally,
perhaps, one might argue that in all of the above cases, the common denomi-
nator is a—conscious or unconscious, individual or collective—misogyny
and homophobia which aims at curbing all manifestations of female sexuality, and thus represents a universal fear and hatred of women which must
be countered by the appeal to a universal approach to human rights, the
only means of protection for female children in misogynist cultures. But to

condemn excision as a violation of human rights is to arbitrarily presume
that such a practice is the only culturally sanctioned form of violence that
deserves to be denounced, whereas we know that many other forms of violence are not repressed by law in the Western context, and that some of our
own practices are objectionable and shocking to Africans.

Erlich expresses doubts about some of the radical Western feminist
arguments, and states that it is "*un étrange paradoxe*/a strange paradox" that
women's right to pleasure and to the integrity of their bodies

> *passe par une législation qui légitime l'avortement, mutilation majeure dont la légali-*
> *sation a effectivement contribué à la libération féminine dans notre société, mais qui est*
> *encore considérée par bon nombre de nos concitoyens comme un crime et jugée en tant*
> *que tel dans ces cultures aux moeurs mutilantes, que notre activisme humanitaire a*
> *décidé de traiter par des moyens eux-mêmes mutilants.*[15]

> [is linked to a legislation that legitimates abortion, a major mutilation the
> legalization of which did indeed contribute to female liberation in our society,
> but which is still considered a crime by many and judged as such in those cul-
> tures that practice mutilations, which our humanitarian activism has decided
> to treat with mutilating means.]

To accept the legality of abortion, but to criminally repress the performance of excision is one of those paradoxes of contemporary legal practice
that seem to arbitrarily condemn "exotic" or "foreign" barbaric practices
regardless of precedents in our own culture that are legal and acceptable
to a majority because they are situated within a particular framework of
rights and gender that no longer shock our sense of fairness or interfere
with our freedom to live according to our own values. Although Erlich
does not elaborate on the parallel he draws with abortion, the suggestion is
provocative and compelling because it seems to put the abortion issue within
a context of reproductive rights that forces a reexamination of both feminist individualism and modern notions of freedom of choice.

Given the social stigmas that still attach to unwed motherhood among
the middle classes, and the financial and emotional difficulties that will
continue to be involved in raising a child as a single parent so long as the
responsibility for doing so is primarily the mother's, one might argue that
there is no real "freedom of choice" for many women who decide to have
an abortion. Indeed, aren't some of them—like the African women influenced by their communities' views on excision—deciding to have an abortion because it is the only possible solution in an economic and cultural
context that might force them to choose between a career and motherhood,
or to gain acceptance within their own social or professional communities
as women who are truly in charge of their own lives and reproductive
capacities? The rhetoric in favor of abortion has stressed the rights of
women to choose, and that is why the law should protect that right and sustain the legality of the procedure. Note also that the parallel Erlich draws

between abortion and excision is *not* based on a religious view of the fetus as different "person" whose rights are in conflict with those of the mother (as the fundamentalist Christian Right would have it), but more on a view of pregnancy as a "natural" consequence of female sexuality, just as we might see the clitoris a "natural" part of the female body. In this view, abortion, like excision, simply imposes cultural constraints on physical reality, and both procedures can arguably be defended by their proponents as cultural steps taken to avoid biological determinism.

The question of choice thus remains problematic when one focuses not just on individual rights, but on the way such rights might be in conflict with the broader social, religious, or communitarian values to which an individual woman has to subscribe if she is to remain a respected member of her community, as opposed to being a "free" agent in our increasingly atomized capitalist culture. Here again, the modern individualist view of freedom leaves much to be desired, since identity remains so closely linked to particularist views of reproductive rights and sexual choices, and in the case of women choosing motherhood, to their—by no means universal—right to health care, day care, and social programs that will help in the task of raising children.

What this suggests is that radical individualism is an empty concept for women, whether they live in "traditional" societies that uphold practices that are shocking to us, citizens of modern states that theoretically protect human rights, or *are* such citizens living under a comforting illusion of choice that does not sustain critical scrutiny whenever we examine the supposedly "voluntary" acts that involve sexuality and reproduction. Similarly, ritual practices are not adhered to "voluntarily": like Sémité Coulibaly, the mother who solicits the services of a woman to excise her daughters believes that she is conforming to the traditions of her community, and that failing to do so would jeopardize her daughters' chances of being accepted by their community of origin. Furthermore, refusal to allow excision of the daughter runs the risk of endangering the mother's opportunity to engage in the slow process of liberation that now allows African women living in France to oppose polygamy, to work, and to enroll in literacy programs *as long as* they are not perceived by the immigrant community as imposing these "new" values on their own daughters: "*Si en plus on s'approprie les filles on sera rejetée par tout le monde, renvoyées au village/*If on top of all this we seem to be appropriating the girls, we'll be rejected by everyone, sent back to the village," as one woman exclaimed. Her fear is echoed by most of the Soninké of Mali who participated in the study conducted in Paris by Catherine Quiminal.[16]

At stake is the definition of tradition itself, the way it forms part of a network of power within which conflicting notions of freedom, community, and authority hold ground. Quiminal is well aware of this, and she points out:

comme toutes les traditions, les mutilations sexuelles des femmes ne sont traditions que dans la mesure où les intéressées n'ont d'autres possibilités que de les subir sous peine d'être exclues de leur communauté. Dès lors qu'elles sont contestées, les traditions apparaissent pour ce qu'elles sont: expression d'un rapport de force, arguments d'autorité.[17]

[Like all traditions, the sexual mutilation of women is "tradition" only to the extent that the women concerned have no choice but submit to it or else be excluded from the community. As soon as they are contested, traditions are revealed to be but the expression of power relations, arguments of authority.]

Excision makes clear how power relations are inscribed on the female body by virtue of its subjection to particular sexual traditions. Indeed, the reasons for this practice have to do with complex definitions of masculinity and femininity that construct the clitoris and the male prepuce as vestiges of the opposite sex that must be eliminated for a "proper" sexual identity to exist. Thus, the female body is considered "too masculine" and socially unacceptable when not marked by excision. Malian women are culturally dependent on this view of sexuality that forms the basis of their feminine identity. This situation illustrates well Michel Foucault's insight that "the political technology of the body" amounts to a "system of subjection"[18] of individual persons within a specific cultural code.

It is interesting to note that in the African context, the discourse on female sexuality defines femininity in terms of binary *cultural* inscriptions (male circumcision/female excision) rather than purely biological categories of male/female.[19] One becomes a female person after having submitted to a cultural process; one is not simply born a "woman." Similarly, a "person" is not a person until he/she has been marked by society in a way that gives him/her dignity and social status within a specific ethnic group. Isaac Nguema has stressed that throughout "traditional" Africa "*la personne humaine n'a de valeur qu'à l'intérieur de son groupe éthnique, . . . la personalité juridique . . . s'acquiert au fur et à mesure que la personne franchit les étapes de la vie: à l'occasion de la circoncision . . . du mariage . . . de la naissance des enfants/*the individual has value only as a member of her ethnic group, . . . the legal personality . . . develops as one goes through different stages of life: on the occasion of circumcision . . . marriage . . . and the birth of children."[20] Thus, he argues, the African notion of "person" is a more interactive and dynamic one compared to the Western one, which he sees as "*abstraite, mécanique, statique, matérialiste/*abstract, mechanistic, static, materialistic," and intolerant of genuine solidarity since an absolute view of individual rights will necessarily enter in conflict with a genuine form of familial or cultural solidarity.

Problems then arise because the power of Malian culture to invest meaning in the individual body is at odds with the French state's power to construct that body's biological integrity according to modern notions of individual rights. When Malians fall under the authority of the French courts on French territory, their bodies are invested with full responsibility for their actions and intentions, and they become liable to imprisonment, not so much because the performance and/or abetting of excision is a violation of the rights of children, as the application of Article 312-3 would suggest, but because the state locates meaning and identity in the individual, autonomous body of its *citizens*. Because the Coulibalys reside in France, it is the authority and sovereignty of the French courts that are exercised. It is the Coulibalys' identity derived from their immigrant status that supersedes their "Africanness." Sylvie Fainzang is well aware of the specifically legal aspect of a dilemma which is increasingly familiar in a pluralistic society, and which faces all those who live in two cultures with a foot in each world:

> *L'excision est donc pratiquée pour se conformer à une loi; elle est le résultat d'une conformité à une pratique collective et de la soumission à une contrainte sociale. Les individus se retrouvent pris comme dans un étau entre deux lois contraires: la conformité à l'une entraînant* ipso facto *le non-respect de l'autre.*[21]

> [Excision is thus performed in order to obey a law; it results from the need to conform to a collective practice, and from the fact of being subjected to a social constraint. Individuals are thus caught as in a vise between two opposing laws; to obey the one ipso facto leads to breaking the other.]

Both laws represent two systems of power that hold sway over individual responsibility, undermining the very possibility of assigning individual blame. These cases demystify the fiction of the sovereign subject since the subjectivity of the defendants can easily be shown to be the site of conflicting and contradictory constraints. The "power-knowledge relations"[22] created by the courts' intransigence is a reflection of the absolute noncommensurability of the two cultural systems that interface in these cases.

Indeed, since excision can very well be defined as a "custom" in the technical sense allowed by French law (according to Article 327 of the penal code), this should exempt it from criminalization, just as corporeal punishment of children is exempt because it is considered an acceptable form of parental behavior sanctioned by "custom" as understood by this law.[23] The crux of the matter here is clearly a question of which jurisdiction has authority over the persons accused and what constitutes "custom" or tradition or precedent under that jurisdiction. Giudicelli-Delage puts it clearly:

> *Tout comme notre ordre public ne pourrait s'accommoder d'un ordre contraire de la loi étrangère, il ne peut s'accommoder d'une coutume étrangère contraire.*[24] *Dans le conflit de cultures que constitue l'excision, toute position qui pourrait laisser croire à une tolérance de cette pratique sur le territoire français est condamnée au nom de l'ordre public interne et des principes fondamentaux de l'homme. La culture qui est la nôtre ne peut qu'affirmer haut et fort son rejet de l'excision. Mais par quelle voie l'affirmer? La voie judiciaire actuellement pratiquée, la voie législative, ou encore une "troisième voie"?*[25]

[Just as our public order/system of law and order could not accommodate an opposing order based on a foreign system of laws, it cannot tolerate a foreign and opposed practice/custom. Within the conflict of cultures that excision foregrounds, any position that might suggest a tolerant attitude toward this practice on French territory is condemned in the name of our own internal public order, and of fundamental human principles. Our culture can only proclaim its vigorous opposition to excision. But by which means can it do so? The judicial way as it is currently done, the legislative way, or yet a "third way"?]

For Giudicelli-Delage, there is no doubt that the only worthwhile and effective approach is the "third" one, that is, cooperation with those African countries that are slowly struggling to put in place new cultural forms by educational, and not repressive, means: "*Il faut pour chasser une ancienne coutume qu'une nouvelle prenne sa place, qu'une nouvelle culture se forge at non se voit imposer*/The way to phase out an ancient custom is to allow a new one to replace it, to let a new culture forge itself, not to impose one from above."[26] To apply abstract Enlightenment values in a rigidly intolerant legal way is to undermine the system's own claim to universality since it thereby condemns practices that form part of a network of social values which are the scaffolding upon which rests the global equilibrium of a *different* culture. These practices are not just irrational and aberrant abuses as many uninformed Western critics would like to believe. It is in fact possible to see them as part of a coherent, rational, and workable system, albeit one as flawed and unfair to women as our own can be.

The March 8, 1991, ruling marks the Coulibalys as subjects of/to the French state. Ironically, their identity is thus reconstructed by the same court that might ultimately decide whether or not to grant them citizenship, in accordance with recent decisions about the right of immigrants to full French citizenship. Interestingly, then, it is the same sort of power relations that impose a different "national" identity (and the customs that go with it) on immigrant families whose right to citizenship is not even clear that is also central to the construction of sexual identity in the cultures that allow excision. As Sylvie Fainzang explains,

> *l'analyse des discours relatifs à cette pratique révèle qu'il s'agit en fait, avec les mutilations sexuelles, de façonner les individus de manière à les rendre aptes à assumer le rôle social qui leur est réservé en raison de leur sexe. Cette différenciation sexuelle est motivée par une volonté de différenciation des statuts sociaux. . . . Le marquage sexuel que réalise l'excision est la condition de l'accès à un statut social spécifique, celui de* femme, soumise à l'autorité de l'homme. *La pratique de l'excision repose donc sur la volonté de créer les conditions (physiques) de la domination (sociale) de l'homme sur la femme.*[27]

[The analysis of discourses relating to the practice reveals that sexual mutilations are a means of disciplining individuals, of rendering them fit for the social role which is reserved for them because of their gender. The sexual differentiation is motivated by the will to distinguish among different statuses. . . . The sexual marking provided by excision is the necessary condition of access to a specific social status, that of woman subjected to the authority of men. The practice of excision thus depends on the will to create the (physical) conditions of the (social) domination of woman by man.]

On the one hand, we have immigrants who are subordinated to French law, on the other, females brought under the authority of males. In either case, it would seem that we are very far indeed from any individualist conception of rights. It is a conception of identity as subordinate to either the state (France) or the ruling patriarchy (in Mali) that governs the (il)legitimacy of parental behavior. It is therefore pointless to claim that the issue opposes communitarian values to universal ones, since the actual conflict hinges on the opposing claims of two different communities, one of which would like to believe that its culture is a "universal" one.

What does appear to be "universal" when we carefully examine the whole cultural contexts within which the debate is situated is the way in which *different* cultures, for better or for worse, impose *similar* constraints on the bodies of their members, especially when those bodies are already marked by the sign of the feminine. Both cultures—the French and the African—have ways of disciplining and socializing the body that denote highly complex sociocultural organizations, and the work done by the *Centre Droit et Cultures* attests to the long-term educational process that still needs to take place in order for African immigrants to liberate themselves from age-old customs, and for the French legal system to accommodate the increasing diversity that is now French society. This diversity has the incontestable merit of underscoring the injustices and inequities of our own culture, and of reminding us that "*le barbare, c'est d'abord l'homme qui croit à la barbarie/*the barbarian is first and foremost the one who believes in barbarism,"[28] as Lévi-Strauss once put it.

The changes that were put in place in the 1990s in Senegal are proof that this long-term educational process has begun to meet with success. Indeed, it is through respect for the "other's" culture and its collective symbolic and ritual dimensions that "public declarations" and exchange of views has led to the monumental changes of the last few years, as documented by Melching.[29]

NOTES

An earlier version of this chapter appears in *Contemporary French Civilization* 16 (2) (1992): 294–307.

1. See Melching 2001, 157.
2. United Nations 1973.
3. See Slack 1988.
4. Howard 1986, 17.

5. Giudicelli-Delage 1990, 207.
6. Giudicelli-Delage 1990, 208.
7. Peyrot 1991, 16.
8. Peyrot 1991, 15–16.
9. Peyrot 1991, 16.
10. Giudicelli-Delage 1990, 205.
11. Erlich 1986.
12. Koso-Thomas 1987.
13. Verdier 1990, 149.
14. See Erlich 1990, 156, 159. This medical "solution" to the "problems" of female sexuality reaches its apex during the Victorian era in Britain, and continues to be performed until the 1950s in the United States: "*Reprise par LEVRET, cette solution radical inaugure une stratégie répressive de la sexualité féminine dont le sadisme va s'accentuer tout au long du XIXe siècle. Appliquée pour la première fois en 1822 par GRAEFE au traitement de la 'folie masturbatoire,' la clitoridectomie est érigée en panacée quarante ans plus tard par BAKER-BROWN, chirurgien britannique de renom qui passe à la postérité comme le champion de l'excision 'thérapeutique.' A la même époque, l'Américain BATTEY, autre grand mutilateur propose l'ovariectomie qu'il qualifie de 'normale,' c'est-à-dire la castration féminine, en guise de triatement de divers troubles nerveux. Culminant à l'époque victorienne en Angleterre et aux Etats-Unis, cette mysoginie médicalisée va se prolonger dans ce dernier pays jusqu'au courant du XXe siècle, où elle trouvera encore d'ultimes adeptes jusque dans les années cinquante. Ainsi les indications médicales des mutilations sexuelles évoluent du domaine de la pathologie morphologique à celui de la pathologie psychologique*" (156). [Adopted by Levret, this radical medical solution inaugurates a strategy of repression of female sexuality the sadism of which will be on the increase during the nineteenth century. Cliteridectomy was first used in 1822 by Graefe to treat "masturbatory madness," and forty years later, it was chosen as a panacea by Baker-Brown, the famed British surgeon who will be remembered by posterity as the champion of "therapeutic" excision. At about the same time, Battey, an American, and another great mutilator, proposed ovatiectomy (that is female castration) which he defines as "normal," as a means of treatment for a number of nervous ailments. The medicalized form of misogyny culminated in England during the Victorian era, but in the United States, it continued to be performed during the twentieth century, and some doctors were prescribing it into the 1950s. This is how the medical uses of sexual mutilation evolve from the domain of physical pathology to that of psychological pathology.]

15. Erlich 1990, 161.
16. Quiminal 1990, 190.
17. Quiminal 1990, 183.
18. Foucault 1979, 26.
19. See Erlich 1986; Lionnet 1990, 1992.
20. Nguema 1990, 215.
21. Fainzang 1990, 180.
22. Foucault 1979, 27.
23. See Merle and Vitu 1984.
24. Giudicelli-Delage 1990, 203.
25. Giudicelli-Delage 1990, 206–207.
26. Giudicelli-Delage 1990, 210.
27. Fainzang 1990, 177–178.
28. See Lévi-Strauss 1961, 22. On January 10, 1993, a year after this essay was written, the *New York Times* reported that under this Article, a Gambian woman, Mrs. Teneng Jahate, had been sentenced to five years imprisonment, four of them

suspended, on charges of causing the wounding and mutilation of her two daughters, aged one and two years, respectively.

29. See Melching 2001.

WORKS CITED

Erlich, Michel. 1986. *La Femme blessée: Essai sur les mutilations sexuelles féminines.* Paris: L'Harmattan.

———. 1990. "Notions de mutilation et criminalisation de l'excision en France." *Droit et Cultures* 20:151–162.

Fainzang, Sylvie. 1990. "Excision et ordre social." *Droit et Cultures* 20:177–182.

Foucault, Michel. 1979. *Discipline and Punish: The Birth of the Prison.* Trans. Alan Sheridan. New York: Vintage Books.

Giudicelli-Delage, Geneviève. 1990. "Excision et droit pénal." *Droit et Cultures* 20:201–211.

Howard, Rhonda E. 1986. *Human Rights in Commonwealth Africa.* Lanham, MD: Rowman & Littlefield.

Koso-Thomas, Olayinka. 1987. *The Circumcision of Women: A Strategy for Eradication.* London: Zed Books.

Lévi-Strauss, Claude. 1961. *Race et histoire.* Paris: Gonthier.

Lionnet, Françoise. 1990. "Feminism, Universalism, and the Practice of Female Excision." *Passages* 1:2–4.

———. 1992. "Identity, Sexuality, and Criminality: The Legal Debate around the Issue of Female Excision in France," *Contemporary French Civilization* 16 (2): 294–307.

Melching, Molly. 2001. "Abandoning Female Genital Cutting in Africa." In *Eye to Eye: Women Practicing Development across Cultures,* ed. Celeste Schenck and Susan Perry, 156–170. London: Zed Press.

Merle, Phillippe, and André Vitu. 1984. *Traité de droit criminel.* Paris: Cujas.

Nguema, Isaac 1990. "Universalité et spécificité des droits de l'homme en Afrique: La Conception traditionnelle de la personne humaine. *Droit et Cultures* 19:215.

Peyrot, Maurice. 1991. "L'excision, crime coutumier." *Le Monde,* March 8, 15–16.

Quiminal, Catherine. 1990. "Les Soninké en France et au Mali: Le Débat sur les mutilations sexuelles. *Droit et Cultures* 20:183–190.

Slack, Allison, T. 1988. "Female Circumcision: A Critical Appraisal." *Human Rights Quarterly* 10:437–486.

United Nations. 1973. *Human Rights: A Compilation of International Instruments of the United Nations.* New York: United Nations.

Verdier, Raymond. 1990. "Chercher remède à l'excision. Une nécessaire concertation." *Droit et Cultures* 20:149.

"Other" Bodies: Western Feminism, Race, and Representation in Female Circumcision Discourse

Chima Korieh

> There is no vantage outside the actuality of relationships between cultures,
> between unequal imperial and non-imperial powers, between different Others,
> a vantage that might allow one the epistemological privilege of somehow
> judging, evaluating and interpreting free of the encumbering interests,
> emotions and engagements of the ongoing relationships themselves.
>
> EDWARD SAID[1]

The worldwide debate on female circumcision has come under increasing scrutiny partly because it is fuelled by feminist discourses that position the West as the arbiter of cultural values and meanings. Western feminist discourses on female circumcision have produced powerful images of African and Middle Eastern societies. The images, embedded in a salvationist and liberationist message, describe female circumcision as emblematic of a backward and uncivilized society. A critique of these discourses has become evident as scholars and other commentators break out of the binary construct of the West/The Rest of Us or the civilized/uncivilized confinements of Eurocentric literature and knowledge production. In the ongoing debate about female circumcision, in particular, it has meant looking critically at Western feminism in its continued privileging of Western cultural ideas and practices. It has also meant looking critically at the salvationist agenda of Western feminism and its mission of speaking across differences of race, gender, sexuality, and cultures.

This chapter explores the ways in which some arguments central to female circumcision discourse contribute to promoting a racist culture grounded in unequal power relations. It will specifically examine recent arguments in the female circumcision debate in order to situate the arguments in their historical context and to point to the polemics as representing cultural imperialism and functionalist theorizing. The chapter will also probe the definition of the Western self, identify what assumptions underlie this definition, and attempt to reveal some of what remains suppressed. In order to contextualize the discourse, I undertake the task with an understanding, as Penelope Hetherington argues, "that there is no pure or uncontaminated speech as our language employs categories in all fields of so called 'knowledge' to make distinctions between things, including the separate categories of polemic and history."[2]

FEMALE CIRCUMCISION THROUGH THE LENS OF RACE AND HISTORY

Female circumcision has been given different names in different contexts by people with different agendas. Basically, female circumcision denotes a set of surgeries performed on females in some African and Islamic societies. They range from the removal of the prepuce (*sunna*) to the more severe procedures that entail the removal of the clitoris (excision), to infibulation, which involves the removal of the clitoris, the labia minora, and the labia majora. In pharaonic circumcision, the remaining flesh is stitched together leaving a small aperture.[3] While "female circumcision" and "clitoridectomy" are used for any of these procedures, the preferred term used by feminists is "female genital mutilation (FGM)."[4]

The deleterious health consequences of certain female circumcision practices cannot be overemphasized. For the severe types of female circumcision, the health implications include hemorrhaging, shock, infection, urinary retention, and urinary tract infections. Other long term physical complications and health effects of female circumcision include urethral and bladder stones, excessive scar tissue formation, dermoid cysts, and obstructed labor.[5] Certainly, female circumcision has become problematic in recent time for both Western and non-Western societies. For non-Western societies, it is problematic not only because it lies at the intersection of a number of Western discourses that have become very powerful in the late twentieth century. It is also problematic because the consideration of the issue by Westerners often revives memories of the cultural arrogance that underpinned some missionary activities during the colonial period, resulting at least in one case in the retention of the practice till the present time.[6] As a result of the problematic nature of the subject, it has also produced a burgeoning academic and professional literature seeking to understand the sociology of the practice and offer suggestions for its "eradication." A considerable proportion of the literature includes polemic tracts by Western feminists and commentators in the Western media propaganda against the practice.[7] From the 1970s, female circumcision was condemned widely in the Western scholarly circles and popular culture, variously labeled as a "crime of gender," "torture," "barbarism," and "ritualized torturous abuse."[8]

In the 1990s, it took on a particular significance because of the way it emerged not only as a concern for feminists, but also for physicians, ethicists, governments, and development agencies. Through such organizations as Women International Network (WIN), feminists have mounted increased campaigns to "eradicate" female circumcision. Western governments, for their part, have instituted legislation prohibiting female circumcision among immigrant communities.[9] Medical literature has increasingly lent its weight to efforts to stop the practice.[10] Other insurgents have their origin in academia.[11] From the 1980s, female circumcision increasingly became part of the development agenda and a human rights issue in the West.[12] More recently, African women have contributed to the female circumcision debate[13] by producing a counterdiscourse to the Western feminist-informed arguments in the debate. For many of the African critics, Western feminist discourses are denigrating and reflective of "Eurocentric preoccupation with sex, individualism, and other concerns valued in Western societies."[14]

That the literature has grown exponentially since the 1980s lies in what Hetherington observes as the development of several intersecting discourses which find the issue of female circumcision an ideal "site" for the expression of deeply held convictions.[15] There is no doubt, however, that the development of the female circumcision discourse hinges on the issue of female sexuality and the politics of the body in feminist discourses. The awareness amongst feminists of the clitoris as a site of women's sexual pleasure and the rejection of the primacy of vaginal orgasm particularly fueled the debate over female circumcision from the 1980s. Although many societies that practice female circumcision may be aware of the importance of the clitoris as an area that increases sexual pleasure, female circumcision may not be rationalized as suppressing women's sexuality. For example, genital surgeries were known and had been studied by anthropologists as early as the 1950s, at least since Bruno Bettelheim's 1955 psychoanalytical analysis of indigenous genital alterations. But such investigations were undertaken in the context of cultural relativism without making any moral judgment.[16]

However, a number of developments unrelated to female circumcision discourse in the late 1960s and early 1970s also imbued the debate with its current passion, at least from the Western perspective. One of these developments was Masters and Johnson's 1966 publication of *Human Sexual Response*,[17] which established the centrality of the clitoris in female orgasm, debunking Freud's notion of the mature vaginal orgasm.[18] The discovery implied that women's orgasm could readily be achieved without male penetration, or even male participation.[19] In a period that saw the growth of radical and separatist feminist politics, the acceptance of lesbian sexuality, and the growing body of criticism of aggressive and sexist male behavior, symbolized by the phallus, "the clitoris came to symbolize female sexuality and feminist concern."[20] As a result, feminists, particularly in the United

States linked their aspiration for autonomy and self-determination with control over their sexuality, and rejected notions that women's genitals were shameful, ugly, and dirty. Sandra Lane and Robert Rubinstine rightly suggest that by the late 1970s, "the clitoris had undeniably become a metaphor for women's power and self-determination."[21]

While circumcision is widely practiced in many parts of the Middle East and Africa, its severity and sociological implications vary widely. Their variations, however, are not always clearly identified in Western feminist discourse. Implicit in current circumcision discourse, therefore, are many generalizations that concur on the harmful effects of particular circumcision procedures, but ignore the differences between the various kinds of circumcision procedures and fail to establish their character, extent, and implications for African women and societies at large. An unfortunate legacy of the discourse is the neglect of cultural particularities and unequal power relations between the West and other societies and the failure to take into account the colonial and imperialist contexts of these relations dating back to the nineteenth century.

Apparently, female circumcision is not unique to non-Western societies. But the West makes it look so. By the nineteenth century and up till the 1940s, women and girls in Europe and America were circumcised to "cure" female nervousness and masturbation.[22] In March 1866, for example, Isaac B. Brown published his book *On the Curability of Certain Forms of Insanity, Epilepsy, Catalepsy, and Hysteria in Females*[23] and proposed that all forms of feminine illnesses referred to in the book's title could be cured by excision of the clitoris. Encouraged by Brown's work, the church in England supported female circumcision and encouraged the clergy to bring the procedure to the attention of male physicians.[24] Till the late nineteenth century, the medical reasoning behind excision of the clitoris was not discredited in America. Charles Meigs in his 1859 study,[25] *Woman: Her Diseases and Remedies*, had proposed the excision of the clitoris to cure certain diseases in women, citing the case of a nine-year-old nymphomaniac. And by 1897, Thomas Allbutt's *A System of Gynaecology* stated that in cases of nervous disorder thought to be caused by enlarged clitoris, it may be necessary to amputate the clitoris, or to excise the nymphae.[26] Furthermore, Barbara Ehrenreich and Deirdre English note that as late as the 1940s, clitoridectomy was performed on a five-year-old girl to correct emotional disorder.[27] Ironically, however, the present attention focused on female circumcision has allowed some Westerners and social scientists (feminists included) "to view such practices as being rooted in ideologies totally foreign to the West."[28] I agree with Elizabeth Sheehan's argument that criticism too deeply imbued with a sense of ethical and scientific superiority deflects attention from the cultural contexts in which female circumcision takes place while also denying Western medicine's use of similar procedures.[29] An appropriate approach to understanding female circumcision and its global reach would require situating it in all its complexities in a historical context. We must not only acknowledge the history and global nature of circumcision and clitoridectomy,[30] but also situate the debate in time and place. Only then can the self-denial on the part of Western commentators and attempts to impose their views on others be unveiled. Only then can Western approaches in the circumcision discourse be understood as a continuing legacy of Western cultural imperialism.

COLONIALISM, FEMINISM, AND HISTORICAL CONTINUITIES

Nineteenth-century Europe, in particular Victorian England, fostered a notion of "normality" and what Susie Prestney has described as a penchant for the "perverse" in science in particular and in culture in general.[31] During the colonial period, the so-called "natives" were made accessible to the anthropologist as tools of his knowledge production that ultimately provided a road map for the effective "governing" of the "natives." Indeed, knowledge production and utility are central issues in the postcolonial context as well. The Western imagination of geographical worlds and difference is now rooted in information from personal narratives, the print and electronic media, and films. Since non-Western societies do not have equal access to information technology, there continues till today an imbalance in flow of information and cultural knowledge.

To a large extent, this inequality of relationship stems essentially from the fact that the West has more resources and power with which to force its own assumptions on other societies. In the circumcision discourse in particular, Western feminism, like anthropology, constructs stereotypical images of cultural "others" with little attempt made to truly understand women in other societies.

Essentially, histories of feminist discourse in the West have focused primarily on the image of the colonized women as helpless and suffering from the backwardness, savagery, and wretchedness of their own cultures.[32] For instance, scholars have focused on *sati* and the veil in Hindu and Moslem societies as emblematic of women's dismal status in India and Egypt respectively.[33] In the case of Egypt, for instance, Leila Ahmed highlights some of the problems of the representation of the veil as a symbol of women's oppression in colonial narratives.[34] In the rhetoric about the veil, Ahmed argues that:

> What was created was a fusion between the issues of women, their oppression, and the culture of Other men. The idea that Other men, men in colonized societies beyond the border of the civilized West, oppressed women was to be used, in the rhetoric of colonialism, to render morally justifiable its project of undermining or eradicating the cultures of colonized peoples. [W]hatever the disagreements of feminism with white male domination within

Western societies, outside their borders feminists turned from being the critics of the system of white male dominance to being its docile servant. Anthropology, it has often been said, served as the handmaid of colonialism. Perhaps it must also be said that feminism, or the idea of feminism, served as its other handmaid.[35]

In the same vein, Frederique Apffel-Marglin and Suzanne Simon argue that "colonialists and Victorian feminists combined to conflate women and culture. The comparison of womanhood in 'civilized' Britain and in the colonies made it possible for someone like Lord Cromer (then Governor of Egypt) to oppose Victorian feminists at home while simultaneously using Victorian feminist arguments in respect of Egyptian women to argue for the wholesale overhaul of Egyptian ways of life."[36] Indeed, Frantz Fanon points out in his analysis of French colonial attitudes and strategies concerning the veil in Algeria that the colonialist's goal, here as elsewhere in the world, was "converting the woman, winning her over to the foreign values, wrenching her free from her status" as a means of "shaking up the (native) man" and gaining control of him.[37] With this and other motives, those outsiders who would "develop" the Third World have often seen the advancement of non-Western women as the first goal to be achieved, with their men's program thought to follow rather than precede it.[38]

Colonial discourse and the current feminist discourse on female circumcision assume the same binary trajectory of a civilized, emancipated, and autonomous Western woman, on the one hand, and the oppressed and backward non-Western woman bound by tradition, superstition, and male suppression on the other. Such binaries are possible only with the Western subject as the primary reference point.[39]

However, as issues of power and representation continue to assume a central role in contemporary theory, what has been largely neglected is the imperial context that gave rise to various forms of racial representation.[40] Radicalized knowledge, deriving from contemporary feminist circumcision discourse, rests upon what Edward Said describes as an "almost insuperable contradiction between political actuality based on force, and a scientific and humane desire to understand the 'Other' . . . in modes not influenced by force."[41] Whether this knowledge is used for purposes that are repressive or liberatory, interpretation of "other" cultures, as Said points out, appears to be delivered "directly into a universalism free from attachment, inhibition and interest."[42] What is being increasingly acknowledged, however, is that international relations, like imperial relations, proceed on the basis of hierarchy and unequal power relations. The principle of hierarchy, as Susie Prestney argues, has been intrinsic not only to how we think about the system "out there," but to the formulation of knowledge itself.[43] In today's context, as I have noted, it takes the form of cultural imperialism through which Western cultural norms are imposed on other cultures.

In the female circumcision debate, in particular, the argument as presented in the West relies heavily on a discourse of normalcy and natural-ness on the one hand, and primitivism versus modernity on the other. These arguments are buoyed, as in the natural childbirth discourse, by visual imagery of the sex organs caught in the web of sexist and racist artistic conventions, informed in part by colonial and postcolonial unequal power relations.[44] I shall discuss the ways African women's bodies have been exposed to photo-graphic scrutiny later in this chapter. What is evident, however, is that con-temporary Western feminist and media representations often objectify peoples in non-Western societies.

By portraying female circumcision as a central feature of African societ-ies, Western feminists see the "elimination" of the practice as a worthy lib-eratory project aimed at restoring women's control over their sexuality. Such knowledge production suppresses the heterogeneity and historical particularity of non-Western, "nonmodern," and "nonintegrated" women, while simultaneously reproducing the prevailing notion that they are voice-less, passive, and unable to speak truthfully or objectively about themselves.[45] Thus, the image of a "Third World" oppressed woman exists in universal, ahistorical splendor, setting in motion a colonialist discourse which exer-cises a very specific power in defining, encoding, and maintaining existing First/Third World dichotomies.[46] To a large extent, the invention of "Third World" woman by Western/ized feminists is tantamount to recolonization at the level of knowledge production.

Incidentally, just as Victorian culture was shaped by imperial propaganda, the twentieth century has been shaped by the more subtle, "humanistic," imperial propaganda of development.[47] As I have noted earlier, in the nineteenth century, the colonized woman was an object of British "civiliz-ing" mission. In the late twentieth century, the postcolonial woman has become the subject of a *planned* "liberation" called development.[48] The terms of such liberation are set by the dominant discourse of feminism and women in development. However, the focus on women in development discourses that took place in the 1980s is significant in opening up the space for reevaluating the development discourse itself. With the dominant ideology of integrating women in development, the West attempts an overhaul of non-Western societies. But it is inaccurate, for instance, to talk about inte-grating women in development for women who are already integrated. The reevaluation process should involve a more critical attitude towards West-ern conceptualization of modernity and the modernizing process, as well as engaging Eurocentric imperial legacies that have continued in the post-colonial era through the ideology of development.

Furthermore, the 1980s brought in its wake a radical questioning of the universal "sisterhood" based on the commonality of sex and "common oppression"[49] that pervaded feminist thinking in the 1960s and 1970s. The idea of "common oppression," as bell hooks observes, is a "false and cor-rupt platform disguising and mystifying the true nature of women's varied and complex social reality."[50] Like hooks, other feminist women of color insist that "it was primarily bourgeois white women, both liberal and radical in perspective, who professed belief in the notion of "common oppression."[51] At the ideological level, therefore, the notion of universal sisterhood fails to acknowledge the changes happening as a result of the activities of African activists. As Chandra Mohanty sums it up, the representation of "Third World" women in scholarly, feminist discourse is largely a product of the "self-representation" of the historically mediated and culturally specific experiences of women in modern industrial societies. Mohanty maintains that beyond sisterhood there is still racism, colonialism, and imperialism.[52] Therefore, Western feminists should reevaluate their objectification of African women and recognize the historical and cultural diversity between and amongst women as well as the internal African challenges to female circumcision and other issues that affect women's lives.

For their part, African feminists—indeed, all women of color—should continue to challenge Western feminist thinking and ideology of "common oppression." The interrogation of white, bourgeois, liberal, feminist thinking demands a reevaluation of "universalist" feminist agenda and a reenactment of a global feminist agenda that allows the voices of women of color and non-Western women to be heard in matters concerning them. As Wang Jailing concludes, the feminist movement and the demands in any particular country grow out of the reality of that country, and "it's wrong to say that what we want is what everybody should want and what we don't want nobody should ask for."[53] Hira Jhamatani argues further that Western-style feminism is not relevant to the "Third World," as its strategies are based upon the cultures and experiences of Western women. She rejects the most prominent view in Western feminism that only men are the culprits of women's oppression.[54] Thus, contemporary feminist discourse on female circumcision grounded in the obsession with sexuality provides a point of entry into reassessing the continuities of imperialist domination.

In my view, to reconceptualize the circumcision discourse and Western feminist attitude is to abandon what Apffel-Marglin and Simon have called "historical baggage" in another context. In postmodernist terms, "historical baggage" is a direct continuity from colonialist discourses mostly undetected, clothed in a language that gives the illusion of discontinuity.[55] In the circumcision discourse in particular, Hetherington argues that the development of certain ways of constructing social reality and certain bodies of knowledge make it possible that female circumcision would be described as "mutilation" and that Western women mount a strong, polemical challenge to the practice.[56]

Hetherington and others are not the first and will probably not be the last critics of Western feminism to call for a reevaluation of the whole feminist agenda, especially in representing non-Western women. The call is a legitimate one in view of the fact that Western feminist arguments against female circumcision, produced and sustained by various forms of anthropological knowledge have been used by radical feminists and development agencies to advocate for the "eradication" of female circumcision. Together with the visual images in the print and electronic media, Western feminist circumcision debate forms a powerful discursive weapon in contemporary representations of African peoples and non-Western cultural practices. However, the images, the salience of the arguments, and the representations of African women in the circumcision discourse derive primarily from the ability of the West to construct a racialized "Other."[57] As Soheir Morsy aptly notes, "Western interest in the discourse is a 'paternalistic' reminder of the bygone era of colonial domination."[58]

ISSUES IN THE CIRCUMCISION DEBATE

In contemporary Western societies, every woman "knows" that the uncircumcised clitoris plays an important part in her enjoyment of sexuality. The removal of the clitoris has, therefore, become one of the most patriarchal and sexist acts imaginable.[59] The point, according to Hetherington, is not to agree or disagree with such a view, but to point out that, in poststructuralist terms, this "knowledge" about the clitoris may have no power in many African societies where women "know" that the proper expression of sexuality involves the removal of the clitoris. Such "knowledge," in other words, is socially constructed.[60] What then do I question about Western feminist approach to the circumcision discourse?

First, the feminist insurgencies and Western media propaganda that inform recent circumcision discourse are direct offshoots of colonialist ideology and imperialist propaganda, which feminists and other commentators have neither abandoned nor reformed. The inscription in the female circumcision polemics of nineteenth century anthropological terms—"savage," "primitive," and "barbaric" used to describe non-Western societies—raises questions about the insensitivity inherent in Western representations of other peoples.[61] Among feminists in particular, the polemics have depended largely on emotive language, distortion, and even elements of exaggeration aimed at achieving political outcomes.[62] Lane and Rubinstine maintain that the debate often reaches an impasse between two well-meaning but seemingly irreconcilable positions: cultural relativism and universalism. The clash between these two positions is an implicit obstacle in a great number of issues in bioethics, human rights, and social theory.[63]

I do not advocate a continuation of female circumcision but rather call attention to the implications and consequences of the overall tone and scope of feminist "mission" in this regard. It is hypocritical, for example, that many Western feminists and governments have devoted themselves to criminalizing female circumcision, while blatantly supporting abortions and pro-choice extremism. Just as people in the West may find female circumcision repulsive, many non-Westerners find repulsive pro-choice extremism that supports abortion. One wonders, for instance, which procedure is more morally shocking, female circumcision or partial-birth abortion and forced sterilization practiced in many Western societies. I agree with Obioma Nnaemeka when she asserts that "we must not be distracted by the arrogance that names one procedure breast reduction and the other sexual mutilation, with all the attached connotations of barbarism." In both instances, she argues, some part of the female body is excised."[64] I, therefore, find particularly problematic the double standards of some Western feminists. If women in the West have a right to express their sexuality and are pro-choice, why should other women not have the right to express their sexuality in ways they deem appropriate?

An important caveat in the discourse is that many members of societies that practice female circumcision do not view it as mutilation. Among these groups, in fact, the resulting appearance is considered an improvement over the genitalia in their natural state,[65] in the same way that breast implants and cosmetic surgeries are considered "improvement" in the West. As Nnaemeka rightly concludes, the issue is not just about barbaric Africa and control of African women's sexuality but about the abuse of the female body on a global scale.

> Some women undergo breast reduction for some of the reasons that some young girls undergo clitoridectomy—to be more attractive, desirable, and acceptable. For the women in areas where clitoridectomy is performed, beauty is inextricably linked with chastity and motherhood. The crucial questions we must ask are: For whom are these operations undertaken? For whom must women be desirable and acceptable? Women's inability to control their bodies is not country-specific. Abuse of the female body is global and should be studied and interpreted within the context of oppressive conditions under patriarchy.[66]

Consequently, I call attention to the epistemological issues involved in cross-cultural understandings and the place of culture in shaping perceived reality. By recognizing the role of Western value judgments in contemporary social relations, we can develop a deeper and more nuanced understanding of cultural practices that are now the focus of ethical, legal, and moral debates.[67] Thus, "it is only in understanding the practice, its meaning to those who undergo it—indeed, the extent to which its meaning inform women's sense of self and are embedded in the commonplace details of everyday life—that those who are committed to its eradication might approach the problem with the sensitivity it demands."[68]

Another important issue that needs reexamination is the gender dimension of female circumcision discourse. Gender perceptions in the context of male control and domination have traditionally ordered feminist discourse in the West. Therefore, the dominance of gender in Western feminist movements historically makes the issue of gender central in understanding women's positions in society. The circumcision debate in Western feminist discourses, therefore, hinges on gender arguments that foreclose attention to other factors such as culture, politics, and economics. It is an essential assumption by advocates for the "eradication" of female circumcision that African men are the problem to confront. For example, Berhane Ras-Work argues that female genital mutilation continues because of "male dominance in Africa as well as the lack of protection and action on the part of men in other countries, especially, those in international affairs."[69] Similarly, Robin M. Maher sees female circumcision as male domination of women in Africa communities and a method that men use to exert power over women's sexuality.[70]

Of all the reasons given for the persistence of female circumcision, those referring to the control of women's sexuality seem to be the most persuasive.[71] But, is female circumcision just about control of women's sexuality? Rose Oldfield Hayes argues with regards to pharonic circumcision in Sudan where it is assumed that circumcision is carried out to preserve virginity: "The concept of virginity in the Sudan is an anomaly to the Western world. Virginity, from our [Western] point of view, is a physical condition which is absolutely (and irrevocably) changed by a certain specific behavior. Virginity in Sudan can be thought of as a social category, in the sense that the physiological manifestations can be socially controlled."[72]

It is apparent here that many Western commentators generally lack a theoretical knowledge and understanding of what gender and sexuality mean in many non-Western societies. The body, sex, sexuality, and gender are all collapsed into an existential significance and biological determinism. In doing so, Western feminists have only translated female circumcision into a template of sexuality and women's domination. However, one can rightly argue that Western feminist gender ideology is not relevant to Africa because its strategies are based on the cultures and experiences of Western women. I agree with Hira Jhamatani's rejection of the most prominent view in Western feminism that "only men are the culprits of women's oppression."[73] In its focus on men alone, Western feminist attitude negates the roles, interests, and investments which women themselves have in female circumcision. In many respects, Western feminist patronizing and imperialistic insurgency focus primarily on female circumcision with little or no concern for the priorities of women in non-Western societies which include education, poverty, and health issues.

In their fight to "eradicate" female circumcision, Western feminists and development agencies have over sensationalized the issue by making it seem as if they are dealing with a plague instead of with peoples, societies, cultures, and values.[74] As Nnaemeka rightly observes, "the pervasive sensationalization of clitoridectomy in Western media and scholarship leads to the equally pervasive belief in the incompleteness of most African women, a belief that basically questions our humanity."[75] Similarly, Nahid Toubia argues: "The West has acted as though they have suddenly discovered a dangerous epidemic which they then sensationalized in international women's forums creating a backlash of over-sensitivity in the concerned communities. They portrayed it as irrefutable evidence of the barbarism and vulgarity of underdeveloped countries. . . . It becomes a conclusive validation of the view of the primitiveness of Arabs, Muslims, and Africans all in one blow."[76] In the same vein, Belkis Wolde Georgis notes that, in trying to reach their public, (Western) crusaders have fallen back to sensationalism, and have become insensitive to the dignity of the very women they want to save. In their oversensationalism, some Western activists have become totally unconscious of the latent racism their campaign evokes.[77]

Furthermore, the religious justifications that sustain the practice in many Moslem societies are ignored or condemned as religious fundamentalism. Undoubtedly, the human rights, health, and psychological concerns are valid, but they are not seen in the context of a broader development agenda not only for African women, but also for African societies as a whole. As noted earlier, the voices that speak against female circumcision from the West only echo the notion of "otherness," which has informed perceptions of non-Western societies. Accordingly, Western feminist circumcision discourse is only able to produce a body of knowledge full of emotions and lacking empirical and sociological interpretations, thereby increasingly objectifying African and Arab women.

"OTHER" BODIES AND
WESTERN/FEMINIST DISCOURSES

Finally, I will examine how female circumcision discourse serves the objectification of African women by Western feminists and media. In this debate, African women are presented as mutilated, abject bodies.[78] Here, the truth of the body's deficiency is uncovered for us, pinned down between inquiring pages, opened out to photographic scrutiny, or simply documented in textual forms.[79] For instance, the *News Photographer* reported in its July 1996 issue how "capturing a brutal genital mutilation rite on film won twenty-two-year old Syracuse University graduate, Stephanie Welsh, the 1996 Pulitzer Prize for Feature Photography."[80] The report indicates that although some of the women did not want Welsh to photograph the ceremony, she edged her way in and photographed the circumcision of sixteen-year old Seita Lengila of Wamba, a small town in Kenya. With a $3,000 Pulitzer cash award, Welsh said she has been overwhelmed by the "very, very positive and compassionate response" to the publication of the photos and intends to use part of the award to pay off her school loan.[81] I therefore ask who has the right to profit from another's "pain"? In this case, there is no doubt that profit and career advancement were the motives behind Welsh's mission in

Wamba. The implication of Welsh's comments belies a self-serving interest, all on the back of Seita Lengila, whose nude photographs have been published in twelve American newspapers and submitted for many competitions without her consent.[82] Like many Western missionary and civilizing endeavors in Africa, all we can conclude from this case is that there is no sincerity in some of these "benefactors," as they continue to profit from objectifying African women in particular and Africans in general.

Another widely circulated source of racialized knowledge employed to further the argument for "eradication" of female circumcision is the *Childbirth Picture Books (CBPB) and Their Additions to Prevent Excision and Infibulation.*[83] Developed together by medical artist, Marcia L. Williams, and WIN, the book has been widely distributed in Africa. From the perspective of African men and women, the pictures act as a powerful symbol of their objectification. Excerpts of letters from readers of the *Childbirth Picture Books* published by *WIN News* are full of testimonies of African men and women begging for additional copies of this visual imagery as if it represented the only authentic body of knowledge about reproduction and the effects of female circumcision.[84] The activities of WIN are located within a framework of coercion/imposition. Prospective recipients of the *Childbirth Book* are made to sign an undertaking that their children would not be circumcised before these books are distributed to them. The following testimonies reported in the *WIN News*[85] reveal the objectification of African peoples in the context of Western knowledge production and dissemination. For example, a community health officer from Nigeria whose letter was published in the *Progress Report on WIN Grassroots Campaign to Stop Female Genital Mutilation* states: "I hereby promise that my daughter will not be circumcised and I shall teach others about the dangers of female circumcision. I shall ask them to join me to stop circumcising girls in our family and the families of friends (a list of 12 signatures follows). The above named people are those I teach and are in full support of not circumcising girls."[86]

Other testimonies attest to Africans signing an undertaking as a condition for receiving the book that is supposed to teach them about their bodies and the dangers of female circumcision. Mr. O. B. from Techima, Ghana, in his letter to WIN added, "enclosed [is] the statement signed by me and the executive members."[87] Still others wrote in similar contexts:

> I have received your package and I hurry to write about the *Childbirth Picture Book* and to send you attached the names and addresses of members of our group of Gobe. We would like more books to teach. The drawings are very well understood by all (*Nine signatures attached*).[88]

> Thank you very much for the 78 copies of the *Childbirth Book with the additions to prevent excision*. As pointed out in my first letter, I would like to reaffirm that the books will be put to good use. Meanwhile, all the people who signed the statement (that their daughters will not be circumcised) sent to you have received their own copies and they have promised to do all they can to spread the message.[89]

I have received the copy of the *Childbirth Picture with the additions to prevent excision*. Thank you very much indeed. The usefulness of this book is limitless especially in my country due to excision. I and my staff hereby promise that our daughters will not be circumcised and we shall teach about the dangers of excision. With the help of the pictures, we shall prevent this practice.[90]

The above testimonies expose the ways in which media spectacles and feminist discourse intersect as female circumcision becomes a moving picture. African men and women are portrayed as lacking the basic knowledge of their bodies. As one recipient of the *Childbirth Book* notes, "your book is very important and teaches people about their bodies. The pictures speak for themselves. We hope you will send more books."[91]

Western feminists and other advocates for "eradication" of female circumcision have all ceded what Rosalind P. Petchesky calls the "visual terrain."[92] However, these visual images rely on our predisposition to "see" what they wants us to "see" because of a range of influences that come out of a particular culture and history.[93] As Petchesky observes, "evidentiary uses of photographic images (as in the circumcision discourse) are usually enlisted in the service of some kind of action—to monitor, control, and possibly intervene."[94] In the female circumcision discourse in particular, the power of the Western media in conjunction with Western medicine, and decades of female circumcision images make Western contextualization appear credible. However, many images of female circumcision presented by the Western media are viewed not from the perspective of the African women involved, but from the perspective of Western feminists. This is an aspect that many African and non-Western activists have commented on. For instance, Seble Dawit and Salem Mekuria in a 1993 *New York Times* review of Alice Walker's film on female circumcision, *Warrior Marks*, criticized Walker for her portrayal of "respected elder women of the village's secret society . . . [as] slit-eyed murderers wielding rusted weapons with which to butcher children."[95] This critique is well founded, as Walker's *Warrior Marks* and other related films/documentaries on female circumcision are judgmental representations from Western perspectives.

To further illustrate the role of the Western media in the circumcision discourse, I cite from a transcript of a recent interview on 20/20 with Somali model, Walis Dirie titled "A Healing Journey: Somalian Born Fashion Model's Painful Story" on June 20, 1997. Hugh Downs began the interview in these words: "Tonight, we tackle a shocking and *barbaric* subject with the help of a remarkable woman. . . . Looking at her you'd never guess the ordeal that she's has been through, but now, she wants the world to know her secret and to take action."[96] Barbara Walters, the co-anchor of the program, had this to say of Walis Dirie: "Her mission is to stop a centuries' old practice— ritual often called female circumcision, but this model calls it torture. . . . For thousands of years, women like her have been forced to submit to this genital mutilation. . . . Why would anyone do this to females?"[97]

Dirie whose voice spoke through that of Walters for most of the interview argued that her campaign to stop female circumcision in Africa was motivated by her own experience of circumcision as a child. In Dirie's view, female circumcision exists because men want to control women and guarantee their fidelity. Throughout the interview, both Hugh Down and Barbara Walters portrayed Walis Dirie as one who was able to escape the "brutality" and "barbaric" activities of a "backward," "nomadic" African society. The contrast between the primitive and the civilized as emphasized in this interview serves to highlight again the perception of non-Western cultural practices as barbaric and uncivilized. Presenting a reductionist view of female circumcision, they saw it not only as a mark of an "uncivilized society," but again as control of women's sexuality. Displaying an obvious contradiction, Barbara Walters rationalized male circumcision on religious and medical grounds, a rationalization that was not extended to African and Arab women. Walters concluded that male circumcision is a totally different process of just cutting the foreskin and has nothing to do with their sexual enjoyment.[98]

Unfortunately, this interview also shares the problems that have distorted the understanding of female circumcision in African societies. What concerns me are some of the subjects used by the Western media. It is important to get the perspective of someone who has experienced female circumcision, but in this particular interview, all the questions Dirie answered were leading questions, requiring a yes answer, affirming the "cruelty" of female circumcision. Dirie's only credential is that she is a successful model and was circumcised as a teenager. As I read the transcript of this interview with amazement, I could not help but conclude that Dirie is just being used as a propaganda tool as she does not show that she has a grip on the complex web of critical issues involved in the female circumcision debate. Needless to say that we are not presented a counter perspective, an error of which Western feminists, media, and other agencies are guilty.

CONCLUSION

Since the nineteenth century, the West has generated powerful images of non-Western societies and the people who live in them. In reviewing the female circumcision discourse, I have attempted to show that although female circumcision is practiced in many Africa societies, its cultural, political, and historical particularities are summarily negated while medical discourse and sexuality alone provide the basis for Western/feminist conceptualization. Various motivations and agendas fuel the insurgency against female circumcision. Some have intended women's liberation and gender equality especially within feminism. This essay argues that Western feminists have increasingly appropriated African and Arab women's experiences for their own purposes, practicing what Chilla Bulbeck calls "epistemological imperialism."[99]

This chapter suggests that the benevolent intent of feminists, humanists, and ethicists should not be the final word in the moral justification of Western judgments. I have called attention throughout the essay to the fact that beneath the polemics of the discourse are embedded notions of cultural superiority and arrogance. Like nineteenth century anthropological and colonial knowledge of non-Western societies, present day Western feminists are engaged in a system of knowledge production that implicitly denies self-determination while claiming to advance such ideals. At the heart of the conceptualization of non-Western societies lies the racist, imperialistic assumption of a special right to liberate and manage the affairs of Africans.

While calling attention to the sociocultural implications of the approach adopted so far, I have not suggested a relativist position wherein female circumcision, regardless of its harmful effects, is legitimized within its cultural context. Rather, taking account of contemporary and historical relationships of power and privilege are essential first steps towards arriving at a sensitive and nuanced approach to engagement. The search for a way to successfully confront female circumcision and to move beyond the impasse of the confrontation between universalism and cultural relativism depends upon finding a language and constructing an approach that is respectful of diverse cultural concerns.[100] Western feminists in particular must not deny the complexity of Third World women's experiences and must eschew any demand for a certain speaking position as "authentic" as an unproblematic self.[101] Female circumcision, in my opinion, is an issue that Africans are capable of resolving themselves based on the knowledge and appreciation of their specific locations and contexts.

ACKNOWLEDGMENTS

I am indebted to Margie Ripper, Tanya Lyons, and Simon Stratton for their insightful suggestions and thorough readings of this chapter.

NOTES

1. Said 1989, 216.

2. See Hetherington 1997 for a critique of Western feminist approaches in the circumcision debate.

3. Available data show that 85 percent of female circumcision worldwide involves clitoridectomy while infibulation accounts for 15 percent of all procedures. See Lane and Rubinstine 1996 for details.

4. See, for example, Donna Haraway 1989, 290 for a discussion of the use of the term "mutilation" in Western feminist discourses. However, my preferred term for all forms of female genital surgeries is "female circumcision."

5. These health implications are more evident in the Sudan and Somalia where severe infibulations are practiced. See, for example, Nahid Toubia 1985, 148–159. Toubia further discusses the health implications of female circumcision (Toubia 1988, 98–109). See also Rushwan 1980; AbouZahr and Royston 1991.

6. For instance, Hetherington (1997, 4) argues that the attempt by several missions among the Kikuyu in Kenya in the late 1920s to force church members to abandon female circumcision led to the creation of The Independent Church which still approves of the practice even though it has otherwise been abandoned in the Central Provinces. See also Bass 1994; Bass observes that some black feminists now believe that female circumcision is being continued as a form of rebellion against the alien values imposed on African cultural heritage by the West.

7. See, for example, Hosken 1982. This publication opened a whole new debate on female circumcision in Africa. See also Sanderson 1986; McLean and Efu 1983; Walker and Parmar 1993.

8. See Lane and Rubinstine 1996.

9. Governments in the United Kingdom, Sweden, and The Netherlands have passed legislation prohibiting female circumcision. In France, legal action has been taken against migrant families for circumcising their children. In the United States and Canada, attempts have been made since the early 1990s to prohibit female circumcision. See, for example, Sochart 1988; Simons 1993.

10. For the discourse in the medical fields, see Adetoro 1986; Heise 1989; Aziz 1980; Kluge 1993; Adamson 1993.

11. See, for example, Kouba and Muasher 1985; Kirby 1987; Mohamed 1997; Hetherington 1997.

12. In the United States, for example, immigration judges have granted asylum in cases involving potential genital mutilation. As an issue on the development agenda, the World Health Organization (1992) describes female circumcision as significantly associated with poverty, illiteracy, and low status of women in communities where people face hunger, ill health, overwork, and lack of clear water.

13. Many African and Arab activists feel that Western feminist attitude is nothing but a dictate of the "correct" agenda. Female circumcision, however, has had very strong advocates of "eradication" within the African and Arab societies as well. See, for example, Toubia 1985.

14. Lane and Rubinstine 1996; see also Nnaemeka 1994.

15. Hetherington 1997, 6.

16. For a discussion on the need to be culturally sensitive in the female circumcision discourse, see Lane and Rubinstine 1996.

17. Masters and Johnson 1966.

18. Lane and Rubinstine 1996.

19. Hetherington 1997, 6.

20. Hetherington 1997, 6. See also Apffel-Marglin and Simon 1994.

21. Lane and Rubinstine 1996.

22. For a discussion of the use of clitoridectomy in Victorian England and its consequences for a gynecological surgeon named Isaac Baker Brown, see Sheehan 1981.

23. Brown 1866.

24. *Church Times* of 1866 quoted in the *British Medical Journal* 1866a: 456. Cited in Sheehan 1981, 13.

25. Meigs 1859.

26. Allbutt and Playfair 1897.

27. See Meigs 1859; Allbutt and Playfair 1897, especially 97; Ehrenreich and English, 1973, 34.

28. Sheehan 1981, 14.

29. Sheehan 1981, 14.

30. See Nnaemeka 1994, 314.

31. Prestney 1997.

32. Apffel-Marglin and Simon 1994.

33. See, for example, Ahmed 1992; Nupur and Strobel 1992; Lata 1989; Ware 1992.

34. Ahmed 1992, 154.

35. Ahmed 1992, 154–155.

36. Apffel-Marglin and Simon 1994, 28.

37. See Fanon 1965, cited in Lutz and Collins 1997.

38. See Lutz and Collins 1997, 301.

39. See Apffel-Marglin and Simon 1994.

40. For an analysis of imperialism and representations of colonized peoples, see Said 1993.

41. Said 1989.

42. See Said 1993, 56, cited in Nestel 1994, 5.

43. See Prestney 1997.

44. For an analysis of Western feminist critics of technological childbirth and the presentation of "native/primitive" women and natural childbirth, see Nestel 1994.

45. See Mohanty 1991, 71–72.

46. Mohanty 1991, 73.

47. Mohanty 1991, 73.

48. See Apffel-Marglin and Simon 1994, 35. This attitude was informed by the nineteenth-century evolutionary theory claim that the move upward from savagery to barbarism to civilization was indexed by the treatment of women, in particular by their liberation "from the burden of overwork, sexual abuse, and male violence," see Tiffany and Adams 1985, 8; see also Etienne and Leacock (1980, 1) who argue that colonialists saw women in non-Western societies as chattels who could be bought and sold, eventually to be liberated by "civilization" or "progress," thus attaining the enviable position of women in the Western society, who were then expected to be happy in their place.

49. See hooks 1997, 396.

50. hooks 1997.

51. hooks 1997.

52. Mohanty 1991.

53. Wang 1995.

54. Hira 1991.

55. Apffel-Marglin and Simon 1994.

56. Apffel-Marglin and Simon 1994.

57. For an excellent analysis of the ability of the West to construct racial and sexual Others, see Nestel 1994, 10–16.

58. See Morsey 1991.

59. Hetherington 1997, 6.

60. Hetherington 1997.

61. For an excellent analysis, see Kirby 1987.

62. Hetherington 1997, 4.

63. Lane and Rubinstine 1996.

64. See Nnaemeka 1994, 314.

65. See Lane and Rubinstine 1996.

66. Nnaemeka 1994, 314.

67. See Lane and Rubinstine 1996.

68. See Boddy 1997, 310. Boddy shows that the Sudanese women's perceptions of female circumcision differ significantly from Western feminists' perceptions of the practice. Consequently, she argues for a deeper understanding of the sociological implications of the practice.

69. Ras-Work 1994.

70. Maher 1996. See also Montagu 1995, 12–16. Montagu postulates that there may be a correlation between male dominance of a society and the practice of female genital circumcision.

71. I am indebted here to Boddy 1997, 313. In speaking about the explanations for pharonic circumcision in Northern Sudan, Boddy argues that "preservation of chastity and the cubing of sexual desires are most persuasive, given that in the Sudan, as elsewhere in the Muslin world, a family's dignity and honor are vested in the conduct of its womenfolk."

72. See Hayes 1975, 622.

73. Hira 1991.

74. Sensational headlines have appeared here and there. See, for example, Cooperman 1997; Welsh 1995; Benneth 1994.

75. Nnaemeka 1994, 313.

76. See Toubia 1988.

77. Georgis 1981, 57.

78. See Kirby 1987, 36.

79. Kirby 1987.

80. As a result of fifteen photos depicting female circumcision, Stephaine Welsh became an overnight success. The photos, distributed by the Newhouse News Service, were published in twelve U.S. newspapers. The photographs also earned her a second-place prize in the World Press photo contest. I doubt if photos depicting starving children would have made similar impressions. For some of the newspaper reports on Welsh see, for example, Sader 1996; Lieblich 1996; Liberman 1996.

81. I think it is an insult to the dignity of Seita Lengila that all Welsh could do was to write her and enclose $5 and $10 at different times after exploiting her and her community. See Sader 1996 on Welsh.

82. Sader 1996.

83. See WIN 1997.

84. WIN 1997.

85. WIN 1992.

86. Mr. M. M., Chief Community Health Officer, Niger State, Nigeria (WIN 1997).

87. Mr. O. B. is a health educator (WIN 1997).

88. Testimony from student, Atakpame, Togo (WIN 1997).

89. Mr. B. M. J., September 1996, Banjul, Gambia (WIN 1997).

90. From A. M., 1996, Ethiopia (WIN 1997).

91. From a teacher, Agricultural Training Centre, Parakou, June 1996, Benin (WIN 1997).

92. Petchesky 1997, 134–150.

93. Petchesky 1997, 134–150

94. Petchesky 1997, 140

95. Dawit and Mekuria 1993.

96. ABC News 1997 (emphasis added). Transcript of a 20/20 (an ABC News magazine) show on female genital mutilation with Somali fashion model, Walis Dirie. Dirie is part of a United Nations campaign team working to stop female circumcision.

97. ABC News 1997.

98. ABC News 1997.

99. For an excellent example of a Western feminist's concern with the issue of representing non-Western women, see Bulbeck 1991.

100. Lane and Rubinstine 1996.

101. See Bulbeck 1991, 88.

WORKS CITED

ABC News. 1997. "20/20: A Healing Journey: Somalian Born Fashion Model's Painful Story."

AbouZahr, Carla, and Erica Royston. 1991. *Maternity Mortality: A Global Fact Book.* Geneva: World Health Organization.

Adamson, F. 1993. *Female Genital Mutilation: A Counseling Guide for Professionals.* London: The Foundation for Women's Health Research and Development.

Adetoro, O. O. 1986. "Health Implications of Traditional Female Circumcision in Pregnancy." *Asia-Oceania Journal of Obstetrics and Gynaecology* 12 (4): 489–492.

Ahmed, Leila. 1992. *Women and Gender in Islam.* New Haven, CT: Yale University Press.

Allbutt, Thomas, and W. S. Playfair, eds. 1897. *A System of Gynaecology.* New York: Macmillan.

Apffel-Marglin, Frederique, and Suzanne L. Simon. 1994. "Feminist Orientalism and Development." In *Feminist Perspectives on Sustainable Development,* ed. W. Harcourt, 26–45. London: Zed Books.

Aziz, F. A. 1980. "Genealogic and Obstetric Complications of Female Circumcision." *International Journal of Gynecology and Obstetrics* 17:560–563.

Bass, Margaret Kent. 1994. "Alice's Secret: Alice Walker's Novel *Possessing the Secret of Joy.*" *CLA Journal* 38 (1): 1–10.

Benneth, Kathryn O. 1994. "Castrating Women." *Off Our Back* 24 (1): 16.

Boddy, Janice. 1997. "Wombs as Oasis: The Symbolic Context of Pharonic Circumcision in Rural Northern Sudan." In *The Gender/Sexuality Reader: Culture, History, Political Economy,* ed. Roger N. Lancaster and Micaela di Leonardo, 309–324. London: Routledge.

Brown, Isaac B. 1866. *On the Curability of Certain Forms of Insanity, Epilepsy, Catalepsy, and Hysteria in Females.* London: Robert Hardwicke

Bulbeck, Chilla. 1991. "First and Third World Feminisms." *Asian Studies Review* 15 (1): 77–90.

Cooperman, Alan. 1997. "No End in Sight for a Gruesome and Widespread Ritual." *U.S. News and World Report* 123 (1): 51.

Dawit, Seble, and Salem Mekuria. 1993. "The West Just Doesn't Get It." *New York Times,* December 7, A13.

Ehrenreich, Barbra, and Deirdre English. 1973. *Complaints and Disorder: The Sexual Politics of Sickness.* Old Westbury, NY: Feminist Press.

Etienne, Mona, and Eleanor Leacock. 1980. *Women and Colonization: Anthropological Perspectives.* New York: Praeger.

Fanon, Frantz. 1965. *A Dying Colonialism.* New York: Grove Press.

Georgis, Belkis Wolde. 1981. *Female Circumcision in Africa.* New York: United Nations.

Haraway, Donna. 1989. *Primitive Visions.* New York: Routledge.

Hayes, Rose Oldfield. 1975. "Female Genital Mutilation, Fertility Control, Women's Roles and the Patrilineage in Modern Sudan: A Functional Analysis." *American Ethnologist* 2 (4): 617–633.

Heise, Lori. 1989. *Crime of Gender.* New York: Worldwatch Institute.

Hetherington, Penelope. 1997. "The Politics of the Clitoris: Contaminated Speech, Feminism and Female Circumcision." *African Studies of Australia and the Pacific Review* 19 (1): 4–10.

hooks, bell. 1997. "Sisterhood: Political Solidarity between Women." In *Dangerous Liaisons: Gender, Nation and Postcolonial Perspectives,* ed. Anne McClintock, Aamir Mufti, and Ella Shohat, 396–411. Minneapolis: University of Minnesota Press.

Hosken, Fran P. 1982. *The Hosken Report: Genital and Sexual Mutilation of Females.* Lexington, MA: Women's International Network.

Jhamatani, Hira. 1991. "Redefining Feminism as the Women's Movement." *Asia Studies Review* 15 (1): 96–100.

Kirby, Vicki. 1987. "On the Cutting Edge: Feminism and Clitoridectomy." *Australian Feminist Studies* 5:35–55.

Kluge, Eike-Henner. 1993. "Female Circumcision: When Medical Ethics Confront Cultural Values." *Canadian Medical Association Journal* 148 (2): 288–289.

Kouba, Leonard, and Judith Muasher. 1985. "Female Circumcision in Africa: An Overview." *African Studies Review* 28 (1): 95–110.

Lane, Sandra D., and Robert A. Rubinstine. 1996. "Judging the Other: Responding to Traditional Female Genital Surgeries." *The Hastings Center Report* 26 (3): 31–40.

Lata, Mani. 1989. "Contentious Tradition: The Debate on Sati in Colonial India." In *Recasting Women: Essays in Colonial History,* ed. S.Kumkum and S. Vaid, 88–126. New Delhi: Kali for Women.

Liberman, Si. 1996. "Blood, Sweat, Tears: A Pulitzer Story; 22 year-old College Dropout Paid Extraordinary Price to Capture Prize-winning Photos." *Editor and Publisher* 129 (38): 12.

Lieblich, Julia. 1996. "How Stephanie Welsh, Age 22, Won a Pulitzer in Africa." *American Photo* 7 (5): 24.

Lutz, Catherine A., and Jane L. Collins. 1997. "The Color of Sex: Postwar Photographic Histories of Race and Gender in *National Geographic Magazines.*" In *The Gender/Sexuality Reader: Culture, History, Political Economy,* ed. Roger N. Lancaster and Micaela di Leonardo, 291–306. London: Routledge.

Maher, Robin M. 1996. "Female Genital Mutilation: The Struggle to Eradicate this Rite of Passage." *Human Rights* 23 (4): 12–16.

Masters, William H., and Virginia E. Johnson. 1966. *Human Sexual Response.* Boston: Little, Brown.

McLean, Scilla, and Stella Graham Efu. 1983. *Female Circumcision, Excision and Infibulation: Report No. 47.* London: Minority Rights Groups.

Meigs, Charles D. 1859. *Woman: Her Diseases and Remedies.* Philadelphia: Blanchard and Leas.

Mohamed, Khadra. 1997. "Female Genital Mutilation: A Violation of Human Rights and a Development Issue." Unpublished paper, University of Toronto.

Mohanty, Chandra Talpade. 1991. "Under Western Eyes: Feminist Scholarship and Colonial Discourses." *Third World Women and the Politics of Feminism,* ed. Chandra Talpade Mohanty, Ann Russo, and Lourdes Torres, 51–80. Bloomington, IN: Indiana University Press.

Montagu, Ashley. 1995. "Mutilated Humanity." *The Humanist* 55 (4): 12–16.

Morsy, Soheir A. 1991. "Safeguarding Women's Bodies: The White Man's Burden Medicalized." *Medical Anthropological Quarterly* 5 (1): 19–23.

Nestel, Sheryl. 1994. "'Other' Mothers: Race and Representation in Natural Childbirth Discourse." *Resources for Feminist Research/Documentation sur la recherche féministe* 23 (4): 5–19.

Nnaemeka, Obioma. 1994. "Bringing African Women into the Classroom: Rethinking Pedagogy and Epistemology." In *Borderwork: Feminist Engagements with Comparative Literature,* ed. Margaret R. Higonnet, 301–318. Ithaca, NY: Cornell University Press.

Nupur, Chaudhuri, and Magaret Strobel. 1992. *Western Women and Imperialism: Complicity and Resistance.* Bloomington, IN: Indiana University Press.

Parmar, Pratibha, producer/director. 1993. *Warrior Marks* [videorecording]. A Rawlence Hauer Production. New York: Women Make Movies (distributor).

Petchesky, Rosalind Pollack. 1997. "Fetal Images: The Power of Visual Culture in the Politics of Reproduction." In *The Gender/Sexuality Reader: Culture, History, Political Economy*, ed. Roger N. Lancaster and Micaela di Leonardo, 134–150. London: Routledge.

Prestney, Susie. 1997. "Inscribing the Hottentot Venus: Generating Data for Difference." In *At the Edge of International Relations: Colonialism, Gender and Dependency*, ed. Phillip Darby, 86–105. London and New York: Pinter.

Ras-Work, Berhane. 1994. "The Facts about Female Genital Mutilation in Egypt: An Overview," *WIN News* 20 (4): 1.

Rushwan, Hamid. 1980. "Etiological Factors in Pelvic Inflammatory Disease in Sudanese Women." *American Journal of Obstetrics and Gynecology* 138 (7): 877–879.

Sader, Jennifer. 1996. "22-year-old Photo Intern Documents Grisly Female Genital Mutilation Rite." *News Photographer* 51 (7): 24.

Said, Edward. 1989. "Representing the Colonized: Anthropology's Interlocutors." *Critical Inquiry* 15: 207–227.

———. 1993. *Culture and Imperialism*. New York: Knopf.

Sanderson, Lillian Passmore. 1986. *Female Genital Mutilation, Excision and Infibulation*. London: Antislavery Society for the Protection of Human Rights.

Sheehan, Elizabeth. 1981. "Victorian Clitoridectomy: Isaac Baker Brown and His Harmless Operative Procedure." *Medical Anthropology Newsletter* 12:10–15.

Simons, Marlise. 1993. "French Court Jails Mother for Girl's Ritual Mutilation." *New York Times*, January 17, late edition, 2.

Sochart, Elise. 1988. "Agenda Setting, the Role of Groups and the Legislative Process: The Prohibition of Female Circumcision in Britain." *Parliamentary Affairs* 41:508–526.

Tiffany, Sharon, and Kathleen Adams. 1985. *The Wild Woman: An Inquiry into the Anthropology of an Idea*. Cambridge, MA.: Schenkman.

Toubia, Nahid. 1985. "The Social Implications of Female Circumcision: The Case of Sudan." *Women and the Family in the Middle East*, ed. Elizabeth Femea, 148–159. Austin: University of Texas Press.

———. 1988. "Women and Health in Sudan." In *Women of the Arab World: The Coming Challenge*, ed. Toubia Nahid, 98–109. London: Zed Books.

Walker, Alice, and Pratibha Parma. 1993. *Warrior Marks: Female Genital Mutilation and the Sexual Blinding of Women*. New York: Harcourt Brace.

Wang, Jiaxiang. 1995. "A Chinese View of Feminism." *Asian Studies Review* 15 (2): 177–180.

Ware, Vron. 1992. *Beyond the Pale: White Women, Racism and History*. London: Verso.

Welsh, Stephanie. 1995. "A Dangerous Rite of Passage." *World Press Review* 42 (10): 39.

Women International Network (WIN). 1992. "Canada: Policy on Female Genital Mutilation." *WIN News* 18 (2): 45.

———. 1997. "Progress Report: Women's International Grassroots Campaign to Stop Female Genital Mutilation." *WIN News* 23 (1): 27–30.

World Health Organization/International Federation of Gynecology and Obstetrics. 1992. "Female Circumcision." *European Journal of Obstetrics, Gynecology, Reproductive Biology* 45:153–154.

PART IV

Imperial Gaze and Fictions

Libidinal Quicksand: Imperial Fictions, African Femininity, and Representation

Jude G. Akudinobi

A rather complicated and problematic relationship exists between the representation of African femininity in imperial/colonial fictions and Western notions of self. These complications are not incidental. They mutate in the various forms of contradictions, conflicts, and ambivalence through which Africa is generally coded as "dilemma." In this configuration Africa is not just a geographical entity, but a network of projections through which the relief of Western identity is formed. As "dilemma," Africa generates crises and, with respect to African femininity, overwrought representational lattices. The preceding is particularly significant if we note, as has been argued by Ronald Hyam, that "sexual dynamics crucially underpinned the whole operation of British Empire and Victorian expansion. Without the easy range of sexual opportunities which imperial systems provided, the long-term administration and exploitation of tropical territories, in the nineteenth-century conditions, might well have been impossible."[1]

In examining *Mountains of the Moon*[2] and *Mister Johnson*,[3] it will be argued that both films not only valorize European masculinity but also oppositionally define African femininity not just against European femininity per se but through a nexus of needs and desires. As masquerade, African femininity is "made up"; that is, conjured and conditioned, through the discourses of imperial/colonial racial hierarchies and forced to wear a guise fabricated from the disfigured aspects of the colonialists' unconscious desires. This not only reflects the imperial/colonialist ambiguities about women in general; additionally, African femininity is represented as an effigy of womanhood endowed with a form of "bewitching" sexuality, enticing yet abhorrent. Thus positioned, African femininity serves the additional function of propagating certain ideas of race and desire.

Generally, the function of African femininity in imperial fictions lies precisely in its definition as enigma. It is in this context that this inquiry will expand by examining how *Warrior Marks*,[4] a documentary on "genital mutilation,"[5] inserts itself in the discourse of African femininity. Here, it will be argued that despite the director's concern about how the film can "challenge the imperialist imagery of Africa and Africans as perpetuated in Hollywood films,"[6] certain continuities link this film to the tenets established by imperial fictions and dominant discourses of the practice which according to Françoise Lionnet are as follows: "In contemporary Western medical and anthropological literature, and in journalistic reports, the subject of excision has often been treated peremptorily, in an impassioned, reductionist and/or ethnocentric mode which represents the people who practice it as backwards [*sic*], misogynist, and generally lacking in humane and compassionate inclinations."[7]

Of particular concern here are the ways conventional understanding of the practice, exemplified by the preceding quote, permeate the film. Touted as a critical, questioning, and important intervention, *Warrior Marks* generates, more like colonial discourse, a lack which it hopes to fill while scuttling around the ideological tensions inherent in the exercise and the cultural complexities which it can neither grasp nor resolve. It is not just that the film's reductive framework, consistent with an imperial point of view, fictionalizes the status of African femininity insofar as a caricatured African femininity is used to establish the "meaning" and "significance" of "female genital mutilation," and to the extent that the sum of her complex realities and existence is reductively presented as an effect of "mutilation"; crucially, the film furthers the scandalizing of African female sexuality by constructing it as an object of sensational investigation and voyeuristic mystification.

This leaves us with the question about why Africa is the principal site of the discourse on female circumcision despite a global distribution.[8] Could it be that African women evoke a special interest, concern, or privilege? Answers to this question will be found in how scandal, difference, and "photogenicity" govern the appropriation, commodification, and consumption of Africa in contemporary Western cultural orbits. Else, how can one explain the assertion by Maria Rosa Cutrufelli, writing in the 1980s, that "either overtly or covertly, prostitution is still the main if not the only source of work for African women"[9] or a *Newsweek* article which assuages American fears of AIDS thus: "Africa is different, experts theorize, because of astounding (by US standards) levels of heterosexual promiscuity and assorted sexual diseases, including open genital ulcers."[10] The attribution of the latter quote to experts carries with it the imprimatur of scientific certitude while the former touts its outrageous claim as an existential fact. Not surprisingly, dominant discursive regimes now inscribe an intrinsic relationship between female circumcision, the myths of African sexuality, and AIDS. But then how do they explain the fact that Somalia, Djibouti, Egypt, and Sudan, where female circumcision is the most widespread, are among the countries with the lowest incidence of AIDS?[11]

Be that as it may, it would not be enough to reduce this inquiry to patterns of projections, understandings, constructions, and so on. Attempts would, therefore, be made to situate it squarely within the institution of myth making and its attendant functions. After all, as has been noted by Dorothy Hammond and Alta Jablow, "myths have a place and function in the societies which create them. They support cultural values and mediate points of stress."[12]

DIRECTIONS

The film *Mountains of the Moon* is based on William Harrison's novel, *Burton and Speke*, which chronicles the Royal Geographical Society–sponsored expeditions of Richard Francis Burton and John Hanning Speke to find the source of the Nile. As adventure, their exploits are coded around social displacement, psychological turmoil, and assorted "symptoms" of Africa, chief among which are its "strangeness" and unpredictability. As an infernal sphere, Africa not only heightens the thrill of adventure but emphasizes what has been described by Rebecca Stott as "the androcentric mystique of exploration."[13] Appropriately then, our "heroes" fight the continent, display strong male-bonding, instigate "scientific" debates, fall out with each other and eventually, following Speke's apparent suicide, and part ways eternally. A review effuses, without any equivocation, that the film is "a dazzling, meticulous re-creation of 19th Century East-Africa—of its strange tribes and customs, of vicious slavers and violent natives, of inhospitable geography and climates."[14] This sentiment is echoed in Peter Rainer's declaration that the director (Bob Rafelson) "is on much firmer ground in his portrayal of the Africans."[15] Matters are not helped by Rafelson's self-serving response to concerns about the film's violent sequences. According to him, "The things that I portray in the film did happen, and much worse."[16] Put together, these views purport that the film *documents* an essential African reality.

Based on the novel of the same name by Joyce Cary, an erstwhile colonial administrator, *Mister Johnson*, which was "chosen by the Queen of England as the one film a year she deems worthy of a Royal Command Performance,"[17] is ostensibly about a "native clerk" in the colonial administration. Johnson, a chronic debtor, colonial pawn, and egregious anglophile, behind in his "bride-price" payments and faced with the imminent prospects of losing his wife, Bamu, to an extortive father-in-law, kills his erstwhile employer, Sargy Gollup, in a robbery attempt. Consequently, he is convicted, condemned, and executed by the district officer, Harry Rudbeck, whose act reestablishes the British moral authority/superiority over the "benighted" empire. Notably, Peter Rainer describes Johnson as "a marvel of spirit" but laments that "it's his very spirit, his frolicky Africanness, that dooms his attempts to become a proper British squire."[18]

Proposed as "a delicate exploration of the tidal zone between two very different cultures,"[19] the film is appraised as "both insightful and educational,"[20] lauded for its restraint "from emphasizing snap liberal judgments that usually accompany films dealing with imperialism and its attendant racial issues"[21] and defended in a *Los Angeles Times* article as illustrative of "the history of race relations."[22] Significantly, these views, like the previous ones, are impaired by their unexacting appraisal of the film as *objective representation*—a claim to "realism" favored, apparently, by the knowledge that Joyce Cary was a British colonial officer, Bruce Beresford a former employee of the Nigerian government and that the screenwriter, William Boyd, was born in Ghana and "spent his childhood and teens there and in Nigeria."[23]

Interestingly, both films open with captions. For *Mountains of the Moon* it is "East African Coast, 1854"; for *Mister Johnson*, it reads, "West Africa, 1923." These captions do not just allude to a geographical and/or historical context; they appropriate a documentary aesthetic/practice, which proposes an understanding of the subsequent narrative as "factual."

DISCOURSES

Patrick Brantlinger cites the myth of the "Dark Continent" as a Victorian concoction which ever since, and along with imperialism, is responsible for the Africa of "popular" Western consciousness.[24] Undoubtedly, the task of these explorers was "to incorporate a particular reality into a series of interlocking information orders"[25] but "the journeys of exploration did not simply produce 'knowledge,' they were also large-scale explorations in myth-making."[26] The works of the explorers are, therefore, crucial to the constitution of Africa as a discursive object. For the explorers, the dilemma of making sense and constructing order in the face of bewildering physical/cultural complexities soon gave way to a racist and masculinist pattern.

First, the encounters were reduced to a series of oppositions, and "lacks" (for the Africans); then, the explorers invented roles for themselves, recasting their bewilderment as chaos endemic to the continent. Evoking metaphors of suffering, they spoke of tribulations; not in such a way that would question their masculinity, but in a manner through which those became enactments of masculinity and by extension, means of self reassurance. Furthermore, it is not simply that the myths supplied a heuristic portrait of Africa; more important, they provided the framework for its subsequent feminization; that is, to the extent that "the continent appears as an irresistible woman, but one whose beauty is a snare and an enticement to destruction."[27]

The implications of the foregoing, as shall be shown later, are far reaching.

There may be a temptation for some spectators to read *Mountains of the Moon* as a nonfictional narrative insofar as its main characters are historical figures and the film's raison d'être, the "discovery" of the Nile's source, a documented event. For these spectators, the film becomes an affirmation of past glories. It is, for instance, no accident that Speke names the Nile's source Lake Victoria. This deed conflates the idea of the heroic to the patriotic. His status as hero, it should be noted, is a residual construct of Victorian patriarchal society through which Africa as an exotic and "appropriate" setting enhances anxieties/excitement evoked by the narrative. Under these circumstances, the racial implications would not be difficult to see especially if we acknowledge the tension which exists between hero and villain. As has been argued by Paul Hoch: "Almost by definition, the villain is threatening and immoral—a representative of the *dark, bestial* forces of lust and perdition, an embodiment of the lower and *sexual,* as against the higher and spiritual ties of the hero's conscience."[28]

According to this configuration, what determines the hero is a system of representation analogous to the ideas of African femininity in dominant circulation. This is largely because the "perversity" often attributed to African femininity is a function of repressed desires. In examining the representation of African femininity, we must note that discourses about her intuitively, and often manifestly, depend upon masking any attraction to her as disturbing. It is this grotesque image of her that is prominent in the films under consideration.

CONTOURS

Mister Johnson opens with Johnson himself depicted as a figure of seduction. Visiting Bamu at the riverside, he "extols" her beauty through concentration on body parts. This rather crude courting prefigures the equally caricatured wedding which vulgarizes African social values, specifically regarding kinship and marriage, by juxtaposing them disparagingly with the codes of European "civility" and marriage. To a large extent, the wedding scene dramatizes the differences between "us" and "them" insofar as Johnson's "white" wedding, as mimicry, is a pale shadow of the "real thing."

Furthermore, reference to the notion of daughters as objects of exchange between two men (usually husband and father) is given a new twist with the introduction of a "bride price." The negative correlation this parody establishes between connubiality and monetary exchange is that of purchase. By focusing on the means and superficialities of the exchange, African marriage systems are not only invalidated; Johnson seems to have acquired proprietary rather than marital rights. This, (1) mocks the sociohistorical specificity of African marital and kinship systems; (2) introduces a hegemonic (European) discourse of marital systems; (3) reinstates the discourse of Euro-femininity as ideal, especially since Johnson had promised to teach

Bamu to be "a civilized lady"; and (4) incites the very restrictions through which African femininity will be represented.

As the film suggests, Bamu marries Johnson for money rather than love, any "honorable" sentiment or reason. Thus, the "bride price" is devoid of the social meanings for which, in its cultural framework, it was meant to account for. Consequently, as "puzzle," ground is cleared for its insertion within a structure of meanings offered by the colonialists. In other words, the "bride price" has no meaning in and of itself except that assigned it within the film's diegesis. Furthermore, since it is not shown as part of a social system with its unique rationale, except that African women are chattel, this scene displaces the meaning of the symbolic exchange to that of a market economy and encourages the spectator to believe that what is (re)presented is *meaningful revelation*. But there is a problem. The film, set in northern Nigeria does not depict a marriage tradition indigenous to the area. Furthermore, Bamu's father speaks to her in Yoruba, a language neither indigenous to the area nor widely spoken there. But what is depicted is not a Yoruba marriage tradition, either. By divesting the ceremony of any cultural specificity, the scene appropriates an *important* African cultural system as a site for the construction of British identity. Furthermore, inventing an "African" tradition through homogenization and obfuscation, it seems, relieves the filmmakers of the "burden" of presenting an authentic ceremony— that is, with culturally distinct features. In this respect, African femininity is derided and humiliated.

In one of the film's early scenes, Sargy Gollup, set up as a "fall guy" for colonial racism, beats his African concubine for drinking his gin. As she is chased through their compound, Johnson and his companions who witness this do not intervene. Obi Ajalli, one of the men states approvingly: "A man should beat his woman." Taking a cue, the other fellow, Benjamin asks: "Do you beat your wife, Mister Johnson?" To which Johnson replies, "In England, we do not beat our wives." Interestingly, the spectators' objections to Sargy Gollup's violation of European "civility" are overruled by "native custom" which essentially upholds his rights to abuse the African woman and conceals the racial privilege underlying his actions. This invocation of "African tradition" simultaneously provides justification and defense for Sargy Gollup. The larger consequence of the preceding scenario is that it "normalizes" the sexual exploitation of the African female insofar as she is positioned within an incarcerating "tradition." Following this logic, what is being called into question here is, fundamentally, the position of African women within their "primitive" setting rather than Gollup's barbarity. Besides, her position as concubine, it seems, relieves Gollup of any obligation to protect, love, and cherish. Thus, this reinscription of "domestic violence" primarily supports European male dominance but ironically reveals the intersection between sexual exploitation and colonial logic.

As has been indicated, Johnson's goal is to "civilize" his wife. This under-taking, however, not only mirrors Johnson's colonialist concept of feminin-ity but has an honorific effect on Euro-femininity since he sees his wife in terms of lacks. As Johnson's "civilizing project," Bamu fits into a key issue central to the colonialist discourse; that is, the task of "reforming" the Afri-can. This point is very important because the "African woman," in compar-ison with the "European woman," was seen as primeval, promiscuous, and inferior. In this spirit, the "European woman" was projected as a signifier of "femininity," virtue, and "civilization." An exemplary writing on this topic by a doyen of the early explorer-mythmakers, Winwood W. Reade, sums it up: "The negress is not a woman; she is a parody of a woman; she is a pretty toy, an affectionate brute."[29]

While Bamu is indeed pretty and does not exhibit any brutish disposi-tion, her beauty is, nonetheless, defined within the parameters set by Mrs. Rudbeck. Having met Mrs. Rudbeck on arrival, an enthralled Johnson nar-rates the experience thus: "Bamu, that Mrs. Rudbeck is a beautiful woman. Her cheeks are as white as ivory, her breasts, hey, my God! When you see her breasts, it big like pumpkin, the two of them. The king of England him-self wanted to marry her but she refused." At this point, Bamu sweeps dust all over him. Framing Bamu's reaction as a laughable act of jealousy dilutes and, indeed, displaces her resistance to the ideological linings of Johnson's entrancement.

Even though Mr. and Mrs. Rudbeck have their spats, essentially over his musical and literary tastes, part of their discord is displaced on the envi-ronment and her difficulties in adjusting to its harshness. The Johnsons' marriage, on the other hand, is problematized by the in-laws frequent "repos-session" of Bamu each time Johnson falls behind in his "bride price" pay-ments. The point here is not so much that African femininity is constructed according to the cultural legislatures of colonialism, but that Mrs. Rudbeck measured against prostitutes, a concubine, and Bamu, comes out shining. As sinister shadows, the African women collectively articulate her as the legitimate and ideal object of desire.

It is also worthy of note that Sargy Gollup's companion is never given a voice, in part because of her social and sexual status as African/female/concubine. Facing an imminent beating at some point in the film, Sargy orders her to get her, "fat bum in here on the double, you ungrateful cow." While reference to her "fat bum" could be an index of her physical stature, it also evokes images of the nineteenth century European fixation on cer-tain anatomical regions of the so-called Hottentot Venus.[30] Calling her "an ungrateful cow" grants Gollup the racial/masculine "privilege" to identify with and disavow his desire. His simulated hurt at her ingratitude is an excul-patory measure which reroutes critical attention to her "failing" (ingrate) and Gollup's "magnanimity" (provider).

CODES

If *Mister Johnson* treats African femininity ambivalently, *Mountains of the Moon* revels in its profanation. Each preposterous encounter with African females, except in the beginning where she is veiled and featured as mystery, exploits the stereotypic lascivious African woman. The film is not just about adventures. Largely, it is about sexual adventurism. Early in the film we learn that Richard Burton "is interested in tribal practices" and "for centuries Somali women have been circumcised and the men believe it keeps them home where they belong," but that "Burton has single-handedly disproved that theory." For good measure the camera allows a view of relaxed Somali women, one of whom examines a telescope with childlike fascination. Here, the Somali women become central to establishing Burton's virility and potency. Put another way, they constitute his libidinal trophies. As "representatives" of their society, these women's presence in the explorers' camp not only puts them in Burton's "protective custody" but could be symbolically interpreted as illustrative of Europe's capacity to domesticate. Ordinarily, interest in "tribal practices" does not translate into sexual dalliance but in the film, this linkage is strengthened by the theme of exploration, domestication, and domination.

Interestingly, Lord Ngola's territory poses a unique dilemma for Burton and Speke. According to Sidi Bombay, their guide and translator, "The king's sister is very much sick and needs a beautiful, white doctor man." We also learn that "her husband died, she has very much desire." As a bewildered Speke begins to leave, Lema, the king's sister grabs his hand and places it about her mid-region. Soon after, Sidi Bombay tells Speke that his "touch makes her feel better and he should come every day." Clearly flustered, Speke asks for permission to leave but is told that would happen if and when she got better. His further protestations are lost in her rapacious embrace. Later, Burton's voice tells us that Speke was granted permission to leave and he (Burton) was held as collateral. This scene, arguably, amplifies the imperial, masculinist fascination with the relationship between sex and subjugation.

In any case, Lema is represented as a castrating figure—a point emphasized by her aggressive advances and Speke's own castration anxiety evidenced in a concern he has earlier shared with Burton in the following words: "I've heard the tribes in these areas castrate their victims." Lema's, of course, is a symbolic kind of castration specifically in relation to the shock it (re)presents for Speke who is white, male, and homosexual. Notably, she is not attractive, since making her so would signify desirable sexuality. Further, since this encounter feeds the established view of black female sexuality as perverse, pathological, and easily accessible, it is also a threat to English "virtue," rationality, and discipline, whose abdication collapses the boundary between "us" and "them." At another level, Lema, along with other African women featured in the film, serve to articulate the ideal(ized) womanhood, Isabel, Richard's love interest and eventual wife.

Remarkably, the film does not fully disclose the "terms of settlement" under which Speke is released. Be that as it may, Lema's libidinal assertion marks a rupture of the imperialist prowess. She constitutes effrontery to Speke's personal liberty, if he is coerced into intimacy with her, and the imperial system from which his power emanates, if taken hostage. Either way, these intimations of impotence are certainly problematic, especially if we understand that they have roots in the psychic/mythic subtexts of the adventure stories set in Africa. Jan Nederveen Pieterse, in tying these adventure tales to European notions of self, notes: "Among recurring themes are the fantasy of fear: the European as prisoner of the savages and the fantasy of power: the European as king over the savages, with secondary roles for the savages themselves, either as threatening or servile."[31] Regardless of the filmmakers' intent which, arguably, is to represent the lasciviousness of African femininity, Lema brings into question, in fact subverts, Victorian patriarchal notions of power and privilege.

More so, a closely related, claustrophobic sequence, with Richard Burton flat on his back and an ambiguously androgynous African figure dominantly over him, is used to further problematize African femininity. Pointedly, it is the power of such an arresting image, emblematic of "heathen" ritualistic practice, to elicit shock, horror, and disgust, as well as its amalgamation with "naturalized" notions of African femininity, that augment and animate racial anxieties. In and through the androgynous figure, African female sexuality is codified and reified. Here, more than elsewhere, the film elaborates the mysteriousness attributed to African femininity but adds to that another dimension, the fetishistic. Significantly, this scene puts Burton in a position of victimhood—victim of loyalty to his friend, Speke, and of the perversity of African femininity which he had earlier, and laudably, been credited with taming.

Ostensibly, the scene depicts "tribal" healing practices, with Burton being nursed back to health. What we see here, however, is "witch doctoring" and sorcerous sexuality. Either way, this and the previous scene with Speke are thematically linked; they conflate autonomous African female desire with illness.

MATRICES

An exonerative argument could, of course, be made by the filmmakers that these films under consideration were adaptations and as such required a certain fidelity to their original sources. Granted. But that argument can only go so far. As adaptations, the directors also have liberties of interpretation that allow for a vision other than, or not necessarily that of, the original sources. What is of essence here, then, is the relationship between the filmmakers' cultural histories, their intended audience, and the discourse of Africa. Attention, therefore, must be paid to this cultural positioning and how it is articulated in the films. Let us begin with the idea of "bride price" as it is elaborated in *Mister Johnson* and address its relationship to the concept of African femininity. In the film, the issue of "bride price" is a recurring gag. As comic motif, its value resides in the ability to shock and simultaneously amuse. As caricature, it alludes to the commodification of African femininity. Interestingly, as early as 1931, E. E. Evans-Pritchard had called for the abandonment of the term "bride price" since, amongst other things, "it encourages the layman to think that 'price' used in this context is synonymous with 'purchase' in common English parlance."[32] There is a corollary to this important point. The concern here, it must be pointed out, is not just over terminology since the meaning of the term "bride price" is explicit in the cultures where it is prevalent. The problem is its meaning *in relation* to the observing Western self. Put another way, since the term does not have any cultural equivalent in the observer's culture, its assigned meaning names the interpreter's relationship, in terms of understanding, to the practice, and as such is coterminous with the interpretive framework used.

In the main, both films deploy the issue of African female sexuality as a fundamental problem. In *Mountains of the Moon*, the connection between African femininity and the "unusual" is not just related to the fact they establish Burton's virility or interest in "tribal practices." Additionally, it allows for the translation of Africa's exploration and exploitation into sexual terms. In *Mister Johnson*, one of Rudbeck's initial "administrative" duties includes the adjudication of the fate of local prostitutes. While this sequence, ostensibly, shows the range of Rudbeck's "administrative headaches," it also performs the function of hinting at a concupiscent African femininity. Interestingly, Bamu rejects Johnson's request that she put on her wedding gown for their reception on the grounds that it is a prostitute's dress. Intended to show her laughable ignorance, this statement undermines colonial hypocrisy, especially if we note that at the height of the empire, "Britain did not merely sell cotton clothes to all the world: it also exported nude erotic photographs."[33] Since there is nothing about a wedding gown that points to prostitution, it then follows that Bamu's deprecating reaction emanates from either exposure to British erotica in which similar attire feature or the local prostitutes' appropriation of it, following, also, exposure to imperial pornography. This is not far-fetched especially if we recall Richard Burton's salacious predilection typified by his book, *The Perfumed Garden*, which contains pornographic illustrations.

From the foregoing, it is not difficult to see that African femininity as a discursive category is a feature of certain historical and ideological processes. In sum, the ascription of certain, immutable attributes to African femininity correspond to its abstraction as mystery and exotic oddity. Now, let us turn our attention to *Warrior Marks*.

EXTENSIONS

As has been stated earlier, the concern of this section is to analyze how *Warrior Marks* inserts itself in the discourse of African femininity, particularly given the film's claim to reveal the "secrets" and "truths" about female circumcision. Before that, however, some clarifications are necessary for the ideological and subtextual interstices of the film to be accurately identified and addressed. Conventional wisdom posits a documentary's claim to "realism" as intrinsic, and absolute rather than relative and a product of specific ideological/intertextual oscillations. But, as has been noted by Bill Nichols, the documentary "is a fiction (un)like any other."[34] In other words, the documentary as a representational form must be considered in its paradoxical relationship to fiction since its "truths" are mediated and somewhat fictive. Michael Renov elaborates, further:

> Indeed, nonfiction contains any number of "fictive" elements, moments at which a presumably objective representation of the world encounters the necessity of creative intervention. Among these fictive ingredients we may include the construction of character . . . emerging through recourse to ideal and imagined categories of hero or genius, the use of poetic language, narration or musical accompaniment to heighten emotional impact or the creation of suspense via the agency of embedded narratives (e.g. tales told by interview subjects) or various dramatic arcs (here, the "crisis structure" comes to mind).[35]

Thus, the documentary is coterminous with fictional representation in so far as it proposes certain types of identifications and foregrounds certain meanings while actively excluding others. For *Warrior Marks*, our concerns are with how its construction of characters and embedded narratives are mediated by the cultural logic of imperial fictions. To reiterate, *Warrior Marks* is not fictional in the sense that female circumcision is not practiced in parts of Africa; it is fictional in the sense that the procedure's existence in the film is chimerical. Viewed closely, the film's key to the construction of meaning around female circumcision and African femininity fits well into the mold of a specific cultural/ideological peephole which engenders a voyeuristic fascination with African femininity/African female sexuality.

Warrior Marks is structured around the issues raised in an earlier novel by Alice Walker, *Possessing the Secret of Joy*. A brief critique of the novel is, therefore, necessary. According to Gina Dent, "Walker's novel forces us to confront not the history of female circumcision, but the mythical use of that particularity as a point of entry into the analysis of our ever elusive connections to Africa."[36] But in the opinion of Gay Wilentz, "there is an aspect of voyeurism in Walker's approach," which "unfortunately puts her in the company of other Western writers before her for whom 'Africa' merely represented the exotic or the grotesque."[37] This last observation is echoed by Diane C. Menya who writes that "by taking circumcision out of its cultural context, Walker has clearly displayed the ethnocentric view of an outsider."[38] The preceding observation is especially pertinent to *Warrior Marks* and merits attention now. Interestingly, Walker's "insider status" is framed within the axes of ancestry, sororal solidarity, and a supramaternal figure, especially, if we understand the "bad guys" to be sadistic grandmothers, hideous fathers, and ignorant mothers. Pratibha Parmar, born in Kenya of Indian parentage, institutes her claims thus: "I did not go in as an outsider but as a [person] of color, lesbian, woman, looking at female mutilation as violence against women. In India a woman is burnt every three minutes for not bringing in enough dowry."[39]

Be that as it may, at the center of these "treatises" on female circumcision is a key element of imperial fictions: pernicious homogenization. According to Chandra Mohanty, the average (stereotypical) Third World woman is seen as "sexually constrained . . . ignorant, poor, uneducated, tradition bound, religious, domesticated, family oriented, victimized, etc." and in "contrast to the (implicit) self-representation of Western women as educated, modern, as having control over their own bodies and sexualities, and the 'freedom' to make their own decisions."[40] To understand the import of these observations, one should note Walker's comments about the writing of *Possessing the Secret of Joy*. According to her, "To write it, I went to Mexico. I needed to be in a Third World country, where I could feel more clearly what it would be like to have a major operation without anesthetics or antiseptics, because that is what happens to little girls when they are genitally mutilated."[41] The importance of her statement does not just lie with defining the Third World in terms of lacks, absences, and easy substitutability but, in hitching those definitional elements to an *inspirational, visionary realm*. Further, Walker's debt to imperial ideology could not have been better acknowledged than in her prefatory appropriation of a colonialist memoir for inspiration and title. The preface is from Mirella Ricciardi's *African Saga* in which she writes:

> I had always got on well with the Africans and enjoyed their company, but commanding the people on the farm, many of whom had watched us grow up, was different. With the added experience of my safaris behind me, I had begun to understand the code of "birth, copulation and death" by which they lived. Black people are natural, they possess the secret of joy, which is why they can survive the suffering and humiliation inflicted upon them. They are alive physically and emotionally, which makes them easy to live with. What I had not yet learned to deal with was their cunning and natural instinct for self-preservation.[42]

The racist implications of the preface are self-evident and should have been quite clear to Walker. A key element here is Ricciardi's assumed mastery of "native" psychology and culture. In addition, her objectification of the "natives" subscribes to and reinforces racist hierarchies, especially as it is undergirded by a concern for establishing and maintaining dominance. Walker's attempt at damage control in a subsequent preface is problematic; in the paper back edition of *Possessing the Secret of Joy,* it reads: "There are those who believe Black people possess the secret of joy and that it is this that will sustain them through any spiritual or moral or physical devastation."

As disclaimer, the preceding quote denies complicity by trying to evade the implications of its forebear rather than challenge its racist assumptions. Put differently, the subsequent preface retains the patronizing tenor of its forebear, assigns no origins or histories, except as an opinion of an amorphous *some people,* and neither goes beyond nor reverses/revises the former preface's constitutive arrogance. In any case, the ostensibly intrinsic capacity of black people to bear pain sidesteps the dynamics of their oppression and resilience, in addition to naturalizing their suffering. The preceding has been an attempt to sketch the various ways in which *Warrior Marks* is indexed in specific discursive imperatives.

References will also be made to the film's companion book, *Warrior Marks: Female Genital Mutilation and the Sexual Blinding of Women,* which though published "on a crash basis," generated such phenomenal interest that advance orders accounted for 75,000 of its initial run of 100,000 copies.[43] Of interest here is how the book's main structural elements correspond to various elements of imperial fictions, and how these elements form the psychic and mythic skeins which run through the film. Chiefly concerned with emphasizing how this "hideous" practice, female circumcision, relates to the issue of African female subjugation, Walker opines that "the result is women with downcast eyes and stiff backs and necks (they are of course beaten by fathers and brothers and husbands). And men who look at a woman's body as if it is a meal. On the other hand, there are all the Africans, women and men, I'm finding to love."[44] These comments, ironically, document narcissism, ignorance, and arrogance. Predictably, "cartographies of pain"[45] dominate the filmmakers' accounts of their efforts so much so that, in the words of a reviewer: "Parmar has nightmares, Walker insomnia. . . . The images are cataclysmic, oppressive, dramatic, insufferable. . . . Walker and Parmar lead us like brave guides into the charnel house."[46] The chamber of horrors projected on the discourse of female circumcision is consistent with imperial mythologies which present a phantasmagoric spectacle of Africa necessary to highlight our "heroes" of piety, charity, stoicism, fortitude, and so forth. In the book, the filmmakers' sense of mission is complicated by their inordinate reliance on constructing African femininity as a figure of abjection. African women, we are told, wear expressive colors as emotional conduits; clamp the chewing-stick, a dentifrice, between their teeth in order not to bite their tongues in sorrow. Parmar finds lots of prostitutes; Walker finds most African women overweight, pitiable, and quite a few, predatory.

Examining the positioning of African femininity in the discourse of cultures, Ama Ata Aidoo argues for a bifocal approach which would reveal that her status is neither peculiar nor pathetic; in fact, she contends that African women are not only at par with other women but ahead of some societies including "the self-congratulatory West."[47] Achola O. Pala argues further that "the position of women in contemporary Africa is to be considered at every level of analysis as an outcome of structural and conceptual mechanisms by which African societies have continued to respond to and resist the global processes of economic exploitation and cultural domination."[48] From the foregoing, what links Walker and Parmar's book with imperial fictions is a penchant for easy categorization and an insistence on equating a grotesque African femininity with the real. Now, let us examine the film.

Warrior Marks is, ostensibly, a "call-to-consciousness" story of Alice Walker and a fictional, generic, African dancer whose respective destinies, the film suggests, are inextricable. Its focus is on circumscriptions: Walker's personal tragedy and the dancer's clitoridectomy, variously interpreted as mutilation, torture, and enslavement. The film's repertoire includes letters, interviews, touristic and folkloric footage, dramatization, and evocative camera work. At the climax, the ubiquitous dancer is forcibly excised but despite her extreme condition manages to limp away. Her fighting spirit is celebrated in the end through dance; Walker's through a benedictory sense of accomplishment. Within this framework, the film serves as a coming-of-age narrative for the dancer and for Walker; the film is about coming to terms. As the credits roll, a song of transcendence, "Something Inside So Strong," harmonizes the film's raison d'être.

Warrior Marks, "despite its painful and distinctively unphotogenic subject,"[49] has been praised as "compelling,"[50] "engaging, passionate and inspiring";[51] a "powerful and affecting film" which takes the spectator to "a world where women are kept as children, subjugated to the primitive ritual of genital mutilation."[52] Even so, Natalie Nichols notes that "plenty of African women oppose the conventional wisdom" and that the film "wisely affords these dissident women ample opportunity to speak for themselves."[53] Another review assures the potential spectator that while "the subject is horrific, this candid and understanding exploration of a demeaning cultural tradition is produced with surprising beauty and sensitivity."[54] In the same vein, William Raspberry surmises that "probably the greatest contribution of *Warrior Marks*, which manages to be surprisingly tasteful in its treatment of the subject, is to drive home just how awful—and dangerous—FGM can be."[55] These reviews should not be understood merely in terms of the aesthetic and moral registers they evoke. Actually, they establish an epistemological field inscribed with cryptic questions like: What is wrong with those people? Significantly, a claim in the Women Make Movies *Film and Video Catalogue* which carries enormous implications for this essay states that "this remarkable film unlocks some of the cultural and political complexities surrounding this issue."[56]

In *Warrior Marks*, the spectator position is established early through the dancer, from whom the spectator is invited to engage, investigate, and (de)construct the ideological meanings of female circumcision. The dancer's status as spectacle is established in the opening shot which tracks her from toe to head. Her superficially constructed "Africanness"—cloth, earrings, "dreads," dance—epitomizes exoticism and fetishization. The dominance of this fictive African femininity will persist until it is ousted by Walker's controlling discourse. In any case, both Walker and the dancer do not just specify the points of identification; they structure the terms, too. Thus, our fictive model of African femininity pops up nonetheless throughout the film in a choric role. Her significance, as has been advanced by Parmar, is to redress the desexualization of women, which ostensibly circumcision does. Following this logic, the dancer is meant to collapse the boundaries between performance, representation, and resistance. It would be argued nonetheless that the artificiality of her characterization valorizes contrivance and spectacle, rather than an understanding of the women on whose behalf intervention is sought.

In the opening sequence the dancer performs against a spectral back projection of a woman, whom we later understand is a circumciser, leading a procession. As shadowy characters, African femininity provides a surrealistic backdrop necessary to constitute the dancer as spectacle. Here, *difference* is color-coded. The African women's realities are stark, frozen, so to speak, in a monochromatic "*other* worldness," and in remarkable contrast to the dancer's which is colorful, alive, and infinite. Even then, a color shot of African girls that immediately follows positions the spectator to acknowledge the dancer as the girls' object of gaze and admiration. The dancer is thus given visual and discursive priority—a position inconsistent with the ostensible aim of understanding the meanings of excision, at least through the eyes of the newly excised. Somewhat like the girls, the circumcisers are excluded from any autonomous intelligibility since they are singularly identified as handmaids of what Walker's calls "mutilating cultures."[57] Cylena Simmonds puts their representation thus: "The only women interviewed who support the tradition are the elder and highly-respected practitioners, who are presented as poorly educated, and uncivilized. In *Warrior Marks* they are treated with less respect and empathy, granted fewer opportunities to express their positions, and viewed as unimaginably insensitive and cruel."[58]

Interestingly, Walker intimates that an interview with a circumciser in the Gambia "was in many ways the interview I came to Africa to get."[59] This statement ostensibly posits the circumciser as an important source of meaning. Even then, comprehension of her position would constitute a significant but not the paramount reason, understanding, and justification of female circumcision since the meanings are steeped, diffused in the intricate folds of her culture and as such would require a much more complex articulation. Even if a charitable reading credits Walker's perspective to "procedural error" one cannot also discount that it anticipates and supports a structure of revelation premised on confrontation, suspense, and drama. Thus, the circumciser is introduced exclusively by her craft. But since her calling inhabits no professional register in the West, the meaning of her craft is foreclosed, positioned against Western notions of medical/surgical practice and "witch doctoring." Thus positioned, the circumciser is forced to respond to her displacement against which any attempt to assert an autonomous identity is read as cold, callous, even evil. In this context, the circumciser is located outside reason, intelligibility, and understanding; her assertion of subjectivity misnamed and rerouted. Interestingly, the circumciser's insistence on tradition offers other possible readings not consonant with the film's intentions: it exposes the impulses which seek to transport her outside of a specific cultural framework, and as such could be read as a resistance to objectification and the truncated extrinsic definitions of what constitute her essence.

Parmar's recollection of an interview with another circumciser is even more telling. She writes: "This was a very chilling and harrowing interview, as she kept on picking up her knife. [It is *her* knife that appears throughout the film.]"[60] In the film, the circumciser does not speak. Her knife is made to speak for her according to the aesthetic cadence and ideological accents of imperial fictions. Having established her knife as the locus of meaning, Parmar exacerbates the situation through its use as background against which the dancer gyrates, through close shots of her hand, slow-motion photography, and haunting music; juxtapositions which ironically foreground the director's relationship to her subject more than they express a complex understanding of female circumcision. Here, technique does not work to encourage spectator recognition of the pedantic mediation of meaning; the knife is animated, displayed, and displaced. As an iconic cue, the knife is imbued with a perverse photogenicity; shock value inaugurates a distancing from the circumciser and repudiates any compassionate identification with her. While this may have some worth, at least in the director's mind, of focusing attention on circumcision as mutilation, it nonetheless abandons the film's avowed rhetoric of elucidation for that of visual terrorism, since the meaning of female circumcision lies beyond the reach of artifice, technique, and fetishization.

Obviously, the filmmakers understand that the assertion of autonomous identity by their subjects is "problematic" since it signals a dissatisfaction with the immobilizing roles/space consigned them and poses the larger threat of disruption of representational power. Two interview subjects described as "recently circumcised girls"[61] who support the tradition, for instance, are *no-named*, just like the circumcisers, who are identified in the book by numbers one, two and three, and on the screen by malevolence; nor do the girls make it to the screen. By dismissing the girls, the filmmakers assign themselves the sole prerogative of limiting and interpreting African femininity but, in addition, display their ideological allegiance to imperial/ colonial authorship, in so far as "colonialism works in part by policing the boundaries of cultural intelligibility, legislating and regulating which identities attain full cultural signification and which do not."[62]

Arguably, the girls' imperviousness is premised on what they see as a nullification of a critical aspect of their identity, their culture and tradition. A contrary reading, nonetheless, would see them as pitiable prisoners of patriarchy. To be sure, circumcision may not be the inevitable essence of their identity, but it cannot be discounted that identities are complex, and often, mosaic. In a similar instance Mary, whose daughter, Little Mary, is featured in the film, is asked about her sex life. Her affirmative response elicits this rather patronizing response from Walker: "How would you know, though, I thought."[63] How could Walker know *better*? Arguably, anxieties about the autonomous subjectivity of African femininity play substantial parts in activating the film's mechanism of meaning containment and regulation. Not surprising, the prescriptive feminism advocated by the filmmakers operates within the dynamics of colonization, especially if it is understood that "the colonized are constrained to impersonate the image the colonizer offers them of themselves; they are commanded to imitate the colonizer's version of their essential difference."[64]

If the dancer is emblematic of African femininity, as the director suggests, her status operates within a charade. With her, Parmar wants to "evoke a sense of women loving their own bodies, reveling in their capacity to enjoy sexual pleasure through oral sexual practices."[65] Here, sexual proclivity is proposed as liberation, but it also mutes some questions in relation to what liberatory potentials or priority that has for African women. In criticizing what she calls the "missionary aspect" of the women's movement, Filomina Chioma Steady notes that "the fact that alternative systems exist which recognize other loci of power, authority, and rewards are often overlooked."[66] Thus, while it could be argued that the film attacks ostensibly patriarchal prescriptions of an ideal femininity, it nonetheless supplants those concerns by exalting a clone: "Western matriarchy that, in the name of feminism, is at least as controlling and self-serving as its male counterpart."[67] Hence, by eliding initiative from characters, like "Big" Mary and others, who are trying to negotiate viable identities within culturally specific paradoxes, the film fosters a *catechismal feminism* which makes for their progression to be read as *conversion* rather than a logical outcome of specific social dynamics. The preceding is very important if we note, as has been argued, that "becoming westernized is not a necessary precondition for female emancipation."[68]

STRUCTURES

At the core of *Warrior Marks* is a discursive order which becomes for Walker a means of comprehending a personal tragedy. Walker's introductory monologue which traces her involvement in the movement is framed within the context of childhood and the Civil Rights movement in the United States. This proposes an understanding of the film as irrevocably tied to (self)emancipation and liberation. Her revelations, especially about a painful childhood, create a sense of connectedness between excision and an emergent sense of self. The inclusion of other stories, of penitence (Comfort Ottah), ostracism (Aminata Diop), "betrayal" (Little Mary) and hope (Mam Yassin), which propose an understanding of the film as a meditation on personal histories/*her*stories does not detract from the fact that Walker's is the *master* narrative, at least to the extent that these stories are subordinated to Walker's who has been positioned as a victim of male violence and surrogate victim of "genital mutilation."

As has been noted, "all scenes in the film are centered around Walker's emotional commitment to this issue."[69] This is important because in the film authority or dominance is delegated, in part, according to the allocation of space. In other words, it is through space that hierarchy of characters and discourses follow. A reviewer has this to say about Walker's childhood story: "As a point of departure, it served the film well. The only problem is that Walker doesn't 'depart.'"[70] Elizabeth Pincus is more elaborate:

> The problem? Too much Alice Walker. During a lengthy setup, Walker describes how she was maimed as a child—a bullet from her brother's gun blinded her in one eye. Throughout the documentary, she returns again and again to this incident, comparing her own "patriarchal wound" with the ravaged genitals of entire nations of women. Hmm, a bit of a stretch? Worse, Walker assumes the role of the American crusader; she confronts village elders with bold—some would say condescending—questions about why the tradition continues, then fails to draw articulate conclusions from the information she gathers.[71]

This critique underscores, amongst other things, the film's inability to penetrate the realities of the women and/or the practice. Within this context, the "realities" are condensed to spontaneous expressions of outrage. While Walker's point about her childhood serves to develop the film's theme of child-as-victim and show how childhood experiences structure identity, it nonetheless imbues the film with an aura of narcissism. To a greater extent, what is at play here is *narcissistic rage* which according to Heinz Kohut is predicated on "the unconditional availability of the approving functions of an admiring self-object or on the ever present opportunity for a merger with an idealized one."[72] More on this, later. From the preceding quote, one can discern the network of exchange through which the film's representation of African femininity merges with Walker's quest for a newly validated self. Her presence does not just provide possibilities for a transition from restriction to liberation; in the film, she is *the* model—an idealized image of feminist consciousness and personal agency. In this light, Seble Dawit and Salem Mekuria's observations, which put Walker in a messianic role, are especially important: "As is common in Western depiction of Africa, Ms. Walker and her collaborator, Pratibha Parmar, portray the continent as a monolith. African women and children are props, and the village the background against which Alice Walker, *heroine-savior*, comes to articulate their pain and condemn those who inflict it."[73]

From the above, Walker's status as heroine is integral with "revealing" African femininity as a pathetic victim of African cultures. Accordingly, Aminata Diop is abstracted as a poster/foster femme and Walker's involvement heralded as haute cause célèbre. Put another way, Walker's status is concomitant with constructing African femininity as lacking and relegating it to passivity. This is important, especially, if we understand that imperial fictions often construct an inchoate, chaotic *other* world, a space for fictive possibilities, for excitement, for anxieties to be worked out. Significantly, this chaotic fictive realm secures the designation of central characters, important narrative anchors without which unwieldy reality reigns and other "supporting characters" whose importance lies in unintrusive presence in the text. It is not that African women do not have some moments in the film. They do. But it also brings to the surface the ambiguities surrounding agency in the film, especially if we understand agency to mean autonomous and personal control over the definitional elements through which a particular subjectivity is constituted, anchored, and expressed. Interestingly, the few moments of "speech" by African women are often recuperated by the appearance of Walker, Parmar and the dancer who have been positioned for the spectator as self-determining. In this sense, African women's "presence" and "testimonies" could be read as vehicles to navigate through some of the textual turbulence caused in good measure by their confinement as mannequins, mascots, marionettes, and domestic assistants. Not surprisingly, the spectator is ushered into identification with their "presence" and "testimonies" without attention to the textual discrepancies, and the anxieties deriving from the filmmakers' need to choreograph meanings and dominate elucidation.

Incidentally, a film festival brochure notes the "leading players: Alice Walker and Awa Thiam."[74] As lead players they are abstracted as best suited to voice the unconscious and "stifled" emotions of African femininity. This categorization, nonetheless, implies a hierarchy, a distinction between the principals and the supporting cast. As a publicity ploy, it is structured around Walker's status as Pulitzer Prize winner and, probably, the recognition of Thiam, in the words of Parmar, as "Africa's *first* and *leading* feminist."[75] A couple issues deserve mention here. Arguably, Parmar's meretricious anointment of Thiam is integral to her (Thiam's) conscription into the film's credentialing process. What is more, Parmar's reckless periodization of oppositional African female consciousness not only subordinates it to campaign against female circumcision but, importantly, retains the imperial "privilege" of *ranking* and *appointing*. It is not surprising, therefore, that Dawit and Mekuria hold that the film, "portrays an African village where women and children are without personality, dancing and gazing blankly through some stranger's script of their lives."[76] In essence, analysis of the discourse on circumcision in *Warrior Marks* should not glibly separate identity from position, and agency from *positioning*. Clearly, the position constructed for Walker in the film is one that disassembles the individual identities of her representational subjects and dramatizes, in the words of Ama Ata Aidoo, "the accepted notion of them as mute beasts of burden."[77]

Concretely, the film's reluctance to give primacy to the voices of African women secures Walker's position as "spokesperson"; not surprising if we understand, as has been argued by Roland Barthes, that "Myth is speech *stolen and restored,*"[78] and as has been pointed out by Linda Alcoff that speaking for others necessarily invites erasure and reinscription of hierarchies and "is often born of a desire for mastery, to privilege oneself as the one who more correctly understands the truth about another's situation or as one who can champion just cause and thus achieve glory and praise."[79] In this sense, questioning Walker's discursive authority should not be narrowly focused on the issue of mandate; importantly, it should include querying the translation of "individual conscience" into privilege, (melo)drama, opportunity.[80]

BORDERS

Inevitably, the discourse of circumcision must either engage or confront the specific cultural contexts of its location. Typically then, the Western discourse of excision limits the debate to simplistic binaries, blotting out and blocking off "disruptive" viewpoints. By contrast, the noted African scholar and clergyman, John S. Mbiti, places circumcision, the individual, and society in a complex cultural and ancestral continuum. According to him, "The blood which is shed during the physical operation binds the person to the land and consequently to the departed members of his society. . . . This circumcision blood is like *making a covenant* or a solemn agreement between the individual and his people."[81]

Notably, the category of social relations the preceding observation weaves, places identity, its construction and affirmation, in a unique configuration. But as has been hinted, a staple of imperial fictions is the destabilization of other cultures. Fundamentally, destabilization performs three roles: (1) it creates an epistemological vacuum by restricting access to certain meanings; (2) it clears grounds for the deliberate and pervasive invocation of *difference*; and (3) it secures the (re)production of narcissistic points of identification. In *Warrior Marks* these categories, singularly or severally, augment the reinscription of primitivism in the discourse of African peoples and cultural institutions. Put another way, the film advocates a common-sense, transparent, and unproblematic association between the practice and savagery. Advertised as a "gentle film on a harsh reality,"[82] the film privileges "harshness" so much so that the "realities" forfeit their meanings to it. In other words, "harsh" does not become a guide to comprehending a specific reality; it becomes, instead, a penumbra which mystifies African female sexuality, and a diffuse metaphor for, in Walker's words, "all that is wrong with Africa."

Interestingly, the film proposes an understanding of the meaning of the practice (its realities) as existing independently and unproblematically outside of certain constitutive discourses. But as has been argued by Roland Barthes, the substance of myths draws its "luminary" current or coercive appeal by presenting its "truths" as instinctive and autonomous. Myth making, according to Barthes, "abolishes the complexity of human acts, it gives them the simplicity of essences. It does away with all dialectics, with any going back beyond what is immediately visible, it organizes a world which is without contradictions because it is without depth, a world wide open and wallowing in the evident, *it establishes a blissful clarity*: things appear to mean something by themselves."[83]

In other words, myth making transforms complex realities into a common-sense show-and-tell. At one moment in the film, a chicken is beheaded. The camera zooms in and lingers on the chicken's death throes. The close-up, interestingly, does not work to foster insight but rather to contain it; to adhere it to a *specified* viewpoint. As spectacle, this moment is enigmatic— unintelligible except as a sign of barbarism. No mention of it as sacrifice is made, except in the film's companion book; even then, it receives preposterous "explanation." For Alice Walker, who claims to have "understood the message of the sacrifice," it means a threat: "Next time, we cut off your head."[84] In saying this, Walker subordinates other notions of sacrifice such as atonement, supplication, and communion to primitivist cliché, thereby stripping the moment of any vestige of spirituality. Furthermore, her "explanation" typifies what Obioma Nnaemeka terms "the incorporation of feminism into world systems of power and privilege."[85] But that is not all. Noting the centrality of sacrifices in African spirituality, John S. Mbiti, who defines them as instances "where animal life is destroyed in order to present the animal, in part, or in whole to God, supernatural beings, spirits or the living-dead," points out that "as a rule, there are no sacrifices without prayers."[86] Whatever invocation there was during the ceremony was reduced to background noise in the film, and in the film's companion book, a crude exhortation to maintain tradition.

Another issue deserves mention here. In the film's companion book, Walker notes the presence of women, including the "butcher," whose dressing and mannerisms make them virtually indistinguishable from men. The self-reflexive potentials and dynamics of the women's masquerade are, however, subsumed to specious speculations about the women's sexual orientation. Certainly, there is more to it than whether they are "dykes";[87] especially if we consider, for instance, that the Maasai initiation rites for males, similarly, include circumcision and seclusion "after which they emerge *dressed like women*."[88] As with the sacrifice, naive assumptions incapable of discerning or insufficient to explain complex cultural matrices are imposed.

At another point in the film, Walker declares that women are circumcisers because men do not want to do it since they are decidedly indifferent to certain "maternal" functions like child grooming. This "insight" neglects that the circumcisers have traditionally functioned as midwives, even gynecologists and that contemporary class distinctions account, in part, for their prevalence among certain groups. Be that as it may, the assumed indifference of African men to sexual subjugation is not just a theme in *Warrior Marks*. Concretely, it is a principal axis of its meaning and aesthetic construction. African men are, so to speak, repressed in the film; structured, fixed in the film as haunting presence. While their silence and near effacement may be read as (1) part of transference of agency to women, and (2) subversion of male privilege, it also could be argued that the men's position, marked as it is by exclusion, describes a convenient arc for sidetracking the multiple layers of the issue, since showing African males ambivalent about, even opposed to, the practice disrupts the binary opposition of bad male/innocent female necessary for the constitution of African femininity as victimized. This imposed binary is antithetical to the spirit of African feminism, which does not see men as inevitable/eternal foes but wants to incorporate men as partners in progress, and places the film within the realm of revenge fantasies. This is more significant if we note that "those who are in the grip of narcissistic rage show total lack of empathy toward the offender,"[89] or imagined offenders. In the film then, hatred for men becomes hatred for female circumcision and *vice versa*.[90]

We seem to be dealing here with much more than revenge, however. An instance during the shooting of the film offers further insight. According to Parmar, "There was one shot of Alice gazing across the river, and behind her were two men looking into the water, where the sunlight was reflected. They were totally absorbed and didn't mind that we filmed them."[91] This statement is illustrative of the relationship between the imperial observing eye and its subjects; between Parmar and the "natives" who constitute her representational putty. That they *didn't mind* does not ameliorate not seeking their permission first. Courtesy, fairness, respect, would suggest that. But the "natives" are different. In imperial fictions they are expendable to scenery.

As an imperial fiction, *Warrior Marks* tries to institute a totalizing context for analysis of female circumcision. The film cripples understanding of the practice by urging a reading of it in solely patriarchal terms. Following this forfeiture of rigorous analysis, condemnation, not contemplation, is the key note. The film's critique of the practice is formulated around absolutist terms, including oppression, repression, and inhumanity, and around metaphors of infanticide and enslavement, while dispersing the discourse in multiple historical and institutional spaces, in a way, insulates the film from rigorous analysis, since such questioning runs the risk of being called callous, unprogressive, or worse. Concerted calls by Western feminists for economic sanctions against "erring" societies replicate an imperial era during which renouncement of the practice was "a condition of baptism and church membership . . . eligibility for school entry . . . part of teachers' condition of employment."[92] Sanctions direct appeals to institutions they have written off as irredeemably patriarchal and dismiss the wishes of the African women on whose behalf the efforts are (ostensibly) being made, but who have spoken clearly like Asha Mohamud, a Somali-born pediatrician, who states that "sanctions are stupid. . . . The goal should be to improve the economic and educational status of women."[93] Or like Wilkista Onsando, a Kenyan women's rights activist: "Let indigenous people fight it according to their own traditions. It will die faster than if others tell us what to do."[94] Interestingly, the *Newsweek* article from which the preceding quote is taken is titled: "Is It Torture or Tradition?" Not only does the title propose a sophistic understanding of the issues at hand, the article dismisses Onsando's wishes thus: "That may be. But for Westerners like Walker, patience in the face of savagery is no virtue."[95] Here, the nullification of African women's agency, through the invocation of primitivism and haughty moralizing, also denies her identity any complexity, depth, or autonomous/full expression; especially, as has been pointed out by Carole Boyce Davies, since African feminism "examines African societies for institutions which are of value to women and rejects those which work to their detriment and does not simply import Western women's agenda."[96] Seen this way, African feminism is simultaneously political and cultural. But with *Warrior Marks*, the possibilities of establishing or forging a resistance based on the cultural values of its representational subjects are obliterated. The last point is especially cogent if we consider that Parmar's essay with Valerie Amos, "Challenging Imperial Feminism," not only questioned the foundations of hegemonic/orthodox feminism but argued, quite vividly, that feminist solidarity should neither be simply an expression of positional sameness nor ahistorical, acultural uniformity.

As was indicated earlier, the imposition of a unitary reading/meaning upon a complex reality is inextricably connected with a specific way of seeing Africa and, particularly here, African femininity. We also have to understand that as a campaign against female circumcision *Warrior Marks* stresses negativity and as a campaign focused outside of Africa, structures an understanding of the practice in distinctively Western terms; here, the contrastive elements of "the other" culture are elaborated to signal a preferred identificatory configuration. Ultimately, an appeal to the meaning of the practice inevitably becomes an appeal to the difference between "us" and "them." How else can one account for the fact that "barbaric," "primitive," and "savage" are the defining elements of female circumcision in the West?

It would be unfair to blame *Warrior Marks* wholly for the preceding views since ignorance and prejudice had been the defining features of the discourse on Africa in the West. However, it is pertinent to note that the film, through a representational rhetoric that may not be in marked disagreement with popular "understandings" of the continent, gives African femininity a *pathetic, perverted,* and *ornamental* existence.

CONCLUSION

The films discussed, as should be clear by now, have ideological affinities with imperial mythologies. Significantly, their identification with imperial cultural chauvinism is not restricted to the definition of self as ideal; concretely, it is characterized by a host of discourses in which reductiveness, gaps, and silences merge with the boundaries established by the Western discourse of "civilization." Accordingly, African femininity, habitually constructed outside normalcy and "civilization," exists in these films as a category to be measured against a normative femininity. The disembodied African femininity of these films, however, does not merely exist to draw parallels. At its center is a scene of fantasy of imperial potency and erasure of imperial self-ambiguities. But that is not all. The deployment of African femininity in imperial fictions, it should be noted, is also juxtaposed with subtextual narratives. Hence, the specters of African femininity encountered in the films under discussion actually are, amongst other things, embedded narratives—in *Mountains of the Moon* and *Mister Johnson,* of desire incapacitated by the same forces which evoke them; in *Warrior Marks,* of disavowal through incessant reworking of similarity and difference.

NOTES

1. Hyam 1990, 1.
2. Rafelson 1990.
3. Snow 1991, quoting Beresford 1990.
4. Walker and Parmar 1993.
5. This term is put in quotation marks because a productive critique of the practice should involve much more than presenting it as a spectacle of primitive, dismembering revelry. Besides, the facile and voguish usage of the term gives primacy to (re)naming as a hermeneutic magic wand; in other words, that an acknowledgment of the practice as "hideous" necessarily offers a crucial understanding of the issue of African female subjugation. That said, I am against female circumcision.
6. Walker and Parmar 1993, 95.
7. Lionnet 1991, 2. Lionnet's explanation accounts for the views like the following: "The strongest considerations involved are economic ones. Many Africans believe that unless females are excised no one will marry them, and they will therefore deprive their family of a dowry. Moreover, if an African woman is not married, she is commonly deemed worthless" (Bardarch 1993, 126). The preceding quote is notable because of how it slides certain spurious understandings of Africa in relation to "existential truths" about the practice. Be that as it may, another piece declares

without equivocation that: "In other regions, such as parts of Nigeria, girls are circumcised in the street with no more ceremony than Americans devote to piercing a child's ears" (Brownlee et al. 1994, 58). Yet another asserts that: "The chants intoned as the cuts are made are often confused cocktails of Koranic text and pagan spell" (Foster 1994, 244).

8. According to Cutner, "The practice of female circumcision is nearly global in its distribution; Africa, Malaysia, Indonesia, and the southern parts of the Arab peninsula, Pakistan, and Russia (some sects), United Arab Emirates, Oman, Bahrain, and South Yemen. The practice is also found in Peru, Brazil, Eastern Mexico, and among the aboriginal tribes of Australia" (cited in Slack 1988). Nawal El Saadawi is more emphatic: "It is known in history that it was performed in Europe and America, Asia and Africa" (cited in Patterson and Gillam 1983).

9. Cutrufelli 1983, 33.

10. Kaus et al. 1987, 46.

11. Geshekter 1995, 10 (emphasis added).

12. Hammond and Jablow 1977, 15.

13. Stott 1989, 70.

14. Honeycutt 1990.

15. Rainer 1990.

16. Cited in Kroll 1990, 65.

17. Benenson 1991, H23.

18. Rainer 1990.

19. Brosnan 1990, F3.

20. Major 1991, 23.

21. Cover 1991, R9.

22. Snow 1991.

23. Pym 1990, 95.

24. Brantlinger 1985, 199.

25. Pratt 1985, 125.

26. Pieterse 1992, 64.

27. Hammond and Jablow 1977, 148.

28. Hoch 1979, 45.

29. Cited in Hammond and Jablow 1977, 71.

30. See Gilman 1985. Chapter three is especially pertinent.

31. Pieterse 1992, 108.

32. Evans-Pritchard 1931, 36.

33. Hyam 1990, 3.

34. B. Nichols 1991, 105; see 105–198 for the full argument.

35. Renov 1993, 2.

36. Dent 1992, 3.

37. Wilentz 1993, 15.

38. Menya 1993, 423.

39. Coleman 1994, 58.

40. Mohanty 1988, 65.

41. Walker and Parmar 1993, 268.

42. Ricciardi 1982, preface.

43. O'Brien 1993, 13.

44. Walker and Parmar 1993, 69.

45. Nnaemeka 1994, 317

46. Brownworth 1994, 37.

47. Aidoo 1992, 324.

48. Pala 1981, 209.

49. *Cork Film Festival Brochure* 1994, 44.
50. Minor 1994, 7.
51. *Melbourne International Film Festival Brochure* 1994, 46.
52. Herrick 1994, 103.
53. N. Nichols 1994.
54. Wood 1994, 342.
55. Raspberry 1993, A21.
56. Women Make Movies 1995, 42.
57. Walker and Parmar 1993, 73.
58. Simmonds 1994, 3.
59. Walker and Parmar 1993, 301 (emphasis in the original).
60. Walker and Parmar 1993, 317 (emphasis in the original).
61. Walker and Parmar 1993, 310.
62. Fuss 1994, 21.
63. Walker and Parmar 1993, 44.
64. Fuss 1994, 24.
65. Walker and Parmar 1993, 225.
66. Steady 1981, 25.
67. Bass 1994, 5.
68. Steady 1981, 26.
69. Simmonds 1994, 3.
70. Farrar-Frazer 1993, 41.
71. Pincus 1994, 50.
72. Kohut 1973, 386.
73. Dawit and Mekuria 1993, A13.
74. *Cork Film Festival Brochure* 1994, 44.
75. Walker and Parmar 1993, 109 (emphasis added).
76. Dawit and Mekuria 1993, A13.
77. Aidoo 1992, 321.
78. Barthes 1972, 125 (emphasis in the original).
79. Alcoff 1994, 306.
80. Other references to opportunism and exploitation could be found in an attempt by an American television crew to sabotage Walker's documentary (Walker and Parmar 1993, 165); Fran P. Hosken's charge that the writings on the topic by A. M. Rosenthal, a *New York Times* columnist, appear designed to raise the paper's readership (Hosken 1994, 30); grounds for political asylum in Canada (Fennell 1994, 18); and the United States (Gregory 1994) and A. M. Rosenthal's declaration that female circumcision is "the world's most prevalent human rights violation (Rosenthal 1993, PA15)." Interestingly, Nawal El Saadawi identifies the same exploitative and even, remarkably, censorial penchant in Beacon Press, publisher of her book, *The Hidden Face of Eve*, and Fran P. Hosken (Patterson and Gilliam 1983, 190–191).
81. Mbiti 1975, 93 (emphasis added).
82. Hamilton 1993, 2.
83. Barthes 1972, 143 (emphasis added).
84. Walker and Parmar 1993, 47.
85. Nnaemeka 1995, 81.
86. Mbiti 1975, 58, 61.
87. Walker and Parmar 1993, 44.
88. Mbiti 1975, 123 (emphasis added).
89. Kohut 1973, 386.
90. Walker's description of African males is generalized, rigid, and allows no room for difference. According to her, "The men around here are blandly gra-

cious, like all slave-masters, I suppose" (Walker and Parmar 1993, 43). But as has been argued by Chandra Mohanty, "there is . . . no universal patriarchal framework . . . unless one posits an international male conspiracy or a monolithic, transhistorical power structure" (Mohanty 1988, 63). Moreover, "the problem with Western feminist interpretations of women's position in Africa is that they have often been projections of male/female antagonisms that derive from Western middle-class experiences. There is often very little concern shown for the oppression by world economic systems on African *men* as well as women" (Steady 1981, 28, emphasis in the original). Not surprisingly, Walker links the "hordes of intrusive men on the beach" (Walker and Parmar 1993, 53) to "mutilation," rather than an obvious tourist sex-economy; similarly, Parmar writes: "We have noticed many older white women tourists accompanied by young Gambian men. Interesting" (Walker and Parmar 1993, 200). Just interesting? The import of Parmar's "observation" lies in her glib evasion of the unsettling questions and ideological stress the situation raises, and which an article, "Seeking Sex in the Gambia," addresses. In the article, a fifty-eight-year-old English woman is quoted thus: "I had four different boys that holiday and the best sex I have ever had. I came back a new woman. It was very empowering as a woman to be able to have my pick of a bunch of beautiful men" (Aziz 1994, 12). At any rate, the Gambian president is unequivocal about the tourist sex-economy: "We are not sex machines. I want that to be clear to anyone who comes here. This behavior will no longer be tolerated" (*New African* 1994, 39).

91. Walker and Parmar 1993, 193.
92. Hyam 1990, 192.
93. Cited in Gregory 1994, 45.
94. Cited in Kaplan et al. 1993, 124.
95. Cited in Kaplan et al. 1993, 124 (emphasis added).
96. Davies 1986, 9.

WORKS CITED

Aidoo, Ama Ata. 1992. "The African Woman Today." *Dissent* 39:319–325.
Alcoff, Linda. 1994. "The Problem of Speaking for Others." In *Feminist Nightmares: Women at Odds*, ed. Susan Ostrov Weisser and Jennifer Fleischner, 285–309. New York: New York University Press.
Amos, Valerie, and Pratibha Parmar. 1984. "Challenging Imperial Feminism." *Feminist Review* 17:3–19.
Aziz, Christine. 1994. "Seeking Sex in the Gambia." *Marie Claire/UK Edition*, May 10–18.
Bardarch, Ann Louise. 1993. "Tearing Off the Veil." *Vanity Fair*, August, 123.
Barthes, Roland. 1972. *Mythologies*. Trans. Annette Lavers. New York: Hill and Wang.
Bass, Margaret Kent. 1994. "Alice's Secret." *CLA Journal* 38 (1): 1–10.
Benenson, Laurie Halpern. 1991. "By Royal Command: It Was a Night at the Movies." *New York Times*, January 6, H23.
Beresford, Bruce, director. 1990. *Mister Johnson* (Film).
Brantlinger, Patrick. 1985. "Victorians and Africans: The Genealogy of the Myth of the Dark Continent." *Critical Inquiry* 12 (1): 166–203.
Brosnan, Pierce. 1990. "Handicap Not Lest Ye Be Handicapped." *Los Angeles Times*, December 3, F3.
Brownlee, Shannon, et al. 1994. "In the Name of Ritual." *US News and World Report*, February 7, 56–58.
Brownworth, Victoria A. 1994. "*Warrior Marks: Female Genital Mutilation and the Sexual Blinding of Women*." (Review.) *Lambda Book Report* 4 (September/October): 37.

Coleman, Beth. 1994. "Warrior Women: Pratibha Parmar Joins Forces with Novelist Alice Walker." *Out*, December/January, 58.

Cork Film Festival Brochure. 1994. Cork, Ireland: Cork Film Festival Association, 44.

Cover, Arthur Byron. 1991. "Review of *Warrior Marks*." *Box Office* 127 (1): R9.

Cutrufelli, Maria Rosa. 1983. *Women of Africa: Roots of Oppression.* London: Zed Press.

Davies, Carole Boyce. 1986. "Introduction: Feminist Consciousness and African Literary Criticism." In *Ngambika: Studies of Women in African Literature*, ed. Carole Boyce Davies and Anne Adams Graves, 1–23. Trenton, NJ: Africa World Press.

Dawit, Seble, and Salem Mekuria. 1993. "The West Just Doesn't Get It." *New York Times*, December 7, A13.

Dent, Gina. 1992. "Introduction: The Truth about Non-Fiction." In *Black Popular Culture*, ed. Gina Dent, 1–19. Seattle, WA: Bay Press.

Evans-Pritchard, E. E. 1931. "An Alternative Term for Brideprice." *Man* 31:36–39.

Farrar-Frazer, Leasa. 1993. "An Opportunity Missed: A Review of *Warrior Marks*." *Black Film Review* 8 (2): 41–42.

Fennell, Tom. 1994. "Finding New Grounds for Refuge: A Somali Woman Wins a Fight to Keep Her Daughter in Canada." *Macleans*, August 8, 18–20.

Foster, Charles. 1994. "On the Trail of a Taboo: Female Circumcision in the Islamic World." *Contemporary Review* 264 (1540): 244–249.

Fuss, Diana. 1994. "Interior Colonies: Frantz Fanon and the Politics of Identification." *Diacritics* 24 (2/3): 20–42.

Geshekter, Charles L. 1995. "Outbreak? AIDS, Africa, and the Medicalization of Poverty." *Transition* 67:4–16.

Gilman, Sander L. 1985. *Difference and Pathology: Stereotypes of Sexuality, Race, and Madness.* Ithaca, NY: Cornell University Press.

Gregory, Sophfronia Scott. 1994. "At Risk of Mutilation." *Time*, March 21.

Hamilton, Amy. 1993. "*Warrior Marks: Female Genital Mutilation and the Sexual Blinding of Women*." (Review.) *Off Our Backs* 23 (11): 2.

Hammond, Dorothy, and Alta Jablow. 1977. *The Myth of Africa.* New York: The Library of Social Sciences.

Herrick, Roxanna. 1994. "Warrior Marks Narrated by Alice Walker" (Review). *Library Journal* (November): 103.

Hoch, Paul. 1979. *White Hero, Black Beast: Racism, Sexism and the Mask of Masculinity.* London: Pluto Press.

Honeycutt, Kirk. 1990. "Review of *Mountains of the Moon*." *Hollywood Reporter*, February 7.

Hosken, Fran P. 1994. "FGM and the Media: A Critical Perspective." *WIN News* 20 (1): 30–31.

Hyam, Ronald. 1990. *Empire and Sexuality: The British Experience.* Manchester: Manchester University Press.

Kaplan, David A., et al. 1993. "Is It Torture or Tradition?" *Newsweek*, December 20, 124.

Kaus, Mickey, et al. 1987. "The 'Small Health Problem' of AIDS." *Newsweek*, July 13, 46.

Kohut, Heinz. 1973. "Thoughts on Narcissism and Narcissistic Rage." In *The Psychoanalytic Study of the Child*, ed. Ruth S. Eissler, 360–400. New York: Quadrangle Books.

Kroll, Jack. 1990. "How to Get a Bug to Crawl on Cue." *Newsweek*, February 26, 65.

Lionnet, Françoise. 1991. "Dissymmetry Embodied: Feminism, Universalism and the Practice of Excision." *Passages* 1:2–4.

Major, Wade. 1991. "Mister Johnson/'Magic' Johnson." *Entertainment Today*, April 5, 23.

Mbiti, John S. 1975. *An Introduction to African Religion*. London: Heinemann.

Melbourne International Film Festival Brochure. 1994. Melbourne: Filmfest Ltd., 46.

Menya, Diane C. 1993. "Bookshelf: *Possessing the Secret of Joy* by Alice Walker." (Review.) *The Lancet*, February 13, 423.

Minor, Diane. 1994. "Warrior Marks: Joyous Resistance at Walker Film Debut." *National NOW Times*, January, 7.

Mohanty, Chandra. 1988. "Under Western Eyes: Feminist Scholarship and Colonial Discourses." *Feminist Review* 30:61–68.

New African. 1994. "Gambians Are Not Sex Machines." *New African*, October, 39.

Nichols, Bill. 1991. *Representing Reality: Issues and Concepts in Documentary*. Bloomington: Indiana University Press.

Nichols, Natalie. 1994. "Scarred, but Not Scared: Scenes from the War on Female Genital Mutilation." *Los Angeles Reader*, May 20.

Nnaemeka, Obioma. 1994. "Bringing African Women into the Classroom: Rethinking Pedagogy and Epistemology." In *Borderwork: Feminist Engagements with Comparative Literature*, ed. Margaret R. Higonnet, 301–318. Ithaca, NY: Cornell University Press.

———. 1995. "Feminism, Rebellious Women, and Cultural Boundaries: Re-reading Flora Nwapa and Her Compatriots." *Research in African Literature* 26 (2): 80–113.

O'Brien, Maureen. 1993. "Alice Walker Offers a New Book and a Film with a Cause." *Publisher's Weekly*, October 25, 13.

Pala, Achola O. 1981. "Definitions of Women and Development: An African Perspective." In *The Black Woman Cross-culturally*, ed. Filomina Chioma Steady, 209–214. Cambridge: Schenkman Publishing.

Parmar, Pratibha, producer/director. 1993. *Warrior Marks* [videorecording]. A Hauer Rawlence Production. New York: Women Make Movies (distributor).

Patterson, Tiffany R., and Angela M. Gilliam. 1983. "Out of Egypt: A Talk with Nawal El Saadawi." *Freedomways* 23 (3): 186–194.

Pieterse, Jan Nederveen. 1992. *White on Black: Images of Africa and Blacks in Western Popular Culture*. New Haven, CT: Yale University Press.

Pincus, Elizabeth. 1994. "Review of *Warrior Marks*." *L. A. Weekly*, May 20–26, 50.

Pratt, Mary Louise. 1985. "Scratches on the Face of the Country; or, What Mr. Barrow Saw in the Land of the Bushmen." *Critical Inquiry* 12 (1): 119–143.

Pym, John. 1990. "Mister Johnson." *Sight and Sound* 59 (2): 94–95.

Rafelson, Bob, director. 1990. *Mountains of the Moon* (Film).

Rainer, Peter. 1990. "The Other Richard Burton." *Los Angeles Times*, February 23.

Raspberry, William. 1993. "Women and a Brutal 'Tradition.'" *Washington Post*, November 8, A21.

Renov, Michael. 1993. "Introduction: The Truth about Non-Fiction." In *Theorizing Documentary*, ed. Michael Renov, 1–11. New York: Routledge.

Ricciardi, Mirella. 1982. *African Saga*. London: Collins.

Rosenthal, A.M. 1993. "Female Genital Torture (Ending the World's Most Prevalent Human Rights Violation)." *New York Times*, November 12, PA15.

Simmonds, Cylena. 1994. "Missing the Mark." *Afterimage*, March, 3.

Slack, Alison T. 1988. "Female Circumcision: A Critical Appraisal." *Human Rights Quarterly* 10 (4): 437–486.

Snow, Shauna. 1991. "Beresford Defends New Film." *Los Angeles Times*, February 25.

Steady, Filomina Chioma, ed. 1981. *The Black Woman Cross-culturally*. Cambridge: Schenkman Publishing.

Stott, Rebecca. 1989. "The Dark Continent: Africa as Female Body in Haggard's Adventure Fiction." *Feminist Review* 32:69–89.

Walker, Alice. 1992. *Possessing the Secret of Joy*. New York: Harcourt Brace Jovanovich.

Walker, Alice, and Pratibha Parmar. 1993. *Warrior Marks: Female Genital Mutilation and the Sexual Blinding of Women.* New York: Harcourt Brace.

Wilentz, Gay. 1993. "Healing the Wounds of Time." *The Women's Review of Books* 10 (5): 15.

Women Make Movies, Inc. 1995. *Film and Video Catalogue,* 42. New York: Women Make Movies.

Wood, Irene. 1994. "Video: *Warrior Marks* produced by Alice Walker" (Review). *Booklist* (October 1): 342.

Confronting the Western Gaze

Eloïse A. Brière

The Western gaze has constructed Africa since Herodotus's early descriptions of the continent. An example of contemporary construction of Africa will be examined here through perspectives provided by two women filmmakers, one who is Western, and one who is not. Since both films define African women, I will compare representation and self-representation as they relate to the concepts of the "other" and "voice." It is most often the gaze of Western media and the sound of Western voices that frame the African subject—whether it be CNN in Mogadishu or Kinshasa or early films like *Tarzan the Ape Man* or the more contemporary *Greystoke*. The African subject is framed as a voiceless "other," dependent on the strong Western hand, whether it is that of the character created by Edgar Rice Burroughs or that of United Nations relief agencies.[1]

The films under consideration are in the documentary style and focus on the controversial issue of female excision in Africa. As Françoise Lionnet, quoting Renée Saurel, states in *Postcolonial Representations*, "these practices have caused much blood to be shed for thousands of years and much ink for the past two."[2] Now, celluloid images and African languages have entered the debate, starting with Oumar Cheikh Sissoko's film.[3] His film dramatizes, in the Bambara language, the plight of a young urbanized Malian woman who is forced to submit to excision.

Two later films by Pratibha Parmar and Alice Walker[4] and Anne Laure Folly (from Togo)[5] have added other dimensions to the ongoing debate. Although Folly's film was released shortly after the Parmar/Walker film and is available in the United States from California Newsreel, it is known far less than the Parmar/Walker film.[6] In addition to the wealth of information in Walker's controversial film is the companion book—a journal, also called *Warrior Marks*, kept by Walker and Parmar during the filming.[7] Because of her power, access to information, and reputation, race, and gender, Walker becomes an implicit spokesperson for African women, appropriating their voice, replacing the missionary or colonial administrator of the past, once the only Westerners to speak with authority about Africa.[8]

As V. Y. Mudimbe states, "It takes little imagination to realize that missionary discourses on Africans were powerful. They were both signs and symbols of a cultural model."[9] Walker's voice in *Warrior Marks* functions in much the same way.[10] Contrasting with Walker, Folly, who is unknown and new to the debate, provides a forum where women appear to speak for themselves. The discursive stances taken by both filmmakers raise questions relating to authority and power since, as Michel Foucault argues, to speak about sex in the West is to wield power.[11] Hence the Western gaze and the African gaze, as they look upon African women tell us about struggle to control voice.

The excision of African women has become a hot-button issue in the United States, as the recent spate of articles in the press testify.[12] The textual space allotted to African women in the U.S. media revolves around a single issue because of the increasing number of African women seeking protection from excision by requesting asylum in this country.[13] Variously called female circumcision, clitoridectomy, female genital mutilation, and most recently, genital cutting, in the United States, the practice is becoming a defining characteristic of African women.[14] Forgetting that in the nineteenth century it was practiced on U.S. soil by U.S. doctors as a way of curing a host of ills, the West today constructs excision as the prism through which all African women are viewed, a sign of their "otherness."[15] The current American concern with excision is, according to Opportune Zongo, due to a central issue which, as she says, "has plagued the field of African women's studies: the overemphasis on African women's genitalia and sex lives."[16] This should come as no surprise, if, as Foucault has pointed out, "the deployment of sexuality has its reason for being, not in reproducing itself, but in proliferating, innovating, annexing, creating, and penetrating bodies in an increasingly detailed way, and in controlling populations."[17]

This kind of control is consonant with the Westernization of the world, which, as Samir Amin has suggested, would impose on everyone the adoption of the recipes for European superiority—free enterprise and the market, secularism and pluralist electoral democracy.[18] Thus what appears to be overemphasis from Zongo's African perspective is to be expected in the West where the function of sex has changed from an emphasis on reproduction to pleasure, which has in turn become the means of disciplining the body and regulating populations.[19]

The American tendency to focus exclusively on one corner of Africa or one aspect of African culture corresponds to an imperialistic totalizing strategy wherein a chosen element stands as a metaphor for the whole. As a result, the information on excision tends to exoticize African women by decontextualing their circumstances and constituting them as the West's "other." Exoticism effaces contexts and hard facts and lends itself to sensationalism. For instance the fact that excision is not practiced throughout the fifty countries of the African continent, but in only twenty-eight of them is rarely if ever mentioned.

By the same token, numbers of women affected vary wildly. For example, the *Economist*[20] states that 6,000 women are excised daily, adding up to more than 216 million women per year. Somewhat more conservative, a *Christian Science Monitor* article,[21] citing a World Health Organization (WHO) report, states that 120 million women are circumcised each year, which is about half of the figure stated in the *Economist*. Now, if we take the two figures just quoted—annual rates of circumcision of either 200 million or 120 million—and compare them to the total number of women on the African continent of approximately 350 million, we see that Africa is going to run out of women to excise! In fact the World Health Organization figure is a world figure, but is used in such a way by the writer that it appears to be the African rate of excision. Moreover, the WHO report actually states that there are an estimated total of 85 to 115 million women in Africa who have been circumcised; this is clearly not a yearly rate of excision. The report also states that the numbers are not definitive "because there have been few scientific surveys."[22] As Melissa Parker cautions, "anthropological understanding of female circumcision will remain partial until data is collected and analyzed in more authentic ways. Emotional bias of Western research teams creeps into their selection of data and interpretations."[23]

As is well known, images of the "other" are projections from the "self" and do not represent reality.[24] Focusing on genital mutilation enables the West to view itself in a positive light, just as Keith Richburg's obsession with all that is wrong with Africa enables him to view U.S. culture favorably and to be thankful that slavery brought his ancestors to the New World.[25] Like the deviant subjectivities in horror cinema opposite which the normal, the healthy, and the pure can be known, the "barbaric" acts carried out "over there," enable those of us who are living "over here" to know that we are "civilized." This is why the representation of African women in connection with excision can be a way for us to see how the Western gaze functions to create the "otherness" that reinforces ethnocentrism.

The attempt to eradicate excision is most definitely a postcolonial phenomenon.[26] During the colonial period, for example, French administrators saw the practice as being outside of their purview and turned a blind eye to it, while the White Sisters pled *for* excision so that the little girls would be considered normal in their own environment.[27] On the British side, the issue of clitoridectomy was raised in the House of Commons in 1930. However, the committee investigating the matter "agreed that the best way to tackle the problem was through education and not by force of an enactment and that the best way was to leave the people concerned free to choose what custom was best suited to their changing conditions."[28] Before the current attention given excision in the United States, it became an issue in Europe after the end of the colonial period because postcolonial immigration created a new awareness of excision among the former British and French colonial powers. Suddenly the African "other" was no longer situated "out there" in the "Dark Continent," but located squarely in the heart of the French or British capitals. Immigrant parents tended to continue the practice, believing it was essential for their daughters' wellbeing. As a result, during the 1980s a number of European countries passed legislation making excision illegal.[29]

In France controversy over excision has been the nexus of cross-cultural clashes, given the large numbers of immigrants who have settled in major French cities.[30] Starting in October 1980 with what was called "l'Affaire Doucara" (when a father was charged with mutilating his three-month-old daughter), a number of African parents (from Mali and Senegal in particular) have been sentenced for the excision-related mutilation and in some cases the deaths of their daughters.[31] At the same time as the immigrant phenomenon was developing, in the 1970s and 1980s the French women's movement became increasingly concerned with excision.

One of the earliest to speak out against the practice was the French feminist, Benoîte Groult, whose work[32] explores the complexity of patriarchy. Containing an overview of various practices including excision, Groult's work draws parallels between African and French patriarchy to show that the subjugation of women is not specific to Africa.[33] She posits that both forms of patriarchy subjugate women for the same reason: fear of women's unbridled sexuality.[34] Following on the heels of Groult's exposé, the Senegalese sociologist, Awa Thiam, published a bombshell in Paris in 1978.[35] With a preface by Groult, Thiam's book contained a series of interviews of African women who discussed concerns ranging from polygamy and repudiation to excision. The following year the Canadian writer, Louky Bersianik, published *Pique-nique sur l'Acropole* in which patriarchal power is symbolized by clitoridectomy. The illustrated book even contains a photograph of an African child about to be excised.[36]

We can see a convergence occurring in the postcolonial world as excision travels with immigrant communities from the Third to the First World, while at the same time, women of the First World are becoming aware of the politics involved in the control of their bodies. As a result of this newfound awareness, handbooks about the female body began to be published.[37] Such guides to the female body were needed because, as Simone de Beauvoir suggests, "the feminine sex organ is mysterious even to the woman herself. . . . Woman does not recognize herself in it and this explains in large part why she does not recognize its desires as hers."[38] The convergence in the West between awareness of excision and the reappropriation by women of their bodies explains, to some degree, works by Francophone

writers such as Groult, Thiam, and Bersianik. At the same time, women artists in the United States were exploring the representation of the female
genitalia, not only as art forms or incarnations of sexual or generative prop-
erties, but as political or social symbols. In an article on "Vaginal Iconology"
Barbara Rose notes that

> this category of women's art is profoundly radical in that it attacks the basis of
> male supremacy from the point of view of depth psychology. . . . At issue in
> vaginal iconology is an overt assault on the Freudian doctrine of penis envy. . . .
> The self-examination movement among women that strives at familiarizing
> women with their own sex organs and images in art of non-menacing and
> obviously complete vaginas are linked in their efforts to convince women that
> they are not missing anything. . . . [Such art] is in effect, propaganda for sexual
> equality.[39]

Perhaps the best-known work of art in this category is Judy Chicago's
1979 painting, *The Dinner Party*, which has thirteen place settings as in the
all-male *Last Supper*, but here each place setting represents a famous woman
and consists of a plate containing female genitalia.[40] Chicago herself has
said that "the woman artist . . . takes that very mark of her otherness . . .
and . . . establishes a vehicle by which to state the truth and beauty of her
identity."[41]

Against the background of a women's movement that reappropriates
the body through making a crucial link between female genitalia, pleasure,
and identity, one is not surprised that when the issue of excision reached
American shores it would have a very peculiar resonance for feminists who
"relentlessly scrutinized the historical and global oppression of women."[42]
The mutilated genitalia of African women hearkened back to the darkest
days of patriarchy, before self-discovery and self-appropriation ushered in
the sexual revolution in the United States. Shere Hite in her investigation
of female sexuality in North America reveals that "there is a social pressure
[in North America] that says a woman who has an orgasm is more of a
woman, a 'real' woman."[43] Not only did excision suggest that its victims were
not "real" women, it also generated fears of castration among men: only a
"real" man knows how to satisfy a woman sexually. As Parker points out,
"the chances of a man sexually satisfying a circumcised woman (that is,
enabling her to become a "real" woman) are much diminished.[44]

Seen through a Western paradigm where femininity and masculinity are
no longer tied so closely to reproduction, it comes as no surprise then that
Alice Walker should want genital wholeness for her African sisters.[45] Thus
the film purports to show—via dance—"the inner turmoil and devastation
associated with the loss of sexual pleasure."[46] If only the slow shuffle of the
downtrodden African girls we are shown in *Warrior Marks* and the Olinka
women Walker describes in *Possessing the Secret of Joy* could be replaced by
the confident stride of the liberated African-American woman! Like Celie,[47]

they would then experience what Marjorie Pryse describes as "life, liberty and the pursuit of happiness by finding again the 'ancient power' of great-great-great-grandmother Walker."[48] Because the right to sexual pleasure was part of self-appropriation in the women's movement in the United States, it is assumed that a return to primordial female power through the eradication of genital mutilation provides a solution to Africa's problems.[49]

With excision, Walker's viewers are given a key to understanding Africa: it is suggested that excision is the only tool we need for understanding poverty, underdevelopment, postcolonial tyrants, neocolonial dependency, disease, and so on. Remove excision—it is suggested—and Africa will catch up to the rest of the world. While it may well be true that women are central to the development of Africa and that the end of excision is concomitant with modernization, this Western gaze is blind to the fact that within some traditional African worldviews, genital wholeness is abhorrent and femininity is dissociated from sexual pleasure. Those who see excision from this perspective suggest that it is an "assertive and symbolic act, controlled by women, which emphasizes the essence of femininity: morally appropriate fertility, the potential to reproduce the lineage or to found a lineage section."[50] This is a voice that one does not hear in *Warrior Marks* or *Women with Open Eyes*.[51] The question to be underlined here is who enables whom to speak about excision?

While Walker has long insisted on the necessity for African American women to engage in self-definition as a way of validating Black women's power as human subjects, this power is not always granted to the African women in *Warrior Marks*.[52] As a result, characterized by the slow shuffle of the mutilated female object, they stand in stark contrast to the powerful, striding, speaking subject incarnated by Alice Walker. Walker's "deliberate effort to stand with mutilated women"[53] is laudable; at times however, it is reminiscent of the stance taken by nineteenth century missionaries. The religious convictions that once propelled African American missionaries to "elevate African womanhood" for Christ, have been replaced by a blinding conviction that genital wholeness will improve African womanhood.[54]

Anne Laure Folly's film also uses a documentary approach and interviews the same types of women we see in *Warrior Marks*. Like Walker, Folly focuses on three categories of women—the activists, the excisers, and women who are victims of tradition. They are interviewed in French, sometimes in Bambara or Wolof, and in the case of Walker's film, in English. However, the impact of Folly's film is quite different because the process of self-definition is never denied African women themselves. Moreover Folly's film was intended for African audiences and, according to film notes from California Newsreel, has apparently screened to enthusiastic female audiences across West Africa, helping to reinforce women's demands for a place at the center of the development process.[55] How then does *Warrior Marks*, despite the filmmaker's best intentions, silence the women we see on the screen?

Walker's film uses narrative and visual strategies that effectively act to muffle these women's voices. While they start out as speaking subjects in the various interviews that make up the film, the women are continually interrupted either by Walker's voice-over, shots of Walker herself, or by sequences of an African American dancer. In the film, African women are silenced. As a result, the women end up playing the role of the "native informant." We see them just long enough to be convinced of the seriousness of the problem that Walker is bringing to the fore.[56] The implicit message is that the voices of such women do not matter, since they can be replaced by that of Alice Walker or by images of the African American dancer.[57] In the end the film constructs images of incomplete African women in impoverished situations whose experience becomes secondary under the Western gaze.[58] Moreover, the shots of the dancer play into the commonplace clichés of Africa under the Western gaze.

Such clichés range from the "terra incognita" of antiquity and the land of nightmare[59] to the convention of terrifying, horrific, and frequently fatal native savagery present in a great number of feature films set in Africa, not to mention unbridled female sexuality.[60] Intervening when the discussion of excision by the African woman speaking becomes graphic, the camera leaves her face and focuses solely on the dancer. All discussion is brought to an end by filling the screen with the towering female body of an exquisitely beautiful African American woman. Her writhing movements may be variously interpreted: from the erotic, to the suggestion of boundless pain and fear.[61] Such use of movement and sound suggests that there are things capable of creating such immense terror in Africa that they are unspeakable, that they lie beyond the limits of language. Thus, the viewer is left to fill in the blanks, as it were, with her own imagination, rather than keeping open eyes.[62]

Two sequences from *Warrior Marks* are typical of how the Western gaze intrudes and silences. The first (1218–1263) illustrates how Alice Walker's voice occupies the soundtrack as she describes the childhood mutilation of her eye by her older brother, while we see little girls—presumably candidates for excision—who are silent, followed by a full-frontal shot that focuses on Walker as she is interviewed by Parmar. The second sequence (1345–1389) is an interview in French of the sociologist Awa Thiam. As Thiam describes excision the camera shifts to shots of a knife held in the gnarled hand of an old exciser. Finally, this is interrupted by the dancer writhing before a gigantic blow-up of the exciser whose hand has now clearly become a gigantic claw. While their intent are opposite, such images recall those that have been central to the dehumanization of black women in their dialectical construction as a voiceless other, suggesting that the existence of a female Caliban just as necessary to the Western female Prospero. If she is monstrous as voiceless mutilator, then the Western woman can be eloquent in her self-possession.[63] This part of the film ends with Alice Walker again talking about the experience of her childhood visual mutilation as a privileged way of understanding the experience of African women, thereby becoming their spokesperson.

In Anne Laure Folly's *Femmes aux yeux ouverts/Women with Open Eyes* women are given the opportunity to define themselves; they occupy the entire visual space while their uninterrupted voices fill the soundtrack. Contrary to the women in Walker's film, Folly's women need no Western interpreters in order to be fully conscious of the issues that matter to them. In contrast to the dance imagery that makes the African women invisible in Walker's film, the women in Folly's film face controversial issues directly, as the film's title suggests. Moreover, this film produces a greater sense of balance because there is no ostensible Western gaze to produce "otherness," and because the film does not focus on a single issue, nor is it limited in terms of geography and social class: it avoids creating exotic specimens of African women. As the introductory voiceover reminds us of the multiple roles women play in Africa as mothers, teachers, farmers, traders, and organizers of social life from birth to death, we see shots of women engaged in ordinary activities of daily life. This is in sharp contrast to *Warrior Marks*, in which we never see images of women involved in normal everyday activities such as caring for their children, cooking, working, or eating.[64] In fact women have been defamiliarized because the familiar everyday life of women has been traded for ritual space of the excision rite of passage.

While the issue of female genital mutilation is present in *Women with Open Eyes*, it is embedded in a matrix of six other concerns that impinge directly on the quality of women's lives. Women from four countries—Burkina Faso, Mali, Senegal, and Republic of Benin—not only speak about these concerns, but show us the solutions they have developed. The film is divided into seven sections; each is clearly identified and deals solely with the issue under consideration. The first three sections focus on matters of personal freedom and health: excision, forced marriages, and AIDS. The last four sections deal with political and economic power. Located squarely in the middle, the powerful section on political struggle makes an eloquent case for women as key players in the change from oppressive neocolonial governments to those that are committed to democratic change. Alternating actual news footage taken of women as they joined the 1991 revolution in Mali with the interview of a participant who lost her daughter in the uprising, it becomes clear that excision is not the only threat to women in Africa. Acting as "natural feminists,"[65] women took matters into their own hands, put their lives on the line by descending into the streets, initiating the overthrow of Mali's military government and ushering in significant democratic reforms.[66]

The next two sections, titled "economic survival" and "economic power," show two extremes of the economic spectrum as it concerns women. The Senegalese women who prepare fish for drying or who tan hides are members of castes, living in virtual slavery, never enjoying the fruits of their labor. Standing in stark contrast to such exploitation, in the next section we return to Benin where we see that the largest market on the African continent, Danktopa, is run entirely by women. It is not unusual for the annual earnings of these strong, powerful, and intelligent women to run into millions of dollars.[67] With this segment, the film comes full circle, returning to Benin where it began with the section on excision, establishing a counterpoint between these two sections. The economic power of women in Benin provides a context with which to frame the issue of excision. Not that it is discounted as a serious problem, but at the same time contextualization prevents generalizations about the women of Benin that make "othering" and exoticization less likely.

The variety of powerful female images in this film provides a much fuller spectrum of African womanhood. For example, the interview with the exciser in the early part of the film clearly shows her absence of consciousness as she willingly describes her role in performing the tradition of cutting on female children, but this contrasts sharply with the eloquence and militancy of the younger women who are calling for an end to the practice. When Aïcha Tamboura of Benin, holding her baby on her lap, speaks, it is as a mother who does not want her daughter to go through the pain of excision and as a woman who understands that her culture's infringement on women's bodily integrity is wrong.

Image after image of thoughtful, assertive African women—from the community health worker demonstrating the use of condoms in a busy marketplace, to the woman who became Governor of Bamako in Mali after the revolution, to the entrepreneurs who control trade in Benin—add up to a very different view of African women from the one Alice Walker's film imparts. A comparative study of the films stresses the importance of the power dynamics underlying the very process of definition itself. In the case of Walker's film, definition resides in the voices of the Western spokespersons. Although we do see African women speaking out, the film's narrative and visual strategies conspire to silence them, reinforcing stereotypical images of African womanhood that enhance the Western other's view of herself. Anne Laure Folly puts the speaking African subject on center stage, releasing her from the grip of exoticism and from the reductionism inherent in seeing all African women through a single lens, that of excision.

Warrior Marks and *Women with Open Eyes* also enable us see how differing views of female sexuality condition the portrayal of African women.[68] Both films place women at the center of the problem of modernization that is rooted in the clash produced by the colonial encounter. On the one hand a single issue—excision—holds the key to an improved lot for African women whereas on the other, excision is placed within a matrix of interconnected issues relating to freedom in general: personal, political, and economic. In situations where all of these freedoms are not accessible to women, freedom from excision is nothing more than a partial victory. As a matter of fact, the economic insecurity currently rampant on the African continent is fueling excision. As Calixthe Beyala reports, unscrupulous *marabouts* and healers use excision to guarantee their clients' eligibility for marriage and concomitant economic security.[69] Walker's analysis is based on the assumption that certain universal values hold true in Africa; Folly's approach shows us that such values are not universal, but that they are indeed making progress precisely because African women themselves are working hard to create their own bridge between tradition and modernity.

NOTES

1. Dunn 1996, 150.
2. Lionnet 1995, 129.
3. Sissoko 1990.
4. Parmar 1993.
5. Folly 1994.
6. Folly's documentary, *Les Oubliées*, was shown at FESTPACO in January 1997. Previous films include *Le Gardien des forces* (1991); *Femmes du Niger* (1992), a twenty-six-minute video discusses problems of polygamy in an Islamic nation: men vote by proxy for their wives and daughters; women who speak out are physically harmed; women work together to gain equal rights; *Les Femmes africaines face à la démocratie* (1993); and *Femmes aux yeux ouverts* (1994), a fifty-two-minute video that shows a panorama of African women and the issues they face—clitoridectomy, precocious and polygamous marriages, AIDS, absence of democracy, and health and economic problems.
7. For a discussion of the various responses to Walker's film, see Cheryl Johnson-Odim (1996). The seven-city U.S. tour of the film with its producer and director raised funds for such groups as the Women's Foundation, the Bay Area Black Women's Health Project, and the Women's Funding Alliance in Seattle (Walker and Parmar 1993, xx).
8. The need to redeem Africa has a long history in the United States. In her study of African American women missionaries in Africa, Suzan Jacobs (1987) states that American blacks endorsed the perception of Africa as a "dark" continent, "believing that the exposure of Africa to Western religious and cultural influences would make the continent acceptable to the world, seeing the 'redemption' of Africa as their 'special duty'" (121).
9. Mudimbe 1988, 44.
10. As Eliott Butler-Evans (1989) points out, this stands in contrast to Walker's womanist stance in *The Color Purple*. The experiences of Celie and the African women Nettie describes in her letters emphasize the universal oppression of black women (170–171).
11. See Foucault 1990, 11. According to Foucault, a distinguishing characteristic of the West is its proliferating discourses on sex: "and these discourses on sex did not multiply apart from or against power, but in the very space and as the means of its exercise" (32).
12. FGM became the object of a legislative initiative by Representative Pat Schroeder, and was followed by the precedent-setting decision by the U.S. Immigration and Naturalization Service to grant asylum to Fauziya Kasinga, who feared being forcibly subjected to female genital mutilation in her home country, Togo. USAID has subsequently created a working group on FGM.

13. See *New York Times* 1997b; French 1997a; *New York Times* 1997a; French 1997b; Dugger 1996; McKinley 1996; Katz and Christian 1997; Hetcht 1996; Gauch 1996; Ragab 1994.

14. The evolution of the vocabulary is interesting and instructive in itself since it marks a definite change from "female circumcision," which was first used in the 1920s, to the graphic precision of the term "genital cutting," used in McKinley (1996). Rosenthal (1993) notes that the *Washington Post*'s William Raspberry "dared risk the charges of bias by referring to the practice as 'mutilation' rather than the more benign [term] circumcision" (Ragab 1994, 11).

15. Marie-José Ragab states that the "Orificial Surgical Society" (forerunner of today's association of obstetricians and gynecologists) recommended excision for curing everything from masturbation to measles (Ragab 1994, 6). In a 1992 letter to Parmar, Walker states that the West has its equivalent of genital mutilation ("spread over the entire body") and that she wanted to include this in the film "because otherwise there will be a tendency for Westerners to assume that genital mutilation is more foolish and 'barbaric' than the stuff they do" (Walker and Parmar 1993). Françoise Lionnet, quoting Michel Erlich, points out that while abortion is legal and acceptable to a majority in the West it is shocking to Africans, "a major mutilation . . . which is still considered a crime by many and judged as such in those cultures that practice mutilations" (1995, 160).

16. Zongo 1996, 179.

17. See Foucault 1990, 107. It is interesting to note that USAID's recent involvement in eradicating FGM relates to the aid agency's main goals: "stabilizing global population and protecting human health; and building democracy."

18. Amin 1989, 108.

19. See Foucault 1990, 146. In describing the paradigmatic shift from a society that values blood to one that values sex, Foucault states, "Where power spoke through blood: the honor of war, the fear of executioners, and tortures; blood was a *reality with a symbolic function*. We, on the other hand, are in a society of 'sex' or rather a society 'with a sexuality': the mechanisms of power are addressed to the body, to life, to what causes it to proliferate."

20. *Economist* 1996.

21. Gauch 1996.

22. McKinley 1996.

23. Parker 1995, 506.

24. As Pieterse (1992) notes, "Ideology of *alter* involves an ideology of *ego*. Representations of otherness are therefore also indirectly representations of the self" (232).

25. See Richburg 1995. Richburg left Africa feeling not at all "African," and "quietly celebrating the passage of my ancestor who made it out [as a slave]" (quoted in Press 1997, 12).

26. While the fate of African women was also the concern of missionaries in French West Africa, controversy over excision does not seem to have occurred, largely because missionary activity was most intense in non-Islamic territories. Missionaries worked for women's rights. For instance, in Cameroon they created training centers for monogamy; in Senegal, the Sisters of St. Joseph of Cluny opened schools for women in St. Louis and Dakar; Soeur Marie André, a French missionary, used her legal training to draft legislation for the protection of African women that was passed by the French National Assembly in 1939 and 1951.

27. Coquery-Vidrovitch 1997, 209.

28. See Kenyatta 1965, 126. Kenyatta gives an anthropological description of the customs of his own ethnic group, the Kikuyu of Kenya. The book contains one of the first accounts of the excision controversy that pitted the Church of Scotland

Mission against the Kikuyu people in the 1920s in the British colony of Kenya. In an attempt to break down the custom, admission to missionary schools was based on a pledge to not observe the custom. Although the push to obtain missionary education was very strong, such missionary interference with traditional customs was far from successful, and even resulted in the creation of Kikuyu independent schools where access to education and the renouncing of excision were not linked.

29. Sugier 1984, 95–98.

30. One of the earliest French colonial references to the practice can be found in Moreau de St. Méry's 1797 work (vol. 1, 52), where the author stated that it was extant among female slaves from the Arada group (from the city of Alada in Dahomey).

31. See Sugier 1984, 68–70. In her discussion of excision in France, Françoise Lionnet points to the clash between Western and African concepts that define the nature of the human being, making excision an "ideal test case, since it . . . illustrates absolute and total cultural conflict between the rights of the individual to bodily integrity and the individual's need to be satisfactorily integrated into a community" (1995, 159). See the chapter in this book titled "Women's Rights, Bodies, and Identities: The Limits of Universalism and the Legal Debate around Excision in France" for a full discussion of the clash between the French legal system (based on Enlightenment values) and African cultural practices.

32. Groult 1975.

33. According to Groult, "*Je trouve même que l'analogie est terrible entre les propos des exciseurs, muphtis et autres sorciers et les phrases prononcées par certains de nos élus que nous avons continué à élire, hélas!*" (106).

34. From the European perspective, this fear is based on Christian notions of morality and proper conduct. In the African context, it is related to the fact that such women run the risk of not fulfilling their primary role of reproduction of the lineage.

35. Thiam 1978.

36. The latest in this ongoing debate was penned by Calixthe Beyala in 1995: *Lettre d'une Africaine à ses soeurs occidentales.* Having just barely escaped excision at age six, Beyala states that despite the "errors of feminism" (78) against Africa, the eradication of excision must be a priority. She goes on to say that the "most dangerous" positions are those that "intellectualize the oppression and mutilation of women on the basis of tradition" (88).

37. For example, Boston Women's Health Book Collective 1998.

38. See de Beauvoir 1952. As Germaine Greer says, if the vagina had been relatively invisible in the expression of culture, for many women it had also been literally unseen (quoted in Ardener 1987, 124).

39. Ardener 1987, 130.

40. Ardener 1987, 131.

41. Ardener 1987, 133.

42. Walker and Parmar 1993, xiv.

43. Hite 1976, 131.

44. Parker 1995, 519.

45. Included in the appendix of Walker and Parmar (1993) is a passage from *The Hite Report* arguing that the "clitoral system" is the equivalent to the male penile system: "women's sex organs, thought internal and not as easily visible as men's, expand during arousal to approximately the same volume as an erect penis" (Walker and Parmar, 365).

46. Walker and Parmar 1993, 222.

47. See Walker 1982.

48. Pryse and Spillers 1985, 20.

49. In July 1996, the practice was outlawed in Egypt and doctors were prohibited from performing the operation. But the following year, June 1997, the prohibition was lifted after the death of five girls within the one year of prohibition. As was the case with the prohibition of abortion in Europe and the United States, the practice continued under unsanitary conditions, putting women's lives at even greater risk (Gauch 1996, 7).

50. Parker 1995, 517.

51. The recent excision of 600 girls and women in Sierra Leone at the Grafton Displaced Persons' Camp was seen by the participants as a way of celebrating the end of war and their imminent return home. Sponsored by the Bondo, an exclusive female "secret society" which draws Sierra Leonean women from across all ethnic and religious lines, the practices "persist because they are a rare female preserve in a society otherwise heavily dominated by men" (French 1997b, A4). According to gynecologist Dr. Olayinka Kosso-Thomas, a leading campaigner against genital cutting, "it is just about the only time they can drink and dance, let their hair down and enjoy a bit of freedom"(French 1997b, A4).

52. See Collins 1991, 38–39. This objectification accounts for what Stephen A. Zacks identifies as the reason *Warrior Marks* is seen as "offensive and paternalistic toward Africans . . . despite its . . . clearly committed anti-oppression pan-Africanist political positions" (1995, 9).

53. Walker and Parmar 1993, 13.

54. The first unmarried black woman missionary from the United States to work in Africa, Nancy Jones, stated in 1888: "He [the Lord] directs my mind and heart to Africa, the land of my Forefathers. To those who are living in darkness and sin. To those who are calling to their sons and daughters to come and help them" (Jacobs 1987, 124).

55. See California Newsreel 1995, 6. In her introduction to *Warrior Marks*, Walker says her film was shown to women's groups in Africa (xv).

56. For a discussion of the problematic of the "native informant" role usually reserved for Africans (academics, feminists, the uneducated, etc.) by researchers from the North, see Abbenyi 1997, 145–147.

57. Parmar states that the dancer was used as a way of "celebrating the sensuality of women's bodies, as well as to express the inner turmoil and devastation associated with the loss of sexual pleasure" (Walker and Parmar 1993, 222). She goes on to say that "this film is about bodies and body language, a celebration of women's bodies despite their mutilation" (Walker and Parmar 1993, 225).

58. This "silencing" occurs even in interviews of women who are leaders in the fight against excision, such as the Senegalese gynecologist, Dr. Kouyate, and Awa Thiam of the Commission pour l'Abolition des Mutilations Sexuelles. Both interviews are interrupted by shots of the African American dancer.

59. See Conrad 2000.

60. Dunn 1996, 154.

61. I wish to thank Judith Miller for pointing out the erotic possibilities of the dance. It is interesting to note Walker's reaction to a dance performed for her in Dakar during a meeting of a woman's association: "The dance the women did for us was erotic to the extreme. Several women danced, sticking out their tongues and with their eyes rolled back, presumably in ecstasy. So curious to see in a mutilating culture" (Walker and Parmar 1993, 73).

62. The African location of several of sequences emphasizes poverty, lack of hygiene (dirty fingernails, buzzing flies), suggesting a narrative that is concerned with issues of primitivism versus civilization. The interviews conducted in the United States or London reinforce the idea of Africa as dangerous and unsafe, suggesting that the only "safe" place from which one can speak is Alice Walker's living

room, or some other similar space in the West. This is also evident in the journal to the film where other women either "lack a strong sense of self," or are dangerous: "there will occasionally be an extremely loud, brash woman, like the one who pressed us to buy her wares with such vigor that she ran us out her stall. These are the women whose pent-up anger seems to be a powder keg" (Walker and Parmar 1993, 53–54).

63. Melissa Parker (1995) cautions: "The tendency to exaggerate, twist and distort, however unconsciously, may also be linked with the researcher perceiving female circumcision as an attack on their own complex associations between sexuality, femininity and reproduction. Whatever the reasons, judgment is often impaired" (521).

64. Abbenyi (1997) cautions that "academic feminist discourses have, on the whole, failed to identify grassroots feminists as custodians of ways of knowing, of knowledge that academics do not possess" (5).

65. This term is inspired by the expression "natural democrats," which the Cameroonian feminist scholar, Nalova Lyonga, coined to designate the political action of ordinary African women. It is also inspired by the work of Juliana Abbenyi, also a Cameroonian feminist scholar, who pleads for a space in Western feminist discourse for persons like her mother who are "illiterate, African, grass-roots feminists" (Abbenyi 1997, 10).

66. In 1991, when Malian women and students took to the streets to drive out the dictator Moussa Traoré, they were joined by the men. Today great strides have been made by women: Two women are ministers in Alpha Oumar Konaré's government (Coquery-Vidrovitch 1997, 182) and in the April 1997 elections, fifteen women contested parliamentary seats (Engels 1997, 2). In *Warrior Marks*, although Walker recounts her visit to the grave of the Thomas Sankara, the Burkinabé President who opposed excision and was assassinated in 1987, she does not seem to be aware of the political gains made by women under Konaré.

67. The "Nana Benz" of Lomé, named for the Mercedes-Benz they own, began to take over the cloth business in the 1930s (Coquery-Vidrovitch 1997, 100).

68. Pertinent to this discussion is Françoise Lionnet's study of Nawal El Saadawi's novel, *Woman at Point Zero*. In addition to examining questions related to cultural relativism and the conflict between Western abolitionists and African traditionalists, Lionnet explores the ways in which El Saadawi's novel touches upon "the possibility of resistance to hegemonic pressures and to the cultural master narrative" (Lionnet 1995, 141).

69. Beyala 1995, 82–83.

WORKS CITED

Abbenyi, Juliana. 1997. "Bridging North and South: Notes towards True Dialogue and Transformation." *Canadian Woman Studies* 17 (2): 145–148.

Amin, Samir. *Eurocentrism*. 1989. New York: Monthly Review Press.

Ardener, Shirley. 1987. "A Note on Gender Iconography: The Vagina." In *Construction of Sexuality*, ed. Patricia Caplan, 113–142. New York: Travistock Publications.

Beauvoir, Simone de. 1952. *The Second Sex*. Trans. H. M. Parshley. New York: Knopf.

Bersianik, Louky. 1979. *Le Pique-nique sur l'Acropole*. Montreal: L'Hexagone.

Beyala, Calixthe. 1995. *Lettre d'une Africaine à ses soeurs occidentales*. Paris: Spengler.

Boston Women's Health Book Collective. 1998. *Our Bodies Ourselves*. New York: Simon & Schuster.

Butler-Evans, Elliott. 1989. *Race, Gender and Desire*. Philadelphia: Temple University Press.

California Newsreel. 1995. *Library of African Cinema 1995–96*. San Francisco, CA: California Newsreel.

Collins, Patricia Hill. 1991. "Learning from the Outsider Within: The Sociological Significance of Black Feminist Thought." In *Beyond Methodology*, ed. Mary Maragaret Fonow and Judith A. Cook, 34–59. Bloomington, IN: Indiana University Press.

Conrad, Joseph. 2000. *Heart of Darkness*, ed. Nicolas Tredell. New York: Columbia University Press.

Coquery-Vidrovitch, Catherine. 1997. *African Women: A Modern History*. Boulder, CO: Westview Press.

Dugger, Celia W. 1996. "Tug of Taboos: African Genital Rite vs. U.S. Law (Cover Story)" *New York Times*, December 28, 1.

Dunn, Kevin. 1996. "Lights . . . Camera . . . Africa: Images of Africa and Africans in Western Popular Films of the 1930's." *African Studies Review* 39 (1): 149–176.

Economist. 1996. "Men's Traditional Culture (Women Campaign against Female Circumcision in Africa)." *Economist*, August 10, 34

Engels, John. 1997. "President Konaré Seeks to Build Consensus in Mali." *African Voices* 2:2.

Folly, Anne Laure, director. 1994. *Femme aux yeux ouverts/Women with Open Eyes* [videorecording]. Amanou Production. San Francisco, CA: California Newsreel.

Foucault, Michel. 1990. *The History of Sexuality*. New York: Vintage Books.

French, Howard W. 1997a. "Africa's Culture War: Old Customs, New Values." *New York Times*, February 2, Sec. 4, 1

———. 1997b. "The Ritual: Disfiguring, Hurtful, Wildly Festive." *New York Times*, January 31, A4.

Gauch, Sarah. 1996. "In Egypt, Movement to Ban Ancient Practice Expands." *Christian Science Monitor*, December 19, 7.

Groult, Benoîte. 1975. *Ainsi soit-elle*. Paris: Grasset.

Hetcht, David. 1996. "How A Woman's Fakery Helps Save Thousands." *Christian Science Monitor*, December 19, 7.

Hite, Shere. 1976. *The Hite Report: A Nationwide Study on Female Sexuality*. New York: Macmillan.

Jacobs, Suzan. 1987. "Afro-American Women Missionnaires Confront the African Way of Life." In *Women in Africa and the Diaspora*, ed. Rosalyn Terborg-Penn and Andrea Benton Rushing, 121–132. Washington, DC: Howard University Press.

Johnson-Odim, Cheryl. 1996. "Mirror Images and Shared Standpoints: Black Women in Africa and in the African Diaspora." *Issue* 24 (2): 18–22.

Katz, Nancie, and L. Christian. 1997. "Groups Blast US Treatment of Illegal Immigrants." *Christian Science Monitor*, April 10, 6.

Kenyatta, Jomo. 1965. *Facing Mount Kenya*. New York: Viking Press.

Lionnet, Françoise. 1995. *Postcolonial Representations*. Ithaca, NY: Cornell University Press.

McKinley, James C., Jr. 1996. "At a Ceremony in Kenya, a Harsh Rite of Passage for a Brother and a Sister." *New York Times*, October 5, 6.

Mudimbe, V. Y. 1988. *The Invention of Africa*. Bloomington, IN: Indiana University Press.

New York Times. 1997a. "Sierra Leone Women's Group Mutilates 600 Girls." *New York Times*, January 13, A6.

———. 1997b. "U.N. Officials Appeal on Genital Mutilation." *New York Times*, April 10, A6.

Parker, Melissa. 1995. "Rethinking Female Circumcision." *Africa* 65 (4): 504–521.

Parmar, Pratibha, producer/director. 1993. *Warrior Marks* [videorecording]. A Hauer Rawlence Production. New York: Women Make Movies (distributor).

Pieterse, Jan Nederveen. 1992. *White on Black: Images of Africa and Blacks in Western Popular Culture.* New Haven, CT: Yale University Press.

Press, Robert. 1997. "Black Author Turns a Jaded Eye on Africa." *Christian Science Monitor,* April 8, 12.

Pryse, Marjorie, and Hortense J. Spillers, eds. 1985. *Conjuring: Black Women, Fiction and Literary Tradition.* Bloomington, IN: Indiana University Press.

Ragab, Marie-José. 1994. "Genital Mutilation: The Case for International Duplicity." *NOW Times* (Special issue on Female Circumcision) 27:6–12.

Raspberry, William. 1993. "Women and a Brutal 'Tradition.'" *Washington Post,* November 8, A21.

Richburg, Keith. 1995. "A Black American in Africa." *The Washington Post National Weekly Review,* April 1–16, 6–8.

Rosenthal, A. M. 1993. "Female Genital Torture (Ending the World's Most Prevalent Human Rights Violation)." *New York Times,* November 12, PA15.

St. Méry, Moreau de. 1797. *Description topographique, physique, civile, politique et historique de la partie française de l'isle Saint-Domingue.* Paris: Dupont.

Sissoko, Oumar Cheick, director/producer. 1990. *Finzan: A Dance for the Heroes* [videorecording]. Kora Films Production. San Francisco, CA: California Newsreel.

Sugier, Annie, ed. 1984. *Les Mutilations du sexe des femmes aujourd'hui en France.* Paris: Editions Tierce.

Thiam, Awa. 1978. *La Parole aux négresses.* Paris: Denoël-Gonthier.

Walker, Alice. 1982. *The Color Purple.* New York: Simon & Schuster.

———. 1992. *Possessing the Secret of Joy.* New York: Harcourt Brace Jovanovich.

Walker, Alice, and Pratibha Parmar. 1993. *Warrior Marks: Female Genital Mutilation and the Sexual Blinding of Women.* New York: Harcourt Brace.

Zacks, Stephen A. 1995. "Theoretical Construction of African Cinema." *Research in African Literatures* 26 (3): 6–17.

Zongo, Opportune. 1996. "Rethinking African Literary Criticism: Obioma Nnaemeka." *Research in African Literatures* 27 (2): 178–184.

PART V

Transnational Feminist Contentions: Sisterhood and Coalition Politics Revisited

The Anti-Female Circumcision Campaign Deficit

L. Amede Obiora

In many parts of the world, political ideas and positions identified with feminism routinely arouse resistance, even outrage. Some of such reactions derive from the long history of gender moralizing in the discourses of Western colonial expansion. In nineteenth-century British debates around numerous gendered practices in colonized regions, the agenda of rescuing nonwhite women from the barbarity of the culture into which they had the misfortune of being born played an important role in justifying the imperial project. So enduring and influential have been Western modernization-as-redemption narratives that the advocacy even by local, non-Western women of reforms identified as feminist is frequently perceived as pandering to outside pressures and as a betrayal of local cultural norms of gender relations. Such reactions raise a number of pressing questions, including what feminism is—whether it is necessarily a purely Western entity—and the question of the "authenticity" of the local, that is, of what constitutes an outside versus an inside influence. If we seek to avoid essentialized views either of feminism or of local culture, then even the most modest attempt to look for the possibility of common ground for discussion reveals a profound misrecognition.

With particular reference to Alice Walker's critically acclaimed novel, *Possessing the Secret of Joy*,[1] this chapter calls into question the authenticity and validity of the barrage of literature that informs Western feminist protestations against the practice of female circumcision in Africa. Pointing up the shortcomings of the critiques is not intended to discount their underlying vision and purpose, however, for that would be tantamount to throwing out the baby with the bath water. The first section of this chapter outlines certain aspects of the epistemology and praxis of Western feminism that help to frame the problem under review. The second section draws upon

Walker's works to foreground the drawbacks in the campaign against female circumcision. The final part of the chapter focuses on efforts that are reorienting the campaign in ways that showcase women's critical role as forceful agents of change.

BACKGROUND

To the credit of feminist criticism, the world has become more sensitized to the problems that are of particular concern to women. Prior to the inception of concerted feminist activities, these problems were marginalized and often occluded due to the sheer force of the standpoint of men. With a view to remedy this anomaly, feminist theory and practice gives centrality to the experiences, consciousness, and perspectives of women. Feminism emerged in opposition to patronizing and paternalistic politics predicated on phallocentric misconceptions of women's "nature" and "best interests."[2] The feminist critique seeks to redeem women's voices and realities from the eclipsing of male-controlled social discourses and institutions.[3] Insisting that no one community of norms should trump the variegated values and standards of human experience, feminists argue that the white male ideal marginalizes, disempowers, and renders the "other" invisible.[4] Rather than predispose women to uncritically adopt male standards, feminism validates the significance, strengths, values, and positive functions of women's experiences and perceptions. Because it grows out of direct experience and consciousness, feminism emphasizes context and the importance of identifying experience and claiming it for one's own.[5] As a mode of analysis, feminism rejects elitism and vanguardism, its core insights evince the understanding that people are imbued with transformative capacities best suited to champion their own revolution.[6]

Nevertheless, feminism manifests a tendency that betrays the partiality of its makers and is prone to entertain a party line that muzzles voices that do not echo mainstream sentiments. Feminist inquiry's once-inspirational evocation to liberate a balanced reality risks deteriorating into the suppression of difference and ends up reenacting the self-same evil that it confronts in patriarchy.[7] Owing to their attraction to essentializing categories, their unconscious attachment to stereotypes, and their participation in a culture in which power is enforced by dominance over definitions and truth claims, some feminists renege on the principal insights that animate their initiatives—insights about the problems of unstated reference points and about how privileging a particular experience mystifies difference and situatedness.[8] Although challenging patriarchal paradigms of power and knowledge has constituted a key item on the feminist agenda, the actions of these feminists compromise the raison d'être of feminism when, in its name, they betray the ground-level realities of women and resurrect processes that pawn the actual interests of women under the guise of protecting them. To the extent that they recuperate or retreat into some kind of accommodation of transgressions which they ordinarily identify as being endemic to patriarchy, these feminists bring home the paradox that no politics remains innocent of that which it contests.[9]

Several women of color have proffered correctives to mainstream feminist structuration of power relations in terms of a unilateral and undifferentiated source (read as male) and a cumulative reaction to power (read as female). Contrary to original conceptualizations of gender differences as fixed and essential, there is an increasing acknowledgment of gender as a multifaceted and dynamic social phenomenon that is constituted by and constituting of the experiences of race, class, culture, and other attributes of subjective identity. While as a strategy and/or rhetoric for political mobilization, it may be expedient to minimize the divergence of these experiences, the experiences cannot be virtually subsumed and obliterated in the grand scheme. In many instances, the commonalities of women from different backgrounds are discernible only in so far as they are defined in relation to men. Once this preliminary comparison is accomplished, the commonalities are assuaged and the complex heterogeneity of their objective realities becomes obvious.[10]

Audre Lorde poignantly captures the gravamen of the issue in one of her writings. Alluding to the disparate distribution of the benefits and burdens of patriarchy, Lorde explains that to imply that all women suffer the same oppression simply because they are women, "is to lose sight of the many varied tools of patriarchy. It is to ignore how those tools are used by women without awareness against each other."[11] Bell hooks makes the case more bluntly by stating that the idea of a "common oppression" is a corrupt platform which disguises and mystifies the fact that women are divided by sexist attitudes, racism, class privilege, and a host of other prejudices.[12] Juxtaposing the (re)presentation of Third World women as ignorant victims of barbarous sexual practices with the discursive self-representation (not necessarily material reality) of Western women as enlightened and liberated, other commentators delineate the imperialistic roles and interests of certain Western feminist elites.[13] In a similar vein, but with particular reference to scholarly definitions of African womanhood, Filomina Steady extrapolates from the "expert" undertakings and manipulation of data by some of these feminists to underscore her submission that the exploitation of Africa has not been restricted to the historical extraction of natural and human resources.[14]

Relational feminists have vigorously argued that, in comparison with men, women are more attuned to contextual specificities and averse to undue universalizations, or that they are more likely to resist the temptation to trump the practicalities of everyday life in the quest for abstract justice.[15] Notwithstanding, the record shows that this is not always the case. Some feminist activists have been known to be neither exempt from wide-eyed propagandism nor immune to purposeful paternalism.[16] It is not unusual for such feminists, armed with unverifiable dogma and exuding a desiccated passion that shares continuity with the patriarchal paradigm of power that they condemn, to arrogate to themselves prescriptive rights. Rather than exploring the means to transcend the inherent limitations of their pre-ordained prescriptions, they prefer to "preach to the choir,"[17] lend deaf ears to constructive criticisms of their insights or approaches, and thereby replicate some of the fundamental flaws of "patriarchy" in ways that render feminist ideology merely ostensible.

By virtue of fundamental feminist principles, it goes without saying that vehement opposition to any practice that is detrimental to the interest of women is valid, if there is credible evidence to establish the hazards of such a practice. Hence, where it is shown that severe forms of female circumcision jeopardize the health of girls and women, there is a prima facie case for reform. Having said this, however, it must be noted that the relative strength of the case against female circumcision is apt to be undermined by nihilistic and ethnocentric radical feminist campaigns. These campaigns are engineered by activists who often indulge in inexcusable exaggerations, denigrate other legitimate points of view, and co-opt or insist on controversial postures. Although female circumcision is a social practice with health consequences, in order to effectively portray it as indefensible, many of these campaigners are content to resort to decontextualized depictions that fail to illuminate the social dimensions of the practice. Many of the studies on circumcision that they regard as seminal fall short of the canons of feminist and scientific scholarship. They are rife with broad generalizations, poverty of analyses, dearth of evidence, and a host of other limitations that render them questionable.[18]

Female circumcision is a practice of immense diversity. Women are circumcised at different ages depending on the locality. Some women, like Tashi in Alice Walker's novel, appropriate the practice as a form of self-assertion; others may be circumcised when they are underage and unmindful of the implications of the practice. In some instances, the circumcision may involve just a symbolic piercing or the removal of the hood of the clitoral prepuce; in other instances circumcision may mean the thorough excision of the clitoris. One hardly gets a sense of these differences from reading the popular accounts about the practice. The various forms and their concomitant gradations of harm are conflated and designated "mutilation"; the entire continent of Africa, despite its complex heterogeneity, is reduced to a particular research site and the emphasis is on children, as if they were the sole subjects of the practice when, in reality, the ages of the circumcised vary from place to place.[19]

In lieu of rigorous, systematic, and substantiated analyses, many of the studies on female circumcision in Africa settle for hearsay anecdotes that are embellished with speculative and titillating editorials. Typically, the anecdotes do not only capture the worst-case scenario, they also blur various forms and motives of the practice. In the 1970s when the campaign against female circumcision was just beginning to gather momentum in the international arena, some nascent French feminist sponsors relied on the anecdotal despair of a child of no more than ten years of age as their determinative evidence.[20] The reliance on anecdotal evidence is understandable given the reticence and surreptitiousness surrounding the operation. However, this does not warrant the arbitrary manipulation and parade of spiced anecdotes as absolute fact. Moreover, generalizing from such anecdotes to the entire population of women undergoing the procedure is akin to estimating or predicting the incidence of strep in a pediatrician's office from the number of children who come in complaining of sore throat.

The shoddiness of the works on circumcision is further exemplified by *Warrior Marks*, a documentary film which drew extensively, if not exclusively, from the perspectives of selectively solicited and compensated informants and volunteers. The representativeness and reliability of information derived from a minute and arguably stage-managed sample of respondents with overt political agendas and economic interests are open to question.[21] Even Pratibha Parmar, who collaborated with Alice Walker on the project, grew exasperated and thoroughly disgruntled with the mercenary overtone of the endeavor.[22] Witness her lamentation of how she had never depended as much on the contacts and commitments of "people whose motives [she is] not always comfortable with" for her other films.[23] Notwithstanding this telling observation, Parmar proceeded to rely on the uncorroborated information of the very characters that she identified as dubious. To complicate matters, there are grounds to argue that Parmar, congruent with the saying that "[s]he who pays the piper calls the tune," predetermined the structure and outcome of the exchange, while paying lip service to the goal of fostering candid reflections about circumcision.[24]

ILLUSTRATING THE DEFICIT

The furor in the US over female circumcision, where it has taken on the prominence of a cause célèbre, is hardly surprising. There is always something or the other which American women . . . feel bound to take up on behalf of the women world-wide in much the same way as their government sees itself as the world's police.

MARILYNNE CHARLES[25]

As an African-American woman in white patriarchy, I am used to having my archetypal experience distorted and trivialized but it is terribly painful to feel it being done by a woman.

AUDRE LORDE[26]

When the axe came into the forest, the trees said the handle was one of us.

BUMPER STICKER[27]

Much has been written about the conceptual and ideological reservations that Third World women and women of color harbor against the approaches and political priorities of white, Western feminists. However, the analyses that problematize the imperialist propensities and modalities of Western feminists across the board are more pertinent for our present purposes. In this vein, Obioma Nnaemeka's conceptualization of Western feminism as a mindset which is not only racially but fundamentally geographically specific is instructive.[28] The works of Alice Walker, especially *Possessing the Secret of Joy*, lend credence to Nnaemeka's analysis.

Walker, who has been dubbed a "rebel with a cause" by *Ebony* magazine, maintains that she does not write just to tell stories, because her work is at once political and personal. *Possessing the Secret of Joy*, however, raises questions and concerns that Walker fails to address.[29] To begin with, it is difficult to reconcile her purported humanitarian promptings with the monolithic construction of female circumcision as they function in Walker's own personal and cultural context. In addition, her devoted projections of values are of questionable ecological relevance. Commenting on the literal ramifications of Walker's propagandist posturing, Max Davidson notes that unfortunately, Walker dotted her i's and crossed her t's just a little too assiduously for the good of the story.[30] Along similar lines, Carol Anshaw asserts that Walker, in service to her agenda to shock, imposes her voice on her characters and leaves little to the reader's imagination.[31] On a pragmatic level, it bears mention that being "a rebel with a cause" is no justification for countenancing a rebellion that portends a backlash that redounds exclusively on the lives of other persons.

Although Walker validates her involvement in the campaign against female circumcision on grounds of her love for her African roots, her work is peppered with contemptuous remarks about things African. Of graver concern is the fact that her situated angle of vision and unmonitored biases reinforce imperialistic impulses that reify Africa as the morally bankrupt antithesis of the West.[32] Any person with an inkling of the images of Africa in the Western media knows the continent's emphatic but perverted depiction as a jungle inhabited by human beings who are hardly distinguishable from beasts.[33] As far back as the nineteenth century, Henry Stanley postulated that Africans were the "link sought between the average modern humanity and its Darwinian progenitors, and certainly deserving of being classified as an extremely low, degraded, almost bestial type of humanity"[34] When Walker first introduces the heroine of her novel, Tashi, and her imaginary African tribe, she deliberately feeds off truncated and oppressively racist objectifications by describing her as having monkey-like hands.[35]

In one of the many reviews of the novel, Jennifer Mitton observes that its most blatant flaw is that Walker's fictional Olinkans, created to stand for Africans in general, end up unlike anyone anywhere and leave the reader with a vague and stereotyped vision of present-day Africa.[36] This view is echoed by another writer who remarked that "[a]n American of European descent, passing himself off as an expert on Europe, is not likely to make up a pan-European language and meld Germany, France, Russia, Spain and Albania into one country. But Miss Walker does not know enough to have the faintest notion of her fraudulence as an Africanist."[37] Also, in portraying Petit Pierre, a partial product of white blood, as the fountain of knowledge and paragon of virtue, while portraying the black child as an imbecile, Alice Walker resurrects the time-worn and discounted assumption that race is the principal determinant of capabilities and inherent tendencies.[38] Another interesting case in point relates to Walker's failure to explore the possible connections between Tashi's predicament and her husband's infidelity. Instead, she condones and glorifies the infidelity only to condemn polygamy.

Further—and this list is, by no means, exhaustive—in her rendition of Tashi's sister, Dura, who died prematurely at the hands of a circumciser, Walker writes that when Dura was a toddler, she had picked up a burning twig that protruded from the fire and attempted to put it into her mouth. It stuck to her lip and "she cried piteously, her arms outstretched, looking about for help. . . . The twig, ashen, finally dropped away, having burned through the skin. But did [the] mother or a co-wife leap to gather the crying child in her arms?" It stands to reason that heeding the heart-rending scream of a burnt child is a spontaneous instinctual reflex in most human societies. Anyone who sincerely appreciates the value of children in the African worldview would not dare to ask whether the child was rescued, let alone indulge in such unreal reflection.

Tashi, though an African, is entirely Eurocentric. Because her precarious entanglement in a clash of religions and cultures, she becomes predisposed to psychosocial disturbances. In fact, it appears that she resorts to the procedure of circumcision in a bid to resolve the crisis. (Dis)located in the suggestively pristine West, she is compelled to come to terms with her life primarily by probing motive and memory through introspection and analysis.[39] Unequivocal empirical documentation of the emotional security which prevails among African children seems to argue that had Tashi stayed in the confines of her native culture, she might at least have found a modicum of the affirmation and sanity which utterly eluded her in the individualism, narcissism, and racism of the West.[40]

Of particular relevance are the findings of Hanny Lightfoot-Klein who, incidentally, is one of Alice Walker's select and choicest sources. Reading Lightfoot-Klein's report of the unanimity of local psychiatrists about the unflinching support for children, one cannot escape the conclusion that Tashi's alienation from her culture was a major factor for her woebegoneness.[41] After an extensive study of female circumcision in Sudan, a perplexed Lightfoot-Klein found it most enigmatic to observe "the general aura of serenity and balance that [the Africans she encountered] far more commonly exude than a lot of Western women."[42] For all her investment in symbolism, Walker's obsession with a single angle of female circumcision renders its other manifold dimensions inscrutable.[43] Thus, suggesting that the ritual practice is a sadistic venture thoroughly enjoyed by privileged spectators, Walker declares, "it's unbearable to me to think there are little girls in Africa today being held down by their mothers and aunts, deprived of parts of bodies they don't even know they had, with papa proud as punch sitting outside."[44]

Even if the practice is susceptible to flagrant abuse, it is conceivable that such factors as the relative power of the collective of women, the belief and value systems, and the multiplexity and interdependence of relationships, serve to check the extent of the abuse. It is probably as an instrumental measure that lends itself to the expression of social values that the custom has come to gain a foothold. Insinuations of premeditated and misogynistic intent to harm, mutilate, and deliberately impair the circumcised oversimplify the issue and run the risk of thwarting change-oriented endeavors.[45] It is one thing to blame a mother for the plight of her daughter; it is another thing to probe the reason for her apparent "connivance." Less strident and less moralizing scholars who have duly considered the motivations of the average mother whose daughter is circumcised find that she is typically a loving and well-meaning woman who pursues the practice out of concern for her daughter and in sincere belief of its benefits and necessity.[46] As Boulware-Miller points out, dwelling in a vacuum on the risks involved in circumcision does not address its mitigative psychological, social, and economic benefits.[47] Even in *Warrior Marks*, a more sensitized Walker concedes that women circumcise their daughters because they want to ensure that the daughters will be considered eligible—"able to marry and at least have a roof over her head and food."[48]

Despite fleeting intimations of the courage and agency of African women, of how they "made a way out of no way," Walker goes to great length in portraying them as passive pawns of male transactions.[49] In another context in which she largely capitalized on her celebrity to bore her audience with unfounded claims,[50] Walker argues that African women are routinely followed, yelled at, and harassed on the street by men who look at their bodies as if they were meals, and how the women seem so joyless and oppressed with downcast eyes and stiff vertebrae, frequently abused by fathers, brothers, and husbands.[51] Elaborating the claims, she writes: "I can't help but connect this behavior to genital mutilation: the acceptance of domination, the lack of a strong sense of self one sees among the women here."[52] That this passage serves to illustrate the wantonness of Walker's proclivity toward generalization and selective amnesia is evident when one compares it with Pratibha Parmar's recollection that "it was the very image [of proud African women who hold themselves with a noble majesty that speak of their determination and hope that] Alice had described when she'd said she wanted to be filmed with African women celebrating their strength."[53] It is the same Alice Walker who equivocally compares the passive African woman of her imagination with the occasional "extremely loud, brash woman, like the one who pressed us to buy her wares with such vigor that she ran us out of her stall. These are the women whose pent-up anger seems to be a powder keg."[54] Thus, in the same stroke of the pen, she denigrates the assertive as well as the seemingly passive, as if with her, African women are damned if they do and damned if they don't.

In an interview, Paula Giddings anticipated the main thrust of the criticism against Alice Walker and implored her to articulate the basis for her intervention as a Westerner in the cause of African women. Walker retorted that slavery intervened and that she was speaking for her great-great-great-great-grandmother "who came to America with all this pain in her body."[55] She scoffingly proceeded to state that "when Africans get in trouble, they call on everybody and that [t]hey don't have a leg to stand on, so they better not start hopping around [her]."[56] She further pontificated that genital mutilation, as she calls it, makes her wonder about "everything [she has] been taught about African women, that they are 'hot' and 'lascivious.'"[57] In a more lucid tone, she alluded to the reality of human interdependence, but instead of developing this cogent thought, she digressed into a fantasy in which she equated her novel to a psychoanalytic healing device or a mirror which illuminates areas that are not readily observable, such as the posterior of an assessor. Finally, offering her now-too-familiar standard refrain vis-à-vis her visual mutilation and miserable childhood which sent her scurrying off to the woods for solace, she maintained that even though it is extremely difficult for women to blame their mothers, they must begin to confront their mothers' complicity in their distress.

In her remark about the African dependency syndrome, Walker introduced but forfeited a golden opportunity to situate and address the underlying power dimension of her intervention.[58] The gratuitousness of her diminutive about the lasciviousness of African women is too obvious to deserve a response. The several authorities who, as indicated earlier, document the supportive safety net provided by African familial and communitarian orientation refute Walker's correlation between her flights to the woods and her perceived plights of African children.[59] In reductively extolling blame and the "couch approach," she loses sight of the possibility, perhaps the fact, that these may well be culturally specific, not universal, paradigms of conflict resolution.[60] Perhaps some cultures are more oriented towards conciliation and understanding and less obsessed with finger-pointing. Indeed in Igbo land, one of the ways of instilling the preferred value in children is through a dramatization of the irony of finger-pointing, which gets them to realize that when finger-pointing, only the thumb and/or index finger points at the indicted; the remaining three fingers are bent toward the finger-pointer, as if beckoning her to acknowledge her complicity.

In Giddings's interview with Walker, the "how dare this American judge us,"[61] which Giddings considers the crux of the criticism against the author, is not without merits. However, this pales in light of other criticisms. The issue of the mandate for representation is quite peripheral to the issue of *mis*representation that is implicit in Walker's discernibly crass disrespect of the Africa and African women's lives. Mildly put, a person who undertakes to represent but shirks the correlative duty not to misrepresent, and disrespectfully at that, leaves much to be desired. The demonstration of respect and sensitivity will not necessarily valorize the social assets of the subjects. Respect and sensitivity are merely threshold indicators of goodwill. In other words, showing respect for the African women she has chosen to discuss will be more helpful in establishing that Walker has some noble intentions than it will be in altering the material conditions of the women. Additionally, Walker's claim to be a vindicator of her African forebear who was doubly victimized by circumcision and the transatlantic slave trade is, arguably, ahistorical. But for the assertion of Tashi's fictional psychoanalyst, who speculates that African female slaves introduced Western doctors to circumcision, there is not much real documentation of the mutilation of the genitals of slave women. Chattel slaves were purchased for breeding purposes, *inter alia*. In light of the intensity of racism in the antebellum era, coupled with slave dealers' yearnings to exculpate exotica, it is unlikely that an "anomaly" which debilitated the reproductive and productive capacities of slaves and interfered with the slave owners' investment in them would have gone down in history without comment.[62]

On a very facile level, Walker's assumptions are that the practice of female circumcision predated the slave trade, that the practice prevailed in the particular locality from which her putative forebear hailed, and that this forebear had the severe form of the operation. The fact is that data as to the date of origin of the practice is lost to the sands of time, and the issue of frequency in terms of form and geographic location remain largely unresolved and in need of further research.[63] Besides, one cannot imagine that Walker's forebear, if she was circumcised, perceived circumcision as the quintessential manifestation of patriarchal oppression most worthy of vindication, as opposed to the plethora of indignities and dehumanization of slavery.[64]

In this sense, Walker's isolation of circumcision as a cause célèbre is analogous to a legend that underscores a pivotal Igbo philosophy. Oral tradition has it that during the colonial era, the Catholic Church established a presence in the village. On one dry harmattan day, a wild fire torched and razed the mission. The resident Reverend Father, who from popular description bore a striking resemblance to Sigmund Freud, was badly burned. He died shortly thereafter. In the time of his tenure, this Father remarkably worked his way into the heart of every child in the village. These children were particularly fond of what they saw as the sage's awe-inspiring navel-length beard. When news of the devastation and death reached the children, they were dumbstruck. The one child that recollected himself looked the harbinger in the face and gasped: "Did I hear you say that Father was burnt to death? *Ewoo-o-o*, was his beard burnt too?" Obviously, the poor child was more concerned about the father's beard than about the extensive damage done to the Father that eventually took his life. The child's fixation with the reverend gentleman's beard parallels Walker's preoccupation with her great-great-grandmother disembarking on the shores of America without a clitoris.

REINING IN THE EXCESSES: AN OVERVIEW

There are many people who consider [Third World] dwellers marginal, intrinsically wicked and inferior. . . . Such a Manichean attitude is at the source of the impulse to "save" the "demon possessed" Third World, "educating it" and correcting its thinking according to the [savior's] own criteria. [The savior] can never relate to the Third World as partners, since partnership presupposes equals, no matter how different the equal parties may be. . . . Thus, "salvation" of the Third World by the [savior] can only mean its domination.

PAULO FREIRE[65]

We were admonished more than once by the African panelists to eschew the insensitivity and arrogance [of] the "Desert Storm approach.". . . [One white woman was asked what right she had to be on the panel.] She went on to explain that fourteen years ago, while wandering through Egypt, she had discovered the practice of genital mutilation and suddenly found her "purpose in life."

ERICH EICHMAN[66]

The overwhelming majority of the [people] believe that it is the secret aim of those who attack this centuries-old custom to disintegrate their social order.

JOMO KENYATTA[67]

I would advise you to tackle this problem very carefully. . . . From generation to generation, customs tend to disappear. I myself blackened my lips, but our children have categorically refused to do that, and I am convinced that the same thing will happen with circumcision.

HENRIETTE KOUYATE[68]

Female circumcision has been a standing source of conflict between the West and Africa. Ample evidence that previous attempts of abolition have not appreciably changed the situation serve as an inescapable corrective to delusive inscriptions of alien paradigms and modalities of change.[69] For historical reasons, a preponderance of Africans seem to be averse to other-defined and imposed priorities or patterns of cultural chauvinism which masquerade as a sense of moral responsibility of the enlightened to save the benighted.[70] Replete as they are with pedestrian broadsides, tensions, and contradictions, some radical Western feminist efforts against circumcision are likely to reenact mistakes of the past. These efforts do not only run the risk that their legitimacy and effectiveness will be undercut, they also run the risk of tragically erecting walls, instead of bridges, as well as the risk of burning nascent bridges.[71] Rather than locating their campaign against circumcision as part of a continuum of indigenous struggles against the practice, the stalwarts of the problematic efforts tend to arrogate to themselves patronizing prerogatives that divert attention from the reality at issue.[72]

The erasure or usurpation of African initiatives is a throwback to missionary and Eurocentric views that seek to explain events and developments only in terms of an external frame of reference.[73] A variant of this manifests itself when oppositions to circumcision are attributed to the frustration of the foreign-educated African elite. Awareness of the hazards posed by some forms of circumcision to the health of women is not peculiar to the educated elite. If the reports that pertain to circumcision have any modicum of validity, one would think that a reasonable proportion of the affected women are not oblivious of their plights.[74] Even base beasts are capable of perceiving danger. If it is true that self-preservation is a basic instinct, it arguably stands to reason that the value and utility attached to circumcision are predicated on its burdens not exceeding its benefits. Like human beings who have a limited threshold of pain, a culture cannot afford to subscribe to and sustain a practice that threatens its very existence; to do otherwise would be to create the conditions for its own extinction.

For all its discrepancies, one cannot help but concede that there are substantial merits to some aspects of the campaign against female circumcision. Where there is *well-founded* evidence that some practices are harmful, the issue ceases to be whether the custom should be challenged.[75] The issue becomes how to identify and execute the responsibilities of relevant communities for attenuating the danger of harm.[76] This concession does not do away with the corollary issues that revolve around the questions of the logistics of change. A nagging consideration concerns the role of outsiders in directing the change. This issue implicates several questions. These include: What is in the best interest of the affected population of women? Who decides what constitutes the best interest? And who decides who decides this? Is the best interest as obvious and as simple as it seems or are there latent and unintended consequences of change? Can an outsider be so arrogant and disdainful as to assume that she is omniscient or omnipotent enough to unilaterally appropriate a lead role and articulate a viable reform agenda?

The salience of these questions is compounded for the feminist community by feminist discourses that generate profound skepticism about the ability of a select constituency to "know" what is in the interest of all others.[77] A close reading of these discourses reveals the element of hypocrisy that lodges in intoning the highfalutin theory of global sisterhood without backing it up with consistent practice. For one, the feminist concept of sisterhood eschews hierarchy and implies an alliance that is actively forged—not merely theorized or assumed into existence.[78] Additionally, an understanding of the concept suggests that only a person with a vested interest in the status quo assumes that she can project, top-down, a course of action on a perceived subordinate.[79] An unscrupulous and reckless outsider may exploit pertinent power differentials and violate the realities of the lives of the women by refusing to understand these realities through the perceptual prisms of those experiencing them and by imposing her culturally mediated and specific definitions of reality on them. But whether that will take her far in resolving the matter at hand is most improbable, particularly given the peculiar nature of circumcision. Bell hooks offers a critical insight into the limitation of such action. Insisting that the structures and dynamics of domination seldom castrate so-called subordinates, hooks illuminates the potency of their agency and refusal to uncritically swallow the definition of their reality which is put forward by the dominant.[80] Indeed, even Alice Walker would not disavow the agency and resilience of women.[81] About twenty years ago, she delivered a speech at Radcliffe called "In Search of Our Mothers' Gardens," eulogizing mothers who persevere in life, in spite of the many obstacles that threaten to stifle and destroy their creativity.[82] To discount long-standing traditions of agency, power, and strength among African women may well be to stall progress and constructive dialogue.[83]

An Ewe proverb states that, "because a stranger has big eyes does not mean that she sees everything." The Chinese, on the other hand, counter that distance lends enchantment to the view. These seemingly opposed worldviews appear reconciled by Richard Wright, who points out that while an observer who is too close to a subject may suffer a blurred vision, the one who stands far away may have the benefit of detachment but run the risk of neglecting salient issues.[84] Wright's comment is not just apt for articulating the essence of a balanced perspective; it also speaks to the issues of complementarity and cooperation. In organizing for change, effectiveness is better guaranteed if the change has been diligently earmarked as necessary and is supported by the people at the grassroots level.[85] The value of change that is meant to improve their lot must be judged largely from their own point of view.[86] They are more familiar with the dynamics of and conditions for meaningful change than outside experts. As such, they are best suited to engineer and spearhead a program for change.

The relevance of this for the question of female circumcision is that there is no substitute for the involvement of the women who provide the pillar for the practice. A crucial dimension of collaborative schemes and viable strategies entails developing a rapprochement with the affected population, tapping into the indigenous perspectives about the rhythms of change, and conceding the local women the right to take the lead in identifying their needs and formulating their solutions. If female circumcision is an everyday reality or province that they control, it is inconceivable that it could be eradicated without their input. Radical approaches that covertly and overtly shun them bode ill for enduring change and reduce reformist efforts to little more than intellectual masturbation.[87]

To clarify and make the discourses and proposals for change consistent with and relevant to the ground-level realities of women in cultures that perform circumcision, the material basis of the practice of circumcision, as well as the inescapable consequences of the push for eradication, ought to be addressed. Superficial expressions of solidarity and reductive conceptualizations which are ambivalent or disinclined to address the issue in the context of the secondary allocation of resources to women's education, economic participation, health care, and so on, lose sight of the need to fashion a response that embraces the issue in its totality. The meaningful discourses of the practice by seasoned feminist scholars who situate and address female circumcision in a broader developmental context is a laudable step in the proper direction. Apropos are Achola Pala's remarks about the problems posed by misconceived research goals and processes that are insensitive to and incongruent with the structural dimensions of the very realities that they purport to address. Pala writes:

> I have visited villages where, at a time when the village women are asking for better health facilities and lower infant-mortality rates [pipe-borne water and access to agricultural credit], they are presented with questionnaires . . . on female circumcision. There is no denying that certain statistical relationships can be established between such variables, . . . [however] a statistical relationship per se, which can be exercised as an academic exercise, does not necessarily constitute relevant information or a priority from the point of view of those who are made the research subjects.[88]

The unfortunate approach that Pala speaks to is exemplified by Alice Walker. Walker reports that female circumcision is performed with rusty razors, tin-can tops, shared pieces of unwashed glass or a sharpened stone's edge. Nevertheless, and in spite of her reputation for asking big questions,[89] she neglects to engage the rudimentary questions of why such crude implements are utilized and why infection from the grotesque procedure she describes has not escalated to decimating proportions. Walker may have come to terms with the conflicting priorities of outside and indigenous campaigners when she realized that she could not show her film from village to village as planned because many had "absolutely no audio-visual facilities. Barely, sometimes, drinking water."[90] Although she repeatedly alludes to the socioeconomic realities of the women[91] she fails to explore their implications for the change she posits, and offers little if any guidance regarding the actual process of implementing change.[92] Her inability to offer a critical response to the request in the following passage betrays her lack of appreciation of the correlation between circumcision and structures of underdevelopment:

In the middle of this I was stunned to hear Madame Fall, our host, ask me to buy them a refrigerated truck. Having seen some of the splendid gardens the women have, I realize this is just exactly what they need to get their produce to market; still, I assured her that a whole refrigerated truck is a bit out of my range and the film's budget. Maybe I could contribute a couple of tires?[93]

CONCLUSION

It has become a commonplace that "globalization" is an axial principle of our time. One of the paradoxes of globalization is that even some of its most redeeming initiatives come with both radical and conservative effects. As localized communities that are disequilibrated by the so-called forces of globalization strive to maintain affirming systems of meaning and continuity, some cultivate counterpolitics of identity defined by distinctive cultural and religious categories that they deploy to renegotiate globalized spaces. Contentious international interactions act as a catalyst for militant fundamentalist appropriations of cultural traditions. In some communities, objective evidence demonstrates how far reactionaries are willing to go to manipulate culture as a mechanism for controlling the lives of women. Mindful of such tension, enterprises to promote gender rights are best maximized if indigenized and located within the logic of local worldviews.

With the intensification of global cosmopolitanism from the 1980s onward, local gender relations have increasingly been required to justify themselves in dialogue with alternative modes of being. To an increasing extent, African women are gaining recognition for their contributions; indeed, they are being recognized as protagonists of a quite different sort of narrative about Africa. Along these lines, the convergence of historical circumstances that is now reconstituting the political economy of contemporary African states presents an even greater opportunity both to mitigate gender inequities and to reconceive gender-role differences as constitutive of local social and economic formations.

To further this reconceptualization of the position of African women within both African and transnational gender politics, it is important to question representations of gender that ignore the central role of both local history and contemporary global restructuring in creating existing gender systems. One hears much of the complicated construction of personhood and the specific positions of individual men and women in African communities. One would hardly deny that women in Africa and elsewhere are subject to myriad disadvantages imposed on them by virtue of their gender. Yet what we do know does not suggest that African communities have been devoid of protective resources for women. Even where gender-related inequities are pervasive, they are not necessarily regarded as unproblematic—it is not as though individuals have an unconstrained prerogative in the local moral economy to perpetrate them.

The abundant evidence that African women have been constrained and disenfranchised by gender-biased policies and practices does not negate the fact that they have neither been mute nor invisible in the course of history. In striving to buttress its case for gender equity, international feminist scholarship has tended to flatten the specificities and meanings of women's lived experiences. One-dimensional accounts that focus solely on the evils of a putatively universal patriarchy without attending to women's agency and to everyday forms of resistance are no longer defensible even as polemics. Patriarchy is neither total nor totalizing. It could not be so. To imagine otherwise is to erase a long history of resistance by women. The representation of African women as passive victims of patriarchal structures serves to naturalize its own narrative. If women were indeed so passive, then there would be no hope for gender reform.

NOTES

1. Walker 1992.
2. Hawkesworth 1989, 537.
3. Polan 1982, 294; Cixous 1980, 90–91; Payton 1985, 629; Du Bois et al. 1985, 11; Fox-Genovese 1979; Jagger 1983; Jagger and Bordo 1989.
4. Bartlett 1990, 829, 858; Martin 1985; Cannon (undated manuscript).
5. Minow 1988, 47; Rhode 1989.
6. Hartsock 1975, 67–80.
7. Spelman 1988; Griffin 1982.
8. Minow 1988, 47; Carden 1974, 46, 75.
9. Allen 1964; Lasch 1978, 336; Rich 1979, 306; Minow 1988, 47; Spelman 1988, 36.
10. Fanon 1963, 174.
11. See Lorde 1984. Lorde is echoed by Jane Flax (quoted in Bartlett 1990, 876), who observes that without recognizing gender as a social relation, it is difficult to identify the varieties and limitations of different women's powers and oppressions.
12. Zeroing in on the racial dimension, hooks (1984, 43, 54) notes that white women who daily exercise race privilege may not have a conscious understanding of the ideology of white supremacy and the extent to which it shapes their behavior and attitudes towards women unlike themselves.
13. Mohanty 1991; Trinh 1989; Amadiume 1987; El Saadawi 1980; Patterson and Gilliam 1983, 186.
14. See Steady 1986. The politics of publication and exploitations of power that resound in Steady's critique call to mind the tale of a child who, upon reading several expeditions in which the hunter prevailed over the lion, asked the father why the hunter was always triumphant. The father answered that it will be that way until the lion learns to write.
15. See Belenky et al. 1986; Minow and Spelman 1988, 37, 53; Bartlett 1990, 849. Given the history of feminism, it is not unusual that the tendency to represent reality in exclusionary and absolute terms has traditionally been exposed and denigrated in feminist circles as the defining feature and forte of the patriarchal order.
16. These feminists renounce animating feminist insights and convey the impression that only the pool of players, not the game or its dynamics, has changed. See Spelman 1988 for a chronicle of instances of feminist assumptions of unitary, homog-

enizing and fixed standard for "women's experiences," a tendency that feminists have criticized in others. See also hooks 1984 and Harris 1991 for incisive criticisms of the broken promise of feminist method.

17. The metaphor of the choir is used here to describe an audience of moral elites who are conditioned for the spectacular and who see eye to eye with the exponent.

18. Fran P. Hosken, the author of a series, *The Hosken Report*, which prior to the debut of Walker's novel was the "bible" for the "jihad" against circumcision, has been exposed for her lack of professionalism. See also Obioma Nnaemeka, "Reporting Hosken," work-in-progress communicated to author.

19. The obfuscation is comparable to a 1993 Olympic advertisement that featured representatives of *specific* countries in the West with one African, collapsing a continent into a single a country.

20. Russell and Van de Ven 1976, 151.

21. Reliance on sources that tend to be of minimal integrity or of ulterior political motives is not peculiar to Parmar and Walker. Witness the visibility that was given the woman who, upon being hounded by the U.S. Immigration and Naturalization Services as an "illegal alien," evoked the impending danger of circumcision, whether real or imagined, as a refuge from repatriation.

22. Complaining about the haranguing of her local aide, Bilaela, in regard to when she would be remunerated for her assistance in setting up interviews and visits to the villages, Parmar writes, "Right away, I sensed that something didn't feel right about Bilaela" (Walker and Parmar 1993 162, 167). It was this same Bilaela that double-crossed and brought a New York television agent who had previously enlisted her help and remunerated her for her stand against circumcision. As reported by Parmar, "Stephanie had somehow found out that Bilaela was working with another film crew to make a film about female genital mutilation, and was . . . pressuring Bilaela not to cooperate with us. We heard Bilaela say that she had not given the American crew an exclusive and therefore felt free to work with us" (Walker and Parmar 1993, 162).

23. Parmar is scandalized by what she perceives as her contacts' capitalistic disposition, as if such a disposition were abnormal, and without pausing to ruminate on what their actions say about their realities.

24. See Walker and Parmar 1993, 96. On several occasions Parmar expressed her disgust for the practice to her paid informants. In so doing, she did a disservice to the foregrounding of African women's voices of anger, analysis, resistance, and self-determination which she claimed to be one of her fundamental guiding principles (Walker and Parmar 1993, 109).

25. Charles 1994, 1138.

26. Audre Lorde (1984) wrote this passage deploring the errors and discouraging history of white women who are unable to hear black women's words, or to maintain dialogue with them. Concluding, she notes that women-identified women cannot afford to repeat these same old destructive, wasteful errors of recognition.

27. Bumper sticker cited in Walker 1992, no folio.

28. See Obioma Nnaemeka in this volume. Like externally generated insurgencies, presumptuous feminist discourses that emanate within Africa equally underscore imperialism in so far as they negate the voice and agency of other women.

29. Tilzey 1992, 31; Joseph 1992, B1.

30. Davidson 1992, 112.

31. Anshaw 1992, C3.

32. Several contributions in this volume draw upon Walker's missionary intervention to point out the overt and subliminal racist parallels between the contemporary and colonialist discourses about Africa.

33. Stereotypic images of Africa run the gamut from that of Merry Africa to that of a dark continent of unbridled savagery. Images that inhere in the circumcision campaign are on a continuum with the latter model.

34. Stanley 1890, 374–375. Mary Kingsley concurs. She characterizes the African as being on the "border-line that separates man from anthropoid apes"(Kingsley 1897, 458).

35. Walker 1992, 3. Walker's complicity in the production and perpetuation of racist stereotypes is seen in the concern expressed by her film collaborator, Pratibha Parmar: "How can I create a sensitive and respectful representation of a people—and a continent—who have historically been grossly *misrepresented*? How can *Warrior Marks* begin to challenge the cultural imperialist imagery of Africa and Africans, as perpetuated in Hollywood films like *Out of Africa*?" (Walker and Parmar 1993, 95).

36. Mitton 1992.

37. Grenier 1992, G64. Even the *tsunga* tends toward a language of therapy shaped by contemporary Western dialogue, with its presiding metaphor of the lost inner child (Jersild 1992).

38. Darwin 1874; Curtin 1964, 29. Compare with revisionist claims that "hybrids" are not as inferior as "uncrossed negroes" (Knox 1969, 190).

39. Jersild 1992.

40. Toubia (1994, 712, 714), among others, records that the psychological implications of the practice among immigrants differ from those where the practice is prevalent. See also Poivoir 1992, 22.

41. See also Boddy 1989.

42. For the author, Africans—Sudanese to be precise—are a remarkably peaceable, mutually supportive, generous, deeply devout people, who to the Western mind, are inexplicably happy in their desperately poor, monotonously barren, harsh, and bleakly arid land (Lightfoot-Klein 1989, 149).

43. In her opinion, it has "everything to do with control with curbing women's sexuality early and keeping them docile and undemanding" (Holt 1992, 1). In another context her surprise and curiosity in seeing women in a "mutilating culture" gyrating in "exaggeratedly erotic [dances] . . . sticking out their tongues and with their eyes rolled back, presumably in ecstasy." Then one of her interviewees, "big Mary," curtly informed her that "[m]y sex life is perfectly satisfactory, thank you very much!" (Walker and Parmar 1993, 71, 44). Nevertheless, Walker did not make the connection and neglected to rethink or modify her "catch-all" claim that circumcised women were sexually deprived. The interviewee's response is affirmed by several studies discussed in Obiora 1994. See also Lightfoot-Klein 1989 for a related forceful response by an infibulated Sudanese woman. In the words of the woman, "*A body is a body*, and no circumcision can change that!" (25–26).

44. Holt 1992, 1.

45. Boulware-Miller 1985, 155. Compare with Aweria 1975. It would seem that the closer the Africa woman is to tradition, the more seriously she takes her responsibility for her children. Motherhood slavishly inclines her to make the ultimate sacrifices for them.

46. Assaad 1982, 229. These women are mischaracterized as "prisoners of ritual" for their rational choices (Lightfoot-Klein 1989).

47. Boulware-Miller (1985) states, for instance, that mothers in a bid to spare their beloved the stigma and "social ostracism" that attach to nonconformity and difference, make a superficial cut when pressured by their daughters (155). See also Slack 1988, 437. Badri (1984) found an unexpected pattern where high school students indicated that they forced their parents to have them circumcised.

48. Walker and Parmar 1993, 227. Assaad 1982 notes that the suggestion that men do not marry uncircumcised women is not adequately substantiated. Moreover, the premise for such suggestion here is refuted by Walker herself when she observes that circumcision prevails in foreign countries like Holland, Britain, and the United States, where women are not bound to marry men who favor circumcision (229). The premise is also inaccurate in so far as it holds that women in circumcising cultures are economically dependent on their husbands. Marriage is often more a necessity for sociocultural affirmation and acceptance than a financial insurance. There is no definitive correlation between circumcision and low female status (see Obiora 1994). Given the availability of historical data that suggest that European patriarchy and colonialism eroded the traditional power and autonomy of African women, the relatively low status of women in the contemporary society cannot be simply attributed to circumcision (Leacock 1981; Etienne and Leacock 1980; Boserup 1970).

49. Pondering Joan Smith's question regarding why "Alice Walker, who is so moved by Tashi's story, is unable to portray her as anything more than a dolorous puppet," (Smith 1992, 38) one is inclined to affirm the response that the contrary requires a subtlety and insight not much in evidence from a novelist who dedicates her book "With Tenderness and Respect to the Blameless Vulva" and sacrifices character and plot to the imperatives of polemic.

50. Lasch 1978, 47.

51. Walker and Parmar 1993, 53, 69.

52. Walker and Parmar 1993, 144.

53. Walker and Parmar 1993, 185.

54. Walker and Parmar 1993, 53–54.

55. Giddings 1992, 58.

56. Giddings 1992, 58

57. Giddings 1992, 58.

58. Identifying a dependency and equating it to a warranty for the denudation of the intrinsic worth of the supposedly dependent are two different things. The failure to make this distinction leads Walker to replicate the imperious negation of her research subjects' attributes of humanity.

59. Compare with Walker and Parmar 1993: "I also wondered about the role of food, particularly 'sweets,' in the African woman's life. Perhaps the overweight women one sees so frequently are still feeding 'sweets,' to the little frightened and dishonored child inside in an effort to 'reward' her for her loss and to make her forget. I suddenly remembered that my own mother, after I was shot and delirious from pain and fever, cooked an entire chicken just for me."

60. Hughes 1993; Bloom 1987.

61. Giddings 1992, 58.

62. It has been said that people who exploit fellow human beings tend to emphasize the animal rather than the human elements of their victims. Doing so sits easier on the conscience (see Ohaegbulam 1990, 4).

63. Ritual is a process; it is not static in its procedure. What remains far more constant is the symbolic and ideological content of the ritual.

64. With a spirited penchant for flippancy, Walker also quips about the chill she experienced upon the thought that "for many African women this ritual of circumcision is the only real link they have with their ancient African-Egyptian heritage" (Walker and Parmar 1993, 48).

65. Freire 1970, 213.

66. Eichman 1992, 48.

67. Kenyatta 1965, 263.

68. Walker and Parmar 1993, 330.

69. Without understanding why the practice persists in places such as Burkina Faso, Kenya, Sudan, Britain, Sweden, France, Switzerland, and Italy where it has been prohibited, legislative endeavors in other jurisdictions are prone to the same abortive fate (Obiora 1994). See also Miller 1990, 295.

70. This aversion is not just attributable to nationalism and traditionalism. It is also related to the fact that many Africans have witnessed many broken promises and false prophecies related to interventionist "savior complexes" and they are worse off for it. The aversion has fostered the development of a long-standing and pervasive tradition of resistance to imperialist insurgency that dates back to the days of the maiden encounter. That a particularly wild and domineering species of grass has been called Eliza, after Queen Elizabeth II, among the Oguta Igbo is a testament of this.

71. It is ironic that in their efforts to implement their vision of societal transformation, some feminists have ended up aggravating the self-same grievances that they seek to eradicate (Carden 1974, 46). In the course of condemning a New York television crew that paid for a circumcision in order to have a live recording of the procedure, Pratibha Parmar admitted that it is easy for filmmakers to become a part of the problem even while trying to resolve it (Walker and Parmar 1993, 162). Parmar obviously was oblivious of her own blunder.

72. In this vein, it should be noted that Pratibha Parmar realized that she had mistakenly thought that Africans were doing nothing about female circumcision prior to her visit to Africa to film *Warrior Marks* (Walker and Parmar 1993, 242). Similarly, bell hooks argues that white feminists are not yet free of the type of paternalism endemic to white supremacist ideology when they see themselves as providing black women with "the" analysis and "the" program for liberation.

73. Boahen 1987, 62. The absurdity of this Eurocentrism is most apparent with Alice Walker who even denies nature credit for its endowments. Commenting on the scenery in Ougadougou, the capital of Burkina Faso, she writes that "the French, planted lots of trees, which shade the wide boulevards" (Walker and Parmar 1993, 81).

74. Support for this line of thought comes from an unlikely source, Alice Walker's *Possessing the Secret of Joy*. In the novel, Tashi's sister, Dura, had bled to death. Mindful of this, Tashi reacted violently to the sight of blood. As a child, "she played in such a way as to take no risks and even learned to sew in an exaggeratedly careful way, using two thimbles." If one death could make such an impression on a child, how much more the untold hardship and deaths that are alleged to flow from circumcision in a village?

75. Wasserstrom 1971. Does evidence of harm warrant undifferentiated paternalistic attacks? Several critics maintain that unlike an adult, a child lacks the capacity to give an informed consent. Ordinarily, parental consent is a prerequisite for surgical procedures performed on minors. However, there is authority for the view that parental consent is not absolute, but that it is confined to treatment in which there is a demonstrable element of benefit to the child (Hayter 1984, 332; Gunning 1992, 189). Practitioners of female circumcision pursue it in belief of its benefit. Moreover, as Boulware-Miller (1985) reveals, polar invocations of the rights of children conflict with the parents' desires to rear their children in accordance with their culturally molded perceptions of what is in "the best interest of the child" (155).

76. It is important to note that the notion of harm is relative. For an overview of the debate between universalists and relativists, see Renteln 1990; Schwab and Pollis 1979; Weinstein 1983, 173; Howard 1986. The relativity of cultures is underscored by Gloria Steinem, who asserted during a panel discussion in New York that

"[j]ust as African patriarchs have fashioned a brutal practice that would ensure the virginity of their brides, the 'spirit-killing regimes of male dominance' in the West rob women of their 'reproductive rights' by seeking to outlaw abortion" (Eichman 1992, 48). There is a good chance that abortion is as abhorrent to a woman with a strong pronatalistic orientation as circumcision is to Ms. Steinem. In fact, women practice circumcision to enhance their fecundity.

77. Spelman 1988, 3; Hawkesworth 1989, 537; King 1989, 91; Lugones and Spelman 1983.

78. Walker and Parmar 1993, 28.

79. Note also the findings of critical theorists who demonstrate that dominating a discourse is an effective means of exercising, protecting, and perpetuating the privileges of power: "Those who have power can do the talking; those who lack power must do the listening" (Marder 1987, 598). Consistent with the theorists, Carol Gilligan opines that "if you have power, you can opt not to listen. And you do so with impunity" (Marcus and Spiegelman 1985, 62).

80. hooks 1984, 90–93. Elizabeth Janeway (1980) designates the phenomenon as the power to disbelieve. According to Janeway, the exercise of this personal power is an act of resistance and strength.

81. The resilience of victims, or rather victors, of apparent domination also resonates in Maya Angelou's poem, "And Still I Rise" (1978), and in Labi Siffre's song, "Something Inside So Strong," especially in the stanza that begins: "[T]he higher you build your barrier, the taller I become." Interestingly enough, Siffre's song was the concluding score in the film, *Warrior Marks*. See also, Walker and Parmar 1993, 186.

82. However, Walker juxtaposes these nurturing and creative mothers with the betraying African mother who connives "in the literal destruction of the most crucial external side of her [daughter's] womanhood: her vulva itself" (Walker and Parmar 1993, 21).

83. See Lorde (1984), who conceives African female bonding as the epitome of love and female solidarity. See also the foreword of Adrienne Rich's *Of Woman Born* (1986), in which she says that most of us first know both love tenderness and power in the person of a woman.

84. Wright 1971, 341; Nnaemeka 1994, 301.

85. Even Awa Thiam, who grew famous for her iconoclasm, was tamed into interfacing with the existing order by the frustrations she suffered otherwise (Walker and Parmar 1993, 286).

86. Steady 1986, quoting Galt and Smith, 16; Lee 1959, 89.

87. Even in *Possessing the Secret of Joy*, while Tashi communes with Carl Jung, an African American woman therapist, and even with the son born to her husband's French paramour in order to relieve the concomitant psychosis of her clitoridectomy, *it is her own action*—the nemesis of M'Lissa the circumciser—which precipitates her ultimate recovery (see Ansa 1992, 4).

88. Pala 1977, 10–11. See also Paul 1992, 235.

89. Ansa 1992, 4.

90. Then in her idiosyncratic "Alice-go-be-Alice" or "true-to-thy-nature" manner, she added "None that we foreigners could drink. It is the poverty of Africa that stays with me, along with the bright spirits of African children" (Walker and Parmar 1993, 82).

91. In the interview with Giddings, for example, Walker alleges that "at night all the women go in, like chickens. There are no windows, they lock the door—practically nail it shut. . . . There is no air. That's how they sleep. . . . It almost killed me to see women in Kenya and other places who actually have grooves in their foreheads from carrying heavy loads" (Giddings 1992).

92. Her collaborator, Parmar, was equally remiss. She remarked: "It was hard to believe that Banjul is the capital city of the Gambia. There are few paved roads; consequently everything is dusty. Many people live on the streets" (Walker and Parmar 1993, 166). Yet she neglected to analyze the connection and to provide a structural context for her documentary. Ironically, she is more concerned that nobody stops to think of the reality (of circumcision) behind "the usual ethnographic stereotypical images of bare-breasted African women staring into the photographer's lens, images that create exotic other, images of availability for the white male tourist," without realizing how she reenacts the stereotypes (199).

93. Walker and Parmar 1993, 71.

WORKS CITED

Allen, Carleton Kemp. 1964. *Law in the Making.* 7th ed. Oxford: Clarendon Press.

Amadiume, Ifi. 1987. *Male Daughters, Female Husbands: Gender and Sex in an African Society.* London: Zed Books.

Angelou, Maya. 1978. *And Still I Rise.* New York: Random House.

Ansa, Tina. 1992. "Taboo Territory." *Los Angeles Times,* July 15, 4.

Anshaw, Carol. 1992. "The Practice of Cruelty Alice Walker Inveighs against Ritual 'Circumcision' of African Women." *Chicago Tribune,* June 21, C3.

Assaad, Marie Bassili. 1982. "Female Circumcision in Egypt: Current Research and Social Implications." In *Traditional Practices Affecting the Health of Women and Children: Report of a Seminar,* ed. Taha Baasher, 229–250. Alexandria, Egypt: WHO/Regional Office for the Eastern Mediterranean.

Aweria, Thelma. 1975. "For African Women Equal Rights Are Not Enough: The Real Task Is to Rethink the Role of Men in Present-day Society." *UNESCO Courier,* March, 21–25.

Badri, Amna Elsadik. 1984. *Female Circumcision in the Sudan: Change and Continuity.* Omduran, Sudan: Ahfad University College for Women.

Bartlett, Katherine T. 1990. "Feminist Legal Methods." *Harvard Law Review* 103 (4): 829–888.

Belenky, Mary Field, et al. 1986. *Women's Ways of Knowing: The Development of Self, Voice, and Mind.* New York: Basic Books.

Bloom, Alan D. 1987. *The Closing of the American Mind.* New York: Simon and Schuster.

Boahen, Adu A. 1987. *African Perspectives on Colonialism.* Baltimore, MD: The Johns Hopkins University Press.

Boddy, Janice. 1989. *Wombs and Alien Spirits: Women, Men, and the Zar Culture in Northern Sudan.* Madison: University of Wisconsin Press.

Boserup, Ester. 1970. *Women's Role in Economic Development.* London: Allen and Unwin.

Boulware-Miller, Kay. 1985. "Female Circumcision: Challenges to the Practice as a Human Rights Violation." *Harvard Women's Law Journal* 8:155–177.

Cannon, Kate Geneva. (Undated manuscript). "Hitting a Straight Lick with a Crooked Stick: The Womanist Dilemma."

Carden, Maren Lockwood. 1974. *The New Feminist Movement.* New York: Russell Sage Foundation.

Charles, Marilynne. 1994. "An Open Wound." *West Africa,* June 27–July 3, 1138.

Cixous, Hélène. 1980. "Sorties." In *New French Feminisms: An Anthology,* ed. Elaine Marks and Isabelle de Courtivron, 90–98. Amherst: University of Massachusetts Press.

Curtin, Philip D. 1964. *The Image of Africa; British Ideas and Action, 1780–1850.* Madison: University of Wisconsin Press.

Darwin, Charles. 1874. *The Descent of Man and Selection in Relation to Sex.* New York: D. Appleton.

Davidson, Max. 1992. "Genital Interest Defines a Rising New Genre—The Below the Belt Story." *Sunday Telegraph,* October 18, 112.

Du Bois, Ellen C., et al. 1985. "Feminist Discourse, Moral Values and the Law: A Conversation. (The 1984 James McCormick Mitchell Lecture)." *Buffalo Law Review* 34:11–87.

Eichman, Erich. 1992. "The Cutting Edge: Alice Walker's New York, New Book Party." *The National Review* 44:48.

El Saadawi, Nawal. 1980. *The Hidden Face of Eve: Women in the Arab World.* London: Zed Press.

Etienne, Mona, and Eleanor Leacock, eds. 1980. *Women and Colonization: Anthropological Perspectives.* New York: Praeger.

Fanon, Frantz. 1963. *The Wretched of the Earth.* New York: Grove Press.

Fox-Genovese, Elizabeth. 1979. "The Personal Is Not Political Enough." *Marxist Perspectives* 98:94–113.

Freire, Paulo. 1970. "The Adult Literacy Process as Cultural Action for Freedom." *Harvard Educational Review* 40 (2): 205–225.

Giddings, Paula. 1992. "Alice Walker's Appeal." *Essence* 23 (3): 58–102.

Grenier, Richard. 1992. "No 'Joy' for the Reader." *The Washington Times,* July 29, G64.

Griffin, Susan. 1982. "The Way of All Ideology." In *Feminist Theory: A Critique of Ideology,* ed. Nannerl O. Keohane, Michelle Z. Rosaldo, and Barbara C. Gelpi, 273–292. Chicago: University of Chicago Press.

Gunning, Isabelle R. 1992. "Arrogant Perception, World-Traveling and Multicultural Feminism: The Case of Genital Surgeries." *Columbia Human Rights Law Review* 23 (2): 189–248.

Harris, Angela P. 1991. "Race and Esentialism in Feminist Legal Theory." In *Feminist Legal Theory: Readings in Law and Gender,* ed. Katherine T. Bartlett and Rosanne Kennedy, 235–262. Boulder, CO: Westview Press.

Hartsock, Nancy. 1975. "Fundamental Feminism: Process and Perspective." *Quest: A Feminist Quarterly* 2 (2): 67–80.

Hawkesworth, Mary E. 1989. "Knowers, Knowing, Known: Feminist Theory and Claims of Truth." *Signs: Journal of Women in Culture and Society* 14 (3): 533–557.

Hayter, K. 1984. "Female Circumcision—Is There a Legal Solution?" *Journal of Social Welfare and Family Law* (November): 332–333.

Holt, Patricia. 1992. "Scars of a Beloved Culture." *The San Francisco Chronicle,* June 21, 1.

hooks, bell. 1984. *Feminist Theory: From Margin to Center.* Boston: South End Press.

Hosken, Fran P. 1993. *The Hosken Report: Genital and Sexual Mutilation of Females.* 4th ed. Lexington, MA: WIN News.

Howard, Rhoda E. 1986. *Human Rights in Commonwealth Africa.* Totowa, NJ: Rowman and Littlefield.

Hughes, Robert. 1993. *Culture of Complaint: The Fraying of America.* New York: New York Library.

Jagger, Alison M. 1983. *Feminist Politics and Human Nature.* Totowa, NJ: Rowman and Littlefield.

Jagger, Alison, and Susan R. Bordo. 1989. *Gender/Body/Knowledge: Feminist Reconstructions of Being and Knowing.* New Brunswick, NJ: Rutgers University Press.

Janeway, Elizabeth. 1980. *Powers of the Weak.* New York: Knopf.

Jersild, Devon. 1992. "Walker. Baring a Terrible 'Secret.'" *USA Today,* July17, SD.

Joseph, Toni Y. 1992. "Alice Walker the 'Womanist' Says Joy Lies in Universal Healing." *The Atlanta Journal and Constitution,* June 10, B1.

Kenyatta, Jomo. 1965. *Facing Mount Kenya: The Tribal Life of the Gikuyu.* New York: Vintage Books.

King, Deborah. 1989. "Multiple Jeopardy, Multiple Consciousness in the Context of a Black Feminist Ideology." *Signs: Journal of Women in Culture and Society* 14 (1): 42–72.

Kingsley, Mary H. 1897. *Travels in West Africa, Congo Francais, Corisco and Cameroons.* New York: Macmillian.

Knox, Robert. 1969. *Races of Men.* Miami, FL: Mnemosyne Publications.

Lasch, Christopher. 1978. *The Culture of Narcissism: American Life in an Age of Diminishing Expectations.* New York: Norton.

Leacock, Eleanor B. 1981. *Myths of Male Dominance: Collected Articles on Women Cross-Culturally.* New York: Monthly Review Press.

Lee, Dorothy. 1959. *Freedom and Culture.* Englewood Cliffs, NJ: Prentice-Hall.

Lightfoot-Klein, Hanny. 1989. *Prisoners of Ritual: An Odyssey into Female Genital Circumcision in Africa.* New York: Harrington Park Press.

Lorde, Audre. 1984. "An Open Letter to Mary Daly." In *Sister Outsider: Essays and Speeches,* 66–71. Trumansburg, NY: Crossing Press.

Lugones, Maria C., and Elizabeth V. Spelman. 1983. "Have We Got a Theory for You! Feminist Theory, Cultural Imperialism and the Demand for The Woman's Voice." *Women's Studies International Forum* 6 (6): 573–581.

Marcus, Isabel, and Paul J. Spiegelman. 1985. "The 1984 James McCormick Mitchell Lecture: Feminist Discourse, Moral Values, and the Law—A Conversation." *Buffalo Law Review* 34:11–87.

Marder, Nancy S. 1987. "Gender Dynamics and Jury Deliberations." *Yale Law Journal* 96:593–612.

Martin, Jane R. 1985. *Reclaiming a Conversation: The Ideal of the Educated Woman.* New Haven: Yale University Press.

Miller, Christopher L. 1990. *Theories of Africans: Francophone Literature and Anthropology in Africa.* Chicago: University of Chicago Press.

Minow, Martha L. 1988. "Feminist Reason: Getting It and Losing It." *Journal of Legal Education* 38 (2): 47–60.

Minow, Martha L., and Elizabeth V. Spelman. 1988. "Passion for Justice." *Cardozo Law Review* 10 (2): 37–76.

Mitton, Jennifer. 1992. "The Fundamental Question: Why Is the Child Crying." *The Toronto Star,* August 25, H11.

Mohanty, Chandra Talpade. 1991. "Under Western Eyes: Feminist Scholarship and Colonial Discourses." In *Third World Women and the Politics of Feminism,* ed. Chandra Talpade Mohanty, Ann Russo, and Lourdes Torres, 51–80. Bloomington, IN: Indiana University Press.

Nnaemeka, Obioma. 1994. "Bringing African Women into the Classroom? Rethinking Pedagogy and Epistemology." In *Borderwork: Feminist Engagements with Comparative Literature,* ed. Margaret Higonnet, 301–318. Ithaca: Cornell University Press.

———. "Reporting Hosken." Work in progress.

Obiora, L. Amede. 1994. "Reconsidering African Customary Law." *Legal Studies Forum* 17 (3): 219–252.

Ohaegbulam, Ugboaja. 1990. *Toward an Understanding of the African Experience from Historical and Contemporary Perspectives.* Lanham, MD: University Press of America.

Pala, Achola O. 1977. "Definitions of Women and Development: An African Perspective." *Signs: Journal of Women in Culture and Society* 3 (1): 9–13.

Parmar, Pratibha, producer/director. 1993. *Warrior Marks* [videorecording]. A Hauer Rawlence Production. New York: Women Make Movies (distributor).

Patterson, Tiffany R., and Angela M. Gilliam. 1983. "Out of Egypt: A Talk with Nawal El Saadawi." *Freedomways* 23 (3): 186–194.

Paul, James C. N. 1992. "The Human Right to Development: Its Meaning and Importance." *The John Marshall Law Review* 25 (2): 235–265.

Payton, Sallyane. 1985. "Releasing Excellence: Erasing Gender Zoning from the Legal Mind." *Indiana Law Review* 18 (3): 629–642.

Poivoir, Sally. 1992. "Alice Walker Tackles Challenging Task in 'Possessing.'" *Houston Chronicle,* June 21, 22.

Polan, Diane. 1982. "Toward a Theory of Law and Patriarchy." In *The Politics of Law: A Progressive Critique,* ed. David Kairys, 284–303. New York: Pantheon Books.

Renteln, Alison Dundes. 1990. *International Human Rights: Universalism versus Relativism.* Newbury Park: Sage Publications.

Rhode, Deborah L. 1989. *Justice and Gender: Sex Discrimination and the Law.* Cambridge, MA: Harvard University Press.

Rich, Adrienne Cecile. 1979. *On Lies, Secrets, and Silence: Selected Prose, 1966–1978.* New York: Norton.

————. 1986. *Of Woman Born.* New York: Norton.

Russell, Diana E. H., and Nicole Van de Ven, eds. 1976. *The Proceedings of the International Tribunal on Crimes against Women.* Millbrae, CA: Les Femmes.

Schwab, Peter, and Adamantia Pollis, ed. 1979. *Human Rights: Cultural and Ideological Perspectives.* New York: Praeger.

Slack, Alison T. 1988. "Female Circumcision: A Critical Appraisal." *Human Rights Quarterly* 10 (4): 437–486.

Smith, Joan. 1992. "Genitally Does It." *The Independent,* October 18, 38.

Spelman, Elizabeth. 1988. *Inessential Woman: Problems of Exclusion in Feminist Thought.* Boston: Beacon Press.

Stanley, Henry M. 1890. *In Darkest Africa or the Quest, Rescue, Retreat of Emin, Governor of Equatoria.* New York: C. Scribner's Sons.

Steady, Filomina Chioma. 1986. "Research Methodology and Investigative Framework for Social Change: The Case for African Women." In *Seminar on Research on African Women: What Type of Methodology? AAWORD Occasional Paper Series* 1: 12–21. Dakar: AAWORD.

Tilzey, Paul. 1992. "All the Marks of an Identity Crisis." *The Independent,* October 31, 31.

Toubia, Nahid. 1994. "Female Circumcision as a Public Health Issue." *New England Journal of Medicine* 331 (11): 712–716.

Trinh, T. Minh-ha. 1989. *Woman, Native, Other: Writing Postcoloniality and Feminism.* Bloomington, IN: Indiana University Press.

Walker, Alice. 1992. *Possessing the Secret of Joy.* New York: Harcourt Brace Jovanovich.

Walker, Alice, and Pratibha Parmar. 1993. *Warrior Marks: Female Genital Mutilation and the Sexual Blinding of Women.* New York: Harcourt Brace.

Wasserstrom, Richard A., ed. 1971. *Morality and the Law.* Belmont, CA: Wadsworth.

Weinstein, Warren. 1983. "Human Rights and Development in Africa: Dilemmas and Options." *Daedalus* 112 (4): 171–196.

Wright, Richard. 1971. "Introduction: Blueprint for Negro Writing." In *The Black Aesthetics,* ed. Addison Gayle Jr., 333–345. Garden City, NY: Doubleday.

Colonial Discourse and Ethnographic Residuals:
The "Female Circumcision" Debate and the Politics of Knowledge

Sondra Hale

Quicker than the keys of my computer (lest I become part of the problem!), I am obliged to say that this essay is not about "female circumcision." It is, in fact, not even about the debates. It is about knowledge (including research, data, teaching, and community education), and politics and action and their inseparability. It is about the politics of knowledge and what feminist scholar, Marilyn Frye, has called "arrogant perception."[1] It is about relationships among subjects, those dangerous liaisons Anne McClintock mentions between gender, race, and class that shaped so much of European imperialism[2] and that force us to see the relationships among knowledge, history, and politics. It is about the ruminations, rumblings, and rhetoric of empire, hopefully the last gasp of the ethnography of the "other."[3] This time it is about white women's burden (and the burden of those held captive and captivated by white hegemonic culture).

In terms of practice, and perhaps on a simpler plane, I am also asking whether and how we can be allies for each other. How can so-called Western women be allies of so-called Third World women? Overlapping and within that, we might ask if it is only politically and intellectually acceptable for African American women and others in the Diaspora to be allies of African women. To state the questions simply: How can Euro-American women be allies of women of color? And, how can ethnically, racially, and culturally diverse feminists and womanists be allies of each other? This brings us to ask why the process of alliance usually has been unilinear. That is, in our racist and colonial/neocolonial world, do we mainly think of the invitation to alliance from one direction only? This usually results in one group/side being treated or seen as a "welfare group" and recipients of largesse.

With regard to the subject at hand—"female circumcision"—have some or all of us been invited to action? In general, is it problematic to act on behalf of another group/region/society without invitation? In some cases—genocide, for example—might it be problematic to wait for an invitation? How do we determine who is the "legitimate" inviter? What role does silence play?

I began by saying that this is not an essay about "female circumcision" or "female genital surgeries"[4] but about the world in which this subject is now being discussed and debated. What do our points of view reflect about the politics of knowledge? About the world in which we live? About the institutions in which we are taught and where we teach (in my case, the University of California at Los Angeles, African Studies, Women's Studies, and Anthropology)? I will return to these points.

LOCATION/POSITIONALITY

In 1994, I broke a thirty-year-long silence on the subject of "female circumcision" in Sudan. The answers to the questions of why I chose silence in the first place and why I then broke it are embedded in what follows. Naming my location and stating my positionality are important processes in challenging the state of affairs, that is, the politics of knowledge surrounding the "female circumcision" debates. I often introduce myself, only partly in jest, as a "recovering anthropologist"—mostly to underscore the self-transformation I have tried to undergo to shake off (like an *intifada*) some of the ideological trappings embedded in the field. Many of my colleagues were trying to do the same in the late 1960s.[5]

My main research area is Sudan, which many view as the heart of the various practices of "female genital surgeries."[6] I have also recently carried out research in Eritrea, where the operations are also performed.[7] I lived in Sudan for six years over a period of thirty-three years and have made six trips there. The closest friends of my life are circumcised women, and I have witnessed the operation, attended ceremonies celebrating the event, have had many conversations with my friends, and have read much of what has been published on the subject. Among these old and close friends are medical doctors and leading Sudanese feminist intellectuals in the female circumcision eradication campaigns. These friends and I have been very close in our politics and came into our feminisms together. Some of my Sudanese friends have made choices that are different from mine. For example, Dr. Nahid Toubia is playing a leadership role in making female circumcision very visible to an international public, opting to give her booklet on the subject a provocative title: *Female Genital Mutilation: A Call for Global Action*. Yet Dr. Toubia, too, though choosing the more inflammatory term "mutilation" and calling for "global action" (i.e., international interference), has taken offense at the way in which North Americans and Western Europeans have approached the subject matter.[8]

To continue locating myself, I am a Marxist or a socialist feminist who teaches courses on international gender issues. I am a white, middle-class woman born in the United States of working-class, Euro-American parents. Two events in my life, related to the subject of this essay, altered how I see the world.

The first event occurred in 1961, shortly after I had arrived in Khartoum, Sudan, and was happier than I had ever been in my life—loving the place and the people, thinking of the Sudanese as the warmest and most gentle people I had ever met.[9] Then, quite offhandedly, and in the kind of bemused way men talk to women when they know they are about to shock them, I was told by a British doctor (left over from the colonial period), a professor of medicine at the University of Khartoum, in the course of a social conversation over our gin and tonics, that all Sudanese women are circumcised: Muslims, Christians, and Jews. He then, without invitation, went on to describe the operation. I was so stunned and repelled that I could hardly teach my high school class the next day at Unity High School for Girls—a classroom of some forty Muslim, Christian, and Jewish girls. How could I process that information? I asked how such a loving, gentle culture could "do that" to young girls. How could I go on liking the place and the people? How could I fit "it" into my worldview and moral framework? I battled with my ethnocentrism. I had just read Laura Bohannan's barely fictionalized personal account of going through the same sort of crisis in *A Return to Laughter.*[10] In general, cultural relativism had worked for me across the board, although it did not seem to be working this time.

After some many months of brooding, I decided that this was a practice that I could not expect to understand, and that because I could not possibly understand it, I had no right to discuss it in print or in public settings. And I didn't. After some time, probably a result of my ultimate rejection of cultural relativism, I also decided that it was not incumbent on me to embrace the practice or to see it in some positive light.

The second event: Some fifteen years later (I can still recall the room and the people), I was giving one of my first university seminars on Sudanese women. It had taken me that long to embrace Women's Studies, my having resented being nudged in that direction by sexist anthropology professors simply because I was a woman graduate student. In the talk, I was developing ideas about how powerful and emancipated Sudanese women were before colonialism, how progressive they were by 1965 in terms of political and social rights, how many women doctors there were, the childcare and parental leave services they had, and the like. The point I was making was that Sudanese women were far ahead of U.S. women in the same time period. There was a stir in the room, looks of disbelief, and finally one woman spoke up and asked if it was not true that the women are circumcised. When I responded that it is true, but that it had no bearing on what I had just been saying, I could tell that I had lost the audience.

Murmurs told me that no one in the room could possibly believe my point that in many ways Sudanese women were more emancipated than U.S. women. The year of the lecture was at the peak of the so-called "second wave of feminism," and this was a room full of mainly white feminists whom I saw at the time and now as having a genital definition of women.

As the years wore on, it became increasingly difficult to be successful in our work against the anti-Muslim, anti-Arab racism in this country because of the active participation of mainly white feminists keen on showing that Middle Easterners and other Muslims were barbaric toward their women—using "female circumcision" and "veiling" as the definitive indices.

CONTEXT OF THE CONTROVERSY

Though sputtering and dying, this is still a modernist/capitalist world undergirded and sustained by colonialism and racism. It is a world guided by liberalism, the centerpiece ideology of capitalism. The metanarrative or "master narrative" of liberalism is the quest for an egalitarianism built on a social contract that gives each an equal opportunity. Within that liberal, egalitarian stance is the credo of cultural relativism, which became a guiding principle of anthropology/ethnography. The "Truth" of cultural relativism is that all cultures are okay on their own terms.[11]

Often counterposed to liberal cultural relativism are at least two other universalistic master narratives—Marxism and feminism. Some Marxist anthropologists, for example, see cultural relativists in a "state of moral and ethical confusion characterized by contradictory, weak, unconscious or disguised value judgments."[12] Like left feminists, reconstructed Marxists take the position—with their moral goal being the end of class, gender, (and race) oppression—a universal freedom—that there are "universally valid moral beliefs and right and wrong rules and modes of behavior."[13]

Basically, with regard to our subject, I am raising the issue of whether this universalism of feminism (obscured ethnocentrism) is another form of cultural imperialism. Returning to our questions, is it possible to engage in critical thinking vis-à-vis what legal scholar, Isabelle Gunning, calls a "culturally challenging" practice[14] and still be respectful to other perspectives and cultures? She uses the term "to describe any practice that someone outside the culture would view as 'negative' largely because she is culturally unfamiliar with it."[15]

THE DEBATE

What is the "debate" about? Where does it take place? Who is participating? What is at stake in the sense of whose interests are being served or not served? What are some of the problematics of this debate? Let me begin with the last question: One problem, it seems to me, is that there is a great amount of racism and ethnocentrism being expounded in the name of participation in either a feminist struggle or a human rights struggle. Western feminists (white and of color) have been given license to let their ethnocentrism free associate! A broader but related issue is, of course, that one part of the world is defining human rights for the rest of the world.

Another problem is that people in the West, if we want to engage in some critical thinking about the issues, are starting from the wrong place. For example, feminists in the United States might want to begin to look at the abuse of women and children here in the United States: the rape capital, the child abuse capital, arguably the domestic violence capital, and one of the body mutilation capitals of the world! We might want to look at our society, where more women are hurt and killed by the men in their lives than in any other way.[16] In terms of children, we might want to look at the ominous spread of malnutrition, disease, and death brought on by young girls trying to fit the slim image that our society demands of them—starvation for the sake of beauty. Mutilation (called "cosmetic surgery") for the sake of dominant-culture beauty standards is now common among the very young.

Again, with regard to starting with one's own society, feminists would be kept very busy just looking into the clitoridectomies performed in the United States into the 1950's to control female hysteria, masturbation, and the like.[17] We could probably look into other unnecessary surgeries performed on women as well; for example, too-radical mastectomies and hysterectomies.

As for the various positions or stances in the "debate" over "female circumcision," there are a number of them. There are people both "inside" and "outside" (and those "inside" who are "outsiders," that is, marginalized by their own society, those in exile, and the like) of the cultures where we find the practices that hold these views:[18]

1. The practices are not only a part of the culture, but are a positive and necessary part.
2. The practices may not be very pleasant or healthy, but they are necessary to maintain the culture.
3. The practices set the practitioners off from the "West" and other societies so that any threat to the practices from the outside warrants a retrenchment or even a revival/reassertion of the practices. The practices are forms of resistance (sometimes the practices get romanticized in the process of this discourse).
4. The practices are harmful, immoral, repugnant, repressive (or all of the above) and should be stamped out immediately by any means necessary—even from the outside, if necessary.
5. The practices are harmful but elimination/eradication of the practices will come about in due course (through a natural process of change). This may take a long time, but "we" should not hurry the process, nor interfere.

6. The practices as they are carried out by some people in some areas are too severe. There needs to be a lessening of the severity (for example, clitoridectomy instead of infibulation), and a medicalization of the practices (that is, the operation should be performed in a hospital or by medical personnel).
7. The practices are revealing of unequal gender relations—that is, the extreme subordination of women to men. No custom in the world is so symptomatic.
8. The practices are a form of child abuse, crimes against women and children, torture, or human rights violations. Therefore, outside coercion and force should be used to eradicate the practices.
9. The practices are called for in Islam. That is only one more set of reasons to think of the Middle East and Islamic or Arab countries as "barbaric," or at least not as "advanced" as most other reasons.
10. In this country, only African Americans or people of Arab or Muslim descent have a right to speak about the practices.
11. In some areas of Africa, for example, people have a lot more to worry about than these practices (for example, drought, starvation, war, disease, infertility, high infant and mother mortality, and abject poverty—not to mention economic exploitation and neocolonialism).
12. We should stop using cultural excuses for violence against women and children.

There are also people like me who accept the last two points and also believe that the practices are not healthy nor humane and are politically suspect in terms of gender relations, but respect and trust women and some men in those cultures where they are practiced to deal with their own gender issues. So much of what has been said about the occurrence and need for eradication has deemed people engaged in resistance in the countries where the practices are carried out to be invisible. Where there are people already socially, medically, and politically engaged in working on these issues, I maintain I should be an ally only if I am invited by the people involved in the issue, that is, circumcised women living in their cultures. Furthermore, I can make a contribution to gender scholarship and to gender politics by contributing what I know about my own society. The process of change and exchange should be multidirectional, a situation where I can call upon my sisters in African and Middle Eastern countries to help me understand aspects of our gender politics here in the United States. Since I learned my feminism from Sudanese women, it makes sense to me. Obviously there are many different views (inside and outside) on the origins of "female circumcision," the methods we might use for eradication, who should play the leadership roles, and so on. I have only touched the surface in outlining the debate.

Another issue is why we are seeing so much Western scholarship, publicity, and international agency activity about the practice *now*. Perhaps we should ask ourselves what is going on in this country in terms of both gender and race struggles. Laura Nader has fused her ideas with those of Edward Said in *Orientalism* to maintain that men control the women in their own society by trying to control the women of other societies.[19]

The above leads me to raise the sensitive issue of why so many African American women are becoming activists in the campaign against the practice. As a white woman, I do not want to comment on the right or wrong of the public activism against "female circumcision" of such celebrities as Alice Walker. Most of this activism (in the form of writing, making films, appearing on the popular media, and so forth) has developed into a kind of essentialist stance in which Walker and others, because they are black, seem to be taking on the "burden" of "female circumcision" in Africa as, somehow, their preordained cause. Some might say that this is a quite different process from, say, the stance of some American Jews who profess a special responsibility to stop the persecution of Palestinians in Israel. As it has been expressed to me by such American feminists as Sherna Gluck, this position is related, among other things, to the strong Zionist lobby in the United States and its strengthening effect on Israeli state policies.[20]

Returning to the Nader/Said ideas above, what is happening in gender/race relations in the United States that is compelling so many African American women to launch into the campaign? Is it related at all to African (continent) women? Or is it more related to what is happening within the American African community? To the rise of Pan-Africanism? To the increasing poverty and oppression of African Americans? What is the relationship now of dominant white male culture to African American women? These are not questions I can answer just yet, but it is still important to raise them.

We might also ask how and why so many Westerners, especially (but not only), white feminists, are becoming active in either scholarship or politics around this issue without knowing anything about the practices or without having had a single conversation with a circumcised woman! In this sense and in others, we seemed to have engaged in a great deal of "arrogant perception," which really relates not so much to what we think of something, but what we do with that information and, especially, how we use our analyses to set ourselves apart from *them*.

At the nongovernmental (NGO) segment of the United Nations Fourth World Conference on Women, Beijing, 1995, the difference between the number of workshops directly about female circumcision and the number of presentations on other panels was staggering. "FGM" (as it is referred to by "those in the know"), became a celebrity international topic. The visibility of the topic was pointed out to me by any number of feminists who saw this as evidence of the compelling nature of the problem. I was alarmed that no one mentioned how many of these workshops were sponsored by Western-controlled international agencies with their own agendas! Using the terms of discourse and power, who is providing the money, who is benefiting from accepting the money (for example, the making of careers), who is being heard or read (politics of publishing), and who is being addressed?

Also in terms of critical thinking, I am amazed at the lack of complexity in Westerners' approaches to the subject of "female circumcision." First of all, we talk as if there is only one type of operation; that it is performed in the same way and for the same reasons all over; that there is no pride in it, and if there is, then it must be false consciousness. The quote below exemplifies how complex the subject is when one talks directly with Sudanese women, as both Janice Boddy (cited below) and I have done. Instead of presenting genital surgeries as male attempts to control female sexuality, or polemically, to deprive them of their "human rights" or to "torture" little girls, the explanations Sudanese give are far more complex:

1. Some (but not many) talk about the surgery enhancing male sexual pleasure.
2. It is also not common to hear that the surgery restrains female sexuality. This is much disputed, and considering the active sexual life of married and unmarried Sudanese, it is unlikely as a blanket rule.
3. We do hear ideas about protection of family honor, as well as notions of chastity, modesty, and virtuousness.[21]
4. There is an emphasis on fertility[22]—that is, it socializes toward fertility.
5. Mainly, "[Sudanese women] . . . assert that it is performed on young girls so as to make their bodies clean (nazif), smooth (na'im), and pure (tahir), this last term furnishing the Sudanese word for circumcision in general: tahur ('cleansing' or 'purification')."[23]
6. In other words, circumcision prepares her body for womanhood—thereby confers the right to bear children and, therefore, to advance her position.
7. It is also socialization to selfhood.[24]
8. It creates a social boundary.
9. It is part of the creation of gender identity.

CONCLUSION

At the risk of becoming part of the problem, I have broken my silence, calling for *us*—and I am mainly (but not exclusively) addressing white feminists—to self-interrogate, calling on us always to be suspicious of our ideas and beliefs, and to work on ways of being effective *invited* allies. Whenever we become engaged in the affairs of the "other," we should be circumspect. Whenever we take on, uninvited, their plight as ours, in the face of so much political work to do in our own oftentimes pitiful society, it is useful to examine the timing, the actors, and the rhetoric. If the media and academic campaigns aimed at eradicating "female circumcision" are attempts to add to our knowledge bank, to "understanding," to cross-cultural "information," then we might want to examine the politics of knowledge.

I am not making a statement against altruism, nor political activism on behalf of others, nor resistance to gender oppression everywhere, although these always have to be interrogated. It is a call to step back and ask why, oftentimes, the idea of "female circumcision" is the *only* idea an American may hold about Africa, the Middle East, and Muslim societies. Who is keeping that idea alive and why? The process is one of creating cultural differences, a residual of the ethnographic agenda.

NOTES

An earlier version of this essay appeared in *Ufahamu* (UCLA) 22 (3) (1994): 26–35.

1. Frye 1983. I want to thank Isabelle Gunning for reminding me of Frye's useful concept in her article, "Arrogant Perception, World-Traveling and Multi-cultural Feminism: The Case of Female Genital Surgeries," 1992.

2. McClintock 1995.

3. I have borrowed the term "rhetoric of empire" from Spurr 1993.

4. I would defeat my purpose to debate terminology here. It should seem clear that "circumcision" is technically a misnomer, but it has the usefulness here of being a more "neutral" term. Still, it is not completely devoid of impact. More importantly, it is not medicalized, as is the term "female genital surgeries." Of course, Alice Walker and many, many other Americans are opting for the more dramatic term, "female genital mutilation." It is, however, perhaps unfair to imply that only Americans are using that term when Sudanese medical/political activist, Nahid Toubia, has written a booklet entitled *Female Genital Mutilation: A Call for Global Action* (1993). In a later publication, however, Toubia (1994) moves back and forth between "female circumcision" and "female genital mutilation." Language and who uses it are, of course, politically and epistemologically significant.

5. See Hale (1991) for a discussion of this process.

6. Nahid Toubia, for example, estimates that "female circumcision" is performed on 90 percent of northern Sudanese women (1994, 27).

7. Eritrea is recently independent after thirty years' of struggle. During the war the Eritrean People's Liberation Front, in particular, campaigned against the practice, banning it "in the field" (that is, liberated areas). However, I am told, but have not confirmed, that it is still widely practiced in most of the countryside.

8. Personal communication, 1993.

9. I discuss this suspect romanticism in Hale 1991.

10. Bowen 1956.

11. See Benedict 1934.

12. Harris 1968, 163.

13. Harris 1968, 13.

14. Gunning outlines the complicated journey that she, too, had to undergo vis-à-vis the subject of this essay, for example, acknowledging her "arrogant perception" as an African American woman looking at what she calls "female genital surgeries" (which also represents a shift from her earlier terminology of "female genital mutilation").

15. Gunning 1992.
16. Although I do not think it necessary to cite the statistics of violence against women to a mainly American readership, a few numbers might be useful. The *Los Angeles Times* in its "World Report" section (June 29, 1993) reports that "Battering is the greatest single cause of injury among U.S. women, accounting for more emergency room visits than auto accidents, muggings and rape combined." And, "A recent national survey found that each hour, 76 American women over the age of 18 are raped—683,000 rapes per year. One in five American women is likely to be a rape victim in her lifetime." These are highly conservative statistics in comparison to most feminist quantitative analyses.
17. Barker-Benfield 1975.
18. By no means do I mean to suggest that these are the *only* positions.
19. Said 1978; Nader 1989.
20. See Gluck 1994.
21. See Boddy 1989, 55, note 18.
22. Boddy 1989, 53–56.
23. Boddy 1989, 55.
24. Boddy 1989, 57–60.

WORKS CITED

Barker-Benfield, Ben. 1975. "Sexual Surgery in Late-Nineteenth Century America." *International Journal of Health Services* 5 (2): 279–298.
Benedict, Ruth. 1934. *Patterns of Culture.* Boston: Houghton Mifflin.
Boddy, Janice. 1989. *Wombs and Alien Spirits: Women, Men, and the Zar Cult in Northern Sudan.* Madison: Wisconsin University Press.
Bowen, Elenore [Laura Bohannan]. 1956. *A Return to Laughter.* London: Victoria Gollancz.
Frye, Marilyn. 1983. "In and Out of Harm's Way." In *The Politics of Reality: Essays in Feminist Theory,* 52–83. Trumansburg, NY: The Crossing Press.
Gluck, Sherna. 1994. *An American Feminist in Palestine: The Intifada Years.* Philadelphia: Temple University Press.
Gunning, Isabelle. 1992. "Arrogant Perception, World-Traveling and Multi-cultural Feminism: The Case of Female Genital Surgeries." *Columbia Human Rights Law Review* 23 (2): 189–248.
Hale, Sondra. 1991. "Feminist Method, Process, and Self-Criticism: Interviewing Sudanese Women." In *Women's Words: The Feminist Practice of Oral History,* ed. Daphne Patai and Sherna Berger Gluck, 121–136. New York: Routledge.
Harris, Marvin. 1968. *The Rise of Anthropological Theory.* New York: Crowell.
McClintock, Anne. 1995. *Imperial Leather: Race, Gender and Sexuality in the Colonial Context.* New York: Routledge.
Nader, Laura. 1989. "Orientalism, Occidentalism and the Control of Women." *Cultural Dynamics* 2 (3): 323–355.
Said, Edward. 1978. *Orientalism.* New York: Vintage Books.
Spurr, David. 1993. *The Rhetoric of Empire: Colonial Discourse in Journalism, Travel Writing, and Imperial Administration.* Durham, NC: Duke University Press.
Toubia, Nahid. 1993. *Female Genital Mutilation: A Call for Global Action.* New York: Women, Ink.
_____, ed., with Amira Bahyeldin, Nadia Hijab, and Heba Abdel Latif. 1994. *Arab Women: A Profile of Diversity and Change.* New York: Population Council.

Parallax Sightlines: Alice Walker's Sisterhood and the Key to Dreams

Chimalum Nwankwo

THE KEY TO DREAMS

**There is no better key to dreams
than my name sang a bird.**[1]

The tenor of the above two lines are tragic, authoritarian, monocular, irredeemably arrogant, and parallax. They are the opening lines of Tchicaya U Tamsi's poem, "Agony." In the poem, the bird is confidently enlisted for service by a black boatman who claims that his vaunted gift of clairvoyance and sundry powers supported by a tonic love ostensibly and deceptively offered by the bird are all he needs to be cured of the tragic paralysis of a leprous state. Unabashed and confessed in his proud paganism, U Tamsi has never been more acute and inimitable in his surrealistic depiction of the agony of the lopsided imperial combat between the West and Africa. Led by the bird in siren-like seduction, the black boatman sails for three days and three nights, at the end of which he loses his bowels and arms and memory to an unsuspected charnel feast. Before the recourse to all the black boatman's vaunted gifts, it is all over; too late.

It may turn out to be too late for the African thinker who has not panned the motions of the Western feminist from its inception in the morning of the revolt against Western patriarchy to the fortuitous conflation of its ethos in the postmodern, or indeed postcolonial fallacy. It may yet be quite timely for the African thinker, man or woman, who sees in the growth of Western feminism the danger of the charnel house feast on his bowels, his arms, and memory. But timeliness is here contingent upon a recognition that Western feminism, like the bird in U Tamsi's poem, which claims that no one else has a "better key to dreams," exercises in its methods, practices, and vision a similar claim, no whit different from the patriarchal structures which it fights or claims to differ from. And why not? Imperialism and Western feminism share the same ancestry, the same pedigree. That the present vigor and ballast of feminism is a product of the unraveling of a Western cumulus of ideas is an irony no one ponders, especially the Western feminist who ought to appreciate the significance of the following point. All "posts" imply the collapse of the overt imperial/colonial program which expressed tokenistic recognition of diverse realities via the postnihilistic, deconstructionist assertion of the death of "foundations," especially the monistic sweep of foundations. I cannot see how Africa is a player here, and cannot be convinced that Africa has ever been part of all this. In opining this, one thinks of the kind of ideas arising from Rey Chow's reflections on modernity in *Writing Diaspora*: "Modernity is ambivalent in its very origin. . . . In trying to become 'new' and 'novel'—a kind of primary moment—it must incessantly deal with its connection with what precedes it—what was primary to it—in the form of a destruction."[2] Whatever that destruction is, it is on such universalist presumptions that certain kinds of cultural criticisms base an equally deceitful notion of "the cosmopolitanization of humanity,"[3] which sundry modes of interpretive writing such as feminism foist on Africa.

Because Western feminism is what it is, it proceeds genetically in tune with its pedigree, Western patriarchy. Many years ago Will and Ariel Durant[4] told a monumental story of civilization in eleven massive volumes. The center of that compendious exercise was the West, and while the Orient was acknowledged, Africa appears only interstitially. That has remained the pattern of Western discourses on Africa. It is either occlusion or interstitial tokenism. This is also the pattern of all kinds of anthologies dealing with African literary criticism. Much of all this, of course, also has something to do with the economics and politics of publishing. Who funds publications and for which markets? Which names sell and for what cultural environments? Whose opinions receive the wider air and why? The answers to these questions reveal the nature of the popularity of certain writers. For instance, Emecheta, who is celebrated in Britain and North America finds little favor in her native Nigeria, and Alice Walker, who claims to campaign for the salvation of Africa in her works, is regarded with scorn or indifference by much of the African readership she claims to be saving, while she is feted in the United States.

Whatever the case may be, it seems that once the subject is Africa, all and sundry claim with baffling temerity to be "the key to dreams." Critical postures and attitudes appear to have mollified a little since the great debates excited by the aggressive and stimulating ideas pursued in *Toward the Decolonization of African Literature*[5] from the late 1970s through the 1980s. The African Marxists and their fading shibboleths now rest in peace with the unraveling of the Soviet Union. We are now watching with interest the crusades of Western feminism and its prong of cultural imperialism. Happily, it appears that what will finally perpetrate for that feminism its critical catastrophe are texts like Alice Walker's *Warrior Marks: Female Genital Mutilation and the Sexual Blinding of Women*[6] and *Possessing the Secret of Joy*.[7] Those texts reveal recklessly a prototype and blueprint of the action of erstwhile neatly disguised global sisters rushing all over Africa and anything African in pretended aid of the poor African, to see, à la Walker, "basically, if they'd just stop hurting themselves."[8]

There is no better way of marking the character of these Western feminist engagements in Africa than by looking at some of these campaigns without the obscurantist argots popularized by fashionable coteries of the West's academy. Because the questions that this chapter desires to raise initiate from all the ridiculous fanfare over female circumcision, I must insist on staking a position at this point. I must make it clear that the practice makes no sense and deserves no approval for any reason, in the context of today's realities in Africa. Whether it made sense in the past remains debatable within the parameters of specific social and moral circumstances, but because we live in the present, we must concern our selves with present-day realities. Those who are enamored of the habitual judgments of present day life and conduct with moribund or past cultural errors may continue to titillate their senses in that fashion. It is obvious that their programs are quite remote in intent from that of more serious and well-meaning researchers such as Olayinka Koso-Thomas.

To appreciate fully what the issue is requires something as ordinary as a comparison of the title of Koso-Thomas's study of circumcision and the work by Alice Walker and Pratibha Parmar. Against the latter's screaming, sensational, and pretentious title and subtitle is a direct and businesslike *The Circumcision of Women: A Strategy for Eradication*.[9] The study leaves no spaces for the kind of massive discursive gaps shamelessly advertised in Walker and Parmar's exercises. As Koso-Thomas wisely writes,

> the problem of female circumcision does not fall easily into the category of health problems for which solutions may be found through actions outside the domain of the culture of the country affected. . . . It has a strong religious and cultural base without which it would not exist today, and because this base structure has long been shrouded in secrecy and protected by strong emotional and communal ties, it is difficult to dislodge. The eradication of female circumcision must, therefore, involve the social, religious, and cultural transformation of certain communities, rather than overturning or uprooting this base by rapid legal decrees.[10]

The study answers so many questions about the reasons for circumcision in Africa. It carefully describes and details the female anatomy and different kinds of circumcision, clearly emphasizing that it is not merely restricted to certain areas of Africa. It carefully analyzes all the health problems arising from female circumcision. We are told how to deal with circumcised women humanely and what to do to enhance and ensure the continuity of programs of eradication. There are cultural bolsters that fix the practice in the realm of ignorance and a peculiar attitude to sexuality. Nothing is cast in the kind of incorrigible mental plate that in Walker and Parmar makes out Africa ready for Armageddon because of the crime of circumcision. Koso-Thomas's book is as informative and practical as it is humane and sympathetic, delicate, and understanding. It is blunt without insolence or abrasion and recognizes periodically the complexity of a problem that must first need detangling from the cultural web that obscures all logic or reason. It is an insider's work of mercy delivered professionally and humbly and, I imagine, with that tethered pain which all good doctors vicariously share with their patients. Koso-Thomas's work (written in 1987, several years before the excursion of Walker and her friend), with its statistical details and suggestions and projections of how all could be involved nationally and internationally in the eradication of this unfortunate practice, arrives at conclusions that are sensible, obvious, and unimpugnable:

> With the improvement of women's education in Africa and the massive migration from rural areas into the cities, African women have been exposed to an unprecedented extent to a new thinking of female sex roles, fulfillment, and independence and security. Through the continuing flood of information in print, on radio and television, an awareness of the importance of sexual life has been created amongst women who have been taught to disregard this aspect of their lives. Women are therefore more ready now than ever before to learn about themselves and to reassess their position in sexual partnership with their menfolk.[11]

Perhaps to Walker and her global sisters, the results or conclusions of all that research are not good enough, just as certain readings of African literature are not good enough for certain Western feminists in spite of the fact that they have very limited knowledge of Africa or Africans.

HOLDERS OF THE KEY, AND THEIR PARALLAX SIGHTLINES

Those who want to read Alice Walker and fix the orbit of her total art where it belongs must forget her often vociferous claims to this or that race or to African ancestry. Such claims are either wools of confusion or opportunism, or symptoms of an angst which black people all over the globe have to contend with as part of the unfortunate tragedy imposed by the forces of a history that have remained as inexorable as they are interminable. In the preface to *Alice Walker: Critical Perspectives Past and Present*,[12] Henry Louis Gates has this to say about reactions to *The Color Purple*: "Lamentably, its very success exposed its author to charges of male bashing by those who would prefer that the varied forms of violence against women be discreetly ignored by the black literary record."[13] Gates is sadly in error here. I believe that the more careful reading of Donna Haisty Winchell is closer to the truth about Walker's life and works. One does not see any real sustained cheer for the black male in *The Color Purple*. Besides, as Winchell observes, "on screen there appeared not a single positive black role model, and the portrayal of black family life was, at best, demeaning."[14] But all this is beside the point here. The main issue in Walker's life and works is how her attitude to the human body becomes a narcissistic lodestone that appears to threaten all else. Something has to be wrong with everybody. There are seeds for crises in grandparents, mother, father, brothers, daughter, blacks, Africa, and so forth. But a sincere criticism knows that all these crises emanate elsewhere. According to Winchell, "Walker speaks of her early writing as a means of survival, an alternative to despair. Over time, though, her writing has become not only a means of averting crisis but a means of achieving health."[15] What in the life of this writer could cause this depth of despair? What in her life could place her in her relationship with Africa in an orbit that images her in safari khaki and helmet?

From her circumcision excursion, the orbit of her art is clear. It has been trod by the adventurous gangs of the Lander brothers, of Livingstone and Stanley in their journeys of discovery. It has been trod by the wily and supercilious politics of Lugard and Rhodes in their efforts to devise the best for Africa. It has been seen in the hyperbolic humanism of Schweitzer, as it has been seen in the incongruous voyeurism and paternalism of Rider Haggard and Rice Boroughs. Did *The Color Purple* not hold the American gaze as well as or even better than Crichton's *Congo*?[16]

There is nothing really wrong about criticism of blacks by blacks or whoever, but there is a critical posture that reveals the kind of obscenity associated with the folkloric eyes of Ham on his father's nakedness (no patriarchal slap intended)! Walker is lofty, like Christ, but with neither saintly humility nor restraint as she gazes down from the glorious mountain of Western imperialism at her discovered benighted. The motive of Africa's visitors is always salvationism, but it appears here, as in most other cases, that the whole enterprise is riddled with naked disdain. In the case of Walker, one fears lurking somewhere, secure in the deep recesses of her prodigious talent, something terrible, something vengeful, unrelieving, and Calvinistically final, something spawned by a combination of acknowledged and unacknowledged experiences of hurt, or of other secret and incalculable losses. This is beyond the merely physical; it is spiritual and atavistic. It surfaces cold and deadly in the scene in the film *Warrior Marks* where she recalls that a woman playfully tells her that "she is not directly from Africa." Walker's response is, of course, as it should be: "But I smiled and reminded her that this is definitely not my fault."[17] Obviously, it is the woman's fault.

There are echoes of that condition resounding from the pages of Richard Wright's *Black Power*,[18] especially in the expression "you fellows who sold us,"[19] a popular inane charge inflicted on present day Africans in an absurd conflation of a tragic history and destiny. There are echoes of this periodically blessed and promoted by white American media. The most recent is in a *Washington Post* piece by an African American journalist, Keith B. Richburg, who once again submits his consciousness to the electronic picks and mine-lights of such imperial anthropologisms. In his troubling and self-hating article, "A Black American in Africa," you will find a mixture of triumph and spurious dolor in escaping a hapless African citizenship by the grace of slavery! It is a strange return to the indoctrinated consciousness of Phillis Wheatley, the eighteenth century African American poet, who made out Africa as "land of errors and Egyptian gloom." According to Richburg,

> somewhere, sometime, maybe 400 years ago, an ancestor of mine whose name I'll never know was shackled in leg irons, put with thousands of others in a slave ship. . . . Then one of his descendants somehow made it. . . . And if that original ancestor hadn't been forced to make that horrific voyage, I would not have been standing there that day on the Rusumo Falls bridge, a journalist—a mere spectator—watching the bodies glide past me like river logs. No, I might have instead been one of them, or have met some similarly anonymous fate in any one of the countless ongoing civil wars or tribal clashes on this brutal continent. And so I thank God my ancestor made that voyage.[20]

Even though the count has not been made or completed with regard to how many Africans and African Americans are on their knees thanking God for the kind of salvation which Mr. Richburg is celebrating, we know with reasonable certainty the number of planted coups and dreadful dictatorships or wars in that brutal continent that have been instigated to either facilitate the catching of slaves or to create conducive environment for the benefits of certain strategic, economic, political, or ideological interests. But characteristically, as always, the causes of the errors with all their political and callous ghost puppeteers in the land are ignored in favor of sensationalizing the gloom.

There are muted but potent echoes of this in the innocuous but dangerous and portentous utterances of some young African Americans whose self-esteem and development escaped the eyes of parental care. One such black middle schooler dismissed my precocious and politically sensitive daughter (Nnebuchi Nwankwo), who claimed, à la Peter Tosh, that all black people are from Africa with: "Not so, we are English!" That is a retort that buries in marble the centerpiece of Thurgood Marshall's painful but victorious battle in the American courts, where the perception of a black and white doll in the eyes of black children became unshakable instruments of history. Whether Brown versus Board of Education is remembered by Alice Walker and her admiring readers, one does not know. But whether critics and readers know or do not know, a critical appraisal of

Walker's writings, especially her phony salvationism must take into great consideration these following few observations.

After the climactic trumped annunciation/martyrdom/transfiguration of Walker's beloved Tashi in *Possessing the Secret of Joy*, the most ridiculous creature in the history of imperial fictions, the author quickly places her "humanistic" effort in the context and pedigree of "two excellent books" by Asma El Dareer and Hanny Lightfoot-Klein, other African salvationists. To universalize the company, of course, an internal American crusader is identified, G. J. Barker-Benfield. After that, the familiar Alice Walker takes the podium: "I have claimed the story-teller's prerogative to recast or slightly change events alluded to or described in the earlier books, in order to emphasize and enhance the meanings of the present tale."[21] It is this "story-teller's prerogative" that metamorphoses into something dangerously authoritarian, insensitive, and weirdly chauvinistic (considering her "blackness") in her aesthetic and total vision. When an intellectual enterprise involving cultural questions in Africa seeks authenticity in linguistic fabrication, and ignores teeming resources, or recourse to that matchless diversity which marks Africa, one must watch for warps in motives and actuations.

Consider whether the following in the postscript connotes love of one's culture or condescension, care or insouciance, or simply political ignorance, cultural illiteracy or arrogance: "Tsunga, like many of my 'African' words is made up. Perhaps it, and the other words I use are from an African language I used to know, now tossed up by the unconscious."[22] Perhaps this pathetic remark could have been checked with a little study of one of the speculated 3,000 or so languages in Africa. Just one ought to be able to offer Walker vocabulary adequate for her missionary enterprise. But every careful reader knows that this writer has no such respect for the continent, hence the creation of her own *Heart of Darkness*,[23] with a suffering, brutalized, and half-demented waif called Tashi, in a Congo named Olinka. And then follows that Wrightian trade mark, with its characteristic arrogance and blame for being an African American: "*I* do not know from what part of Africa my African ancestors came, and so I claim the continent!"[24]

To claim a continent needs to be understood, especially by angry African readers provoked by Walker's unsolicited benefaction by what we find in the obviously innovative THANKS at the end of the novel: "I thank Carl Jung for becoming so real in my own self-therapy (by reading) that I could imagine him as alive and active in Tashi's treatment. My gift to him. I thank my own therapist, Jane R. C., for helping me loosen some of my own knots and therefore better able to distinguish and tackle Tashi's."[25] The mildest scrutiny of Walker's writing naggingly suggests that the gratitude to the ghost of Carl Jung and Jane R. C. is rather hasty and premature. Clearly, many more knots or nuts remain for those characters to pry loose.

There is something deep and, simultaneously, deceptively humorous, from an African perspective, in Ben Okri's pampering and polysemous declaration with regard to Walker's *In Search of Our Mothers' Gardens*:[26] "This is one of the healthiest collections of essays that I have come across in a long time."[27] Ha! The essays are healthy as part of a Jungian regimen, and no more. Generally one is inclined to see in those essays the early fulcrum of the assault on Africa worked out in much of Walker's writings. Since part of the business of criticism remains for the critic a business of speculation and imposition of subjective meaning, permit a share of that indulgence here. The amazing subtitle of *Warrior Marks* is *Female Genital Mutilation and the Sexual Blinding of Women.* That subtitle is instructively and unashamedly multivocalic. In one breath, it makes Alice Walker all women. The accidental blinding of her eye by her brother is a crime plotted and hatched by her brothers and all men to undo Alice Walker and all women. Not African American, African, or Asian, or Caucasian women. It is simply all women. For an African reader, the most frightening thing about all this is the obvious implication that Walker has clearly not forgiven her family. All Africans know what the word family is all about. But appreciating this insidious process of self-aggrandizement and ill-conceived apotheosis requires a quick revisit to *In Search of Our Mothers' Gardens*. For there, the whole hocus and posturing of this (to any thinking African) inexplicably celebrated writer fizzes along with all the Californianization of spirituality which veneers some of her ink and utterances. So, just as Walker insists in *Warrior Marks* that she must speak, courageous criticism insists here to probe: "Be nobody's darling, / Be an outcast / Qualified to live / Among your dead."[28] Those words are a part of Walker's 1972 convocation speech at Sarah Lawrence College. How can a writer who claims black and (sometimes) African heritage counsel loneliness or the deviance of existentialism? Is community or communality no longer synonymous with that heritage? It is this kind of cultural confusion that baffles the sensitive Walker reader who often finds it difficult to know when the writer has left the podium of self for the commons of community, when "I" becomes "we," and who or what constitutes the referents of individuality and collectivity.

In "Gifts of Power: The Writings of Rebecca Jackson," she confirms this problem when she opines: "I simply feel that naming our own experience after our own fashion (as well as rejecting whatever does not seem to suit) is the least we can do—and in this society may well be our only tangible sign of personal freedom."[29] If Walker and whomever she refers to here accept the importance of naming their own experience, shall we then not assume that Walker thinks that Africans are so infantile and politically or mentally retarded that they ought to be assisted by neocolonial or imperial aliens of all shades to name their own experience? As we shall see later, Walker does not think that anyone has a right to question what she says. Obviously, she is God, the arbiter of what is fair or not, and what is noble or ignoble. She is unaware of one common African (Igbo) proverb which alerts all blind do-gooders to the fact that whenever one thoughtless critical finger is pointing at the public or anyone, there are four other reflexive fingers pointing back at the pointer. So one reads the following from "Duties of the Black Revolutionary Artist" with little surprise at the selective approbation granted to personal failing:

> We must exercise our noblest impulses with our hate, not let it destroy us or destroy our truly precious heritage, which is not, by the way, a heritage of bigotry or intolerance. I've found, in my own way of writing that a little hatred keenly directed, is a useful thing. Once spread about, however, it becomes a web in which I would sit caught and paralyzed like the fly who stepped into the parlor.[30]

How much more in irony does one need to pity Walker's hateful crusade in *Warrior Marks* and *Possessing the Secret of Joy*?

Let us take some portions of *Warrior Marks* (the book) first. In the opening section, "Like the Pupil of an Eye," the author's traumatic childhood accident (a forever obsession) is carefully forged into a cannon ball of vengeance and hurled along with her phony salvationism toward Africa. Walker carefully asserts that her campaign is explained by the fact that "because I was a girl, I did not receive a gun. . . . I had seen my brother after lowering his gun after shooting me and knew the injury was intentional."[31] All that is in readiness for Walker's assumption of the nails of Joan of Arc on behalf of all womanhood, specifically an African womanhood that incrementally grows benighted in her campaign: "What I had was a patriarchal wound."[32] Next is the transfiguration or annunciation in which Walker's patriarchal wound becomes "a warrior mark."[33] To make this mark worth the warrior's universal campaign, a credible mythology, luna-washed, is invoked in which glistens the proverbial "dark" continent. Superstition, of course, is one familiar bold line in the contours: "Women are blamed for their own sexual mutilation. Their genitalia are unclean, it is said. Monstrous. The activity of the unmutilated female vulva frightens men and destroys crops. When erect, the clitoris challenges male authority. It must be destroyed."[34]

The consequence of superstition finds expression in the joyless life of women. If Alice Walker has experienced visual blindness so have African women experienced sexual blindness because: "Without the clitoris and other sexual organs, a woman can never see herself reflected in the healthy, intact body of another. Her sexual vision is impaired, and only the most devoted lover will be sexually 'seen'."[35] One wonders what the entire West feels about Walker's entertaining writing, whether it is fair to present the Western or American attitude to life as totally sex-centered. One also wonders whether, if Walker's excursion is serious or taken seriously, the whole African continent would not be milling with "blind," crazed African women with "warrior marks" howling for vengeance through the streets and forests. What is clear in all this is that the writer has replaced or consistently confused or distorted the relationship between what she calls "love" and "sex." Perhaps this is a Western thing because there are several instances in her text in which one does not really know what is going on with regard to the writer's vaunted spirituality and love for Africa and Africans. The crudity of her undisguised disdain is cameo in sections of the text detailing this tourney of ancestral or cultural schizophrenia. In the same breath that we read of a fantasized kinship with Ayi Kwei Armah, or watch her hyperbolic presentation of a Yoruba priestess and African virtues, we also read that her eyes are also identifying African female rogues: "One of the women in the very crowded room was slowly but steadily working her way toward my hand bag, which I had flung in my chair when I started to dance. I grabbed it just before she pounced."[36] Such clairvoyant certainties no one can ever get used to. Walker knows the African pouncing thief and retrained saint, and knows when to curse and when to exculpate as we find demonstrated in her reflection on Aminata Diop who claims that her mother thinks she is a bad person because she speaks out against genital mutilation. Here Walker is at her histrionic, comic, and melodramatic best:

> There are just some people who you know are good. Aminata is one of them. It grieves me that her own mother could doubt this. And not appreciate what a brave, tenderhearted, and loving daughter she has raised. I want to shout across the miles separating us: *Stand up and be a mother damn it!* Don't make this child suffer when, after all, *she* is right not the society that enslaves both of you! Instead Aminata and I clasp hands; she throws her scarf over her face and head to hide her tears from the camera and I just say fuck it and let mine flow.[37]

But all this pathetic and phony spiritual posturing should not surprise any reader; African or non-African. Elsewhere Walker's declaration should be our watchword: "I have a right to say what I see. I have a right to see what I see. I need not punish myself or be punished for seeing."[38]

Colleagues who have pondered over such statements and this brand of arrogance have characterized and associated them with nationalism and chauvinism, but they are more an individual quirk than any such thing. How can any American, black or white, who understands and appreciates the legacy of Lincoln and Jefferson up to Martin Luther King Jr. with regard to the latitudes and limits of personal freedom write or speak over the rights of others in such vein? By and large, the Africa Walker sees throughout her voyeuristic and pornographic *Warrior Marks* is an Africa that no African can recognize. Samples of her vision follow below; it is a strange monocular vision that is brutally unsparing in its manifestation of the writer's spiritual deracination. Do not miss the author's distance, a commercial kind of examination of Africans as mere silent commodities:

> The men around here are blindly gracious, like all slave masters. . . . The women seemed bored, weary of their own subservience. . . . There is a barren women's club. . . . One of them kept shaking her near naked butt in the children's

faces. I don't know if they *are* dykes. I think they are ridiculed and forced to play this entertainer role so that they, as barren women, can have a place in society at all, since a barren woman is considered of no use whatsoever.[39]

Women are routinely followed, yelled at, harassed on the street. I can't help but connect this behavior to genital mutilation: the acceptance of domination, the lack of a strong sense of self one sees among the women here. Or, conversely there will occasionally be an extremely loud brash woman, like the one who pressed us to buy her wares with such vigor that she ran us out of her stall. These are women whose pent-up anger seems to be a powder keg.[40]

It is probably pointless to cull more fragments from this horrid text. Every other line is an indiscriminate savage bite in its thoughtless regal arrogance and ignorance. This pattern of manipulation and distortion of reality also expresses itself dearly in *Possessing the Secret of Joy*, as it does in *Warrior Marks*, and irks the sensitive African reader. It is probably welcome in some segments of the African American community considering the reluctance of critics to apply appropriate scalpels on such racially or culturally insidious pestilent abscesses. A beleaguered Africa cannot accept such deliberate incision of deceitful discursive spaces and their creation of dichotomous problems to aggravate the multiplex crises in economics and politics and governance. What this invites is a global sisterhood of the Walkers and Parmars and a certain kind of African literary criticism that will be discussed later.

Part of my unstated original intention in this chapter was to pursue the comic bumbling of *Warrior Marks* from the first page to the last, but spatial demand cannot permit that. Even if it did, it would be most offensive to extend attention to "Pratibha's Journey," considering the political and other relationship between the two collaborators. Even if it did, there is something discouraging and disturbing in the fact that Parmar associated herself with "political and cultural activism," with "feminist and antiracist organizing," and with "the Organization of Women of Asian and African Descent" and has "taught a course entitled 'Women, Race, and Culture' at the University of London" and "written many articles and essays on race and feminism and . . . co-edited anthologies of writings by black and Third World Women"; and with all that, she still does not know that the manner of her participation in the circumcision debate exposes an underbelly of foolishness and ignorance about the real meaning of social justice. If such an activist scholar with Kenyan roots is also so goofy as to identify the foremost creative male activist from Kenya, Ngugi wa Thiong'o, as a Nigerian, critiquing anything more is futile. It is like forgiving a Chinese scholar who writes that Mao Tse Tung was Japanese. The cinematic trickery in *Warrior Marks*, which reduces venerable African mothers and grandmothers to gnarled ghouls and ogres in white and red waiting to devour innocent little girls, merits only silence. For such is the moral character of the ingenuity and capability of all those feminists rushing around the African continent pitching tents here and there to prevent Africans from hurting themselves. Such is the capability of those who hold Africa's key to dreams.

WALKER'S FAITH AND THE PARALLAX

To read Walker's *Possessing the Secret of Joy* is to submit to something politically nauseating, to whirl one into a disturbing centripetality of sordid images slyly designed to impress the reader that the author is engaged in a mission of hope, a mission of selfless rescue of Africa and the African woman. The secret of joy is a clever placard of sympathy for Walker's imaginary suffering African sister. "RESISTANCE IS THE SECRET OF JOY!"[41] is trumpeted in the finale of the novel, when Tashi, the novel's fantastic heroine, envisions before death a defiant solidarity against the Olinkan government on her behalf. Some of the lines of that finale are telling in what they reveal about the novel's impetus and raison d'être: "Mbati is unfurling a banner quickly, before the soldiers can stop her (most of them illiterate, and so their response is slow). All of them—Adam, Olivia, Benny, Pierre, Raye, Mbati—hold it firmly and stretch it wide."[42]

Possessing the Secret of Joy sets up a leitmotif of conflict between evil backward forces and countervailing good ones. It is always clear, as we have seen in the final vignette above, that this novel is the story of another group of foreigners—this time blacks, miscegenated, indigenous, or renegade—come to save Africa. Muted or attenuated by the somewhat disingenuous brush strokes of Walker's art, the work periodically bristles with familiar racist stereotypes. For instance, in the citation above, the soldiers cannot stop Mbati because they are illiterate and therefore slow; probably as slow as all the Africans in the novel who cannot see what Walker sees or what she is trying to accomplish through the various images or characters in this novel.

These selected characters generally understand the African world, or the world in general, far better than any African especially because they are mostly imbued with Walker's supreme or ultimate knowledge—the knowledge of the beauty of sex. Also, they are all either versed in the philological relationship between love and sex or the unquestionable similarity between sex as something physical and sex as something spiritual. These characters are sensitive or must seem to be aware of Walker's novel measures of civilization, which include oral sex, masturbation, and "ways to make love without making babies"[43] or should be able to recognize that "childbirth above all should feel sexy."[44]

Atop all these characters of course is Tashi-Evelyn. She has been anointed and saved, having gone through the crucible of the primitivity of genital mutilation. She bears the burden of her sister Dura, who was "murdered" through that primitive practice. Mad, but recuperating through the services of the Jung incarnate and Raye, keepers of the gate of the West's psyche, Tashi returns to avenge, and for canonization. We see in her and her act

Walker's persona, a deputizing puppeteer conflating childhood trauma and the thrill of a Tarzanic espionage with its license to kill, and a biblical heavenly vengeance-is-mine authority. When Tashi does kill the so-called hateful Tsunga, we do not know what kind of lesson this is supposed to be for the African woman. A most likely implication is that all circumcised African women must either go and murder their mothers or perpetrate some grave harm. The author's mask of compassion turns quite ugly here in a heroism that is Western, selfish, and imperialistic, and as tacky as any tabloid art can be. To house the drama itself in a world of shuffling, suffering African women among seemingly prowling and predatory men and old women is an unbearable insult.

We do not need any extraordinary perspicacity to see that the world that Walker conjures up in *Possessing the Secret of Joy* is a hapless, primitive world where the primal encounter between God (man) and the Earth (woman) is conflated into a modern wicked conflict between the custodians of a brutal patriarchal culture and a helpless female population. Of course, the primordial is still in place, ably represented by superstition, by ignorance, illiteracy, and an ostensible, incorrigible foolishness with regard to diseases such as AIDS. Salvation and redemption are represented by Europe and America in various forms ranging from the poorly veiled and indignant authorial intrusions of Walker to those wooden ideological representations that pass for characters.

In all this absurd drama, which Lillie P. Howard in undeserving critical graciousness equivocates as "simultaneously gripping and repelling,"[45] Walker's puppets identify themselves quite clearly, and often as more repelling than they are gripping. To be pitied or destroyed are the ignorant, old, and polygamous Torabe, the callous and misguided and venerated M'Lissa, the malleable Mbati, and of course all the circumcised or mutilated suffering Olinka women who hobble or drag through a miserable life in what Walker sees as a "sliding gait."[46] On the other side, there are other puppets we are supposed to learn from, though they may be sometimes somewhat complicitous in their direct or indirect connection with the structures or inclinations of patriarchy. Most of these characters, of course, are from Europe or America: Adam, Olivia, Lisette and her great uncle, Raye, and the Carl Jung incarnate.

Lillie P. Howard, respectful and admiring in her reading of Walker, writes, "While one has no trouble comprehending the atrocities the novel unveils, the book is difficult to read nonetheless without physical, mental and emotional outrage."[47] But we do not know who or where to direct this outrage because no one knows exactly where to find Olinka except in that silly satirical realm where, according to Howard, the practice Walker rails against "was done . . . without anesthesia or sterilization, for the express pleasure of African men, many of whom enjoyed splitting open their brides on their wedding night 'like a watermelon.'"[48] But even if one knew where to find these African men who enjoyed splitting their brides like watermelon, the chances of that world being redeemed would appear greater if that world were approached with the cautious gait of Margaret Kent Bass.

Bass understands and appreciates the dangers of the parallax, the sensitivities of the underdog, and the pride that even some destitutes keep as a supplication. She is therefore, unlike some members of Walker's virtuous global sisterhood, able to write in the *CLA Journal*, "I have no quarrel with what Walker attempts to do, but rather the way she does it."[49] Continuing, she adds, "I hold the opinion that neither Walker's African heritage nor her First World benevolence protects her from the charge of cultural condescension, and I would suggest that her race and gender, and the establishment of the family tie lend not only tremendous power to Walker's words but also a *misleading authority and authenticity to the narrative*."[50]

The manipulative bent of the art here may escape the sensitivity of the theoretically faddish who imagine that because the novel appears to involve missionary African Americans, or sympathetic ghost-world characters like Carl Jung, that all racial, sexist and class binaries are happily resolved or nullified in the work. In one such opinion, "The Body as a Site of Colonization: Alice Walker and *Possessing the Secret of Joy*," Alyson Buckman claims that "both Western and male ideologies posit the Other (African, female) as a commodity whose definition should be fixed by the power elite; after all the Other is inferior to the dominant self and can be readily displaced within the system of power."[51] This is the kind of pretentious, universalist inanity which would like us all to wish away the various inequities crudely constructed into a glaring global politics of power where all definitions of status are monological inscriptions from one remote center. Because Africans practice circumcision, African men should now be seen as part of a universal "power elite" or "dominant self." This rings like the hackneyed Marxist hallucination of an oppressed block of workers of the world ranged against a nebulous phalanx of predatory bourgeoisie.

SISTERHOOD AND THE CLAIMS OF INSIGHT

The great pretense of Western feminism is kinship claims with African and other women, a so-called global sisterhood. This mean lie is repudiated by past and present history. The circumstances of slavery in Europe and the Americas do not justify it. The circumstances of colonialism in Africa do not justify it. The economics of neocolonial politics do not justify it. The distinct, ontological wall between the West and Africa deny any such relationship. There are too many scenes in *Warrior Marks* that could be replicated in the relationship between African women and Western women. One of the most interesting and curious scenes in all this is this characteristically unguarded depiction of Dakar women by Walker:

> These city women are quite cool and cynical I thought—until we encouraged their offer to dance. Up to the dancing, we were trying to hold a conversation about wife-beating, child-abuse, economic empowerment—in French, Wolof, Mandinka and English. In the middle of this I was stunned to hear Madame Fall, our host, ask me to buy them a refrigerated truck. . . . I assured her that a whole refrigerated truck is a bit out of my range in the film budget. Maybe I could contribute a couple of tires.[52]

It is doubtful whether this request is out of the range of any free-giving, open-hearted celebrated American writer. But this is not the issue from the above. What is clear again here is the gulf between the quotidian needs of the African woman and the culturally distant issues peddled to these women by Walker and her global sisters. It is indicative of the extent of divergence and dichotomy prevalent in numerous definitions and perceptions inflicted on Africa by all kinds of starry-eyed crusaders. Some of such works betray a weird pride and ignorance and reckless inattention to the historical and cultural foundations of the materials in question. Elleke Boehmer's piece[53] in an anthology curiously titled *Motherlands* merits attention in this regard. Others are completely inane in their assumption of their roles of all-knowing and protective mother of the cultural precincts they engage, such as Florence Stratton's piece: "How Could Things Fall Apart for Whom They Are Not Together?" in *Contemporary African Literature and the Politics of Gender.*[54] Let us take a quick look at the methods of these defenders of Walker's faith. As Marimba Ani writes in the vigorous and incisive *Yurugu*:

> There is only one way to break the hold, and that is to be able to recognize the phenomenon of European cultural imperialism, no matter what form it takes. This recognition can be facilitated by a critical examination of the concepts that are used to "package" it. Its disguises range from so-called universal religion to "objective scholarship"; from the abstractions of progress, science and knowledge to the pseudo-altruistic goals of "humanitarianism," "internationalism" and world "peace."[55]

The editorial introduction to *Motherlands* prepares us with similar universal notions. We are told as craftily as possible that "the mythology of 'motherhood,' then, has long been a familiar one in feminist literary debates whether of 'First' or 'Third' worlds"; but we are not told which representative, authoritative African women join voices with Adrienne Rich to argue "that whilst the historical reality is that motherhood is women's experience, the institution is frequently under male control."[56] Before such bland claims, there is need to explore the three thousand or so diverse ethnic groups in the African continent to figure whether their linealities or focalities are in sync with those conclusions. In the absence of such explorations, Elleke Boehmer's Oxford vantage point should not be allowed to read as authoritatively as that of Igbo women who know better than the kind of claims replete in Boehmer's universalistic presumptions and conclusions. We know that in assertions or contentions of this nature, as Chinua Achebe inimitably put it several years ago, "theories and bogeys are no substitutes for insight."[57]

Boehmer pretends that all women accept the implication of territorial deprivation that would then automatically fix all men in a brotherhood of criminality and create for all women a sympathetic sisterhood. There is a rather diligent explanation about why women have or should have a defensive global front, but we do not know, and we are not told why all men cannot be brothers, and are not brothers. Did Camille Paglia, Boehmer's racially closer and more eminent sister, not declare in *Sexual Personae* that such "insupportable feminist dichotomy between sex and power must go"?[58]

It should be quite interesting to engage issues of this nature exhaustively, especially where critics submit Atlas shoulders for problems not quite commensurate with their strength of knowledge. Of course, the crisis here is that critics of literatures in foreign languages, especially African languages, do not take their callings seriously enough to consider reasonable knowledge of the language and culture they work in before the familiar claims or announcements of expertise. In *Contemporary African Literature and the Politics of Gender*, Florence Stratton undertakes "to write African women back into the African literary tradition."[59] Her maternalism is obviously predicated on the presumption that no African woman has been able to accomplish that feat.

Such ill-considered and hasty declarations may be allowed to pass as philosophical and political statements elsewhere, but in their misplaced context must be read as innkeeper's musings. As carefully thought out literary criticism, grave error abides here. I must also hasten to add that no one can tell better stories about affliction than the afflicted. A man will tell the story of men better than most women, just as women will tell the story of women better. As long as the issue is feeling, no surrogate will do. But a cultural insider's understanding rarely pales before that of the outsider. To know a life can never equate to living that life. Certain critics need to appreciate the kind of afterthought which greeted Gerald Graff after his warring briefly with Chinua Achebe's critique of Conrad's *Heart of Darkness*:

> [T]hat literary representations are not simply neutral aesthetic descriptions but interventions that act upon the world they describe. This, in fact, is the point underlying many recent critiques of the idea of *objectivity*, critiques that are poorly understood by their critics; the point is not that there is no truth but that descriptions influence the situations they describe, thereby complicating the problem of truth.[60]

Obviating this realization in preference for presumptions in these matters generate all the parallax sight lines and their errors. Most such errors are aggravated by ontological distance that often is no respecter of outsiders or even the alienated insider. We appreciate writers such as Walker and all her global sisters, non-African and African, but we must draw their attention to the following.

Reflecting on education and the American polity, E. D. Hirsch[61] demands a certain level of cultural literacy without which one cannot function effectively in American society. In outlining the procedure for acquiring that literacy, Hirsch concentrates on apices of American history and crucial seams of the American cultural bric-a-brac. In all this, the ontological and epistemological basics are taken for granted as commonalities, ostensibly because of the near homogeneity imposed on Americans by the predominance of Judaeo-Christianity and other cognate values. If this demand for cultural literacy is considered that seriously given the near homogenous character of the United States of America, imagine the gravity of problems a mere visitor is likely to encounter with zero knowledge of the language or culture of an African informational area. It seems clear that much of the difficulties evident in the work of Walker and her sisters stem from that lack of the barest in cultural literacy.

Because these writers, who probably mean well, and are not really fools, rush in to where angels fear to tread, we have ill-thought-out judgments and conclusions in the understanding or appreciation of the peculiar nature of the African human condition. Elleke Boehemer inscribes her understanding of nationhood into a pluralistic African space, and Walker, of course, refers her partially and really crazily perceived psychosomatic disorder in the African woman to Carl Jung. Carl Jung? One indeed wonders whether Walker would accept any kind of counsel, psychiatric or psychic, from an Igbo traditional medicine man, a Yoruba *babalowo* (diviner), or a modern-day descendant of Mugo wa Kibiro (a mythical Kikuyu diviner).

All these regrettable attitudes are consistent with the prevailing pattern of relationship between the so-called First World and the rest of us. These things are, of course, based on what Izevbaye has clearly explained in a review essay that comes to terms with the notion of universality in international relations. According to Izevbaye, "the concept of universality—understood as the possession of a common human culture, morality, history or a common set of values . . . is an ideal that is not reflected in the world of politics and economics."[62] Such was the virgin impulse of the imperial and colonial program, but nonetheless, these attitudes are in general understandable. For in another review essay of Wendy R. Katz's *Rider Haggard and the Fiction of Empire: A Critical Study of British Imperial Fiction,* Martin Tucker observes the following in his metacriticism of Katz in a vein that eerily applies to Walker and her sisters: "In stating Haggard's ethos and manipulative/creative expression of it in isolation from its wider complexes of socio/cultural force, Katz refuses the stimulus of value judgment. That refusal is an evasion of Haggard's intrusion into Africa, and his arrogance with African mores. According to Katz, Graham Greene said as early as *Journey without Maps* (1936) that one went in the 1930s either to Africa or to a psychoanalyst."[63]

Even though we are in the 1990s, this relationship between Africa and the psychoanalyst (or psychiatrist) appears deathless and intriguingly interchangeable. We are here reminded of Walker's own defensive insistence that she not only has a right to speak about anything she sees anywhere but claims her prerogative to be Teflon to any African challenge as we find her assert arrogantly in an interview granted to Paula Giddings:

> [W]hen Africans get into trouble, who do they call? Everybody. They call on people they shouldn't even talk to—trying to raise money, appealing to people to fight their battles, buying guns from Russia and the United States. They (Africans) invite all of these experts from Europe and the United States to go there to say their bit about AIDS, to sell them condoms. So they can accept what I—someone who loves my former home—am saying. *They don't have a leg to stand on, so they better not start hopping around me!*[64]

No one knows how to describe or respond to all this, given, as we recall, that when some of those hapless Africans (women) requested a refrigerated truck, Walker was stunned! Now, is there nothing roguish here about all this claim of love for a former home? Walker is stunned when Africans invite her to help solve their problems but turns around to blame these same hapless Africans for accepting help from those other foreigners who are not stunned by similar invitations. How can one aspire toward all that imaginary black community she envisages burdened with a morbid fear of integration?

ONTOLOGICAL RELATIVITY, INTERROGATIONS, AND CONCLUSIONS

Genuine universal integration of humanity into one interdependent tapestry of cultures, mores, and values is not part of any program contemplated by Walker and her global sisters. These really feminist politicians desire to keep everyone's key to dreams. They want everything, especially Africa's memory. How else can one understand this journey without a map undertaken by Walker and her friends in *Warrior Marks*? If their big issue is circumcision and other related women's problems, are there no better ways of accessing the minds of these poor Africans and whatever is left of their bankrupt governments other than through vicious lampoons of venerable images? Certainly one can do better than that.

For the thinking African, here is the grave danger. Most of the feminist critical materials out there on African literature are not really engaged in a criticism that is evaluative of creative effort, as we can easily see from the writings of Boehmer, Stratton, and other similar academic adventurers. Where is the commentary on such crucial things like a writer's descriptive power? Where are the commentaries on evocative power and the imagination? Where are those gripping things that we find dear in American women novelists and poets such as Toni Morrison, Gloria Naylor, Maya Angelou, Zora Neale Hurston, Gwendolyn Brooks, Lucille Clifton, and a host of others? Can we for instance pick one female novelist from Africa and stand one of her novels beside *Song of Solomon, Beloved, Their Eyes Were Watching God, Linden Hills*,[65] and so forth? Can criticism not make valid cases about texts that are unappealing for one reason or the other? These are the issues that could determine the future of African literature by men or women, with regard to quality. As soon as a critic raises one technical question about a female African author, the Western feminist brood and their local culturally diffident cohorts run amok in arms. There must be a ready jargon available for a defensive dismissal. Preferably, patriarchy is being deconstructed! How far can such inanities be allowed to go? In the smoke screen of this impish excitation, veritable questions of African dignity in the face of brazen cultural imperialism take back seat. For instance, the issue of motherhood has been so debased and distorted that the real problem which most of these feminist critics are afraid to discuss—equity where workable or social justice for man and woman—is masked.

The most quoted contradictions in African male attitudes to women have been supplied by Mariama Bâ, Ama Ata Aidoo, and Lauretta Ngcobo, respectively, while for the ultimate vilification of the African male's attitude toward women, Buchi Emecheta keeps the patent. Mariama Bâ declares that "we no longer accept the nostalgic praise to the African mother whom, in his anxiety, man confuses with Mother Africa."[66] For Lauretta Ngcobo, "Africa holds two contradictory views of woman—the idealized, if not the idolized mother, and the female reality of woman as wife."[67] "Praise for mother from a distance is not enough," declared Caroline Rooney on behalf of all African men; "It is a question of landing, homecomings, coming down to earth, locally and practically, with the aspiration of creating new societies, a shared world."[68] C. L. Innes has also kindly pointed out to us that "Aidoo has challenged the nostalgic image of 'African mother' as symbol with a series of mothers whose characters and roles as well as their very plurality prevent them from being seen either symbolically or nostalgically."[69] Something is seriously wrong with all these declarations. There is really no known confusion in the representation or characterization of the mother or motherhood by African male writers. The African family knows that incontrovertible preference exists in favor of the mother by both children and adult. The feminist critic may play ostrich about this but that fact will remain unalterable. The issue skirted and obviated by all this is the interminable universal war between husbands and wives. To broach that and master its ramparts will without doubt expose everyone to culpability. A happier feminist substitute, clandestine and short term, has remained these invidious projections of imaginary African male ambivalence about motherhood.

African critics, men or women, who want to go anywhere with feminist discourse whether with the small *f* associated with Emecheta or the Western feminist's gigantic, imperial *F* must go back and look more carefully at the large issues of geography and cultural politics in Chandra Mohanty's *Third World Women and the Politics of Feminism.*[70] Perhaps these critics would better serve their energies by attending to places and things they understand. Those African female critics who are beginning to question their womanhood must go to Camille Paglia's *Sexual Personae.* This recommendation I make with awareness of the great irony involved considering Emecheta's own invitation to white women. The curiously titled work, *Motherlands* is fitful in sincerity and perspicacity. We are entitled to frown at critical postures which appear to endorse for us a Western perception of motherhood in the tradition of *Mommie Dearest,*[71] which African readers are likely to find culturally obnoxious, given a background of unconditional love and loyalty to those parents who are blessed with reliable consistent sanity and responsibility. Here and there in the contributions of *Motherlands* one encounters sobrieties such as:

> Generally speaking, critical discourse can be regarded as a colonizing or imperialist discourse: one which annexes its textual object in order to perpetuate itself, institutionalize itself, and its attendant ideological assumptions, be they derived from the discipline or the particular critic in question. As an index of this, it can be noted that critics are in the habit of expressing themselves in a colonialist or imperialist metaphors . . . a Western/northern critical appropriation of an African text involves the subjection of not only the particular text but its 'world' or cultural and historical context to the homogenizing standards and interests of the so-called 'first' world. The homogenizing or equalizing operation is more than a matter of cultural failure to recognize global inequalities of power.[72]

The pity of this kind of sentiment is that, very often, even those critics who express such sentiments loose their guard and slip into the same manner of omission. We find that even in Alice Walker, who probably means well, there is an inability to understand how rhetorical strategy anchored in alien values is doomed to a dismal reception, to failure and resentment.

What we are dealing with in all this is reductionism, and the chief peril of reductionism is the new blindness produced in the effort to create light and understanding. General terms and their indices emanate from one specific reality with an assumption that the kind of empirical procedure which enables us to understand physical objects is transposable to non-physical conditions, a useless Cartesian certain knowledge. When the arrogance, insouciance and insensitivity of such practices are challenged, there is feigned surprise, and an effort to reverse error and emotional injury, to reassign failing and political criminality to the interlocutor. We have allowed issues of this sort to pass in the politics of culture. We indulge the neomissionary salvationism otherwise called cultural imperialism. We accept or are expected to accept the usurpation of indigenous voices and deny meaning when meaning eludes the alien perception, or when there is obvious parallax in cultural sightlines. This opinion similar to that from *Motherlands* is therefore not uncommon: "When we compare theories, doctrines, points of view, and cultures on the score of what sorts of objects there are said to be," wisely writes V. W. Quine in one of his old pieces in *Ontological Relativity and Other Essays*, "we are comparing them in a respect which itself makes sense only provincially. It makes sense only as far afield as our efforts to translate our domestic idioms of identity and quantification bring encouragement in the way of simple and natural-looking correspondences."[73]

With regard to domestic idioms of identity, one recalls the old, pithy remark, often-quoted from Chinua Achebe: "No man can understand another whose language he does not speak (and language here does not mean simply words, but a man's entire world-view). How many Europeans or Americans know our language? I do not know of any."[74] Despite what should be a truism, one is amazed by the kind of presumptions that power the critical stances under examination.

Let us face it, the best of Walker's creative effort, such as *The Temple of My Familiar*,[75] in the eyes of any sensitive African reader is pseudomysticism. But whether America chooses to celebrate or not celebrate her is not the business of Africa. In Igbo country, one is always concerned by the excessive liberties in the revels of a foreign masquerade—hence, the concern in the other extreme in the spectrum of Walker's efforts, a mere political Eurocentric salvationism, brazen and intolerable. The writer loves the mystical and spiritual, but her writings and utterances and total demeanor, under scrutiny, lack mournfully in the basic principles of any deep way. Those who protect her works from criticism do her no good. The cocoon of arrogance must be broken. She needs to ponder over the possibility of an Olympics of cultural understanding in which people compete as equals, where the winners excite a positive curiosity in the losers, and where the losers wonder how to win, and see what techniques make them winners, winners whose victories should harm no one. In such a forum, it should be clear that all those who encourage or participate in the awkward in human activity, cultural or whatever, would have sense enough to learn and change. All human beings want to be winners; that is clear. But to be driven to win like beasts of burden, to be nailed to the crucifix of Western imperialism and ridiculed and scourged and lashed and bullied to the finish line must be seen as far less than real victory. Whoever engages in such must be educated out of what is clearly a complicity in dehumanization. Many things that pass as culture around the world are wrong, but we must be careful about who makes the judgment, and why or how it is made. We must be careful that the custodians of such practices be only educated out of them carefully and systematically. Cudgels will not do. Who, but a tyrant, saves anyone with blows on the head?

An African reads Toni Morrison and Gloria Naylor, Zora Neale Hurston and Gayle Jones, a lot of Lucille Clifton and much of Maya Angelou, and so forth with sorrow and cathartic delight. We are disturbed by monumental ancestral errors such as slavery and assorted internecine strife that cannot be wished away. Some of these errors and their terrors are dead and buried. Some are moribund. Some, such as the touted circumcision, infibulation, mutilation and so forth, leave resistant stumps here and there bonded to poverty and ignorance rather than to anything from the Western feminist's grotesque realm of patriarchal conspiracies. The custodians of the traditional instruments of a number of these practices are not educated Africans. Here education implies the formal and informal. Here education also includes that of the mind trapped in tangled shibboleths, capsuled in habit and in sometimes the atavistically complex and inexplicable. The combat weapons in these circumstances cannot be selfish psychotic anger and brazen arrogance. A carefully programmed education cautiously directed and delivered at the appropriate addresses of culture and power will eventually prevail.

The history of the salvation of Africa has always been familiarly written with holy books, sabers, and guns. A lot of literary criticism, anthropology, politics, and variegated philanthropy relish, reenact, and collude to effect that history. The key to dreams comes from one source. Rarely do gentle hands move in, cooperatively and symbiotically, to tend with care and understanding the tree of culture, and prune what is wrong or false. So many things are wrong, but an art, creative, critical or hermeneutic which descends on the people of Africa with the brutal arrogance of *The Color Purple*, *Possessing the Secret of Joy*, and *Warrior Marks* (the book and the film) comes with the royal blood of warriors in search of private joys and private stories to either salve secret hurt or palliate egos throbbing for assertion and recognition. With some candor, some humility, and a little tonic love which looks carefully at the faces of the people being saved and their total circumstances, we would all happily display our various keys to dreams, and then, nobility will manifest as nobility, and not a lunatic pilgrimage, with memorials for or at the gravestone of Carl Jung.

NOTES

1. U Tamsi 1970, 3.
2. Chow 1993, 41.
3. Chow 1993, 41.
4. Durant and Durant 1935.
5. Chinweizu, Jemie, and Madubuike 1980.
6. Walker and Parmar 1993.
7. Walker 1992.
8. Walker and Parmar 1993, 50.
9. Koso-Thomas 1987.
10. Koso-Thomas 1987, 1.
11. Koso-Thomas 1987, 37–38.
12. Gates and Appiah 1993.

13. Gates and Appiah 1993, xi.
14. Winchell 1992, 85–86.
15. Winchell 1992, 27.
16. Crichton 1980.
17. Walker and Parmar 1993, 29.
18. Wright 1954.
19. Wright 1954, 36.
20. Richburg 1995, 6.
21. Walker 1992, 281–282.
22. Walker 1992, 282–283.
23. Tredell 1999.
24. Walker and Parmar 1993, 283 (emphasis and exclamation added).
25. Walker and Parmar 1993, 285.
26. Walker 1983.
27. Okri in Walker 1983, back cover.
28. Walker 1983, 39.
29. Walker 1983, 82.
30. Walker 1983, 136–137.
31. Walker and Parmar 1993, 15–16.
32. Walker and Parmar 1993, 17.
33. Walker and Parmar 1993, 17.
34. Walker and Parmar 1993, 18.
35. Walker and Parmar 1993, 19.
36. Walker and Parmar 1993, 28.
37. Walker and Parmar 1993, 33 (emphasis in original).
38. Walker and Parmar 1993, 39.
39. Walker and Parmar 1993, 43–44.
40. Walker and Parmar 1993, 53–54.
41. Walker and Parmar 1993, 279.
42. Walker and Parmar 1993, 278–279.
43. Walker 1992, 31.
44. Walker 1992, 99.
45. Howard 1993, 143.
46. Walker 1992, 150.
47. Howard 1993, 143.
48. Howard 1993, 144.
49. Bass 1994, 3.
50. Bass 1994, 4 (emphasis added).
51. Buckman 1995, 92.
52. Walker and Parmar 1993, 28.
53. Boehmer 1992.
54. Stratton 1994.
55. Ani 1994, 513.
56. Nasta 1992, xx.
57. Achebe 1975, 79.
58. Paglia 1991, 38.
59. Stratton 1994, 13.
60. Graff 1992, 29.
61. Hirsch 1987.
62. Izevbaye 1989, 538.
63. Tucker 1989, 586.
64. Giddings 1992, 60 (emphasis added).
65. Morrison 1977, 1987; Hurston 1937; Naylor1985.

66. Nasta 1992, 5.
67. Nasta 1992, 5.
68. Rooney 1992, 122.
69. Innes 1992, 133.
70. Mohanty, Russo, and Torres 1991.
71. Crawford 1978.
72. Nasta 1992, 101.
73. Quine 1969, 6.
74. Achebe 1975, 79.
75. Walker 1989.

WORKS CITED

Achebe, Chinua. 1975. *Morning Yet on Creation Day.* Garden City, NY: Anchor/ Doubleday.
Ani, Marimba. 1994. *Yurugu: An African Centered Critique of European Cultural Thought and Behavior.* Trenton, NJ: Africa World Press.
Bass, Margaret Kent. 1994. "Alice's Secret." *CLA Journal* 38 (1): 1–10.
Boehmer, Elleke. 1992. "Stories of Women and Mothers: Gender and Nationalism in Early Fiction of Flora Nwapa." In *Motherlands: Black Women's Writing from Africa, the Caribbean, and South Asia,* ed. Susheila Nasta, 3–23. New Brunswick, NJ: Rutgers University Press.
Buckman, Alyson R. 1995. "The Body as a Site of Colonization: Alice Walker's *Possessing the Secret of Joy.*" *Journal of American Culture* 18 (2): 89–94.
Chinweizu, Onwuchekwa Jemie, and Ihechukwu Madubuike. 1980. *Toward the Decolonization of African Literature.* Enugu: Fourth Dimension Publishers.
Chow, Rey. 1993. *Writing Diaspora: Tactics of Intervention in Contemporary Cultural Studies.* Bloomington: Indiana University Press.
Crawford, Christina. 1978. *Mommie Dearest.* New York: W. Morrow.
Crichton, Michael. 1980. *Congo.* New York: Ballantine Books.
Durant, Will, and Ariel Durant. 1935. *The Story of Civilization.* New York: Simon & Schuster.
Gates, Henry Louis, Jr., and Kwame Appiah. 1993. *Alice Walker.* New York: Amistad.
Giddings, Paula. 1992. "Alice Walker's Appeal." *Essence,* July, 60–62.
Graff, Gerald. 1992. *Beyond the Culture Wars.* New York: W. W. Norton and Co.
Greene, Graham. 1936. *Journey without Maps.* London: Heinemann.
Hirsch, E. D., Jr. 1987. *Cultural Literacy: What Every American Needs to Know.* Boston: Houghton Mifflin.
Howard, Lillie P. 1993. "A Benediction: A Few Words about *The Temple of My Familiar, Variously Experienced* and *Possessing the Secret of Joy.*" In *Alice Walker and Zora Neale Hurston: The Common Bond,* ed. Lillie P. Howard, 139–146. Westport, CT: Greenwood Press.
Hurston, Zora Neal. 1937. *Their Eyes Were Watching God.* Greenwich, CT: Fawcett.
Innes, C. L. 1992. "Mothers or Sisters? Identity, Discourse and Audience in the Writing of Ama Ata Aidoo and Mariama Bâ." In *Motherlands: Black Women's Writing from Africa, the Caribbean, and South Asia,* ed. Susheila Nasta, 129–151. New Brunswick, NJ: Rutgers University Press.
Izevbaye, Dan. 1989. "Review Essay." *Research in African Literatures* 20 (3): 536–540.
Katz, Wendy R. 1987. *Rider Haggard and the Fiction of Empire: A Critical Study of British Imperial Fiction.* Cambridge: Cambridge University Press.
Koso-Thomas, Olayinka. 1987. *The Circumcision of Women. A Strategy for Eradication.* London: Zed Books.

Mohanty, Chandra Talpade, Ann Russo, and Lourdes Torres, eds. 1991. *Third World Women and the Politics of Feminism.* Bloomington, IN: Indiana University Press.

Morrison, Toni. 1977. *Song of Solomon.* London: Vintage.

———. 1987. *Beloved.* New York: Vintage.

Nasta, Susheila, ed. 1992. *Motherlands: Black Women's Writing from Africa, the Caribbean, and South Asia.* New Brunswick, NJ: Rutgers University Press.

Naylor, Gloria. 1985. *Linden Hills.* New York: Tichnor and Fields.

Paglia, Camille. 1991. *Sexual Personae.* New York: Vintage Books.

Parmar, Pratibha, producer/director. 1993. *Warrior Marks* [videorecording]. A Hauer Rawlence Production. New York: Women Make Movies (distributor).

Quine, V. W. 1969. *Ontological Relativity and Other Essays.* New York: Columbia University Press.

Richburg, Keith. 1995. "A Black American in Africa." *The Washington Post National Weekly Review* 12 (23): 6–8.

Rooney, Caroline. 1992. "'Dangerous Knowledge' and the Poetics of Survival: A Reading of *Our Sister Killjoy* and *A Question of Power.*" In *Motherlands: Black Women's Writing from Africa, the Caribbean, and South Asia,* ed. Susheila Nasta, 99–128. New Brunswick, NJ: Rutgers University Press.

Stratton, Florence. 1994. *Contemporary African Literature and the Politics of Gender.* London: Routledge.

Tredell, Nicolas, ed. 1999. *Joseph Conrad: Heart of Darkness.* New York: Columbia University Press.

Tucker, Martin. 1989. "Review Essay." *Research in African Literature* 20 (3): 584–586.

U Tamsi, Tchicaya. 1970. *Selected Poems.* London: Heinemann Educational Books.

Walker, Alice. 1982. *The Color Purple.* New York: Harcourt Brace Jovanovich.

———. 1983. *In Search of Our Mothers' Gardens: Womanist Prose.* San Diego, CA: Harcourt Brace Jovanovich.

———. 1989. *The Temple of My Familiar.* San Diego, CA: Harcourt Brace Jovanovich.

———. 1992. *Possessing the Secret of Joy.* New York: Harcourt Brace Jovanovich.

Walker, Alice, and Pratibha Parmar. 1993. *Warrior Marks: Female Genital Mutilation and the Sexual Blinding of Women.* New York: Harcourt Brace.

Winchell, Donna Haisty. 1992. *Alice Walker.* New York: Twayne Publishers.

Wright, Richard. 1954. *Black Power.* New York: Harper.

Overcoming Willful Blindness: Building Egalitarian Multicultural Women's Coalitions

Ange-Marie Hancock

Feminist theory, in its role as a critical theory, has sought to deconstruct the androcentric focus of society by constructing visions of the world that render the experiences of women relevant and significant. Yet many of Western feminist theory's goals are not carried out in practice by certain Western feminists as they traverse cultural boundaries. The ramifications of this disjuncture prevent the building of egalitarian multicultural coalitions among women of various situations as they struggle to attain a common goal of feminisms: empowerment of women. This gulf between Western women and indigenous women is nowhere more evident than in recent debates over methods to end the cultural practice of female genital mutilation (FGM).

In this chapter, I propose a theory of building more egalitarian coalitions across cultures that resides within the theoretical paradigm of feminist theory. The theory overcomes the "blind spots" previously demonstrated by feminists seeking to build coalitions by focusing on practices that encourage participants to see each other as contextualized subjects rather than essentialized stereotypes. Using the method of discourse analysis, I examine the works of African women regarding the topic of FGM. In so doing, I detail the general responses of African feminists to Western feminists' anti-FGM activism as a way of ensuring that their voices are not lost in the discourse. Herein the responses focus on the work of two Western feminists who have made their names synonymous with the anti-FGM movement in the West. This focus does not intend to include all Western feminists, in their many incarnations, into the characterizations I document here.[1] However, the words of African women's experiences across development programs and political activism indicate a persistent gulf between Western and indigenous women that requires our attention.

To repair this broken bond, I propose a theory of egalitarian multicultural coalition building that aspires to repair the linkages broken between Western feminists and African women. This approach builds on work in the areas of feminist theory, politics, and international development in hopes of creating an empowering approach to coalition development. I then apply the theory directly to the issue of FGM, suggesting that the political context of Burkina Faso represents an excellent opportunity for such coalition building to occur. My concluding thoughts return to feminist theory and praxis, which have been mired in the deconstructive mode with comparatively few attempts towards its companion task of reconstructive visions. With the attacks from feminists of color, Western feminist theorists have recently eschewed metatheory for fear of rendering some group's experience invisible. Through the analysis presented here, I suggest that metatheory is possible when it is grounded in an inclusive, multicultural, egalitarian context. As a practical experience, egalitarian multicultural coalition politics can inform feminist theory by discovering ways to talk about women as a group without devolving into meaningless generalizations.

WESTERN FEMINIST THEORY: A SINGULAR VISION FOR FEMINISM?

Feminism, in its broadest sense, seeks to empower women and to transform unequal power relations between the sexes into more egalitarian structures. Western feminist theory has sought to accomplish this in increasingly open-minded ways, due in part to challenges from marginalized women, as well as its construction as a critical theory that involves both internal transformation and external change. The role of a critical theory is simultaneously deconstructive—challenging the dominant practices, theories, and philosophical presuppositions that undergird such epistemologies— and reconstructive, sketching alternative conceptions to avoid previously outlined flaws.[2] Western feminist theory acts as a critical theory via its deconstruction of ahistorical, decontextualized epistemologies that privilege androcentric ways of being in the world. Many Western feminist theorists[3] answer the negation of women's place in the world by crafting "conception[s] of self, knowledge and practice that are better able to address women's experience."[4]

Thus Western feminist theory commonly presupposes the privileged position of women's lived experience as a contributor to theory. Politically speaking, Western feminist theory, in its role as a critical theory, must seek models of political identity that are "participatory and democratic,"[5] leading to a discourse that is of theoretical and practical solidarity. The importance of the relationships between Western feminist theory and feminist political practice cannot be underestimated. Leonard notes that this link clears a theoretical space for political practices that require the oppressed to emancipate themselves.[6] However, as Western feminist theory has sought to empower women of diverse positions in the social hierarchy, Western feminist praxis has not always lived up to the challenge.

From this broad view of Western feminist theory as a theory of women's empowerment, two further presuppositions traditionally emanate. First, historical and cultural contexts matter—the environment in which empowerment occurs is critical to an understanding of the changing power relations. For example, Patricia Hill Collins notes the critical nature of rooting Afrocentric feminist epistemology in the everyday experiences of Black women: "The forms of knowledge allow for subjectivity between the knower and the known, rest in the women themselves (not in higher authorities) and are experienced directly in the world (not through abstractions)."[7]

The second underlying assumption of an empowering feminist theory concerns political practice. Dorothy Smith's *Conceptual Practices of Power* informs this assertion by seeking to place investigations in a framework of social relations via the concept of "insider materialism," the taking of concepts, ideas, ideology, and schemata as dimensions and organizers of ongoing social processes that we can grasp "only as insiders, only by considering our own practices."[8] By envisioning how we ourselves could be constituted as parts of the "other," that is, members of the out-group in our own context, we can better appreciate the perspective of the women at issue.[9] Linking the good intentions of Western feminist theory to daily cross-cultural practice in research, development programs, and politics, however, is not currently a widespread phenomenon.[10]

Contributions from the psychological and development literatures on empowerment can strengthen the bond between feminist theory and praxis, leading Western feminists ever closer to their goal of empowering all women in their respective contexts. Empowerment herein is a process or mechanism by which people, organizations, and communities gain autonomy and mastery over their own affairs.[11] In particular, political empowerment is commonly noted as having several prerequisites, which include resources (financial, educational, and technological) as well as skills, training, and leadership formation.[12]

By specifying empowerment as an integrative, dynamic process with eight dimensions—self-esteem, self-efficacy, knowledge and skills, political awareness, social participation, political participation, political rights and responsibilities, and resources[13]—a feminist approach to empowerment is enriched, capturing both individual- and institutional-level constructs important in evaluating the empowerment status of women.[14]

Three strategies emerging from research on empowerment are essential to the empowerment of broad and diverse groups of women and particularly relevant to coalition building. First, praxis must be rooted in the daily existence of the women seeking empowerment. Second, practices should grant agency to program beneficiaries by casting them as collaborators with the power of self-definition and self-transformation. Third, locally developed solutions are more empowering than a single broad solution applied in various contexts. Policies pursuing these goals can lead to changes in the eight areas documented above as proxies for measuring the change in the condition and position of women.

Unfortunately, the tactics outlined above are often disregarded as Western feminists journey outside of their own cultural contexts to join with women around the globe in struggles for empowerment. MacKinnon notes that "men create the world from their own point of view, which then becomes the truth to be described."[15] Western feminists have been documented for replicating this practice along the spectrum of North-South relations.[16] When taking up the struggles of women in vastly different situations from their own, Western feminist approaches have been castigated for being culturally insensitive, resulting in characterizations that alienate and isolate non-Western women into exotic, primitive beings who lack agency or knowledge.[17]

This is the charge of which some Western feminists stand accused in their activities to eradicate FGM on the continent of Africa. Western feminist practice in this arena hinders the development of knowledge and processes that serve to empower African women because it does not act in compliance with the more recent developments within its own theoretical discourse.[18] This remains a stumbling block for practical coalitions when Western feminists in this vein have yet to recognize the growth in number and sophistication of African women's organizations over the past twenty years. The resulting clash of interests between such indigenous groups and international women's human-rights organizations have stunted the development of lasting alliances focusing on women's empowerment.[19]

Two ramifications of this serious disjuncture result in the fight against FGM. Women undergoing FGM suffer abstraction and decontextualization, directly contradicting the insider materialist position, which argues that feminist theory and practice should focus on the social relations through which we are constituted, rather than remove people from their context.[20] Ignoring the contextual factors of women's lives documented as critical by Western feminists in their own situations leads to the second ramification, demonization of grandmothers, aunts, and *daya* (circumcisers) who maintain the tradition. Neither outcome is acceptable to many African feminists despite their common normative goal—the obliteration of the practice of FGM. The decontextualization and demonization deny African women the very basic power of self-definition. Without this fundamental prerequisite for empowerment,[21] much of the programs and funding designed to empower women by eradicating FGM are like homes built on quicksand—doomed to be engulfed in power struggles—ironically, between groups of women. The failure of many eradication programs, as well as FGM's endurance over nearly three decades of Western feminist and African women's activities against the practice, necessitate an alternative approach.

Coalitions of Western women and African women have tried and failed to effectively bridge the gaps in cross-cultural understanding.[22] Yet multi-cultural coalitions must remain the hope of this struggle as long as African countries' key goal is "freedom from want."[23] Western feminists in many cases possess the financial and technological resources required for successful programs. What has been commonly overlooked by development professionals and Western feminist activists are those resources already possessed by African women. Multicultural alliances must overcome the obstacles of Western imperialism to employ a more comprehensive approach to coalition building. While theorists have described new types of feminism that are receptive to comprehensive approaches,[24] theorizing concomitant praxes remains a rare occurrence.

While the international anti-FGM movement can be analyzed as a case of fatal misunderstandings and misconceptions in past relationships between Western women and African women, we can also envision it as a potential site for egalitarian coalitions. Such an approach would include previously omitted feminist practices in this domain that (1) encourage intersubjective understanding; (2) seek to comprehend women's positions as contextualized social actors with agency; and (3) attempt to minimize the differential power relations among various groups of women. This type of alliance is proposed as empowering for indigenous women because it encourages self-development, the only type of sustainable development.[25]

This chapter is designed to outline a theory that can reconcile the goals of Western feminist theory with Western feminist praxis for the practical purpose of egalitarian multicultural coalition building. Below, I first explore African feminisms (noting varied terminology in this regard), then provide a brief account of Burkina Faso's efforts against FGM.

Charlotte Bunch notes that this kind of reconstructive discourse is glaringly absent from feminist theory.[26] The painful and often discouraging experiences of women in multicultural coalitions have been documented by many feminists of color throughout the late 1970s and 1980s, satisfying the deconstructive aims of feminist theory. The difficulties, however, exist in making the transition back to an empowering project of reconstructing theory. In practice, coalitions necessarily continue the work of feminisms around the globe. Bernice Johnson Reagon puts this fact quite nicely, "You don't go into coalition because you just like it. The only reason you would consider trying to team up with somebody who could possibly kill you, is because that's the only way you can figure you can stay alive."[27]

Both Bunch and Reagon note the shrinking existence of places for "just us" as global feminism evolves to be a unifying (but not uniform) group of methods women use to empower themselves. Western feminists reaching out to indigenous groups of women in Africa are welcome to join the fight against FGM. It is the nature of their role in the fight, not their very legitimacy as fighters, that is at issue in building egalitarian multicultural coalitions.

AFRICAN WOMEN'S RESPONSES TO
WESTERN FEMINIST ACTIONS AGAINST FGM

Feminist women activists continue to raise public awareness about the harm FGM inflicts on female children across Africa. Few, if any, feminist writers (Western or African) have taken a purely scientific, positivist position: all are clear that their ultimate goal is normative—the eradication of this cultural practice from all parts of the world. However, Western feminist writers have faced a tremendous backlash from African women across the Diaspora who view their work as yet another case of Western imperialism.[28] From the dawn of Western interest in FGM, the responses from African women have been scathing and numerous. The charges are largely legitimate, for a number of reasons that point to the discrepancy between various parts of Western feminist theory and its implementation.

Broadly speaking, developing world feminists have lambasted Western feminists for falling into the trap that androcentric discourse has set for researchers and activists.[29] The goal of empowerment inherent in feminism is lost when, as Chandra Talpade Mohanty asserts, Western feminists decontextualize their subjects, presenting them as already constituted subjects thrown into social situations.[30] The political ramifications on the African continent, according to Egyptian anthropologist Soheir Morsy and Egyptian physician Nawal El Saadawi, can be the use of Western feminist activities as a scapegoat to elicit postcolonial outrage against Westerners. Mohanty notes the power of Western feminist actions in the global discourse, "nevertheless, [each act] carries with it the authorizing signature of Western humanist discourse."[31]

Nancy Scheper-Hughes concurs with Mohanty by noting the political consequences of Western influences regarding actions to fight FGM: "Postcolonial Western anthropologists have attempted (albeit unconsciously) to recolonize parts of the Third World by a critically unreflexive, primitivist discourse on the Other, circumscribed and not."[32]

Feminist theory aside, the discourse created by Western feminists around the issue of FGM has material consequences for all involved. African women continue to endure the practice. Western women, when focusing on the topic, often fail to see the links to equally harmful body practices in their own contexts, which could provide perspectives and approaches more conducive to coalition building. One key component of developing an intersubjective, egalitarian, multicultural coalition between Western women and African women that is empowering rather than debilitating lies in exploring how to address Western-African power dynamics in a way that does not negate the experiences of those who live daily under the threat and violence of FGM. Two anti-FGM Western feminists who have suffered harsh criticism from African women are Fran Hosken and Alice Walker.[33]

The notion of "victimology" seems perfectly suited for Hosken's work.[34] However, Hosken's work is problematic less for its actual content, and more for its hegemony in the discourse on FGM—it is commonly accepted to be the most comprehensive and authoritative source for researchers, policymakers, and activists. Those who rely upon Hosken's work to create anti-FGM programs risk the exclusion of African women's expertise, diminishing the chances for women to empower themselves and successfully eradicate FGM.

Hosken's position as "expert" significantly ups the ante in African women's eyes. Her previous formal role with development organizations and her current informal role as one of the most well-known Western anti-FGM activists imbue her characterizations of African women with power because they are accorded a privileged position in the global discourse. By her own admission, Hosken continues to testify before the U.S. Congress, international organizations, and other agencies in this fight. Her quarterly publication, *Women's International Network News*, includes a section in each edition focusing upon the state of the struggle against FGM. She is indeed one of the most prolific Western writers on this topic. Thus her power endures as a voice in debates concerning resources allocated by donor organizations to anti-FGM efforts, the nature of the programs funded by these organizations, and the image of African women in the international arena.

The political consequences of the words of Western feminist activists like Hosken are documented by Morsy: "These are times when 'natives' have increasingly come to read what anthropologists write. It is worth remembering that it was nothing less than emotional reactions—including distress, anger and indignation at domination, which fueled anti-colonial struggles."[35] Addressing the responses of African women to Hosken's work and other Western feminists is a key variable in developing a working model of egalitarian, multicultural coalition politics.

The power of self-definition, asserted by many postcolonial scholars, is echoed by Collins in creating an Afrocentric feminist epistemology that reconstitutes the power dynamics underlying the very process of definition.[36] It is this right of self-definition, protected in most Western feminist frameworks, that Hosken violates in her anti-FGM activism. This represents a transgression of the boundary of human agency and does violence to the experience of African women as socially constituted figures.

Salem Mekuria[37] documents the rhetoric of Western feminists as part of an overall discourse that completely ignores the experience of African women on the continent who daily fight the challenges of FGM. She states, "The current representation of and discussion about female genital mutilation, be it in literature, film or other popular media, not only ignores the critical voices of Africans, but makes no attempt to present the context within which the practice perpetuates itself."[38] Her statement echoes the sentiments of many African women in response to the eagerness of Western feminists to "aid" African women by joining the movement in a disruptive manner. While Hosken's maternalism does not necessitate a complete refutation of her work, it must be situated as a Western feminist response to the dilemma of FGM, since as Mekuria insightfully states, "We talk a lot about power, usually male power, in the women's liberation movement. But seldom is the power some groups of women have in relation to other groups of women acknowledged."[39] Egalitarian multicultural coalition building addresses differential power among women, as we shall see below.

Alice Walker's voice has similarly been a clear attack on FGM. Through her novel, *Possessing the Secret of Joy,* and her film, *Warrior Marks: Female Genital Mutilation and the Sexual Blinding of Women,* Walker has placed herself at the forefront of African American women's discourse on female genital mutilation. Walker straddles a unique position as a woman of African descent from a predominantly Western cultural orientation. Indeed, her strident response to such criticism attempts to engender solidarity with African women, belying the Western socialization that at times infringes upon her anti-FGM work, "These disgusting intellectual conversations over culture and imperialism. . . . How do you think I got here? We came from Africa on slave ships to America, so I share in the victimhood of Western imperialism."[40] Mekuria's response to Walker's film is one of indignation,

> Walker condemns the practice with statements about her deep love for African children. Surely she can't mean to malign African parents' capacity to love their children and protect them from danger! It is hard to believe that Alice Walker is not aware of the implications of such an invasive approach. Are we now to focus our attention on Africa as a continent of physically mutilated, psychologically deficient and mentally deranged women who, as she presumes in her book, have to 'chew on their sticks to keep from exploding'?[41]

It is important to remember at this point that Mekuria, Dawit, and Toubia are not espousing cultural nationalist or cultural relativist positions—they are as much in favor of eradicating FGM as Hosken and Walker profess to be. However, their experiences as women in African countries at the grassroots and institutional levels lead them to different solutions to the dilemma. And their outrage over the relative silence of African women's voices in the debate over a problem that disparately impacts African women certainly is justified.

INCORPORATING POST-COLONIAL EXPERIENCE: AFRICAN FEMINIST THEORY

Many women in various African nations face charges of Western cooptation when asserting their rights as women to attack patriarchy.[42] Molara Ogundipe-Leslie characterizes this tactic as one designed to divide women during democratic transitions, serving to ensure male hegemony even in light of political uncertainty. African males have resorted to portrayals of middle-class women as "too Westernized to be true African women" and romanticized ideals of rural and unlettered women as those who should naturally be excluded from the public realm and political discourse.[43] The material consequences of this kind of attack include the preservation of FGM as a political tool to arouse nationalist, anticolonial/anti-Western sentiment during turbulent times.[44]

To counter charges that African feminists act with "colonized minds," Ogundipe-Leslie suggests an alternative to the construct of feminism— *stiwanism.*[45] Its root, STIWA, is an acronym for Social Transformation Including Women in Africa. Her further justifications for *stiwanism* stem from claims similar to the both/and construction of Collins in claiming a unique standpoint between group identities. As an *African* woman, she refutes the racist tendency of some white feminist movements to see all other human societies as less evolved and less developed. As an African *woman*, she refutes Africans' privileging of race and class over gender as a category of contestation and inequality.[46] From this situated standpoint the discussion moves beyond the single issue of anti-FGM activism to a global analysis of power relations, where white women exhibit patterns of exclusivity, monopolization of resources, and exploitation of Third World women physically, emotionally and intellectually via their shared group identity with the Western world.[47] This recognition of the differential global power is an important step along the coalition-building journey. Western feminist anti-FGM activists must accept and understand the potential psychological reactions to challenges asserted by African women who often are all too experienced with postcolonial, Western domination.

Philomena Okeke takes this analysis of global power relations among women and links it to Western postmodern feminist discourse to evaluate its usefulness for improving "the state of African-Western feminist relations."[48] Recognizing the global inequity of power in production of knowledge and expertise, Okeke reminds us that, "What the global community knows about African women at present is traceable largely to the writings of white female scholars."[49] While neither Okeke nor Ogundipe-Leslie is advocating the eradication of white feminist theory from analyses of African women, both note that it is impossible, in postmodern feminist theory or other Western feminist theories, to deny the differential power relations in the shared intellectual space of global feminism.[50] Moreover, African women's voices must have privileged access to enhance the opportunities for self-definition and contextualized analysis previously omitted from the discourse about FGM. Without equal roles in the discourse, the potential for egalitarian coalitions is stunted, as the Western feminists' premises, prescriptions, and actions are interpreted and rejected by African women, thus leading to diminished opportunities to successfully end FGM.

In reconstructing feminism, Ogundipe-Leslie states that feminist ideologies have always existed in Africa.[51] Unlike the perceived Western feminist focus on African women's bodily integrity, she and others argue that African feminism/*stiwanism* should include but not be limited to issues surrounding women's bodies.[52] This reconstruction of a feminism that is suitable to African women's experiences attempts to address the decontextualizations prevalent in Western feminist research and activism. Thus the African woman's entire person, immediate family, society, nation, continent, and location in the international economic order are all relevant to *stiwanism*. While this characterization is not unique to *stiwanism*, it grants to African feminists what Western feminist theory so clearly grants to itself.

Any study of African women should situate them in a context of social relations in which they are both instruments and agents of power. One potential site identified for this construction is in the struggle for democracy. Ogundipe-Leslie envisions democratic transitions as an opportunity for African countries to do better than the ancient Greeks and eighteenth-century Europeans who excluded women and slaves from their illusions of democratic political grandeur. According to Mahmood Mamdani, democracy, a concept originating from the Western world, must nevertheless be adapted to the cultural peculiarities of African countries and cannot be expected to proceed in the exact linear progression of the modern European nation state.[53] One key example of African women's struggle to act as agents of power despite their positions in a patriarchal social framework exists in the fight to keep anti-FGM efforts on the mainstream political agenda during the ongoing democratic transition in Burkina Faso.

ADJUSTING OUR SIGHTLINES: SEEING THE ENTIRE PICTURE

The ideas of Ogundipe-Leslie and Okeke echo in theory what Mekuria and others call for in practice. African women's experience must be contextualized and not abstracted from its daily existence. While postmodern debates over the potential for universality in feminist democratic theory or politics are beyond the scope of this chapter, what seems critical from this review of African women's responses to Western women feminists is the development of common ground upon which an active coalition can exist. This coalition can only be achieved, however, with recognition of the micro- and macro- levels of differential power among groups, and the disparate impacts of their various interactions to mitigate its effect upon any potential alliances. Only then can we mute the effect of unequal power relations (and the ramifications thereof) to build empowering multicultural alliances.

WHY COALITIONS WITH BURKINABÉ?

I propose the case of Burkina Faso as a site for such multicultural egalitarian coalitions; anti-FGM action to date in this country has reached the limits of its own capabilities.[54] Western feminists may now seek to aid grass-roots groups in Burkina Faso to push forward in the eradication of FGM.

Burkina Faso is a model partner for Western groups (both feminist and international) in a single-issue social movement designed to simultaneously eradicate FGM and empower women. The 1984 Marxist revolution led to the installment of several high-ranking women government officials who support ending female excision, and produced several informational campaigns against FGM as part of larger government programs to ameliorate the status of women in Burkina Faso.[55] The late Burkinabé leader, Thomas Sankara, believed wholeheartedly in the liberation of Burkinabé women, and granted women ministers the opportunity to create safe spaces within the government for work to begin in earnest against FGM.

Since that time, Burkina Faso has become one of only four African countries to have passed legislation against FGM. In 1991, democratic processes began to evolve in Burkina Faso, with the advent of a constitution, parliamentary elections, and the installation of a popularly elected president. Despite the political uncertainty and popular disenchantment with economic reforms that often accompanies these democratic changes, the struggle against FGM seemingly marches on, with the Burkinabé government actually using significant portions of its foreign aid to campaign against FGM. President Blaise Compaore has utilized his more progressive stand on issues like FGM in his pursuit and attainment of the presidency of the Organization of African Unity, while his wife has co-chaired a major women's organization devoted to the fight against FGM. Similarly, grassroots groups such as the Teriya Theater produce dramatic presentations designed to address the risks of FGM. Thus FGM remains an issue to which national, civil, and grassroots institutions commit their resources in Burkina Faso.

STARTING AND SUSTAINING A CULTURAL REVOLUTION: A THEORY OF COALITION POLITICS

Political coalitions traditionally refer to groups or individuals that come together around a particular issue to achieve a particular goal.[56] The theory of coalition politics I develop here will use FGM as an issue of common interest to Western feminists and indigenous women's groups in Africa. Clearly, the standpoints of Western, primarily white, feminists and indigenous women of color differ. A three-pronged approach to building such coalitions will nurture such coalitions in empowering, rather than imperialist, ways. This approach resides within the underlying assumptions and tenets of critical Western feminist theory while being informed by theory from feminists of color across the Diaspora.[57] It remains for Western feminists to practice what their theory preaches.

Multicultural coalition politics includes three goals to be jointly pursued by Western feminists and indigenous African women fighting to end female genital mutilation. First, cross-cultural interactions between groups must encourage intersubjective understanding—women must seek methods of world traveling that "enter into the spirit of difference and find in it an echo of oneself as other than the way one seems to be."[58] By seeking intersubjective understanding, women move towards the second step in egalitarian coalition building: comprehension of women's positions as contextualized social actors with agency. This step emanates from various Western feminist critiques of androcentric forms of discourse that posit humans as ahistorical phenomena. The third step is last but never final: women from diverse backgrounds must attempt to minimize the differential power relations among various groups of women. Coalition politics, as we shall see in this section, resides in a constant state of becoming. By exploring such a process feminists serve the ultimate goal of empowering women and thus societal transformation.

As noted earlier, coalition building is not always nurturing or comfortable—it involves discussion of concrete issues with material consequences—power and privilege that both condition and facilitate the most important material consequence, access to and utilization of resources.[59] Maintenance of the pursuit of women's empowerment via struggles of strategies and tactics remains the project for egalitarian, multicultural coalitions.

The three-step method outlined in this section is posited as an empowering remedy for some of the potentially immobilizing problems arising from previous practical experiences in coalition politics across differences in race, culture, and class. The uniquely close tie between feminist theory and feminist praxis dictates the exploration of the proposed egalitarian multicultural coalition theory's implications upon feminist political practice and public policy.

By encouraging intersubjective understanding among women across difference, envisioning all women as contextualized social agents, and minimizing differential power relations, feminist political activists and policymakers can bridge the gulf of cultural difference to empower women around the world. Using FGM again as an example, I will draw upon alternative theories of empowerment and development to develop strategies within the framework of egalitarian multicultural coalition politics to help women cross the boundary between the West and Africa to end FGM.

Step One: Pursuit of Intersubjective Understanding

The pursuit of an egalitarian, multicultural, coalition-building approach begins with the pursuit of intersubjective understanding, which involves the pursuit of knowledge on all sides of the coalition of out-group members as an even and equal exchange. This is often seen theoretically as an even and equal recognition of each coalition member's comparable ontological significance in the larger discourse. This pursuit is best described by the Western feminist approach to empathy, which involves both caring and cooperation.

The ethic of caring cited here is part of an alternative epistemology utilized by African American women.[60] Three interrelated components can serve to place African women as subjects in the dialogue, rather than objects or topics of discourse. All three serve to encourage intersubjective understanding. First, African American women emphasize individual uniqueness as a way of being in the world that is already different from what exists in the mainstream discourse, which focuses on European males.[61] By envisioning people as individuals both within and outside of their own cohort, women can move towards intersubjective understanding by validating uniqueness rather than seeking conformity in identity or experience. A second component, the appropriateness of emotions, is similarly both a response to and form of action within the larger world subsuming African American women. Using strong emotions as a cue enables them to evaluate the degree to which a speaker commits to a particular claim.[62] Such an emphasis on individuality and emotion directly contradicts Eurocentric, androcentric epistemology that attempts to abstract distinguishing characteristics from knowledge claims in pursuit of universal truths. Both also serve as cultural markers for African American women as they travel within and outside of their worlds.

The third component, the capacity for empathy, empowers African American women psychologically. Collins notes the overlap of Afrocentric and feminist ethics in this aspect of the caring ethic, but also reveals a critical discrepancy. While the capacity for empathy is present as a shared normative good, Eurocentric institutions possess comparatively fewer outlets for pursuit of this good than African American ones.[63] The empowering potential of support emanating from the use of empathy has now been documented by the white middle-class women's movement as well, via studies of the impact of second wave consciousness-raising groups. African American women have long shared this capacity with each other through strong women's groups in many church denominations. Similarly, many African women document traditions of individual and collective activism inspired by cross-generational female relationships.[64] Sylvester takes the capacity for empathy and moves it to the realm of intersubjective understanding in order to develop a politics that "can be used for creative dialogue in, through and around self-differentiated communities."[65] This is the politics that allows Western feminists to build egalitarian, multicultural coalitions with women of lesser privilege in the global arena. Empathetic cooperation in this context is best defined by Norma Alarcón, who argues that Western feminist world travelers must "learn to be unintrusive, unimportant, patient to the point of tears, while at the same time open to learning any possible lessons."[66]

Unlike the aforementioned theorists, however, the empathetic cooperation described here is not solely the task of the dominant group in building multicultural coalitions. While the dominant group is faced with a heavy workload, such an assignment must be completed by all groups in multicultural coalitions, regardless of their hierarchical position. It involves, importantly, the recognition of those in power as situated subjects in a contextualized position by those in lower positions.[67] Previous attempts at coalition theory and coalition practice have stopped with the responsibility of those in power. Appeals that rest solely upon the dominant group's conscience and morality to produce egalitarian behavior have failed.[68] Throughout the twentieth century male scholars writing from sites of oppression (for example, W. E. B. Du Bois and Frantz Fanon) have documented the oppressed consciousness of those without power. The internalization of images and stereotypes from the larger cultural discourse found in oppressed peoples requires them to divorce themselves of such beliefs and replace them with autonomy and responsibility.[69] Essentialist self-constructed victimologies, as previously stated, limit the degree of bridge building possible between groups with power and those without.

The practice of "conscientization,"[70] as Freire describes it, forces all coalition members to recognize sources of both oppression and potential power in their own lives as a way of moving toward empathetic cooperation across lines of race, class, culture, and other differences. The material experience of radicalization is theorized as one of recognition, which views commonalities among the differences. What distinguishes radicalization/recognition from a search for some type of universal sisterhood is the method. The experience is defined *not* (as done in the past) by the presence or absence of certain qualities (for example, all women are potentially biological mothers), but by seeking among the differences commonalities that can be clustered into "family resemblances."[71] Women can then interact across lines of difference as women in appreciation of class, race, culture and experience distinctions, yet in a way that does not seek to preserve some notion of a list of characteristics (biological, social, or otherwise) that are fundamentally constitutive of universal womanhood.

Once women recognize each other in this way, they are pursuing intersubjective understanding—even and equal exchange. Key in the words "even and equal exchange" is the definition of equality—not identical but situational and proportional. This definition of equality is guided by MacKinnon's argument for treatment of women as different from men, not identical to men, and the development of alternative epistemologies as proposed by Western feminist theorists such as Collins and Harding. Intersubjective understanding permits Western feminists and indigenous women in Africa to treat each other as women different from, not identical to, each other. This tactic constitutes both groups of women as subjects in the discourse—a truly empowering prospect in the global arena.

The first strategic step towards such understanding involves centering the terms of empowerment in the reality of the poor by questioning fundamental realities and concepts that are embedded in development and human rights discourse.[72] Psychological empowerment rests also upon an assump-

tion about the importance of language, not solely as a method of communication in the academic or policy arenas, but to those who are beneficiaries
of the study.[73] The quest for intersubjective understanding helps to mute
resistance to building coalitions where distrust is legitimately high.

External policymakers must recognize that the "value-free" pretense
adopted by many donor organizations (grounded in economic growth–
tinged notions of objectivity) is in truth an ontological position that implicitly legitimizes the existing power relations in the developing country.[74]
The material consequences of such a position cannot be underestimated
in its impact on the lives of women, who seek assistance improving their
subsistence status to one of political and socioeconomic empowerment.[75]
It is important to note that removing the claim of objectivity frees those
seeking to build egalitarian multicultural coalitions from a constricting
need to remain removed from the empowerment process. By engaging
with, rather than seeking to help,[76] Western feminists and even privileged
African feminists can work with women threatened by FGM via an ethic of
caring and empathetic cooperation, two key ways to build intersubjective
understanding.

Step Two: Envisioning Women as Contextualized Subjects with Agency

One of the primary critiques of Western feminist work abroad (in research,
activism, or theory) involves many Western feminists' failure to shed the
Eurocentric, positivist trappings they themselves have condemned as androcentric bias. The resulting research, activism, and programs, as discussed
earlier, are plagued by charges of Western imperialism, cultural insensitivity, and paternalism. The second step in egalitarian multicultural coalition
building seeks to develop ways of seeing that situate women in their own
context and do not lock them into "victimology" or powerlessness. Acceptance of all women's potential for self-transformation and thus empowerment, regardless of their current situation, is crucial to building effective
coalitions. However, accepting each woman's potential regardless of her
current context is significantly different from ignoring the extant positions
women find themselves in. On this point, Western and African feminist
theorists have made strides through their use of insider materialism (in the
West) and African feminism (in Africa).

Insider materialism evolves from the process of empathetic cooperation
outlined in step one. By involving themselves in the process of development or political empowerment or consciousness raising as collaborators
rather than leaders, Western feminists are forced to concretely investigate
their own practices as they simultaneously travel across the divide to investigate other women's practices. For example, Alice Walker's words while
making the film, *Warrior Marks*, are instructive as she seeks to include in
the film references to the various machinations Western women endure

for many of the same reasons women enforce FGM upon their daughters. Western women crash diet, undergo plastic surgery and try many other strategies to ensure their marriageability—methods with equally grave potential results as FGM.[77]

This recognition of oneself as a part of an ongoing androcentric system encourages another type of recognition process to take place regarding women facing FGM. It is easier to relate to (though not necessarily support) the position of women who are preserving apparently dangerous traditions or practices do so as a rational response to the context in which they exist (although this is by no means the only option!). This enables feminist world travelers to recognize the agency (or potential) women possess in situations of gender inequality.

Similarly, the actions of African feminists in creating feminisms that respond to their current contexts contribute to the potential for building egalitarian multicultural coalitions. The first benefit of African feminisms has been to contextualize and situate African women as both creators and preservers of feminist tenets appropriate to their cultural background. The recovery of the values of African feminisms serve as a powerful testimony of the agency possessed by various African women since the very beginning of human history.[78] The emphasis on human totality, parallel autonomy, cooperation, self-reliance, adaptation, survival, and liberation in African feminism[79] counter the global discourse of victimology forwarded by certain Western feminist accounts of African women's lives. Ogundipe-Leslie's deconstruction of feminism as popularly understood in Africa accompanies her recovery and reconstruction of African feminisms noted above. Included in eight items listing what feminism is *not*, she includes three corrections of specific interest to women battling multiple oppressions:

- Feminism is *not* dividing the race or "the struggle."
- Feminism is *not* parrotism of Western women's rhetoric.
- Feminism is *not* opposed to African culture and heritage, but culture should not be immobilized in time as most African men wish it to be.[80]

The willingness of African feminist theorists to take the power of self-definition, rather than await its conferral by those in power, cannot be underestimated. This act of contextualizing feminism is itself an empowering act and one that forces non-African women to contend with African women as possessing varying degrees of control over their lives, which can increase via egalitarian multicultural coalitions.

African feminisms proceed beyond deconstructive efforts to respond to Western feminist discourse. While African feminisms resist several strains of Western feminist theory (as noted above), they affirmatively construct theories relevant to the diverse experiences of African women. While terms vary greatly (Africana womanism, Black feminism, African feminism, womanism), much of African feminist theory seeks to be part of a broader category of transformative feminism, sharing four principles:

1. The commitment to questioning everything.
2. Presumption to struggle on all fronts, resisting all domination.
3. Understanding feminism as a perspective that speaks to all of society (not solely women).
4. A belief in the project of building solidarity.[81]

These principles create a theoretical space for egalitarian, multicultural coalition building. Importantly, however, African feminisms cogently argue for reconstructions that are based not on resistance to the West, but on the African environment itself.[82]

As Okeke, Collins, and numerous feminists of color have argued, the development of a group of global feminisms that recognize the diverse cultural contexts of women as well as their potential for self-empowerment is essential to achieving the goal of societal transformation. By seeking to comprehend all women as contextualized social actors, Western women remove themselves from the trap into which Eurocentric training has conditioned them to fall. The androcentric, Eurocentric mode of investigation abstracts women (for example, a mother who has her daughter circumcised) from their context and characterizes them as powerless victims or irrationally sadistic child abusers. Moving out of this tradition into one that utilizes insider materialism to comprehend cultural difference and embraces the actions of African women to empower themselves via definitions of African feminisms comprises step two of an approach to egalitarian multicultural coalition building.

With regard to development programs against FGM, the implications are clear: without consultation of the *daya*, policymakers will not know the incentive structure that sparks them to continue practicing FGM. Continued ignorance of this structure blunts any chance an anti-FGM program may have to successfully eradicate excision. Clearly, visions of women in context are critical to building egalitarian multicultural coalitions that can produce effective anti-FGM programs that empower women.

The study of psychological empowerment also suggests an approach that considers people in their respective contexts.[83] The multiple paths to empowerment have physical, psychological, and material dimensions when considering women in lesser-developed nations[84] like Burkina Faso. Practically speaking, the focus of governments and policymakers upon varying dimensions of disadvantage will help to center development programming on contextualized social agents, rather than individuals in a vacuum. Such a list includes items from all three of the above-mentioned dimensions of empowerment: poverty, social inferiority, isolation, physical weakness (health), economic vulnerability, seasonality, powerlessness, and humiliation.[85] This kind of holistic approach to multicultural coalition building for development purposes can also speak to the egalitarian multicultural coalition building approach feminists can use to join to fight FGM.

The content of the aforementioned holistic approach to development combines with the "insider materialism" approach of multicultural coalition building for an effective campaign against FGM. In order for a social movement to truly empower masses of women, it must "make sense" to them in terms of their own life experiences.[86] At this critical point in Burkinabé women's fight to end FGM, the people who continue this practice should be treated as collaborators in the struggle; it is important to pursue joint involvement to find methods of self-empowerment that are not harmful to others. This will produce psychological empowerment,[87] in addition to material empowerment. Both types are predecessors of political empowerment.

Within this multicultural coalition-building approach to fighting FGM, there exist plenty of opportunities for Western feminists to share their resources and become empowered themselves via the lessons African women can teach them. The key in applying the coalition theory to practical development and political issues is not merely in the content to be pursued (multilevel, multidimensional) but in the method by which such content is analyzed. Feminist theory's contributions of insider materialism and *stiwanism* to the multicultural coalition-building approach provide a bridge beyond feminist theory and feminist praxis to broader issues of psychological, material, and physical empowerment of women.

Step Three: Minimization of Differential Power among Coalition Member Groups

Through the achievements and insights gained from steps one and two, step three requires women to move from changing their visions of self and others to transforming actual intergroup interactions. Minimizing the differential power relations among various groups of women enables the emergence of egalitarian multicultural coalitions to pursue material social changes that serve to empower women—the ultimate goal of feminism.

Women of color, when encouraged to sublimate gender interests in the name of larger class, race, or ethnic struggles, have often fought to attain the power to change the discourse in order to include an analysis of interlocking oppressions that fracture groups with shared interests in social justice. This same struggle has occurred as efforts to build diverse movements of women have at times forced women of color or lower-class women to submerge their class, race, or ethnic interests. The fight to attain power has often been one against the dominant group, which seeks to preserve its superior status, often destroying the cohesion of the coalition in the process. Subordinate groups respond by envisioning the dominant group as less committed to true social change[88] and interested in the perpetuation of inequality among groups.[89] The minimization of differences in power is thus critical to the attainment of an effective egalitarian multicultural coalition.

The interactive approach to social justice blends tenets of pluralist and separatist models into a single vision of society that can analyze multiple, simultaneous oppressions and provide long-term prescriptions for political action.[90] This model of social diversity is more egalitarian than the pluralist model because it recognizes the existence of institutionalized subordination and domination, rather than seeking to view politics as a random game of "sometimes you win and sometimes you lose." It is more multicultural than the separatist model because it emphasizes the complexity of ways oppression interacts to shape and condition diverse women's lives by privileging the existence of multiple identities. Third and finally, the interactive model proposes a type of consciousness raising that requires interaction among groups in order to broaden understanding of both in-group and out-group oppression. It is this foundation upon which minimization of power differences can occur.

This final step of a more egalitarian approach to multicultural coalition building is also the toughest one to make. It requires women to leave their "safe spaces" or "homes" to engage in liberatory learning and interaction with women as different from them as is conceivable. The actual interactions, fraught with emotional, psychological, even economic risks, are a formidable challenge to the aspirations of much of Western feminist theory. In other words the political risk is substantial—for it is one thing to know intellectually the empowering mode of interaction, but quite another to actually practice it.[91]

One of the key actions that is so risky is trust, for as Freire states, "They talk about the people, but they do not trust them, and trusting the people is the indispensable precondition for revolutionary change."[92] Developing the kind of trust necessary for coalition building is epitomized by Freire's cointentional education, which establishes a never-ending relationship of dialogue among coalition members. Members of the coalition not only communicate with each other, they share joint responsibility for "a process in which all grow."[93] The key development from Freire's theory to egalitarian multicultural coalition building is that the element of trust is required of *all* members of the coalition based on their commitment to self-reflection and self-evaluation. This critical element can only be achieved through ongoing dialogue, which must continue past the initial psychological reactions or historical barriers, for "whoever lacks this trust will fail to initiate (or will abandon) dialogue, reflection and communication, and will fall into using slogans, communiqués, monologues and instructions."[94] The breakdown of communication is cited by all of the coalition theorists cited above as the poison dart that kills coalitions.

Coalitions have thrived, survived, or failed based upon the intransigence or mutability of differential power relations.[95] While minimization should not be construed as a sufficient condition for coalition success, it is a necessary one. I will discuss three steps in minimization of power differences that can act as catalysts for egalitarian coalition success. First, group members must overcome immobilizing responses to differences and diversity, second they must engage in active listening and engaged learning across differences, and third, members must recognize the roles all play as both victims and perpetuators of the unequal systems of power currently in place.

Ignorance on the part of Western feminists about various feminisms around the world has interacted with challenges from subordinate women's groups to produce several responses that serve to thwart, rather than facilitate, egalitarian multicultural coalitions. Instead of engaging challenges to the dominant paradigms in feminist theory, many Western feminists have resorted to defensiveness, over-personalization of charges, withdrawal from political engagement, resentment or weariness of hearing "the same old issue," and attempts to pigeonhole outspoken subordinate group members into issues solely relating to that group identity.[96] The reaction of less privileged dominant groups is often one of outrage and withdrawal from political engagement when met with "nods that silence."[97] The role of coalitions in sparking societal transformation on behalf of women has a long and storied history.

Overcoming the initial psychological responses to challenges is necessary to truly engender a minimization of power relations for two reasons. First, this step acts as a preparation for active listening and engaged learning, one in which all coalition groups must participate in order to be equal members of the coalition. Second, all groups (not just the most dominant group) must move beyond initial responses to confrontations in a manner similar to the individual-level "radicalization" mentioned in earlier steps. Without recognizing and challenging each group's position as both victim and oppressor in society, the agency for social change is muted; this can potentially prevent the coalition's opportunity to attempt "meaningful action in the world."[98]

Lynet Uttal describes the need for women to allow themselves to "get messy" in cross-cultural interactions in order to bridge differences in an empowering, rather than debilitating way.[99] Through active listening, groups can avoid the pitfalls of the immobilizing responses Bunch describes and prepare themselves for multicultural political education that empowers women to act together and apart in ways that challenge and transform the norms of their respective societies. Reading, interacting, questioning, and accepting the facts and myths surrounding the differences that separate women prepares women to make a commitment to active struggle for broad, wide-scale, global empowerment.

The recognition of each group's role as both victims and oppressors in the current system of power relations evolves from consideration of the complex, interlocking nature of various oppressions raised by the interactive model. It is also related to the permission participants grant themselves to explore, validate, and discredit the baggage created from prior history, current social context, and future political interests (through active listening and liberatory learning). Yet the recognition step is often difficult because it requires *all* groups to step out of victimology and acknowledge their power as well as their powerlessness in perpetuating the system. The penchant for "willful blindness" on the part of white Western feminists has been documented by feminists of color and from the developing world, who wish for white feminists to acknowledge whiteness as a race and a perspective, rather than a norm.

Yet Tanzanian feminist Marjorie Mbilinyi takes her counterparts in Africa to task for failing to acknowledge their responsibilities in empowering rural indigenous people in their own countries who lack the training and education to interact in the global feminist discourse.[100] Thus, the necessity of all groups participating in each step towards coalition building cannot be underestimated in ensuring development of egalitarian multicultural coalitions. Subordinate groups cannot position themselves as monolithic victims without agency any more than the dominant group can in the larger arena. Recognition of victimhood, while important, is not the destination of the coalition politics journey. Meaningful action designed to empower women and eventually transform society is the goal.

Lack of trust and confidence on the donor side prevents the reinforcement and enhancement of prepolitical constructs such as self-esteem, self-efficacy, and trust in the indigenous women that are so critical to developing civil society, social capital, and thus, sustainable democracy, development, and women's empowerment. Western feminists may find a role in multicultural coalitions that involves developing approaches that can empower indigenous women yet maintain accountability for donor organizations. This achievement would significantly further the cause of societal transformation urged by feminists and outlined earlier from Freire.

One of the first methods suggested to maintain this fragile balance is to pursue multicultural coalitions over a practical political claim (e.g., the struggle to end FGM) first, rather than broadly challenge the strategic position of women overall.[101] In the face of the severe economic deprivation faced by women in developing nations, the solution is to simply ask what can be done, for "women know very well what they need to start on the road to a better life. It is these very practical and immediate concerns that call for devising development programs with the needs of women in mind."[102] Yet the pursuit of this single issue can be approached in a multidimensional fashion, as described in step two. What is required, however, is the equal valuation of resources to be contributed to the political movement.[103] Western feminists may possess the financial and technological resources of use to Burkinabé women, for example. Yet the Burkinabé women speak the indigenous languages, and know the incentive structures rewarding the itinerant circumcisers and the contexts of women's lives in Burkina Faso. Just as Western feminist theory provided an alternative conception of knowledge grounded in Western women's lived experience, so now must Western feminist activists privilege the Burkinabé women's lived experience in any coalition to end FGM.

The second method regards the ideology that accompanies pursuit of women's empowerment. An empowering ideology is necessarily superior to that of a helper-helped approach.[104] With regard to building an egalitarian multicultural coalition, one concrete method of minimizing power relations concerns the requirement of all coalition members to undergo the empowerment process. While the content for members from varying backgrounds might vary, all can proceed through empowerment's four stages: entry, advancement, incorporation, and commitment.[105]

Applying this process to the struggle to build a coalition to end FGM leads to several possible nondominating interpretations by coalition members. Western feminists may recognize the external threat of FGM as an attack on a "sister" in a nondominating fashion. Members of anti-FGM groups in civil society (such as the CNLE—Comité National pour Lutter contre l'Excision/the National Committee for the Fight against FGM; or UFB—Union des Femmes Burkinabé/the Union of Burkinabé Women) may also view the threat of FGM, if they themselves have not experienced it, in this fashion. They may also be mothers who hesitate to send their children to stay with older female relatives for fear that they will be mutilated secretly. Burkinabé women who are subsistence farmers and mothers of daughters not yet subjected to FGM may view this threat in a more immediate fashion. Yet the common threat (despite the various vantage points) acts as a thread to initially bind these different women together for some type of political action. The first critical juncture emerges when coalition members must recognize the divergent perspectives as a strength that requires different egalitarian tactics to address them.

As the thread linking the women together becomes stronger, the use of the interactive model of social diversity enables them to see the external causes for such problems and the interlocking nature of oppressions. While all three groups of women (Western women, anti-FGM and pro-FGM Burkinabé women) have different lived experiences with varying oppressions, it is possible to note the commonalities in a way characteristic of "family resemblances."[106] This advancement phase of empowerment leads to both personal and coalitional empowerment.

As the coalition is strengthened, members of the coalition are increasingly adept at developing strategic abilities to engender local anti-FGM programs and movements. Again, this is experienced differentially. For Western feminists, the development of strategic abilities may involve learning new methods of cross-cultural communication and interaction as well as restraint. Educated Burkinabé women may also learn these skills, as well as a critical consciousness of their privileged position over women from the rural Sahel, which is the poorest section of Burkina Faso. Yet the women from the rural Sahel, when mothers of daughters not yet excised, also have power and privilege. They have the power to actually stop the mutilations in their tracks. Again, while Western feminists may have what Westerners consider "all the resources of power," without a doubt even the most impoverished in this regard, a Sahelian mother deciding whether to enforce a psychically and physically painful cultural tradition upon her daughter, has the ultimate power in the battle: the power to say NO. The recognition of varying dimensions of power and the work required to improve access to all forms of power and resources is the ongoing project of the multicultural coalition process.

IMPLICATIONS OF THIS APPROACH

The three goals of multicultural coalition politics reviewed here are part and parcel of the dynamic, mutually empowering processes of social transformation known as feminism. While multicultural political coalitions have a history dotted with successes and failures, what can be learned from previous attempts at coalition theory is the emphasis upon an egalitarian, rather than hierarchical approach. While Western feminist theory has sought to address the challenges put forth by women of color and women in the developing world, much theory remains immobilized between separatist and pluralist models of social diversity, while an interactive model is in reality more appropriate. Such a model allows women to recognize commonalities amidst differences in ways that concur with actual lived experience. This empowers women by creating a basis for "collaborative multicultural prescriptive theorizing."[107]

By encouraging intersubjective understanding, comprehending women as contextualized social actors and minimizing power differentials, women's groups can join together to form a coalition around common objectives—thus strengthening a particular movement and mutually reinforcing each other's individual movements. Coalition politics here is not distinguished from alliance politics, because the difference in feminist theory appears to be one of semantics. The questions of duration and scope of coalitions are significant yet not distinguishable with regard to the methods utilized to overcome barriers via deconstruction of difference and reconstruction of solidarity. Moreover, in the more colloquial definition of alliance, the history of international relations reflects the strong helping the weak, rather than the strong enhancing the ability of the weak to improve their position in global society.[108] It is this latter definition that I seek to apply to coalition politics.

Regardless of whether coalitions are long-term or grouped around a single concrete political objective, an egalitarian approach is critical to their success. With regard to the topic of female genital mutilation, Western feminists have sought to provide help to African countries to end this practice.

Instead, the nature of their help often has been, as documented in the first section, a hindrance. The good intentions of Western feminists can be channeled into effective tools in the fight against FGM via coalition politics. However, the coalitions to be built across cultural and class lines should be chosen carefully so as to proceed in an egalitarian manner.

Chronicles of failed development programs for women mirror the failures cited regarding coalition politics. African female policymakers argue that collective participation in empowering activities promotes various dimensions of psychological empowerment, which are often prerequisites of political empowerment. The importance of citizen participation has been duplicated in other contexts in order to confirm that multiple paths to empowerment are possible.[109] Varying theories of empowerment across the disciplines of psychology, planning, public policy, and development now propose changing practical approaches from one of "beneficiary aid" to one of "participant involvement."

On the African continent, women policymakers advocate the necessity of organizing collective participation around specific interests.[110] With regard to the movement to end FGM, this shared interest must overcome the perils noted in section one, which distance Western feminists and African anti-FGM activists from each other. Coalitional interventions must occur on multiple levels to address the empowerment of Burkinabé women so that they are no longer faced with a situation where the rational response is to have one's daughter excised. The inspiring efforts of the Burkina government, groups in civil society, and little-known grassroots organizations have made inroads into ending this cultural practice. Yet the centuries-old tradition requires vigilant, enduring multicultural coalitions that empower women. That these coalitions must continue beyond the short term is evident from the construction of empowerment as a lifetime task. In the words of Ahikire, "it is an ongoing process, a process in which women share experiences and devise strategies together."[111]

The three stage approach to multicultural coalition building elaborated herein seeks to grant agency to those Western feminists who wish to engage in egalitarian world traveling as well as indigenous feminists who fight to empower themselves in a feminist discourse riddled with Western hegemony. The three stages of pursuing intersubjective understanding, envisioning all women as contextualized social agents, and minimization of differential power relations are skills to be developed by all coalition members, regardless of their position in the external hierarchies. The processes of empowering women, an explicit goal of global feminisms, are enhanced by participation in this multicultural coalition building approach.

Yet, in order for global feminisms to succeed via genuine societal transformation, empowerment processes must mobilize large numbers of women.[112] What remains for those committed to building egalitarian multicultural coalitions is, unsurprisingly, trial and error. Feminist theory is at its best when it is informed by and responds to feminist practice.[113] In developing an approach to multicultural coalitions that is empowering rather than immobilizing, the task of feminist theory as a critical theory is not left half done. While previous critiques by women of color and women in lesser-developed nations have challenged Western feminist theorists and activists to practice what they preached, the reconstructive project of a theory of multicultural coalitions had stalled with notions of inclusiveness solely on the terms of those already in power. Though the path is rigorous, we can—through egalitarian multicultural coalitions—start and sustain a cultural revolution.

NOTES

1. The various African women's responses cited are often imprecise in this manner. However, in remaining true to the goal of granting African women agency and voices in the discourse (which is dominated by Western feminists such as myself), I allow their words to stand for themselves rather than qualify and interpret their meaning at every turn.

2. Leonard 1990, 215.

3. See, for example, Harding 1987; Collins 1991; MacKinnon 1981; Smith 1990.

4. Leonard 1990, 231.

5. Dietz 1987, 14.

6. Leonard 1990, 212.

7. Collins 1991, 211. See also Leonard 1990, 235.

8. Smith 1990, 205.

9. Leonard 1990, 235.

10. Oloka-Onyango and Tamale 1995.

11. Rappaport 1987, 122.

12. Sen and Grown 1987, 89.

13. Schwerin 1995, 80.

14. Through his study of conflict mediation, Schwerin explores the possibility of including participation as an empowering experience, whereas other authors have sought to sift out social or economic affiliations from concepts of political empowerment. See Waylen 1996 and Tripp 1994. I am inclined to agree with Schwerin's broader definition.

15. MacKinnon 1981, 23.

16. Oloka-Onyango and Tamale 1995, 713.

17. Mohanty 1991, 62.

18. The Western feminist theory I describe here is part of an ever-changing landscape of self-examination. The strains of feminist theory that now urge pursuit of intersubjective understanding have benefited from decades of critiques by feminists of color in the West in this regard. Serious consideration of the same argument with regard to non-Western women is only now occurring in the theoretical discourse.

19. Oloka-Onyango and Tamale 1995, 704.

20. Smith 1990, 201.

21. Schwerin 1995; Collins 1991.

22. Mekuria 1995, 3.

23. Sklar 1996, 11.

24. I am referring here to terms such as transformative feminism (Miles 1998) and Africana womanism (cited in Nnaemeka 1998). Both stress commitment to transformative practices but offer little concrete direction about such practices.

25. Ackoff 1984, 195–196.

26. Hartmann et al. 1996, 933.

27. Reagon 1983, 357.

28. Burkina Faso's capabilities include national government, civil society, and limited grassroots efforts.

29. See, for example, El Saadawi 1980; Morsy 1991; Mekuria 1995; Dolphyne 1991.

30. Mohanty 1991, 62.

31. Mohanty 1991, 53.

32. Scheper-Hughes 1991, 26.

33. See earlier discussion of MacKinnon's comments in Leonard 1990.

34. Other Western feminists charged with imperialist attitudes around this topic include Lillian Passmore Sanderson, Robin Morgan, and Gloria Steinem. I focus on Fran Hosken and Alice Walker because, unlike many others, they have made their names synonymous with anti-FGM struggles.

35. Morsy 1991, 21.

36. Collins 1991, 106–107.

37. Harding (1987) notes that "victimologies have their limitations, too. They tend to create the false impression that women have only been victims, that they have never successfully fought back, that women cannot be effective social agents on behalf of themselves or others. . . . Women have *always* resisted male domination" (5; emphasis added).

38. Mekuria 1995, 3.

39. Mekuria 1995, 3.

40. Walker 1996.

41. Mekuria 1995, 4.

42. The article credited to Mekuria is actually a conglomeration of responses by three African anti-FGM experts/activists: Mekuria, an Ethiopian professor at Wellesley College and independent filmmaker, Seble Dawit, an Ethiopian human rights lawyer, and Nahid Toubia, a Sudanese physician and executive director of the Research Action Information Network for the Bodily Integrity of Women (RAINBOW) at Columbia University.

43. Ogundipe-Leslie 1994, 248.

44. Florence Abena Dolphyne (1991) notes that upon attending a United Nations Conference Forum in 1980 where FGM was discussed, many African women felt they were "under siege"—not radical enough by Western feminist standards and too radical by the standards of the male dominated African delegations (x–xiii).

45. This phenomenon was demonstrated during the Mau-Mau uprising in Kenya, for example.

46. Ogundipe-Leslie 1994, 207.

47. Ogundipe-Leslie 1994, 208.

48. Okeke 1996, 226.

49. Okeke 1996, 227.

50. Ogundipe-Leslie 1994, 208; Okeke 1996, 230; Miles 1998.

51. Ogundipe-Leslie 1994, 224. See also Steady 1987, 4–6; Nnaemeka 1998.

52. Ogundipe-Leslie 1994, 225; Nnaemeka 1998, 6.

53. Mamdani 1995, 607.

54. While *stiwanism* is by no means the only term suggested by African women seeking to empower themselves and resist the Western conceptualization of feminism, space limits constrain me to a detailed discussion of this particular term. See Nnaemeka 1998 for a broader discussion of various alternatives to "Western feminism."

55. Tarrab 1989, 10.

56. Albrecht and Brewer 1990, 3.

57. Although African American and raised in the United States, I must agree with W. E. B. Du Bois, famous male feminist, that my Western socialization is not easily shed. Thus I speak and frame my arguments within a Western feminist perspective.

58. Sylvester 1995, 946.

59. Albrecht and Brewer 1990, 19; Reagon 1983, 368.

60. This ethic of caring differs from maternalist arguments set forth by some Western feminist theorists.

61. Collins 1991, 215.

62. Collins 1991, 216.

63. Collins 1991, 217.

64. Nnaemeka 1998, 13.

65. Sylvester 1995, 952.

66. Alarcón 1990, 363.

67. See Miles 1998 for the theoretical justification for this assertion.

68. Ture and Hamilton 1992, 74.

69. Freire 1993, 29.

70. See Freire 1993. This type of practice is also called "radicalizing ourselves," among American labor activists participating in the Union Summer activities of 1996. It involves, most importantly, the perception that oppression is not a natural, immutable occurrence but a limiting situation that is capable of being transformed (31).

71. Green and Curry 1991, 43.

72. Chambers 1995, 3; Binion 1995, 525.

73. Rappaport 1987, 141.

74. Bezanson 1995, 404.

75. See, for example, Ndwanga 1994.

76. Freire 1993, 31.

77. Walker and Parmar 1993, 9–10.

78. Ogundipe-Leslie 1994, 224. See also Steady 1987; Nnaemeka 1998.

79. Steady 1987, 20; Nnaemeka 1998, 6–9.

80. Ogundipe-Leslie 1994, 221–222.

81. Miles 1998, 172–173.

82. Nnaemeka 1998, 9.

83. Rappaport 1987, 121.

84. Friedmann 1992, 110.

85. Chambers 1995, 9.

86. Friedmann 1992, 115.

87. Rappaport 1987, 140.

88. Ture and Hamilton 1992, 60.

89. Ture and Hamilton 1992, 74.

90. Alperin 1990, 27.

91. Reagon 1983, 359; Bunch 1990, 53.

92. Freire 1993, 42.

93. Freire 1993, 61.

94. Freire 1993, 48.

95. Ture and Hamilton 1992. See also Albrecht and Brewer 1990, 3.

96. Bunch 1990, 54–55.

97. Uttal 1990, 317.

98. Bunch 1990, 56.

99. Uttal 1990, 319

100. Sylvester 1995, 957.

101. Friedmann 1992, 116.

102. Friedmann 1992, 113.

103. Uttal 1990, 318.
104. Rappaport 1987, 141.
105. Schwerin 1995, 84.
106. Green and Curry 1991, 42.
107. Green and Curry 1991, 40.
108. This metaphor refers to common political conceptions of alliances—for example, the North Atlantic Treaty Organizations, where the most powerful nation, the United States, provides additional support and defense of less powerful countries in a protective manner rather than an empowering one.
109. Schwerin 1995, 83.
110. Ahikire 1994, 88.
111. Ahikire 1994, 89.
112. Batliwala 1994, 132.
113. Hartmann et al. 1996, 939.

WORKS CITED

Ackoff, Russell L. 1984. "On the Nature of Development and Planning." In *People-Centered Development: Contributions toward Theory and Planning Frameworks*, ed. David C. Korten and Rudi Klauss, 195–197. West Hartford, CT: Kumarian Press.

Ahikire, Josephine. 1994. "Women's Empowerment: National or Grassroots Organization?" In *African Women: Our Burdens and Struggles*, ed. Ruth M. Besha, 86–89. Johannesburg: Institute for African Alternatives.

Alarcón, Norma. 1990. "The Theoretical Subject(s) of *This Bridge Called My Black* and Anglo-American Feminism." In *Making Face, Making Soul=Haciendo Caras: Creative and Critical Perspectives by Feminists of Color*, ed. Gloria Anzaldúa, 356–369. San Francisco: Aunt Lute Foundation Books.

Albrecht, Lisa, and Rose M. Brewer. 1990. "Bridges of Power: Women's Multicultural Alliances for Social Change." In *Bridges of Power: Women's Multicultural Alliances*, ed. Lisa Albrecht and Rose M. Brewer, 2–22. Philadelphia: New Society Publishers.

Alperin, Davida J. 1990. "Social Diversity and the Necessity of Alliances—A Developing Feminist Perspective." In *Bridges of Power: Multicultural Alliances*, ed. Lisa Albrecht and Rose M. Brewer, 23–33. Philadelphia: New Society Publishers.

Batliwala, Srilatha. 1994. "The Meaning of Women's Empowerment: New Concepts from Action." In *Population Policies Reconsidered: Health, Empowerment and Rights*, ed. Gita Sen, Adrienne Germain, and Lincoln C. Chen, 127–138. Cambridge, MA: Harvard Center for Population and Development Studies.

Bezanson, Keith A. 1995. "Rethinking Development: A New Challenge for International Development Organizations." In *People: From Impoverishment to Empowerment*, ed. Üner Kirdar and Leonard Silk, 398–407. New York: New York University Press.

Binion, Gayle. 1995. "Human Rights: A Feminist Perspective." *Human Rights Quarterly* 17 (3): 509–526.

Bunch, Charlotte. 1990. "Making Common Cause: Diversity and Coalitions." In *Bridges of Power: Women's Multicultural Alliances*, ed. Lisa Albrecht and Rose M. Brewer, 49–56. Philadelphia: New Society Publishers.

Chambers, Robert. 1995. "Poverty and Livelihoods: Whose Reality Counts?" In *People: From Impoverishment to Empowerment*, ed. Üner Kirdar and Leonard Silk, 1–16. New York: New York University Press.

Collins, Patricia Hill. 1991. *Black Feminist Thought: Knowledge, Consciousness and the Politics of Empowerment*. New York: Routledge.

Dietz, Mary. 1987. "Context Is All: Feminism and Theories of Citizenship." *Daedalus* 116 (4): 1–24.
Dolphyne, Florence Abena. 1991. *The Emancipation of Women: An African Perspective.* Accra: Ghana Universities Press.
El Saadawi, Nawal. 1980. *The Hidden Face of Eve.* London: Zed Press.
Freire, Paulo. 1993. *Pedagogy of the Oppressed.* Rev. ed. New York: Continuum.
Friedmann, John. 1992. *Empowerment: The Politics of Alternative Development.* Cambridge: Blackwell Publishers.
Green, Judith Mary, and Blanche Radford Curry. 1991. "Recognizing Each Other amidst Diversity: Beyond Essentialism in Collaborative Multi-Cultural Feminist Theory." *Sage* 8 (1): 39–49.
Harding, Sandra. 1987. "Introduction: Is There a Feminist Method?" In *Feminism and Methodology,* ed. Sandra Harding, 1–14. Bloomington, IN: Indiana University Press.
Hartmann, Heidi, Ellen Bravo, Charlotte Bunch, Nancy Hartsock, Roberta Spalter-Roth, Linda Williams, and Maria Blanco. 1996. "Bringing Together Feminist Theory and Practice: A Collective Interview." *Signs* 21 (4): 917–951.
Hosken, Fran. 1993. *The Hosken Report: Genital and Sexual Mutilation of Females.* Lexington, MA: Women's International Network News.
Leonard, Stephen T. 1990. "Feminist Theory and Critique." In *Critical Theory in Political Practice,* ed. Stephen T. Leonard, 211–248. Princeton: Princeton University Press.
MacKinnon, Catherine. 1981. "Feminism, Marxism, Method and the State: An Agenda for Theory." In *Feminist Theory,* ed. Nannerl Keohane, Michelle Z. Rosaldo, and Barbara C. Gelpi, 1–30. Chicago: University of Chicago Press.
Mamdani, Mahmood. 1995. "A Critique of the State and Civil Society Paradigm in African Studies." In *African Studies in Social Movements and Democracy,* ed. Mahmood Mamdani and Ernest Wamba-dia-Wamba, 602–616. Dakar: CODESRIA.
Mekuria, Salem. 1995. "Female Genital Mutilation in Africa: Some African Views." *ACAS Bulletin* 44–45:2–6.
Miles, Angela. 1998. "North American Feminisms/Global Feminisms—Contradictory or Complementary?" In *Sisterhood, Feminisms and Power: From Africa to the Diaspora,* ed. Obioma Nnaemeka, 163–182. Trenton, NJ: Africa World Press.
Mohanty, Chandra Talpade. 1991. "Under Western Eyes: Feminist Scholarship and Colonial Discourses." In *Third World Women and the Politics of Feminism,* ed. Chandra Talpade Mohanty, Ann Russo, and Lourdes Torres, 51–80. Bloomington, IN: Indiana University Press.
Morsy, Soheir. 1991. "Safeguarding Women's Bodies: The White Man's Burden Medicalized." *Medical Anthropology Quarterly* 5 (1): 19–23.
Ndwanga, Vije Mfaume. 1994. "Constraints on Women's Income-Generating Projects." In *African Women: Our Burdens and Struggles,* ed. Ruth M. Besha, 19–23. Johannesburg: Institute for African Alternatives.
Nnaemeka, Obioma. 1998. "Introduction: Reading the Rainbow." In *Sisterhood, Feminisms and Power: From Africa to the Diaspora,* ed. Obioma Nnaemeka, 1–35. Trenton, NJ: Africa World Press.
Ogundipe-Leslie, Molara. 1994. *Recreating Ourselves: African Women and Critical Transformations.* Trenton, NJ: Africa World Press.
Okeke, Philomena E. 1996. "Postmodern Feminism and Knowledge Production: The African Context." *Africa Today* 43 (3): 223–234.
Oloka-Onyango, J., and Sylvia Tamale. 1995. "The Personal Is Political or Why Women's Rights Are Indeed Human Rights: An African Perspective on International Feminism." *Human Rights Quarterly* 17 (4): 691–731.

Parmar, Pratibha, producer/director. 1993. *Warrior Marks* [videorecording]. A Hauer Rawlence Production. New York: Women Make Movies (distributor).

Rappaport, Julian. 1987. "Terms of Empowerment/Exemplars of Prevention: Toward a Theory for Community Psychology." *American Journal of Community Psychology* 15 (2): 121–148.

Reagon, Bernice Johnson. 1983. "Coalition Politics: Turning the Century." In *Homegirls: A Black Feminist Anthology*, ed. Barbara Smith, 356–368. New York: Kitchen Table Women of Color Press.

Scheper-Hughes, Nancy. 1991. "Virgin Territory: The Male Discovery of the Clitoris." *Medical Anthropology Quarterly* 5 (1): 25–28.

Schwerin, Edward W. 1995. "Empowerment: Transforming Power and Powerlessness." In *Mediation, Citizen Empowerment and Transformational Politics*, ed. Edward W. Schwerin, 55–91. Westport, CT: Praeger.

Sen, Gita, and Caren Grown. 1987. *Development, Crises and Alternative Visions: Third World Women's Perspectives*. New York: Monthly Review Press.

Sklar, Richard. 1996. "Democracy in Africa." *African Studies Review* 26 (3–4): 11–24.

Smith, Dorothy. 1990. *Conceptual Practices of Power*. Boston: Northeastern University Press.

Steady, Filomena Chioma. 1987. "African Feminism: A Worldwide Perspective." In *Women in Africa and the African Diaspora*, ed. Rosalyn Terborg-Penn and Andrea Rushing, 3–24. Washington, DC: Howard University Press.

Sylvester, Christine. 1995. "African and Western Feminisms: World Traveling the Tendencies and Possibilities." *Signs* 20 (4): 941–969.

Tarrab, Gilbert. 1989. *Femmes et pouvoir au Burkina Faso*. Quebec: Editions G. Vermette.

Toubia, Nahid. 1985. "The Social and Political Implications of Female Circumcision: The Case of the Sudan." In *Women and Families in the Middle East: New Voices of Change*, ed. Elizabeth Warnock Fernea, 148–164. Austin: University of Texas Press.

———. 1994. "Female Circumcision as a Public Health Issue." *New England Journal of Medicine* 331:712–716.

Tripp, Aili Mari. 1994. "The Impact of Crisis and Economic Reform on Tanzanian Changing Associational Life." In *The Changing Politics of Non-Governmental Organizations and African States*, ed. Eve Sandberg. Westport, CT: Praeger.

Ture, Kwame, and Charles Hamilton. 1992. "The Myths of Coalition." In *Black Power: The Politics of Liberation in America*, 58–84. New York: Random House.

Uttal, Lynet. 1990. "Nods That Silence." In *Making Face, Making Soul=Haciendo Caras: Creative and Critical Perspectives by Feminists of Color*. ed. Gloria Anzaldúa, 317–320. San Francisco: Aunt Lute Foundation Books.

Walker, Alice. 1996. Group Interview at University of North Carolina at Chapel Hill.

Walker, Alice, and Pratibha Parmar. 1993. *Warrior Marks: Female Genital Mutilation and the Sexual Blinding of Women*. New York: Harcourt Brace.

Waylen, G. 1996. "Analyzing Women in the Politics of the Third World." In *Women and Politics in the Third World*, ed. Haleh Afshar, 7–24. London: Routledge.

Index

About the Contributors

Omofolabo Ajayi-Soyinka is Associate Professor of Theatre and Film and Women's Studies at the University of Kansas, Lawrence, Kansas. She previously taught at the Obafemi Awolowo University (formerly University of Ife), Nigeria, and was also a Visiting Assistant Professor at Cornell University. Dr. Ajayi's numerous publications appear in edited volumes and scholarly journals including *Women's Studies Quarterly, Research Notes,* and *Journal of Dramatic Theory and Criticism.* Her book *The Semiotics of Yoruba Dance* was published in 1998. She is the Treasurer of the Association of African Women Scholars (AAWS).

Jude G. Akudinobi received his Ph.D. in Cinema-Television Critical Studies from the University of Southern California and currently teaches in the Department of Black Studies, University of California, Santa Barbara. His works include essays that have appeared in numerous collections and journals including *Iris, The Black Scholar, Social Identities, Nka,* and *Third Text.* He has written screenplays including an adaptation (with Gerard Pigeon) of Aimé Césaire's *The Black Tempest.* He is coeditor (with Abebe Zegeye) of *African Cinema and Its Imaginaries* and author of *Empire, Colonialism and Representation* (forthcoming).

Eloïse A. Brière is Associate Professor of French Studies at the State University of New York in Albany. She earned a Ph.D. in contemporary Francophone literatures with an emphasis on West Africa. Her numerous articles focus on Cameroonian literature and women writers such as Antonine Maillet, Simone Schwarz-Bart, and Emile Ollivier. Dr. Brière is the author of *Le Roman Camerounais et ses discours* (1993), coauthor of *La Francophonie*

Rendez-vous: La France et la Francophonie, and coeditor of a special issue of *Notre Librarie* on women's writings from Africa, the Maghreb, and the Caribbean—*Les Novelles Ecritures Féminines*.

Nawal El Saadawi, Egyptian medical doctor and prolific author, is one of the world's most influential feminist scholar/activists. Dr. El Saadawi has had a major influence on the lives of women globally. Her outspoken support of political and sexual rights for women has resulted in her arrest and imprisonment. The publication of her work *The Hidden Face of Eve* (1980) was a major global event. One of her recent works, *The Nawal El Saadawi Reader*, focuses on a whole range of issues at the heart of her lifelong commitment—women's rights, women in Islam and the Arab world, development, literature, health, and the global women's movement. She is the author of over forty books including *Woman at Point Zero, The Circling Song, Death of an Ex-Minister, God Dies by the Nile, The Innocence of the Devil, Memoirs from the Women's Prison, Memoirs of a Woman Doctor, Searching, She Has No Place in Paradise*, and *Two Women in One*. Her autobiography, *A Daughter of Isis*, was published in 1999.

Sondra Hale has a Ph.D. in Anthropology from the University of California, Los Angeles, where she is Adjunct Professor of Anthropology and Women's Studies. Her research interests are in gender politics, social movements, and cultural studies—North Africa and the Horn, with special emphasis on Sudan, Eritrea, and Egypt. Her book *Gender Politics in Sudan: Islamism, Socialism, and the State* was published in 1996. Her numerous articles appear in *Citizenship Studies, Cairo Papers in Social Science, South Asia Bulletin, Reviews in Anthropology, Feminist Economics, Journal of African Studies, The Muslim World, Review of African Political Economy, Aljadid*, and *The New Political Science*. Professor Hale is an ex-president of the Association for Middle Eastern Women's Studies.

Ange-Marie Hancock is Assistant Professor of Political Science and African American Studies at Yale University, New Haven, Connecticut. She received her Ph.D. from the University of North Carolina at Chapel Hill in 2000. Her book *The Politics of Disgust: The Public Identity of the "Welfare Queen"* was published by New York University Press. She won the 2003 Betty Nesvold Award for the Best Paper in Women and Politics for her article "Intersectionality, Critical Theory, and Research Methodology." She served as coeditor of a special issue of *Peace Review* entitled "Ubuntu: Success Stories and Humane Solutions from Africa." She is working on her second book, *The Double Consciousness of the Pariah: Identity, Agency, and Citizenship in the Work of Hannah Arendt and W. E. B. DuBois*. Professor Hancock serves as Director of Undergraduate Studies for the Ethics, Politics, and Economics major at Yale.

Vicki Kirby received her Ph.D. from the History of Consciousness Program, University of California at Santa Cruz, and is a Senior Lecturer in the School of Sociology, University of New South Wales in Sydney, Australia. She is the author of *Telling Flesh: The Substance of the Corporeal* (1997) and has contributed to scholarly journals including *Signs, Hypatia: Journal of Feminist Philosophy, Anthropological Quarterly, Semiotic Review of Books, Australian Feminist Studies,* and *Mankind,* as well as to encyclopedias and anthologies, including *Encyclopedia of Semiotics, Derrida Downunder: Deconstruction at the Millennium,* and *Feminist Interpretations of Merleau-ponty.*

Chima Korieh is Assistant Professor of African History at Rowan University, Glassboro, New Jersey. He received his B.A. in history from the University of Nigeria, an M.A. in Education from the University of Helsinki, Finland, an M.Phil in history from the University of Bergen, Norway, and a Ph.D. from the University of Toronto, Canada. He has written several articles and is coeditor of *Religion, History and Politics in Nigeria* (2005).

Françoise Lionnet is Professor and Chair of the Department of French and Francophone Studies and a codirector of the MRG on Transnational and Transcolonial Studies at the University of California, Los Angeles. She is the author of *Autobiographical Voices: Race, Gender, Self-Portraiture* (1998) and *Postcolonial Representations: Women, Literature, Identity* (1995), and coeditor of a special double issue of *Yale French Studies* titled "Post/Colonial Conditions: Exiles, Migrations, Nomadisms" and two special issues of *Signs* on "Postcolonial, Indigenous, and Emergent Feminisms," and on "Development Cultures: New Environments, New Realities, and New Strategies" (2004). Professor Lionnet directed the 1995 NEH Summer Institute in French Cultural Studies on "Identities, Communities, and Cultural Practices."

Obioma Nnaemeka is Director of the Women's Studies Program and Professor of French, Women's Studies, and African American/African Diaspora Studies at Indiana University, Indianapolis. Professor Nnaemeka is President of the Association of African Women Scholars (AAWS). Her articles have appeared in numerous scholarly journals. She coedited a special issue of *Signs* on "Development Cultures: New Environments, New Realities, and New Strategies" (2004) and is editor of *The Politics of (M)Othering* (1997) and *Sisterhood, Feminisms, and Power: From Africa to the Diaspora* (1998). Her forthcoming books are *Marginality: Orality, Writing and the African Woman Writer, Agrippa D'Aubigné and the Poetics of Power and Change,* and *Engendering Human Rights: Cultural and Socioeconomic Realities in Africa.*

Chimalum Nwankwo, poet, playwright, and literary critic, has taught both in his home country, Nigeria, and in the United States, where he is presently an Associate Professor of English at North Carolina State University,

Raleigh. He received a Ph.D. from the University of Texas at Austin. His critical essays have appeared in many journals and anthologies. Winner of the Association of Nigerian Authors Poetry Prize in 1988 for *Toward the Aerial Zone*, Nwankwo has also published a major critical text on Ngugi wa Thiong'o, *Works of Ngugi wa Thiong'o: Toward the Kingdom of Woman and Man*. He is also the author of poetry collections—*Feet of the Limping Dancer, Trumpet Parable, Voices from the Deep*, and *A Womb in the Heart*. He is on the editorial board of academic journals, including *Jouvert: A Journal of Postcolonial Studies* and *Postmodern Culture*.

L. Amede Obiora is Professor of Law at the James E. Rogers College of Law, University of Arizona, and is a former Director of the Women's Division at the World Bank, Washington, DC. She received her LL.M. from Yale Law School and J.S.D. from Stanford Law School. She teaches courses on international human rights law and feminist jurisprudence. She coedited a special issue of *Law and Policy* on the right to development. Her numerous monographs and articles on international law, human rights, environment, development, and feminism appear in scholarly and law journals such as *Human Rights Quarterly, Syracuse Journal of International Law, American Journal of Comparative Law, Canadian Journal of Women and the Law, Hastings International and Comparative Law Review, Legal Studies Forum, Buffalo Women's Journal of Law and Social Policy, Case Western Reserve Law Review, Journal of African Economic History, Law and Policy*, and *Journal of Law and Social Inquiry*.